D0074253

Spaces of Global Cultures

In *Spaces of Global Cultures*, Anthony King brings together a series of contemporary and historical case studies to show how different phases of globalization are transforming the built environment. Taking a broad, interdisciplinary approach the author draws on sociology, geography, cultural and postcolonial studies to provide a critical account of the development of three key contemporary concepts that provide the theoretical framework for the book: global culture, postcolonialism, modernity. Subsequent case studies examine how global economic, political and cultural forces shape the forms of architectural and urban modernity in the 'globurbs' (i.e. globalized suburbs) and spaces of 'villafication' in major cities worldwide: Beijing, Washington DC, Delhi, Jakarta, and also in Britain. As a key sign of economic and political power and a symbol for states making claims to modernity, the high rise tower (and 'tallest building in the world') forms the subject of the opening chapter. Other themes include the writing of transnational planning histories and the contradictory relationship between imperialism and the ideology of Arts and Crafts architecture in Britain. The author's concluding memoir provides clues into how and why the book came to be written.

The first book to combine global and postcolonial theoretical approaches to the built environment, and to illustrate these with concrete examples, *Spaces of Global Cultures* argues for a more historical, differentiated and interdisciplinary understanding of globalization: one that places material space and the built environment at the center and calls for innovative concepts to address new contemporary conditions.

Anthony D. King is Bartle Professor of Art History and of Sociology, State University of New York at Binghamton. He has been Visiting Professor in Architecture, University of California, Berkeley and, for five years, Professor, Humanities and Social Sciences, Indian Institute of Technology, Delhi.

THE ARCHI*TEXT* SERIES

Edited by Thomas A. Markus and Anthony D. King

Architectural discourse has traditionally represented buildings as art objects or technical objects. Yet buildings are also social objects in that they are invested with social meaning and shape social relations. Recognizing these assumptions, the Archi*text* series aims to bring together recent debates in social and cultural theory and the study and practice of architecture and urban design. Critical, comparative and interdisciplinary, the books in the series will, by theorizing architecture, bring the space of the built environment centrally into the social sciences and humanities, as well as bringing the theoretical insights of the latter into the discourses of architecture and urban design. Particular attention will be paid to issues of gender, race, sexuality, and the body, to questions of identity and place, to the cultural politics of representation and language, and to the global and postcolonial contexts in which these are addressed.

Already published:

Framing Places
Mediating power in built form
Kim Dovey

Gender Space Architecture
An interdisciplinary introduction
Edited by Jane Rendell, Barbara Penner and Iain Borden

Behind the Postcolonial
Architecture, urban space and political cultures in Indonesia
Abidin Kusno

The Architecture of Oppression
The SS, forced labor and the Nazi monumental building economy
Paul Jaskot

Words between the Spaces
Building and language
Thomas A. Markus and Deborah Cameron

Embodied Utopias
Gender, social change and the modern metropolis
Rebeccah Zorach, Lise Sanders and Amy Bingaman

Writing Spaces
Discourses of architecture, urbanism, and the built environment, 1960–2000
C. Greig Crysler

Drifting: Migrancy and Architecture
Edited by Stephen Cairns

Beyond Description
Singapore space historicity
Edited by Ryan Bishop, John Phillips, and Wei-Wei Yeo

Spaces of Global Cultures
Architecture urbanism identity
Anthony D. King

Forthcoming titles:

Moderns Abroad
Architecture, cities and Italian imperialism
Mia Fuller

Sustaining Design
Interpreting green architecture
Edited by Simon Guy and Graham Farmer

Anthony D. King

Spaces of Global Cultures

Architecture Urbanism Identity

LONDON AND NEW YORK

First published 2004
by Routledge
11 New Fetter Lane, London EC4P 4EE

Simultaneously published in the USA and Canada
by Routledge
29 West 35th Street, New York, NY 10001

Routledge is an imprint of the Taylor & Francis Group

Typeset in Frutiger by
Florence Production Ltd, Stoodleigh, Devon
Printed and bound in Great Britain by
The Cromwell Press, Trowbridge, Wiltshire

British Library Cataloguing in Publication Data
A catalogue record for this book is available from the British Library

Library of Congress Cataloging in Publication Data
King, Anthony D.
   Spaces of global cultures: architecture, urbanism, identity/
   Anthony Douglas King.
         p. cm. – (Architext series)
      Includes bibliographical references and index.
   1. Architecture and globalization.   2. Architecture and society.
   3. Architecture, British colonial.   4. City planning – Asia – Case studies.
   5. Postcolonialism – Asia – Case studies.
   I. Title.   II. Series.
   NA2543.G46K55 2004
   720'.1'03–dc22   2003025771

ISBN 0–415–19619–1 (hb)
ISBN 0–415–19620–5 (pb)

TO URSULA
FOR YEARS APART
TOGETHER

Contents

Illustrations

Illustration Acknowledgments

I am grateful to the following individuals and/or institutions for permission to reproduce the illustrations indicated: Wisata Legenda Development Company, Jakarta (6.3), Guan Ming and Zhu Ping (7.4 to 7.8), Corporate Leisure Resorts and Hotels Pvt. Ltd, Bangalore (8.1), Dream Valley Resorts Pvt. Ltd, Hyderabad (8.2), Delhi Land and Finance Pvt (9.1, 9.3, 9.5), The British Library (India Office Collection) (10.1, 10.2), private collection (10.9), DeLorme's New York Atlas and Gazetteer™, Yarmouth, Maine (11.3), Sumati Morarjee and Vithalbhai K. Jhaveri (11.21), James Hunt (11.22).

While the author and publisher have made every effort to contact copyright holders of material used in this volume, they would be grateful to hear from any they were unable to contact. All photographs not credited are by the author.

Preface and Introduction

One day in May 1983, when visiting the United States from Britain, I was sitting, waiting for lunch, in a restaurant in Cambridge, Massachusetts, having finished the lecture I had come over to give. I was thinking of the book manuscript I had recently sent off to the publishers just before leaving the UK. Though the manuscript was finished, I was not happy with the subtitle. My intention there was to suggest that, in what had over time increasingly become a capitalist world economy, a particular type of individual and consumer-oriented form of outer suburbanization, as well as occasional leisure space, represented by a distinctive (though varying) form of one storey dwelling (everywhere referred to by the same term, 'bungalow'), had developed in 'advanced' and especially postindustrial societies. This had first occurred in the colonial and postcolonial countries of the English-speaking ecumene, but by the late twentieth century could be found in all five continents of the world (King 1984). More indirectly, I was also using this as a metaphor for an increasingly architecturally homogenized world. The book was about the various historical, economic, social, political and cultural conditions which had been instrumental in the production of both. Just before the waiter arrived, and quite innocent of the logical, epistemological, let alone historical or conceptual problems I was laying ahead for myself, the subtitle I was searching for suddenly came into my head: 'The Production of a Global Culture'.

Since that time, over the last twenty years I have been both intrigued and mystified by the way the phrase 'global culture' has crept into the language, not only in the academy but also in the public domain. As with one's name, a word or phrase we're familiar with invariably jumps off the page. Others must certainly have used this phrase before 1983 but, with the ability to do keyword searches in computer databases, I have, to date, not discovered the term either in a book or journal title prior to 1984.

Like globality, globalism, or globe-wide, 'global culture' is just one of the many terms and phrases introduced into the now widespread discourses on globalization and globalism which, as others have pointed out, are words that were included neither in the *Oxford English Dictionary* nor *Webster's Dictionary* prior to 1960. The first book with 'global culture' as the main title, a collection of essays edited by sociologist of culture Mike Featherstone appeared in 1990. Since then, the phrase has become established in the academy, penetrated parts of the media and no doubt will soon be heard on the street. (In 2003, it could be found in the titles of at least forty books and articles. See Chapter 2.)

This might all, of course, be part of the general 'global babble' (Abu-Lughod 1991) which has massively increased since the 1990s.[1] We might naively think that there really is some phenomenon/phenomena out there which 'global culture' refers to. And a book entitled 'Spaces of Global Cultures' would suggest the spaces in which these global cultures exist, or which they produce, in which they are contained, resisted, or even imagined. We might, in fact, think – not least in the way that I have introduced the term and idea here in this Preface – that the concept is unimportant, trivial or misleading. Nothing could be further from the truth.

If global culture, as some authors have maintained, refers primarily to 'American cultural imperialism' (Patterson 1994: 103), a global consumerist culture as represented, for example, by the US, based on the unbridled spread of capitalism, erasing local difference into a 'larger Americanization of the world' (Rieff 1993: 77), threatening the sacred space of other beliefs and other world views, the events of September 11, 2001 will, for some people in the world, have a very different meaning from that which they have in the location where they happened. The empty space on which New York's World Trade Center once stood is perhaps the most powerful, and also poignant, space of that particular version of global culture. Yet there are other versions and interpretations of this term and it is these that I discuss in Chapter 2.

I first heard of what was to become known as the attack on the World Trade Center on National Public Radio at about 8.55 am on the morning of September 11, 2001. Later that day, NPR decided to relay reports on the events from the BBC World Service. The correspondent (whose remarks, but not name, I noted) spoke of an attack 'on the key symbols of American economic and political power' and later, making specific reference to the World Trade Center's twin towers and the Pentagon, referred to 'the key symbols of America's financial power' and 'a symbol of America's might'. Quite apart from the horror at learning of these events there was also, for me, an uncanny feeling of prescience. Some five years earlier, following the first attack on the World Trade Center (1993), I had written an article on the symbolic function of tall buildings, particularly the phenomenon of 'the tallest building in the world', drawing attention to the fact that, in the contemporary post-Cold War era, the site of growing international conflict had been displaced from the traditional terri- torial frontiers of the nation-state to the space of large symbolic buildings in the city. My intention was to show not only how the signifiying function of *build- ings* was a neglected topic in social and cultural theory but also how buildings, whether blown up or knocked down, were increasingly becoming the instru- ments for political protest. A year before 9/11 I had written elsewhere 'Now . . . that Manhattan was itself largely a heap of ruins . . .' (King 2000b). It is this theme, therefore, concerning the use made by nations, cities, corporations and others, of high rise towers as signifiers of economic, political and cultural power, with which I begin the book. I start with this chapter not only because of the continuing topicality of the subject but also because, in a book about 'global cultures', it also explores how particular 'worlds' are produced through the construction of spectacular buildings and the discourses that are generated to accompany them. And as a chapter that is only lightly theorized, it provides a reader-friendly entry into the text.

THE SHAPE OF THE BOOK

A central aim of the Archi*text* series in which this book is published is to bring together 'debates in social and cultural theory and the study and practice of architecture and urban design'. In the first part of the book (Chapters 2–4) I address some of these recent theoretical debates, specifically, on the topics of global culture(s), postcolonial knowledges and ideas about modernity. The aim of these chapters is to provide theoretical resources on which to draw (or alternatively, theoretical generalizations which can be interrogated) when discussing the more empirical and historical chapters in the second part. These chapters (6 through 10) can be treated as case studies of the way different kinds of contemporary modernity are being produced in architectural and urban form in the suburbs of various cities worldwide, including: India, particularly Delhi; China, particularly Beijing; the US, particularly Washington DC; Indonesia, particularly Jakarta; and historically, Britain; and how these forms are being influenced by transnational processes.

In the first of these, Chapter 6, which addresses features which, in certain ways, can be found in all the cases, I introduce the concept of the *supra*urb (or *supr*urb) or *glob*urb. In contradistinction to the *sub*urb, which refers to spatial, cultural and architectural developments arising from and dependent on an adjoining city, the suprurb or globurb manifests spatial, cultural and architectural developments originating from locations not only outside or away from the 'indigenous' city but often, from outside the country itself.

In writing about 'global culture' and 'globalization' interdisciplinarity has to be taken for granted. Chapter 2, on the topic of global culture(s) draws largely on a literature from sociology, anthropology and cultural studies; Chapter 3, on postcolonial knowledges, from interdisciplinary postcolonial studies, though also from cultural geography and architecture; Chapter 4, on modernity, from sociology, art history and anthropology. In Chapter 5, I make use of some of these ideas to discuss their relevance in providing frameworks for studying the history of transnational urban planning.

Compared to the earlier chapters in Part Two, Chapter 10 is more specifically historical and empirical. In this, I make use of a more conventional architectural history to explore the apparent contradictions between the practices of specific early twentieth century architects sympathetic to the 'Arts and Crafts' movement, which is generally represented as a manifestation of a distinctive 'national English culture', and the world of high imperialism in which some of them actually worked. In contrast to the more theoretical and generalized themes in earlier chapters, in this I discuss specific historical places, subjects and events in the late nineteenth and early twentieth century world created by the overlapping spaces of imperialism, culture and architecture.

Part Three consists of one chapter. Academic work is often seen as 'scientific', where the author, as subject, is removed from the text. Yet writing is essentially a personal experience, even though that fact is rarely, if ever, acknowledged. And personal experience is informed, amongst other things, by our work, homes, travel, ways of seeing and knowing, a variety of social networks, memory and, not least, serendipity. Here, I put the author back in the text in order to provide the reader with some insights into how, why, as well as where and when,

I became interested in the themes of this book and possibly why the argument follows the shape that it does.

While the chapters can be read sequentially, they can also be read at random as each was originally written to be complete in itself. For readers less interested in theoretical issues, or others who might find them heavy going, they may start with the case studies and, if interested, return to those in Part One later. For readers tempted to take a more 'personal' approach, they might start with the semi-autobiographical essay of Chapter 11, though as this picks up on ideas and issues discussed earlier, they may find a conventional 'beginning-to-end' reading more satisfactory. As should be clear from the first paragraph in this Preface, the origins of this book came out of a 'straightforward' historical study. Only subsequently was I lead into investigating some of the theoretical issues it posed.

The book has a number of themes which are set out at the beginning of each chapter. A central theme in the case studies, however, is the examination of architectural and building cultures as they are affected by transnational processes. What are the social and cultural effects of transplanting particular architecture cultures (including particular building typologies and their exterior as well as interior design) from one cultural location to another? What are the larger political, social and economic forces within which this happens? How are these different invasive practices accepted, resisted, rejected, indigenized and hybrid-ized? Mostly, my case studies are concerned, first, with describing what is happening in specific places, and second, with speculating about the social and cultural effects on the multiple identities of subjects or larger social formations. In general, much of the book addresses buildings as embodying social institu-tions, their physical exteriors and the effects of the image of these buildings in transmitting – under particular conditions – certain symbolic messages. Unlike in some of my earlier books (and in other works published in the Archi*text* series), I give less attention here to their internal spatial structure, not least because, as I indicate elsewhere, the interpretation of the social and cultural aspects of the changes being introduced would require a different type of research. I am more concerned here with how built form, urban space and, in cases, architectural style, convey, under certain conditions, social and political meanings of power, status and identity.

Binghamton
October 2003

NOTE

1   In January 1990, the database in my own university library listed a mere 254 entries under 'global'. By June 1996, this number had increased almost ninefold to some 2,200 entries. Six years later (June 2002), it stood at just over 5,900, suggesting that it was the first half of the 1990s when the initial surge of scholarly interest in 'the global' took place. By June 2004, the figure was just over 7,000.

Acknowledgments

I would especially like to thank four people for help of various kinds. Abidin Kusno's insightful and perceptive comments on all the chapters, including earlier versions, have been invaluable throughout the writing of the book. Archi*text* co-editor, Tom Markus, in addition to sharing many fruitful exchanges over the last few years, has also read the entire manuscript and provided many pertinent and insightful suggestions. Deryck Holdsworth's comments on Chapters 1, 10 and 11 (as well as his generally wise and sound counsel) have added greatly to the final product. Ursula King was instrumental in enabling the field-work undertaken for Chapter 7, provided valuable input for Chapters 4 and 11, kept me supplied with innumerable newspaper cuttings over the years and, in other ways far too numerous to mention, has contributed immeasurably to the completion of the book.

Most of the chapters that follow began as conference papers or invited talks, some of which were subsequently published in less accessible journals and formats. In bringing them together I have, with two exceptions (Chapters 3, 8) totally rewritten, updated and developed these earlier versions, taking into account new research and publications. Earlier versions of Chapter 1 were presented at the second Theory, Culture and Society conference, Berlin, in August 1995, the Chinese University of Hong Kong, December 1995, and the Graduate Institute of Building and Planning, National Taiwan University, Taipei, January 1996. Many thanks to Ping Hui Liao, Stephen Chan and Chu-joe Hsia for their kind invitations and hospitality. The paper was also read in the graduate class ('Imaging the World as One: Pre-Modern Representations of the Global') of my colleague, Charles Burroughs. For his invitation, his bibliographic assistance, and many conversations over the years, my many thanks to Charles on this occasion. The present chapter is a greatly revised and developed version of a paper published in *Planning Perspectives* 11, 1996. Chapter 2 began as a short essay (translated in German) in E. Barlosius, E. Kursat-Ahlers and H.-P. Walhoff (eds) *Distanzierte Verstrickungen: Die ambivalente Bindung sociologisch Forschender an ihren Gegenstand*, Berlin 1997, a festschrift for Professor Peter Gleichmann. Extensively revised, this was given as a paper to our departmental seminar, VizCult, in Fall 2002 at the invitation of my colleague, Tom McDonough. I would like to thank Tom and all my departmental colleagues and also graduate students (and many others over the years) for their contributions and especially, the members of my Fall 2002 graduate class, 'Writing Transnational Space', with whom most of these ideas were discussed. Chapter 3 began as a short commentary in a special issue of *Historical Geography* 29, 1999 on 'Colonial

Geographies', subsequently re-written and developed for the *Handbook of Cultural Geography* (2003). Apart from minor changes, it appears here in the same form. I am particularly grateful to Jane Jacobs, and editors Steve Pile and Nigel Thrift for their useful suggestions in writing this. Chapter 4 was given as a paper to the first Theory, Culture and Society conference (Silver Springs, Pennsylvania) and revised (with helpful suggestions from Roland Robertson) for publication in M. Featherstone, S. Lash and R. Robertson (eds) *Global Modernities* (1995). While there has been a narrowing of the gap between 'humanities' and 'social science' interpretations of ideas of 'modernity' in recent years, I believe the arguments in this (much revised and updated) version of that paper are still sufficiently valid to be worth including. The paper also includes parts from an invited lecture given to the Biennial Conference of the German Social Anthropological Association, Göttingen (Fall 2001), subsequently published (in German) in B. Hauser-Schaublin and U. Brankamper (eds) *Ethnologie der Globalisierung: Perspektiven Kultureller Verflechtungen* (2002). I would like to express my thanks to the organizers for their invitation and to Georg Elwert, Verena Stolke and other conferees for their comments. Chapter 5 developed from a talk for a conference on 'Imported and Exported Urbanism', at the American University of Beirut, December 1998. Parts of the chapter draw on an introduction to five papers from that conference published in *City and Society* 12, 1, 2000 and also from an essay in J. Nasr and M. Volait (eds) *Urbanism: Imported or Exported? Native Aspirations and Foreign Plans* (2003). I am much indebted to Joe Nasr and Mercedes Volait for their invitation and for their many helpful comments on my paper.

Chapter 6 began as a paper for a conference in Istanbul, 'Global Flows/ Local Fissures: Urban Antagonisms Revisited' in 1998 and subsequently published in *WP: Working Papers in Local Government and Democracy* 2, 1999; my thanks are due to Caglar Keyder and Ayşe Öncü for the invitation to that conference. Other parts of the chapter are adapted from the Gordon Cherry Memorial Lecture at the 9th International Planning History Conference in Helsinki, 2000 and published in *Planning History* 22, 3, 2001. I would like to extend my thanks to the organizers of that conference. Chapter 7 is based partly on material gathered in Beijing during a visit in Summer 2000. For arranging visits to various 'luxury' housing developments in Beijing, I am greatly indebted to Virginia Wang and for additional material on villa developments in Shanghai and Guang Dong, and also for comments on my chapter, I owe my thanks to Yunxiang (Sam) Liang. I am also grateful to Hugh Raffles and Lisa Rofel, Department of Anthropology, University of California, Santa Cruz, and the Center for Cultural Studies there for the opportunity to present some of this research at their workshop, 'Place, Locality and Globalization' in October 2000. An earlier version of Chapter 8 was given at the 'Cities, Space, Globalization' conference, University of Michigan, Ann Arbor, and published in H. Dandekar (ed.) *City, Space and Globalization* (1998). It was subsequently extensively revised for a talk in the Global Affairs Institute, Syracuse University and published in R. Grant and J. S. Short (eds) *Globalization and the Margins* (2002). Many thanks to Hemalata Dandekar and also John Short for their invitations on these occasions (and for permission to republish this), and also David Page and Colonel C. B. Ramesh of Bangalore for their helpful comments on this paper. Chapter 9 was first given as a paper at a conference, 'City One: The Urban Experience in South Asia', at SARAI, Delhi, in January 2003, and subsequently at the Global Affairs Institute, Syracuse University and the Department of Sociology's Workshop, 'Understanding Transnational Dynamics', University of Illinois, Urbana-Champaign, in Spring 2003. For their invitations to these events and helpful insights, I am indebted to Ravi Sundaram, Deborah Pellow, Jan Nederveen Pieterse, Narayani Gupta and Michael Goldman, and for their thoughtful comments on the paper, Jyoti Hosagrahar, Deborah Pellow, Vini Gupta and Anjuli Gupta. Faizan Ahmed was an outstanding guide round Old Delhi. Chapter 10 was prompted by a visit to the University of British Columbia's Green College, Vancouver, in March 2003, including reading about the architecture of one of the College's original houses, designed by Cecil Fox, a pupil of the British Arts and Crafts architect, C. F. A. Voysey, and an early twentieth century emigrant to Vancouver. I am very grateful to Penny Gurstein for this invitation. The later part of the essay, revised and expanded, is developed from a chapter in Roger Silverstone (ed.) *Visions of Suburbia* (1997). At the risk of some repetition, my aim here has been to re-locate this essentially local material (including some illustrations I have published before) within the larger global context provided by the Indian, Chinese and other case studies discussed in the previous chapters and the theoretical arguments developed earlier. Many thanks both to Roger and also Greig Crysler for their comments on an earlier draft of this (and to Greig, for innumerable stimulating conversations during his time at Binghamton and subsequently) and especially, to Alan Crawford, for his comments and suggestions on earlier and later versions of this chapter. Thanks also to Wendy Hitchmough and Helen Brandon-Jones for help with illustrations. The inspiration for Chapter 11 came from an essay by Janet Wolff whom I thank for her helpful comments on this essay. Chris Focht, as always, has provided outstanding photographic services and Bülent Batuman proved to be an expert and indispensable computer consultant. My many thanks to both. I am also grateful to the American Council of Learned Societies for a Fellowship in the mid 1990s enabling me to develop the foundations for this project.

In writing the book, I have been greatly helped by the always friendly, expert and willing service at Binghamton University's excellent library and also by the admirably inter-disciplinary atmosphere on the campus. Though the names of many friends and colleagues who, in different ways, have added to the intellectual as well as practical completion of this project are too numerous to list, I should particularly like to mention those at the Fernand Braudel Center and the many graduate students who have participated in my classes over the years. At Routledge, Caroline Mallinder and, especially, Helen Ibbotson, have provided ready, willing and expert assistance. I am also much indebted to the editorial department at Florence Production Ltd, in particular Claire Machin for some meticulous proofreading. Finally, the continuous love and support (of many different kinds) of all the members of our growing family have, with the benefit of email, snail mail, telephone and transatlantic flights, been of immeasurable importance in the completion of the book. The responsibility for what follows is, needless to say, entirely my own.

PART ONE

Theories

Chapter 1: Worlds in the City: From Wonders of Modern Design to Weapons of Mass Destruction

A whole history remains to be written of *spaces* which would at the same time be the history of *powers*.

Foucault (1980: 149)

INTRODUCTION

In this chapter,[1] I address three theoretical issues. The first concerns the use made by nations, cities, and religions – and within these larger categories, corporations, individuals, and followers – of spectacular architecture, and especially high rise towers, not only as signifiers of economic, political and cultural power, but also of national, corporate and both individual as well as collective identities.

The second issue concerns the invention and selective appropriation, worldwide, of particular 'signs of modernity' – especially, the high rise tower – whether in urban contexts in the West or outside it. What are the conditions under which particular signs of modernity have been generated? At what socially, politically and geographically specific moments? In which particular 'worlds', secular or religious? And at what conjunctures and locations in the emergence of advanced industrial capitalism have they emerged and then been appropriated or transplanted elsewhere?

In pursuing these two issues, I take the production of architecture (and the built environment more generally) not simply as *one* way of thinking about signs of modernity in the city, the nation, and different discursively constructed worlds – a 'plurality of competing, complementary and overlapping symbolic and spatial orders'[2] – but *the* most important material and visual realm in which this competition takes place.

Third, as part of this already full agenda, I also want to explore how the construction of spectacularly tall buildings promoted as 'the tallest building in the world', and accompanied by a discourse which represents them as such, not only helps to *create* new (though also exclusive) social worlds, but also how it contributes to a more widely disseminated conception of what 'the world' itself might actually be. Here, I draw on the work of Franklin *et al.* who show how, since the late 1960s, images of the 'blue planet' have been 'deployed as a symbol of global unity, international collaboration and shared planetary interdependency' (2000: 28). These and other images have become a 'fact of life through which a global imaginary is becoming an environment, a universe, an identity, a habit or a "second nature"' (ibid.: 20). By means of these images and texts, the discursively constructed 'planet earth' becomes 'a reality'.

In a similar, though more restricted way, the act of constructing 'the world's tallest building', performed at irregular intervals, and accompanied by discourses of texts and images that represent it as such, simultaneously constructs a 'world' but one of a different kind. The same is true, of course, of other important 'mega-events', not least, the World Cup soccer competition, the Olympic Games (Roche 2000), or television coverage of some catastrophic disaster.

Finally, if it is true that the gigantic tower has become 'the most important symbolic product of the world-economy',[3] what evidence is there to support that assertion? I also attempt to trace the invention and development of what was promoted as a *local* city skyline in Manhattan in the late nineteenth century (van Leeuwen 1988) into what is represented as a worldwide, even *global* skyline today (see, for example, www.SkyscraperPage.com).

CONSTRUCTIONS OF, AND IN, THE WORLD

In these competitive representations of architectural spectacle, 'the world' is, first and foremost, an imaginary or virtual world, constructed through the means of different media: the press, film, television, the web and diagrams in published books. We see and know about 'the world's tallest building' [*sic*] only through representations which present the different exhibits in economic, political and cultural terms and belonging, in the present era, to a world of cities and nation states. It is also, however, a *material* world, a world of interactive symbolic discourse and gesture which operates through an 'economy of signs and spaces' (Lash and Urry 1994). This is not just a 'global world', presupposed on ideologies of interdependency and 'consciousness of the world as a whole' (Robertson 1992). It is also a 'worldly globe' where nations, cities, corporations and human subjects – as well as transnational and global institutions – vie with each other, in a very tangible way, to display and represent themselves on the politically and economically uneven territorial surface of the globe. They do this in carefully selected, visible places, and in the sheer size of corporate organizations reflected, for example, in the size of their office buildings as well as the semiotically coded clothing of architectural design.

THE BUILDING AS SIGN

It is this very material, physical-spatial and visually symbolic element of *the building*, and *building form*, which is insufficiently captured by the loosely theorized 'spatial' which too frequently circulates in the discourses of geography or cultural studies.

Recognizing that New York is imagined, and imaged, through its Manhattan skyline, or Moscow by the stark walls of the Kremlin and bulbous towers of St Basil's cathedral, I want to focus attention on the central synecdochal importance of the materiality and visibility of the *building*, in constituting and representing not only the city, but also the nation, as well as different, distinctive worlds.

The building houses (literally, embodies) the political, cultural or administrative institution; it appropriates scarce and capital-invested landscape; it symbolizes the political presence and economic power of each level of spatial organization: the secular, political world of the United Nations or the fiduciary one of the (in Washington, much less visible) World Bank; the political or military realm of the nation state in its national capitol complex (Vale 1992) or the administrative and social space of the urban polity in its city hall.

It is the *building*, whose presence is usually mysteriously absent in every kind of social or cultural theoretical discourse (King 1990c), in which the ideology of all 'imagined communities' (Anderson 1983) and 'imagined environments' is contained, materialized and symbolized. It is within the space and form of the building in which the social is most frequently constituted, in which its visual image announces its presence – in the city, in the nation, and in various distinct worlds. It is also, in this post Cold-War era of 'peace', the presence and structure (as well as media-transmitted images) of the building that we are learning to see as the most important symbol of both live and lost causes: in India, for the communalist Shiv Sena and right wing BJP, the Babri Mosque at Ayodhya; in England, for the negotiating statements of the IRA, the Baltic Exchange building in the City of London; in the United States, for the splinter groups of an Islamic jihad, the World Trade Center in New York; and subsequently, for the right wing, anti-government militia, the Federal Building in Oklahoma City. As the barbed wire and electronic security systems are dismantled from the often ruralized, distant borders of the nation state, they are re-installed around the perimeters of vulnerable icons in the city.

It is not just that the urban public or private building becomes a manageable project for one, or a larger cadre of politically motivated activists; it is also that it is, *already*, a signifier of some organization or ideology which, when invaded, blown up or burnt down, takes on an additional level of signification. It focuses the lens of the journalist's camera, the eye of the camcorder, the direction of the mobile TV. It is always the image of the *building* – rarely the diffuse and ungraspable 'city', and even less, the 'imagined community' of the nation – which is used to fix our gaze on the limited space of the rectangular screen. In what is now a totally institutionalized mimetic televisual convention, it is the White House, the Houses of Parliament, the Duma or the Eiffel Tower which – subliminally elided into the capital city – is used to mediate the meaning of the Nation to the gazes of the World.

Competition between nations, cities, organizations or even individuals that use buildings as a sign (Trump Tower in New York or over 14,000 McDonald's round the world)[4] is obviously not a competition which everyone either recognizes as legitimate or in which every nation, city, or organization wishes to participate. The practice of postcolonial states (Malaysia), or world powers aspiring to leadership (China), of making use of the symbolic language of 'the tallest building in the world' [sic] or, for cities perhaps, the staging of the Olympic Games (Seoul, Sydney, Beijing) to announce their presence to a world of nations is relatively recent. However, recent cases of 'building tall' as a strategy of attracting international attention do provide insight into the conditions surrounding the origin of the practice, in regard to the earliest high rise buildings in modern times.

Historically, the use made of the *height* of buildings as a statement of identity (and, implicitly, superiority or even power), has been limited to specific historical periods and geocultural areas, most obviously, in regard to the churches and cathedrals of medieval Europe, which I discuss below. And in that case, height has generally only been one of a number of attributes, including design, siting, and (variably perceived) aesthetic quality, establishing the aura and repu-tation of a building. What gave rise to the modern phenomenon were not only the competitive conditions of modern American industrial capitalism, particularly as they played out in the corporate world of the newspaper industry but also the emergence onto the world stage of what, compared to the older states of Europe, was a new and youthful United States of America. The first tall build-ings of the US were built primarily with a local, city audience, and then with a continental one (Europe), as their principal referent. Only later was this extended to the rest of the world.

THE AMERICAN SKYSCRAPER: ORIGINS AND SYMBOLISM

The six structures that constituted the first tall building cluster in nineteenth century New York were erected in Park Place in the early 1870s. Of these, the tallest (260 feet/79.3 meters)[5] was the Tribune Building, the headquarters of the *New York Tribune* (1873–5) and its height was the outcome of fierce competi-tion with its corporate rivals (Domosh 1988). Just as many tall buildings that were to follow, and prior to the days of film and television, the disseminated printed image of the building was to contain more advertising power than the visual experience of the building itself, confined as the experience was to a limited number of viewers. Its image displayed on a flyer, the Tribune Building was promoted as 'the largest newspaper office in the world' and 'The highest building on Manhattan Island'. As an advertising device, the success of the Tribune Building was to provoke rival newspaper proprietors to build even higher. By the end of the following decade (1889), Joseph Pulitzer's 'World Building' [*sic*], housing the offices of the *New York World*, not only upstaged the *New York Times* in its 12-storey building of 1888–9, but also 'towered six stories above any other building in the city' (ibid.: 327–9).

The 'world' created by these developments was limited, mainly confined to New York and its main competitor, Chicago, and the wider American read-ership of its newspapers. Equally cut-throat competition within the life insurance industry, accompanied by the rapid speculative construction of other high rise Manhattan offices, meant that, by 1890, not only had New York become 'the capital of American corporate headquarters' but, in Domosh's words, 'the sym-bolism of height had become established in American society' (ibid.: 341; see also Weisman 1970). What Domosh might have added, however, is that the 'symbolism of height' had also been promoted, unilaterally, *vis à vis* an imagined, discursively constructed 'world'.

These early skyscrapers – the term had come into use in the early 1880s though was first applied to Chicago's 20-storey Masonic Temple in 1891 (van Leeuwen 1988: 43) – were, however, also functional in a more strictly econ-omic sense. Given the financial realities of a profit-driven market in land, there was obvious logic in concentrating people vertically in tall buildings on a small lot.

Equally critical was the entry into the discourse on skyscrapers of the term and concept of the *skyline* which, between the mid 1870s and mid 1890s, gets added to its earlier usage of 'the line where earth and sky meet', the further meaning of 'the silhouette of tall buildings against the horizon' (Attoe 1981). What New York writer Montgomery Schuyler was to conclude in 1897 was that the skyline of lower Manhattan was 'not an architectural vision, but it does, most tremendously, look like business' (van Leeuwen 1988: 84).

Van Leeuwen makes the point that early American skyscrapers were about 'fantasy, capital, and the grid' where conditions in the horizontal plane of the grid were equal, but the vertical space was free territory; the principal cause of the skyscraper, therefore, was speculation, to make money out of land.

Yet American commitment to the 'symbolism of height', gauged in relation to a socially constructed and imagined universe, first produced by the world of commerce and fueled by the competitive spirit of New York and Chicago, the two prime centers of American capitalism, was also shared (not surprisingly) by the world of politics. Within a decade of the Tribune Building, the long-delayed completion of the Washington Monument in the nation's capital was again, befitting a 'developing nation', extensively promoted as 'the tallest building in the world'. A claim of this nature, however, not only required the assembling of a substantial body of geographical, historical and architectural knowledge but also its extensive (ideally, worldwide) dissemination. The imaginary 'worldwide skyline' (Figure 1.1), an architectural collage designed to be read from left to right as well as foreground to rear, and accompanied by a table indicating the comparative heights of 78 buildings worldwide, was published four years after the Monument's inauguration (1885). It provides an early, if not necessarily the earliest, example of a 'global skyline'.

Though most buildings represented are from Europe, the diagram also includes others from China, India and Africa. According to the caption, it purports to represent 'the principal high buildings of the old world' [sic]. Despite the key feature (the Washington Monument) being located centrally at the rear of the exhibits and listed at the very end of the accompanying table, the hardly hidden agenda of the whole is to demonstrate the national superiority of the United States, the metropolitan superiority of its capital, and the moral superiority of its first president, by highlighting the height of the Monument – which exceeds them all – at 555 feet/169 meters.[6]

Yet while this discursively produced 'global skyline' aims to distinguish and implicitly compare the 'old world' with the 'new', to the detriment of the former, it can also be said to do the opposite. As Griswold (1986: 715) suggests, as the obelisk originated in the ancient civilization of Egypt, 'the founder of the New World republic is thus tied to the very origins of political life'.

The existence of this (and probably other) politically invested visual statements without which the Washington Monument could not legitimize its most important claim, draws attention to other issues. What was to become, in the later nineteenth century and most of the twentieth century, in New York, Chicago and subsequently, other American cities, a nationalist American obsession with 'the symbolism of height' – an obsession generally not shared (with the one important exception of China as I discuss below) by the majority of other states, cities, or political regimes in the world for another hundred or more years, rested on a continuous generation of knowledge, not only *in* America, but also *by* Americans and largely, *about* America. From the date of this 1889 collage to Judith Dupré's book, *Skyscrapers* of 1996,[7] with photographs and details of the hundred 'tallest buildings in the world' (some 60 percent of which are in the US) as well of the website, SkyscraperPage.com, this exercise in cultural jingoism has continued to the present, a 'local' discourse projected to the rest of the world.

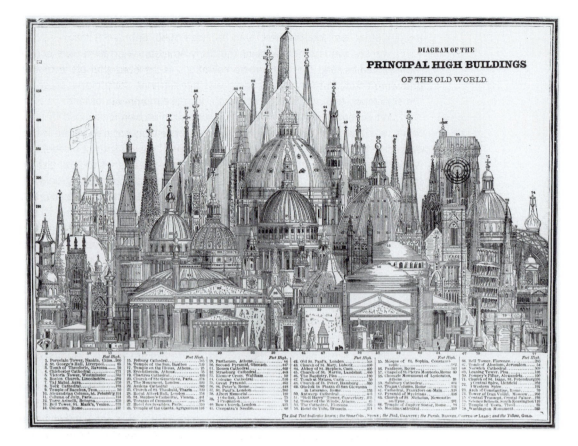

The two 'worlds' in which, in 1889, these building heights are represented are not the 'First World' and 'Third World' familiar to us since the early 1950s (Wolf-Phillips 1987: the 'Second' having largely disappeared), nor the 'modern' and 'traditional worlds' of 1960s 'modernization theory', nor the 'postmodern', 'modern', 'premodern' and 'ancient' world of the 'Western' humanities, but an older, nineteenth-century conception of 'the old world' and 'the new'.

Yet in this, the (implied) 'new' world of the Americas, only one nation state is represented, the US, and only one building (a monumental obelisk). Drawing on the theoretical insights of anthropologist Marilyn Strathern, Franklin *et al.* write that 'a global order that is able to constitute its own context is dependent on a concealing of its own social, political, cultural and economic dimensions'. It produces 'new universalisms which perform specific types of connection' (2000: 20). The 'old world' context constituted here consists of symbolic architectural products belonging to multiple civilizations, religions, empires, states, cities, spread across the world's different continents: the Christian cathedrals of medieval Europe, the Colosseum of the ancient Roman Empire, the Parthenon of the Athenian city-state, the Albert memorial of nineteenth-century imperial London or, moving to other continents, the Third Dynasty Pyramid of ancient Egypt, the Taj Mahal of Moghul India, or the Porcelain Tower of imperial China's Nanking. By representing these buildings only in terms of their height, and not with reference to their various political, cultural, aesthetic, spiritual,

Figure 1.1
'Principal High Buildings of the Old World' 1889: *The People's Illustrative and Descriptive Family Atlas of the World* 1889

constitutional, religious, economic, legal, ethnic, magical or other identities or properties, all are subordinated, reduced in meaning, in order that they can be made inferior, not only to the height of the Washington Monument but to that which it represents. 'The new universalism . . . is achieved through forms of displacement, exclusion and classification' (Franklin *et al.* 2000: 20).

The significance of this and subsequent similar representative diagrams is that they aim to establish (without the consensual involvement of other states, cities or jurisdictions) the *notion* of a global competition not only where it had not existed before, but where it remains a figment of the imagination. This seems a characteristic peculiar to the history of the United States which, for reasons possibly connected to its late arrival on the international stage, has long made a practice of compensating for its comparatively brief history by positioning various of its attributes in relation to similar real or imaginary phenomena in a larger 'world'. The 'world-class' athlete or scholar, or in baseball, the 'World Series' [*sic*], and until quite recently, 'the tallest building in the world', are instances of a peculiar American conceit.[8]

THE WORLD OF CHRISTENDOM

An earlier instance of competition had, however, taken place in the world of religion, though not between representatives of different religious traditions whether Christian, Islamic, Buddhist or Hindu, but rather, within some of them, and in the case of Christianity, within the more limited territory of medieval Europe. Here, the heights of cathedral and church spires of various cities had functioned as symbols of religious power, of clerics over burgesses, or cathedral chapters over each other.[9] In this case, the 'world' of competition was continental, the European and Near Eastern space of Christendom. The medieval Muslim world had run its own competition, quite separate from that of the Christians. The aim in that case was not only to give the mosque dome the greatest height but also the broadest diameter, with Istanbul's Hagia Sophia (originally an Orthodox Christian church) establishing the model following its conversion to a mosque after the conquest of Constantinople (1453). However, the Suleymaniye Mosque in Istanbul, 53 meters in height and 26.5 meters diameter, designed by the great Ottoman architect, Sinan, and built in the 1550s, was still to fall short of its rival by three or four meters in both dimensions.

Despite the massive programs of cathedral and church building from the eleventh to the fourteenth and fifteenth centuries, prior to 1200 no tower or steeple of a Christian church or cathedral had exceeded 100 meters (289 feet). Yet from the first half of the fifteenth century the spires and towers of at least four churches or cathedrals began to rise up to, or exceed, 150 meters/492 feet – St Peter's, Louvain (150 meters/492 feet), begun in 1425 though destroyed by storm in 1606, Strasbourg Cathedral (140 meters/459 feet) completed in 1439, Lincoln Cathedral's central tower (160 meters/522 feet) between 1307 to 1548 (though subsequently to collapse), and Old St Paul's in London (149 meters/489 feet), built between 1315 and 1561. That competition in building height was a well-established practice in medieval Europe is evidenced by the spectacular skyline of towers in Bruges represented in the famous painting, attributed to P. Claessens the elder, 'The Seven Wonders of Bruges' of c.1550 (Girouard 1985).[10]

The construction of spectacularly lofty towers, steeples and spires ascending skywards as a sign (and to heaven), each new manifestation higher than the last and taller than any other building in the world (the height of Old St Paul's, at 149 meters, 2.5 meters higher than the Great Pyramid of Cheops (built c.2580 BC), though that was probably coincidence and not design), lasted until the final decade of the nineteenth century. When Cologne Cathedral, using the available knowledge and skills of an industrialized Germany, was completed in 1880, its final height (at 157 meters/515 feet) was clearly an outcome of 'competitive knowledge', less than ten meters higher than the previous highest spire, that of Old St Paul's. Yet within a decade, and inside the national space of Germany, Cologne was then outdone by the city rivalry of the burghers of Ulm, completing Ulm Cathedral with the highest steeple in Christendom (161 meters/528 feet) in 1890.

At this point, the urban world of European Christianity gave way to the world of American capitalism, commerce and nationalism, as well as egotism. But not, as we have already seen, before establishing the final (European) benchmark for the height of America's national icon, the Washington Monument, built to be 8 meters higher than the cathedral in Ulm.

THE WORLD OF CORPORATE EGOS

That New York office towers at the turn of the century were as much to do with the world of personal egos as corporate identity is well demonstrated by the likes of Joseph Pulitzer who, 'driven with diabolical ambition and the capacity for work', was determined to build the 'highest office building in the world' (van Leeuwen 1988: 103). He was followed in the same goal, first, by Isaac Singer of the Singer Sewing Machine corporation who, in 1906, constructed a 47-storey landmark tower and advertised it with a 'global skyline' (the monument to the nation's founder prominent in its subordination to that of Isaac Singer: see Bacon 1985). The president occupied the thirty-fourth storey with the rest of the offices let to professional and commercial interests. As the first American business to establish branch offices abroad and control 80 percent of the world market, the logic and location of the Singer building were principally in terms of capital accumulation and, like the others, advertisement value (Fenske and Holdsworth 1992: 138–9). Three years later, John R. Hegeman, the 'flamboyant president' of America's largest life insurer, Metropolitan Life, upstaged all his predecessors with a 700 foot (213 meter) tower, again 'the tallest building in the world' (Dupré 1996). Yet the cultural reference for the headquarters tower, modeled (in its re-building, following the collapse of the first attempt) on the Campanile in St Mark's Place, Venice, was still in Europe. Hardly was this finished when F. W. Woolworth's vast landmark headquarters, a visible Gothic skyscraper (again, with its reference to Europe) completed in 1913, topped previous records as 'the largest single office building in the world'. By this time, the distinctively American practice of making the building a metaphor of the owner by naming it after him had become well established. Fenske and Holdsworth conclude:

> The restructuring of New York's urban environment [in the late nineteenth and early twentieth centuries] was not just a matter of changing the skyline. The landmark towers . . . were rarely of any true functional use to their corporate builders . . .

> The only justification was an enterprise's visibility on the urban scene. [Their logic was the] establishment of a physical presence for an unmaterial business such as insurance and the assertion of an individual ego. The unabashed appropriation of a form typically reserved in earlier civilizations for ecclesiastical or civic purposes vividly conveyed the dominance of commercial affairs in American life.
>
> (1992: 154)

Building gigantic towers is an immensely expensive form of advertising, though understandable in the days before television and the saturation campaigns of the press. Yet it is these developments in electronic media technology, combined with other factors discussed below, that have since come to challenge and, in some cases at least, undermine the practice. As Dovey has suggested, there are no real (or permanent) winners in either the local or the global competition for the highest high rise tower: 'Symbolic capital is not so much created as moved around from one temporary landmark to another' (Dovey 1999: 121).

SKYSCRAPER AS AMERICAN SIGN: IDENTITY AND MODERNITY

> Skyscrapers are as much an essential part of America's identity as the Coke bottle, baseball and the Marlboro cowboy.
>
> (Sudjic 1996)

The development of the skyscraper in late nineteenth-century America is generally acknowledged as being not only connected with the growth of nationalism but also the search for a national (American) architectural style (van Leeuwen 1988; Weisman 1970) and a distinctive American identity. By 1900, according to van Leeuwen (from whom much of this paragraph is taken), the skyscraper had achieved the status of an architectural type, and was acknowledged, inside and outside the United States, as characteristic of American civilization. In the twentieth century, it was to become the paradigmatic statement, not only of American architecture and urbanism, but of the economic ideology, mode of production and ethos from which it was largely (if not entirely) produced: capitalist land values, speculative office development and big business materialism in the United States.

It also became a national symbol of modernity, represented in the early twentieth century especially by the 'three monarchs' of New York City, the Chrysler Building, the RCA Building and the Empire State Building, the latter, to be a continuing site of vicious battles between different egos (Yardley 2001).

Yet this is a sign of modernity as understood and represented in the early 1930s, when the Empire State Building was 'the tallest building in the world from 1931 to 1972' (Dupré 1996), having taken over the title, held for one year, by the Chrysler Building. As Welsh author, Jan Morris, writes:

> Every city has its heyday, the moment when its purpose is fulfilled and its spirit bursts into flower . . . Manhattan's occurred I think in the years between the Great Depression and the end of the Second World War . . . In those magnificent years, this small island, no more than a fantastic dream to most peoples of the world, stood everywhere for the fresh start and the soaring conception . . . The memories of that time are legendary already and moving fast into myth.
>
> (Morris 1995)

This, then, is a seventy year old, American version of 'modernity', 'a little old fashioned', to cite Morris (1995; see also Chapter 4); a 'modernity' that has not only become a 'tradition' but, as I discuss below, one that is widely seen as outmoded.

THE SKYSCRAPER AS METAPHOR OF MODERNITY

How the skyscraper moved from being an icon solely of *American* identity and corporate power in its various cities to becoming a signifier of modernity in other parts of the world, and what symbolic meaning might be attached to that, is, as yet, an unwritten story. The *mere height* of a building was never a defining characteristic of what subsequently became known as the 'Modern Movement', either in the United States or Europe. Yet for reasons apparently mimetic of the United States, the spectacular high rise building has become a metaphor of modernity, if not worldwide, at least in some postcolonial or 'emerging' nation states. The most cursory perusal of city view postcards in major cities of the world, from Ankara to Zagreb, would confirm the assumption that popular conceptions of spectacularity and 'modernity' in cities are to be represented by the city's most recent high rise building, irrespective of its architectural design (Figure 1.2).

In the past, cities, particularly in North America, competed with each other and within a national urban hierarchy, in terms of building scale and whether these were large or tall, or even architecturally spectacular. Such architecture was (and is) usually in the interests of boosterism: in Sudjic's words, 'It made nowhere suddenly into somewhere' (1996: 6).

Yet dependent on the international positionality of the observer, the effect can be the opposite: somewhere can suddenly become nowhere. The 420 meter/1371 feet high Millennium Tower proposed for the City of London in 1996 was met by charges that building it would 'simply confirm Britain's status as a Third World country' (*Guardian Weekly*, September 15, 1996: 12). Architect Kim Dovey, criticizing the proposed super gigantic Grollo Tower in Melbourne suggested that if the city were to steal the mantle of the world's tallest building from Kuala Lumpur it would only be a few years before the Grollo Tower was 'overtaken by some fourth rate city with its own identity crisis' (Dovey 1996: 3). For *The Guardian*'s architecture correspondent, Jonathan Glancy, super high rise towers are 'increasingly symptoms of "second-city syndrome"' (December 14, 1998). This issue will be revisited below.

If we consider the modern 'international' history of tall buildings (including important tall structures), we might note that the crude symbolism of height, as established in the American capital by the Washington Monument, was rapidly overtaken in the French capital by Gustav Eiffel's steel tower of 1889, 304.8 meters high (984 feet). As a nationalistic gesture, this was to remain for over four decades the tallest *structure* in the world till the advent of the more than 1,000 feet high Manhattan skyscrapers such as the Chrysler and Empire State Buildings of 1930 and 1931,[11] the height of these buildings was therefore established by reference to a European, particularly French, norm. In other countries, governments, cities or organizations constructed their own cultural, social and spatial worlds within different imperially, nationally or ideologically bounded spaces. The buildings that they put up, and the discourses that were created about them, helped cement the links within these bounded worlds.

Figure 1.2

For most of the twentieth century, few individuals, regimes, or cities outside the United States either recognized, let alone attempted to compete, in the 'world' that the builders of New York skyscrapers had created nor did they conceive of a 'global' or 'worldwide skyline'. Important to mention here, however, not least because it is one of the few attempts at this time to counter capitalist ideology, is the unfulfilled plan, in the wake of the Russian Revolution (1920), to build a towering monument in Moscow to commemorate the Third International. At 412 meters, had it succeeded it would have been by far the highest structure in the world.

In Canada, the office of the *Vancouver World* newspaper, completed in 1913, was for three years known as the tallest building in the – quite different – political and cultural space of the British Empire. Thereafter, both Toronto and Montreal competed for the same title (Gad and Holdsworth 1987). In Melbourne, some years earlier, the 12-storey Australia Building had been completed in 1888. In combining its name with its location, it linked the identity of the city to that of the Australian nation (and perhaps simultaneously thumbed its nose to urban rival, Sydney). It was also perhaps a snub to the imperial center of London, for it was taller than any office building in Australia or, significantly, *in Europe*, and comparable in height with contemporary American skyscrapers (Lewis 1994).

In the early 1930s, with the rest of the world in economic depression, and the American skyscraper craze becoming defunct, the Asian entrepreneur, Victor Sassoon, influenced by American practice, started replacing the old colonial buildings on Shanghai's Bund with some thirty Manhattan-sized and -styled hotels and apartments, the first real skyscrapers both in Asia and outside the United States.[12] The 22-storey Park Hotel, built in 1934 and probably inspired by New York models, at 269 feet/82 meters, remained the tallest building in Asia for some thirty years (Lee 1999: 346).

Yet till the mid 1980s when the massive rash of tall buildings started to go up in Asia, over three quarters of the 70 tallest buildings in the world were still in the United States (Dupré 1996), underlining the fact that this particular practice of urban cultural politics was still a predominantly American, free market phenomenon. Where they existed outside the United States, it was either in emerging 'world cities' such as Toronto (in Canada, America's neighbor to the north), where there were three, Singapore, where in 1991 the Overseas Union Bank Plaza building, at 919 feet/280 meters, was to become the tallest building in southeast Asia and, as a sign of things to come, 'outside the United States' (Yeang 1991), and the postcolonial capitals of Seoul and Kuala Lumpur which were rapidly expanding their presence in the world economy.

TALL BUILDINGS AND WORLD CITIES

By the 1980s, the increasingly fierce (economic) competition and rivalry between actual and potential major financial centers in the world economy ('world cities' as they became increasingly known in the 1990s), fueled in 1989 by the collapse of the Soviet Empire, was already having profound effects on their built environment. The competition was not simply in terms of the costs of office space and labor to attract international banks, finance houses and corporate headquarters but, increasingly, of urban spectacle and cultural gizmos (Zukin 1991). By the 1990s the contest for the tallest, most architecturally unorthodox, postmodern 'signature buildings' was well under way. The producers were architects from geopolitical economies whose societies were most characterized by artistic individualism (cf. Castillo 2001). In Singapore at this time, as also in London, appear the city's tallest and/or most 'spectacular' monuments: Natwest Tower, Lloyd's Insurance Building and Canary Wharf (1991) (777 feet/237 meters), their purpose to reiterate (and reclaim) the historic (and imperial) role of both the City of London as well as the British state in the ever-expanding world of global capitalism. Its 'world city' rival, vying to become the 'New York of Europe' and hosting the European Bank, was Frankfurt, whose Messeturm (259 meters/ 850 feet), completed one year before (1990), along with the Commerzbank (of the same height), were 'the tallest office towers in Europe', institutionalizing the economic world of the European Community.

At the close of the twentieth century, therefore, the 'world' of 'the world's hundred tallest buildings' both confirms, and gives further credence to, the real and discursive realm of the world's 'world cities' (Beaverstock *et al.* 1999; Knox and Taylor 1995). Of Dupré's 'hundred tallest buildings' (updated to 2002), the vast majority exist in what have been categorized as either first or second order 'world cities':

Number of 'The World's 100 Tallest Buildings' in 'World Cities'

US	New York City	19
	Chicago	10
	Los Angeles	5
	Houston	5
	Dallas	2
	San Francisco	2
China	Hong Kong	6
	Shanghai	2

Japan	Tokyo	2
	Osaka	2
Singapore	Singapore	4
Canada	Toronto	4
Australia	Sydney	2
Germany	Frankfurt	2
Malaysia	Kuala Lumpur	2
Korea (S)	Seoul	2
Taiwan	Taipei	1
Indonesia	Jakarta	1
UK	London	1

The figures would also seem to confirm Roger Keil's view that 'the gigantic tower' has, indeed, become 'the most important symbolic product of the world economy', an apparently essential icon in order to be recognized as a 'world city', even though Paris, Milan, Zurich, Brussels, Madrid are among 'world cities' that do not have them (Beaverstock *et al.* 1999).

The 'world' of the world economy has also been signified in other ways, particularly by the construction of World Trade Center buildings, at least thirty of which have been built since the mid 1960s. Though most (11) are (or were) in American cities, Brussels, Mumbai, Taipei, Shenzen, Dalian, Bangkok, Seoul and Dubai all have World Trade Centers in excess of 100 meters high.

And even though the era of American robber barons might be past, the world of personal egos (past and present) continues to flourish. The International Saddam Tower in Baghdad (1994) at 205 meters (673 feet) is somewhat shorter than what was planned to be the height of the minarets (280 meters/919 feet) of the Saddam Hussein mosque, under construction in Iraq in 2002. In New York City, Donald Trump has made four attempts to build 'the world's highest building'. Worth mentioning, too, are the (male) architects and their multinational firms, primarily from the US, but also Japan, the UK, Australia and Canada, who have been at the forefront in the design of the world's tallest towers: Kohn Pederson Fox, Skidmore Owens and Merrill, Sir Norman Foster, Kenzo Tange, Pei Cobb Freed and HOK (see SkyscraperPage.com). As Susan Fainstein (1994) has commented in her study of *The City Builders* in New York and London:

> As I have studied the large projects that have changed the faces of London and New York, I have been struck by the extent to which they have been driven by male egos that find self-expression in building tall buildings and imprinting their personae on the landscape.[13]

The spatial, economic and geocultural 'worlds' of these last cases were all strictly limited – confined to specific 'world units' such as empires, nation states, or continents. Not until a century or more after the earliest claims of a discursively constructed competition for 'the tallest building in the world' does any nation, city, or other entity engage with, or lay claim to, a unilaterally declared American domain. And when a contest is engaged, with one exception, 'the world' is effectively confined to one consisting of two nation states, America and China, and even two or three cities: New York, Chicago and Shanghai.

BUILDING WORLDS

In March 1995, the (now defunct) American magazine, *Progressive Architecture*, ran a leading feature on what were, at that date, about to become 'the world's tallest buildings' being built, or planned, in the nations, and cities, of Asia – Indonesia's Jakarta, Malaysia's Kuala Lumpur, Taiwan's Taipei and China's Shanghai, Chongqing and (after July 1997) Hong Kong. Virtually all were designed by American-based, multinational firms.

At some 1,780 feet (543 meters), China's Nina Tower in Hong Kong was about to be 300 feet (91.5 meters) higher than the then American record-holder, Chicago's Sears Tower which, at 1,454 feet (443 meters), had held the record for the previous twenty years. However, according to these reports, other Asian towers were also out to eclipse the record of 'tower power' which, until the mid 1990s, had been strictly confined to the West. Shanghai's 1,535 foot (468 meter) Oriental Pearl Television Tower, 'more than 150 feet taller than the World Trade Center in New York' was completed in May 1995 (Faison 1995). In Malaysia, the national oil company, Petronas, had recently completed its 1,483 foot twin-towered headquarters (452 meters) which already outranked the Sears Building. That record would only stand till 1997 when another, 114-storey (516 meters/ 1,693 feet) Chongquing Tower, would put both China, as a nation, and Chongqing as a city, back in the lead (Rufford 1995). In either case, it would be the first time since 1891 that the world's highest buildings would be outside North America and, according to a later report in Britain's *Guardian*, the first time since the gothic cathedrals were built that the tallest building on earth was no longer in the West (*Progressive Architecture* 1995: 94; Sudjic 1996: 6).

According to the various reports, the rationale behind these developments was that the new towers were supposedly symbolic of Asia's entry onto the global stage of economic and political power over the coming decade.[14] That claim was subsequently to be discounted following the mini-collapse in the Asian economy. Nonetheless, the new towers were seen as not only marking the emergence of a powerful new space in the world economy but also, at the close of the old millennium, the opening up of a powerful new time, the so-called 'Asian Century'. It was this historical, or temporal gloss which explained another spectacular project supposedly in the offing, the Millennium Tower in Tokyo, designed by Sir Norman Foster and Partners at 2,600 feet (793 meters), three times the height of London's Canary Wharf (Rufford 1995). Other spectacular towers finished in 2003 or planned for the future (including three in China), all well over the height of America's Sears Building, include (in 2003): the Taipei Financial Centre at 508 meters (1,667 feet) ('the tallest building in the world' at that date); Union Square Hong Kong (2005), at 480 meters (1,575 feet); the Shanghai World Trade Center (2007) at 492 meters (1,614 feet); and Suyong Bay Tower, Pusan (2010), at 462 meters (1,516 feet).

According to the editors of *Progressive Architecture,* 'a shift of historic proportions (was) taking place and architecture is the premier symbol of that transformation ... the Chinese, as well as many other Asians, tend to want buildings as tall as possible and in an ostentatiously Modern style as can be found' (*Progressive Architecture* 1995: 44, 66). In the view of Eugene Kohn of New York architects, Kohn Pederson Fox, the reason was 'to catch up with the West. They don't think of themselves as Third World. They've chosen the tower for its skyline image, which immediately puts them in the First World' (ibid.: 46). In July 1995, the Oriental Pearl Television Tower was said to be 'the symbol of a new Shanghai' for its 13 million inhabitants, 'a firm sign that their city . . . is rising from the depths in which it has brooded for the first four decades of Communist rule' (Faison 1995). In Malaysia, the aim was reported to be to advertize 'the country's arrival as a modern industrial nation' (ibid.) and enable its Prime Minister, Mahathir Mohammed, according to another source, 'to stand tall among Asia's tiger economies' (Rufford 1995).

However, for Mahathir Mohammed, when the Petronas building was erected, it was not just – at that time – the world's tallest building but also one where the design embodies and draws consciously on Islamic motives. The world to which it speaks is not only that of the global media but especially, that of the Malaysian nation state and, not least, the larger world of Islam (Figure 1.3). Its symbolic role is 'in realizing a state vision of national development, the so-called 'Vision 2020' by which Malaysia becomes 'a fully developed country' by that year (Bunnell 1999: 2). Its function was to project Malaysia as a 'world class player' on the international scene, put Kuala Lumpur as a 'world city' on the 'world map' and at the same time, promote 'new ways of seeing' among its national citizens (ibid.: 4–5).

If Eugene Kohn's statement is correct, therefore, the massive high rise tower – 'the tallest building in the world' – is now being used by China and other countries in Asia as a magic wand, stuck into the terrestrial globe, to transform what used to be known (in the categories left over from the early 1950s), as the 'Third World' into the 'First'.

Yet according to the website, SkyscraperPage.com, by 2005, the world in which the 'contest' for 'the highest building' takes place seems likely to be restricted to two states. Since the middle of the 1990s, not only have the world's tallest buildings been in Asia but, by 2005, the ten 'tallest buildings in the world' will all be in China, and mostly in Shanghai. In the 1990s, then President Jiang Zemin and his Prime Minister Zhu Rongji decided to transform Shanghai into China's center for global capitalism, capable of vying with Los Angeles and New York. They were not interested in competing with Europe or even Japan but only with the United States. According to one account, this is what explains 'the copycat architecture and the race to build higher in recognition of a universal symbol of power; as if by reproducing the form of the desired object it is possible to appropriate its force'. Not only will the 'Oriental Manhattan' being built across the Huangpu river contain 'the world's highest building', the Shanghai World Trade Center, and the Jin Mau Building, but also a Ferris Wheel, 50 percent taller (660 feet/201 meters) than the London Eye. It will also have the world's tallest hotel (August 2002).

The explanation for this is not difficult to grasp. In the planning of the financial district, according to Olds, skyscrapers were chosen 'in keeping with the planners' ideas about what a central business district skyline should look like. Their model Central Business Districts (CBDs) were Manhattan in New York, Central in Hong Kong, Shinjuku in Tokyo and La Defense in Paris'. The desire to 'encourage the skyscraper form was based upon the association of towers with modernization . . . The most appropriate method to express the reform era', in the mind of Shanghai planners, 'was through the emergence of gleaming skyscrapers that thrust upwards' (Olds 2001: 203–4). Hence, in an era of

Figure 1.3
Petronas Building, Kuala Lumpur,
Malaysia, 2002

electronic communication, and irrespective of the functional need to concentrate workers in high rise towers, this obsolescent practice was followed, despite its acknowledged redundance in the US, with the world's leading company, Microsoft, based in its Seattle headquarters just three storeys high (see King 1996b).

MODERNITY'S SIGNS TRANSPOSED

That China should choose not merely to symbolize its own national identity and progress through the language and architectural codes of American capitalism but should also employ American architectural firms and design practices in order to do this, has more than a touch of irony.

Throughout its 5,000 years of urban civilization, the Chinese architectural tradition has been especially characterized by architectural principles that have emphasized harmony with the landscape, 'building with nature' and the spiritual ecology of *feng shui*. In domestic as well as more formal architecture, single-storey building has predominated, often with courtyard forms; and whether in imperial palaces, gardens or temples, as in the Forbidden City of Peking, the spatial representation of power and authority has traditionally been effected *horizontally* rather than *vertically* (Liu 1989). The principles of Chinese design, according to Kostof, were rectilinearity and axiality, and with these went 'the horizontal aesthetic, the conscious preference for a uniform range of heights that shifted the environmental burden of social distinctions to the placement of buildings in the general scheme of the city, the level of the terraces on which they invariably stood, the area they covered and the degree of their ornamentation' (Kostof 1995). The principal exception to this is the Buddhist pagoda which, in any case, was not indigenous to China but derived from India (Liu 1989: 56).

Even with the Communist Revolution, Mao's spatially symbolic commemorative space was horizontal not vertical: the demolition of vast tracts of central Beijing aimed to enlarge Tiananmen Square in order to hold an assembly 'of one billion' as 'only the biggest public, thus the biggest square, could match the supreme power of the Chairman and the (Tiananmen) Gate' (Hung 1991). Mao's square, in its massive horizontality, was not only the symbolic center of a new Beijing but also of a new China. At 98 acres, it is the biggest square in the world.

In this long-term historical and cultural context, therefore, the shift away from a horizontal symbolic representation of power to a vertical one is to be explained less by reference to the overwhelmingly patriarchal (hence, phallic) nature of China's political establishment[15] but rather, to the acceptance by them of an increasingly universal system of signifying economic and political power, originating in the United States, produced by the logic of a private, profit-driven system of capitalist land values, and classically represented by Manhattan or Hong Kong.

Yet in Beijing's longer historical context where neo-imperial architecture has later been used to represent the glory of the socialist state, the meaning invested in architectural styles can change from one regime to the next (Broudehoux 2001). The Chinese public has doubtless become accustomed to both contradictions and paradoxes. In Kuala Lumpur, meanings invested in the Petronas building, designed by American architect, Cesar Pelli, are apparently bound up with rivalries between the Chinese and non-Chinese business class, between Muslim and non-Muslim. Like other subjects, and objects, skyscrapers can have many identities.

For the vast majority of people who consume them as a spectacle, the meanings they are invested with are derived from their locality, through history, memory and a knowledge of difference. Asked what meanings were associated with Taipei's Shin Kong Tower, one response was 'It's modern, international, and gives us hope.'[16] Yet as local, and place-related as such an interpretation is, it clearly depends on what historically Western, specifically American market capitalist definitions of modernity suggest which, in being adopted by other nations and places, have also become a sign of the so-called 'international'.

In a somewhat different sense, the high rise building is also a sign of a particular function at the heart of the accumulation process characterizing that mode of production – the financial services center. Thus, according to a 1996 report,[17] Zhuang Yulin, the developer responsible for the 88-storey Jin Mao Building, suggests that 'Just one (high rise) building is inadequate, you need more to create the environment (of a financial center)' for Pudong's Lujiazui's Finance and Trade Zone. Here, we have ample confirmation of the argument that social and economic functions are constantly thought of through the images of existing building types (Franck and Schneekloth 1994) and ones developed in particular places, particular times, and within particular modes of production. Though as the recent development of virtually 'shed-based' telephone banking has confirmed, using TV and hoardings to advertise their services, a given architectural form is no more necessary for a banking function than it is for financial services. Yet high rise buildings, 'the tallest in the world', exist in other worlds and also, with their accompanying discourse, effectively construct them. In Jabalpur, seen by many as the 'navel' or center of India according to Vedic calculations, Maharishi Mahesh Yogi and his spiritual followers are in the process of building the Karondi Temple (2,222 feet/678 meters) high, almost twice the height of the Empire State Building and over 700 feet higher than the Petronas Tower. Begun in 1999 and designed like a multistorey Lingaraj Temple, with 20 million square feet on 144 floors, the temple is a 'mega campus of the spirit where 2,500 priests . . . chant Vedic mantras 24 hours a day to save the world'. Along with eleven similar buildings planned throughout the twelve (Maharishi) time zones in the world, the Mararishi believes that if 100,000 Brahmins sit and chant the Vedic mantras simultaneously at the same place, it will 'create coherence in world consciousness' (*India Today* 2001).[18] However, in 2003, the Maharishi's 'Global Community of World Peace' with its 10 million citizens and a presence in 108 countries had tragically to compete with the presence of the US army in 140 countries.

As a contemporary (and particularly 'global') sign of modernity, the irony of the new Asian (and particularly Chinese) skyscrapers, as discussed elsewhere (King 1995b), emerges from the paradigm shifts that have taken place in Western notions of urban modernity in recent years: the displacement of monolithic, gargantuan architectural icons of corporate capitalism by a range of environmental indicators that put ecological, energy, social and health concerns as more appropriate measures and signifiers of the modern city: clean air, public and private safety, quality of housing standards, environmental efficiency, steady traffic flows. On these criteria, among the world's hundred largest cities, Shanghai and Beijing ranked at number 48 and 49, Chongqing at 69. New York, once seen long ago as a model, ranked no better than twenty-seventh. The city with the highest score, at number 1 in the table, was Melbourne, Australia, principally a vast, single-storey suburb with a modest high rise core (Population Crisis Committee, 1991) (see Chapter 4, note 6).

EPILOGUE

The different worlds created by 'the world's tallest buildings' have profoundly changed since September 11, 2001. In the country where the skyscraper originated and where the discourse and contest developed, both have largely disappeared. Overnight, the spectacularly tall building, once a massive baton with which to boast to the rest of the world, has become a potentially terrifying weapon for wreaking chaos and carnage in the city. Where, at the close of the twentieth century, the doyenne of America's urban sociologists and admirer of its two most prominent cities could write 'by 1989, Manhattan had become the undisputed champion of high profile buildings with 117 structures at least 500 feet in height whereas Chicago had only 39' (Abu-Lughod, 1999a: 234), two years later each of these 156 buildings (and many more) were being viewed as potential time-bombs capable of bringing death and mass destruction to their occupants and surroundings.

Not everyone, however, has assumed that the implosion of New York's Twin Towers signals the beginning of 'a new era in architecture' (Glancy 2002) without the high rise tower. But for many in the world of its origin, what the absence of the Twin Towers has revealed is the presence of a new world where other people, with other values, are demanding radically different global priorities.[19]

NOTES

1   An earlier, shorter version of this chapter was published in *Planning Perspectives* 11, 1996: 97–114. While the original version has been extensively revised and developed. I have made virtually no alterations to the section on 'The Building as Sign' at the beginning of the chapter which, in the light of events of September 11, 2001, took on a sinister, tragic, though not altogether unforeseen sense of the prescient. To write, not least in an expository mode, about the symbolic functions of tall buildings after this date has, in many ways, become redundant.

2   The phrase is from the Second *Theory, Society, Culture* conference prospectus, 'Culture and Identity: City, Nation, World', Berlin, August 10–14, 1995 at which an earlier version of this paper was first presented.

3   The phrase was used by Roger Keil at the conference in 2 above.

4   Except where otherwise stated, all dimensions are derived from *The Guinness Book of World Records* (1996 and later editions), New York: Sterling Publishing Co., *The Guinness Book of World Records 1492* and www.SkyscraperPage.com.

5   Providing 'objective measurements' of these buildings in feet and meters throughout should not be read as a detraction from the major theme I wish to pursue. In giving these units, I have followed as far as possible what is historically and culturally appropriate rather than simply being 'consistent' in giving feet before meters.

6   *The People's Illustrative and Descriptive Family Atlas of the World* (1889), Rochester, NY: W. H. Stewart and Co.

7   Dupré's declarative subtitle, 'The world's tallest and most important skyscrapers' makes the assumption that 'the world' as such – all its various continents, peoples, nation states, religions or political regimes – is not only eager to *have* skyscrapers but that they should all engage in the gross competition.

8   The National Football League and National Basketball Association in the United States also proclaim their league winners as 'world champions' even though the leagues are solely American. Many thanks to Deryck Holdsworth.

9   I am indebted to Barbara Abou-el-Haj for this insight.

10   In terms of spectacular buildings giving distinctive identities to medieval cities, deserving mention is Brunelleschi's dome for the Duomo Santa Maria del Fiore in Florence of the Medicis built between 1420 and 1436; no other structure would exceed its dimensions, 138.5 feet (42 meters) diameter at the base and 330 feet high, until the dome of St Peter's, Rome was built 150 years later.

11   van Leeuwen (1988). K. Baedeker, *Paris and Environs*, Leipsic, 1900 gives the correct height of 984 feet.

12   H. Parker James, Skyscrapers of Shanghai: Victor Sassoon and the Depression-Era Property Boom. Paper for the *First International Symposium on Asia Pacific Architecture*, Session on 'The Colonial Experience', School of Architecture, University of Hawai'i at Manoa and the East-West Center, Honolulu, Hawai'i, March 22–25, 1995. Ward suggests that the twin Kungstornen built in the Swedish capital of Stockholm in 1924 and 1925 'were probably Europe's first skyscrapers' (2003: 94).

13   For an excellent study of architects (e.g. Renzo Piano, Sir Norman Foster, Richard Rogers, Rem Koolhaas, Jean Nouvel) as celebrities, as members of the 'Global Intelligence Corps', their role in the global culture of architecture, and particularly, for the views of architect Richard Rogers on urbanism and the city, see Olds (2001: Chapter 5). For architect Rem Koolhaas on architecture and globalization, see J. Signler, (ed.) (1995), *Small, Medium, Large, Extra-Large. Office for Metropolitan Architecture*. R. Koolhaas and B. Mau. Rotterdam: The Monacelli Press: 363–9.

14 Rufford attributes this view to the chairman of the architecture department at the Chinese University of Hong Kong, Tunny Lee.

15 As was suggested to me by a feminist colleague.

16 The response of a graduate from the Taiwan National University Graduate Institute of Building and Planning, January 1996.

17 *South China Morning Post* (Property Post), January 3, 1996: 1.

18 One of the Maharishi's buildings originally intended for Rio de Janeiro, was turned down by the city planning department. Rio has avoided excessively tall buildings. I am indebted to Dr Bianca Freire Medeiros for this information.

19 It is appropriate to end this chapter by referring to Daniel Libeskind's design for the buildings to replace the World Trade Center. Though office workers will occupy only around 60 floors of the various – much lower – buildings (as 'it was felt that no one would want to work in a building so high again' as the 110 storeys of the previous Center) the design includes a narrow tower, at 1,776 feet/541 meters, referring to the year of America's independence as well as being, in height, globally competitive (Teather 2003: 13).

Chapter 2: Interrogating Global Culture(s)

When I use a word . . . it means just what I choose it to mean – neither more nor less. Humpty Dumpty.

Lewis Carroll, *Through the Looking Glass*.
(*Oxford Dictionary of Literary Quotations*, 1997)

INTRODUCTION

Since starting the writing of this book I have been perpetually ambivalent about the title. As Appadurai has written, 'any book about globalization is a mild exercise in megalomania' (1996: 18). And that applies equally to 'global culture'. In one sense, the term is outrageous, the ultimate hubris, impossibly over ambitious in appropriating the largest thinkable spatial unit, as adjective, and applying it to everything encompassed by the noun it describes; the most recent example of the epistemic violence with which the (Eurocentric) Occident attempts to retain its epistemological control over representations of the world (Spivak 1988: 172).

From another perspective, however, it could perhaps be prescient and transformative, suggesting, in the very juxtaposition of the two words themselves, a historically new way of representing, understanding or resisting both the world and the culture(s) of the peoples in it.

In contemporary academic circles, the word 'culture' is increasingly being replaced by 'identity'. But whether we continue to use the term in the more everyday sense to refer to ways of life, or to the arts and media, or for a use that encompasses both these meanings, intellectual controversies persist: how, when and in what circumstances is/are 'culture/s' produced (and how is, or are culture/s the producer?). Within this book, whatever the meanings invested in the term, I will take culture to be a human, social and cultural phenomenon. Distinguished from nature, it refers in some way to historical and contemporary social life, which is why, speaking *literally*, I have two serious problems with the phrase 'global culture'.

Like globality and globalism, 'global culture' is part of the contemporary discourse on globalization. And while researchers in different fields may agree that there is a phenomenon generally represented by that term, an increasing number of them have become conscious that 'globalization' may not be the best word to describe it. As many authors have pointed out, understandings and analyses of that idea differ quite fundamentally: Brenner has termed it an 'essentially contested concept' (cited in Weldes 2001).

In what has, by now, become a well known phrase, Robertson (1992) has defined globalization as a process by which 'the world becomes a single place'. More recently, Held *et al.* spell out that process in more detail: 'a widening, deepening and speeding up of world-wide inter-connectedness in all aspects of contemporary social life, from the cultural to the criminal, the financial to the spiritual' (1999: 2). In one sense, this representation reflects the change in popular use of the term 'global' charted by the *OED* in the roughly two decades between 1971 and 1989.[1] It also accords with what the *Oxford Dictionary of New Words* documents as the emergence of a notion of global consciousness, a phrase it first identifies (probably belatedly) for 1989.[2]

Yet for whom is the world 'global', for whom is it 'a single place'? For whom – to use the other sense of the term – can 'global' be equated with 'comprehensive, all-inclusive, unified and total'? For whom is this hegemonic, totalizing gaze a realistic possibility? As Massey writes in regard to questions of gender, 'the universal, the theoretical, the conceptual, are in current Western ways of thinking, (all) coded masculine. They are the terms of a free-floating generalized science' (1994: 9; see also Hooper 2000). This seems only a slightly modified version of what Blaut (1993) refers to as the 'colonizer's view of the world'.

Nor is it always clear whether the term, global, is being used in a consciously metaphorical way, in the sense of embracing the totality, being all-inclusive, or in its more recent, specialized sense of 'the whole world, or world-wide' (which can also, in the conditions described below, only be a metaphorical use, as implicit in the 1989 *OED* definition).

If we are speaking of 'culture' as a human and social phenomenon, we might remember that three-quarters or more of the terrestrial globe consists of oceans, mountains, deserts and uninhabitable places. Of the remaining quarter of the earth's surface, climatic, resource, and countless other constraints powerfully limit the abilities of human populations to live there. While it is certainly possible to speak, literally, of global climate change, global pollution or the global reach of satellite communications (and these phenomena obviously, and massively, affect human populations in the world), in cases where our main interest is in human, social, and cultural phenomena, the term 'global' has either to be accepted as a metaphor, an exaggeration (in many cases), or, as I shall argue below, a category error. The most obvious example of the latter is in using 'global' where 'postcolonial', anglophone, international or transnational would be more appropriate, particularly where the latter two reflect and help to constitute the still powerful agency of the nation.

Yet in the context of everyday linguistic realities, such epistemological hesitations have obviously become irrelevant. Despite its ambiguities, since the last decade of the twentieth century, the phrase 'global culture' has become commonplace, whether in the academy, the media, or in public culture more generally. And as the aim of this book is to chart and comment on 'the spaces of global cultures', this increasing popularity of the term might be seen as valuable in identifying what I wish to address. From another perspective, however, so far as not only its *use* but also the many different *meanings* invested in the term have proliferated, it can also be seen as a poisoned chalice. None the less, in examining some, if not all, of these different meanings in this chapter, I have two aims in mind.

My first objective is simply to understand how, at the beginning of the twenty-first century, academics and others are constructing the world in which we live, a task which also includes examining the discourses and concepts with which they describe it. As Weldes has written: '(D)iscourses are deeply political, producing significant material and ideological effects . . . the representations that most people entertain about globalization – what they think it is and how they think it works – affect how they act' (2001: 648). The same is equally true of 'global culture'. If, as Robertson (1992) suggests, the idea of global culture is in the process of becoming as meaningful as the idea of national-societal, or local culture, is it replacing, or simply existing alongside of other 'non-global' forms? (such as national, or regional culture)?[3] Moreover, is global culture merely a phrase for something existing long before but under another label? Cosmopolitanism, internationalism, universalism?

My second aim is to see how useful the concept, as well as the epistemological problems its interrogation presents, might be for understanding both the production of an architectural, built environment and spatial culture worldwide as well as its consumption and reception. As others have commented (Cvetkovich and Kellner 1997; Short 2001), after well over a decade of often abstract, theoretical debates about globalization, postnationalism and other conceptual notions, where can we point to the material, concrete manifestations of their existence? What are the spaces produced by this putative global culture (or global cultures)? Where are the places where it can be found, contained or imagined? How does the imagining, construction or 'reality' of global culture put new meanings into the spaces, places and built forms which have existed since times immemorial?

In the conclusion of this chapter, therefore, I will draw on the earlier discussion to make some brief comments about the internationalization of architectural practice and how it may be understood as one example of a global culture, but only under specific conditions.

In the pages that follow, my aim is not to examine or deconstruct every instance of the use of the term to be found but rather, to set out some of the debates developed around them.[4]

'GLOBAL CULTURE' AS DISCOURSE

Like Franklin *et al.* (2000) and Weldes (2001), we can treat globalization, in the first instance, simply as a discourse, and global culture as a constituent part of that discourse. 'Globalization', Franklin *et al.* (2000: 4) write, 'is not simply an empirical force . . . but it is a *discursive condition* currently being reproduced within academia and outside it'.

For Weldes (2001: 650), an 'increasingly global culture', along with other themes – including 'a well worn Enlightenment narrative of progress . . . (and) . . . a utopian narrative of technological advance' – are all seen as 'intertwined elements which permeate the discourse of globalization'. They are all part of a 'discursively constructed *fait accompli* – and hence, a fantasy' . . . a 'self-fulfilled prophesy'. Weldes argues – with a double negative – 'not that "globalization" does not exist but that (these) phenomena are made meaningful and especially political, through discourse' (2001: 648, note 12).

How is the term culture to be understood in these instances? In addition to the common sense ways mentioned above, recent interpretations have stressed the essentially transnational conditions that gave rise to the term. For James Clifford, the anthropological definition of culture(s) emerged as an alternative to racist classifications of human diversity in a 'highly colonial context of unprecedented global interconnection' (1988: 234). Contemporary anthropological conceptualizations of culture emphasize its use as a way of understanding and thinking about difference. It is:

> a contrastive rather than a substantive property of certain things . . . and better regarded as a dimension of phenomena . . . Stressing the dimensionality of culture rather than its substantiality permits our thinking of culture less as a property of individuals and groups and more as a heuristic device to talk about difference . . . especially difference in the realm of group identity.
>
> (Appadurai 1996: 12–13)

It is not, simply, 'an object waiting to be found in the external world' (Franklin *et al.* 2000: 5) but rather, a relational interpretative framework.

In the sampling below, garnered from some of the academics, journalists and others who use the term 'global culture', or write about it, it is clear that, irrespective of the different meanings invested in the phrase itself, we are also dealing with different understandings of *culture* as such. A more detailed discussion of these conceptualizations follows the listing.

CONCEPTUALIZATIONS OF 'GLOBAL CULTURE'

1   Emphasizing plurality and spatialization

- All the different cultures, or cultural forms, characterized by their differences, one from another, that exist in the world (Appadurai 1996; Hannerz 1996; Pieterse 1995, 2004; Street 2000).
- The cultural outcome(s) of different people(s) from various (but not all) parts of the world which, through processes of migration, electronic communication, etc. come to be represented in a single place (Olwig 1993; Works 1993).
- Cultural forms and practices which, at some earlier historical stage, have been characteristic of only one location or region but which have been diffused over many different (though not all) parts of the world (King 1984; Nurse 1999; Poewe 1994).
- Multicentered, non-isomorphic cultural flows around the globe (Appadurai 1990).
- An assortment of cultural artefacts or phenomena from different parts of the world in one location, previously not perceived as belonging there, but now so perceived (Zwingle 1999).

2   Emphasizing the deconstruction of the nation state

- 'Sets of practices, bodies of knowledge, conventions, and lifestyles which have developed in ways which have become increasingly independent of nation-states' (Featherstone 1996: 60; see also Axford 2000: 105; Mathews 2000).

- Forms of media and the arts, originating in many different nations and regions, which are transmitted or diffused across national borders (Crane *et al.* 2002).
- Global culture, 'in the . . . sense that the globe is a finite, knowable bounded space, a field into which all nation-states and collectivities will inevitably be drawn' (Featherstone 1996: 60).

3   Emphasizing (American) cultural imperialism

- 'Global culture is nothing more than American cultural imperialism' (Patterson 1994: 103).
- 'American media culture, commodities, fast food and malls are creating a new global culture that is remarkably similar on all continents' (Cvetkovich and Kellner 1997: 8; see also Ashley 2002).

4   Emphasizing a new (or in some cases 'homogenized') system of culture

- 'the emergence of a new set of universally shared images and practices . . . and thus, *an altered condition of universality*' (Franklin *et al.* 2000: 2) citing other authors.
- A completely new cultural system, or system of culture, emerging from the diffusion of cultural values, beliefs and practices worldwide and which takes on new attributes, and becomes transformed in the process (Hexham and Poewe 1997).
- Global culture: 'a single 'homogenized' system of meaning' (Tomlinson 1999: 71).

5   'Out of this world': Emphasizing the planetary

- Global culture: 'a practical impossibility, except in inter-planetary terms' (Smith 1990).
- 'a global common culture' – developed as 'the response to a perceived threat to the continued viability of life on the planet through some ecological disaster' (Featherstone 1995: 90).
- The general rhetoric and discourse of globality, globalization and internationalism including 'thinking about the world'; the cultural process of thinking the world (Robertson 1991: 88, 1992: 113; see also Surin 1995).

Other classes mentioned in the literature include various qualified derivatives of the term.[5]

Whatever notion of global culture is addressed, we can assume that, as a discursive construction, the concept: a) is 'an aspiration rather than an achievement, as much an effect as a condition' (Franklin *et al.* 2000: 5); b) is ideologically informed; c) if inherently material and spatial, the extent of its 'global reach' must necessarily be exaggerated; and d) has an historical origin, specific historical, social and political conditions under which it is constituted, and a spatial and cultural location firmly situated in a geographical place.

In this latter context, we might also note that the perception of the earth as a sphere and its representation in the form of a globe are historical phenomena of the late fifteenth and early to mid sixteenth centuries, a period when the terms 'globe' and 'global' came into use. Culture, in the sense described by Clifford above, comes into general use from the mid nineteenth century (Williams 1984). The term 'global culture', as I have suggested, has come into more widespread use from the last decade of the twentieth century. It also needs stating that what I address in the following are, with a couple of exceptions, texts produced by academics which, on the whole, come from an anglophone monoglot culture.[6] This is a language culture which, in different contexts, can be described as postcolonial, or postimperial (see Pennycook 1998; Fishman *et al.* 1996) or equally, as neo-imperial or neo-colonial. While a discourse on 'cultura global' can certainly be found in Spanish, any serious understanding of the universality of the term and the meaning(s) it purports to represent would need to be ascertained in other world (and imperial/postimperial) languages (e.g. Mandarin Chinese, Arabic, Ottoman, Hindi, Japanese, Portuguese, French).

This latter, cross-cultural and implicitly geographical context also directs our attention to the necessity of examining the notion of globalization (and global culture) over time. Here, the collection of essays on *Globalization in World History* provides a much needed historical input into what editor Anthony Hopkins calls 'the most important single debate in the social sciences' (2002: 1).[7] The book, the first major venture of historians into the topic according to the editor, focuses on two themes: one emphasizing the non-Western dimensions of globalization; the other exploring its historical forms and sequences. Noting that different definitions of globalization fit different assessments of its causes and consequences, Hopkins and his collaborators, drawing on Held's definition above, suggest that historically globalization has taken different forms which they categorize as archaic (prior to 1600), proto (from the eighteenth century), modern (from the nineteenth century) and postcolonial (after 1950 or 1970). The essays, including studies on Eurasia, Africa, China, and Islam as well as Europe and the Americas, 'underline the antiquity and importance of non-Western forms of globalization and demonstrate that encounters with the West produced a world order . . . jointly, if also unequally, created' (2002: 2). This latter category of 'postcolonial globalization' provides a much needed link between two discourses – on postcolonialism and globalization – which, to date, have been largely kept apart by the different disciplines (principally literary studies for the first and sociology for the second) which have developed the two fields. Pieterse also treats globalization as a 'long term historical process involving ancient population movements, long distance cross-cultural trade, the spread of world religions and the diffusion and development of technologies due to inter-cultural contact' (2004: 24–5).

In the following, all cases are from anglophone sources and all stem from a particular Western perspective and also episteme, a point echoed by both Featherstone (1990: 11) and Hopkins (2002: 30, 32, 36).[8] And not only a Western perspective but one, according to various authors, that comes from a privileged social position. Knauft, for example, suggests that notions of cultural globalization 'still tend to be vague and upper class' (2002: 39). Fellow anthropologist Appadurai states that academic debates (on globalization) 'which still set the standard for the global professoriate . . . have an increasingly parochial quality' (2000: 2). In an important article, he points to the growing divorce between these debates and those that 'characterize the vernacular discourses about the global', typically concerned with 'how to protect cultural autonomy and economic survival in some local, national or regional sphere in the era of "reform" and "openness"'. Focusing on strategies of globalization on behalf of the poor, he argues for an understanding of 'globalization from below' (ibid.: 3). As Pieterse (1995: 95) insists, we need to recognize a 'plurality of globalizations'. With these cautionary notes, we can examine, in more detail, some of these various interpretations.

SPATIALIZING GLOBAL CULTURES

Of all disciplines, the term global belongs most closely to geography. It is, above all, a spatial expression. But representations of the political economy and social organization of the human populations on the globe has, over the last couple of centuries, provided many different options – from a discourse of civilizations, races, empires, tribes, peoples and the oikumene, to more recent notions of the international, transnational, global, world system (with its center–periphery conceptualizations), postnational, postcolonial, neoimperial, neocolonial, postmodern and others. All of these alternatives attempt to pinpoint the significant loci of power, influence and hegemony in the world and the strength and direction in which economic, political or cultural power flows from one part of the world to another through history.

Viewed from this predominantly spatial perspective, therefore, we might categorize some different uses of the concept of global culture as to whether they are centripetal or centrifugal (while recognizing that the positions of both centers and peripheries will change, multiply, or be irrelevant, at different historical times). In the first, centripetal flows of cultural forms and practices from many parts of the world, though invariably transformed, indigenized and adapted to the locality (Appadurai 1996) manifest themselves in one or more places, or among a particular place-related population, a process now called glocalization (Robertson 1994). The obvious example here is of global cultures present in the (inadequately named) 'global city'.[9] This also applies to anthropologist Karen Olwig's use of the term to describe the 'island identity' of the Afro-Caribbean community in Nevis (1993). Other centripetal flows to places outside a narrow understanding of 'the West' are illustrated in Martha Works' study of 'Trade and the emergence of global culture in Spanish Colonial New Mexico'. On the basis of archival research, the author shows how the material culture of sixteenth-century colonial New Mexico represented 'a blend of influences from Spain, other parts of Europe, from Western and Central Mexico, the Far East and Plains and Pueblo Indians'. The events and exchanges Works describes 'represent an *emerging* world or global culture' (1993: 170) (italics added).

In the centrifugal case, cultural influences or practices stemming, initially and historically, from one location or region, are found, again in various indigenized or 'translated' forms, in many parts of the globe. An illustration here is Nurse's study of the 'global spread' of the Caribbean carnival (1999). As Nurse suggests, much of the literature on cultural globalization tends to chart a centrifugal process, with the center located firmly in the West: 'the literature . . . is really a depolitical interpretation of the long standing process of Westernization and imperialism'. Nurse points out that 'in the debate about globalization . . . and the growth of a global culture' the tendency is to focus on the accelerated flow of technology, people and resources in a 'North to South or center to periphery direction'. His own research is based on the premise that – using a center–periphery model – while the periphery is greatly influenced by the society of the center 'the reverse is also the case'. He therefore examines 'the implications for global culture [*sic*] of periphery to center cultural flows' (1994: 661).

With over sixty overseas Caribbean carnivals in North American and European cities, including 31 in the UK, 21 in the US, 7 in Canada and 3 in Europe (Rotterdam, Nice, Stockholm) in the mid 1990s, Nurse maintains that 'Trinidad's carnival . . . is now truly global'. On the evidence presented of these primarily anglophonic and, from a religious/cultural perspective, once primarily Christian urban sites, 'postcolonial' would obviously be more accurate.[10]

Other examples of centrifugal flows are Poewe's study of *Charismatic Christianity as a Global Culture* (1994). By 'global' here Poewe refers to the 'unbound spatial, institutional and linguistic reach of charismatic Christianity' which she maintains has become 'a global culture or way of life based on perceptions and identities that are transmitted worldwide'. Interesting here is that Poewe's 'global culture', indifferent to both institutions and language, has developed over a span of time from 'the first century AD to the present'. In other words, while it has grown over two thousand years – drawing our attention to the longitudinal, and temporal rather than spatial dimension of a 'global culture' – it has also, however, been strictly limited to the Christian era as well as Christian space. In this context, what some see as global cultures may both flourish as well as disappear. And while Poewe represents charismatic Christianity as a global culture 'because it transcends national, ethnic, racial and class boundaries' (she significantly omits reference to gender, coloniality and sexuality) it 'does not transcend, or rarely transcends, other world religions'. In terms of the global positioning of 'global cultures', we might note that all of the major world religions had their origin in what today is represented (by the West) as the 'Third World'. Other 'centrifugal' cases include my own study of the bungalow (King 1984) and examples described in Waters (1995).

While sophisticated debates take place in the texts and journals of the academy, in the popular imagination, 'global culture' often means the discovery of something, either 'at home' or in a place one is not familiar with, which, when experienced for the first few times, is not expected to be there. In the *National Geographic*'s special issue on 'Global Culture' (196, 2, 1999) the phenomenon is described as 'hanging around a pub in New Delhi that serves Lebanese cuisine to the music of a Filipino band in rooms decorated with barrels of Irish stout, a stuffed hippo head and a vintage poster announcing the Grand Old Opry concert to be given at the high school in Douglas, Georgia' (Zwingle 1999).

In all the cases above, whether centripetal or centrifugal, we might note that the 'global culture' described is, if we take the term *literally*, distinctly *sub*global and that the phenomena described have been going on throughout history – if not quite so rapidly as in more recent times.

GLOBAL CULTURE AS DECONSTRUCTION OF THE NATION-STATE

Much of the debate around global culture concerns questions of logic and grammar but also refers to the future of the nation state. For instance, in 1990 Featherstone asked in the introduction to his edited book, *Global Culture:*

Nationalism, Globalization and Modernity, 'Is there a global culture?', suggesting that the term might mean something 'akin to the culture of the nation-state writ large'. As there is no world state, Featherstone's answer to this question is categorically 'no'. Nonetheless, there could be, in his view, a 'globalization of culture', that is, 'cultural integration and cultural disintegration processes which transcend the state-society unit, occurring on a transnational or trans-societal level' (Featherstone 1990: 1; see also 1995, 1996). Used with the indefinite article, ('a') global culture, in the singular, somehow implies processes of cultural homogenization taking place on a global scale. While some authors still maintain this position (Barnett and Cavanagh 1996; Rieff 1993; Patterson 1994; Tomlinson 1999), this is not a view held by many scholars. In the introduction to *Global Culture: Media, Arts, Policy, and Globalisation* (2002), Diana Crane writes 'Cultural globalization is no longer conceptualized in terms of the emergence of a homogenized global culture corresponding to Marshall McCluhan's global village. Instead, cultural globalization is recognized as a complex of diverse phenomena consisting of global cultures originating from many different nations and regions' (Crane *et al.* 2002: 1) a view that accords with Featherstone; '(T)here is', he writes, 'little prospect of a unified global culture; rather there are global cultures in the plural' (1990: 10).

Crane defines what she calls 'cultural globalization' as referring to 'the transmission, or diffusion across national borders of various forms of media and the arts'; culture, she adds, could also refer to 'ways of life', religions and popular attitudes, though space does not allow her to develop these themes (Crane *et al.* 2002: 1). Though not defining 'global culture' as such, she sees globalization as 'a complex and diverse phenomenon consisting of global cultures from many different nations and regions'. Two assumptions are evident from this definition: that while the terms are new, the phenomena – of cultural forms and practices transgressing national boundaries – are clearly not, even though most would agree with Crane that the phenomenon of globalization has massively increased in recent years. Second, the fact that cultural phenomena cross national boundaries (even when electronically transmitted) does not make them, in either a literal, nor realist sense, global. And just where they go, why they go there, what technical or political boundaries inhibit them, how they are consumed, suppressed, resisted or imitated, and with what results, are important questions that need to be addressed. What Crane's conceptualization does, however, is to imply that constructions of culture are 'naturally' and inherently 'national' without acknowledging either the historical nature or contexts of their production (Anderson 1983).

These various examples suggest that contemporary anglophone social and cultural theory is clearly lacking the appropriate language to describe socially, spatially and culturally transmitted cultural phenomena that are more than local, regional, national, or continental (i.e. multinational, transnational, transcontinental), each geographical (rather than social) term falsely reifing and essentializing what it attempts to describe, i.e. phenomena that are clearly *not* found all over the world, as implied by the literal – rather than metaphorical – use of the term global. In Crane's use of the term, all that global infers is nonlocal and non-national.[11] Global culture often tends to mean what local culture is not. In this sense, social theory is still stuck in a paradigm created by an age of nation-states, described by Taylor (1996) as 'embedded statism'.

As for the question of homogenization, Appadurai suggests that 'as rapidly as forces from various metropolises are brought into new societies they tend to become indigenized in one or another way: this is as true of music and housing styles as much as it is true of science and terrorism, spectacles and constitutions' (1996: 32). And indigenization mostly means hybridization.

The idea of 'globalization as hybridization' is particularly associated with the work of Jan Nederveen Pieterse (1995). As against older perspectives which emphasize continuing cultural differentiation ('lasting difference'), or cultural convergence ('growing sameness' or homogenization), Pieterse makes a powerful argument for cultural hybridization as 'ongoing mixing' where the cultural outcome of the globalization process is 'open-ended' (2004: Chapter 3). Hybridization represents transgression and subversion but it always results in something new, a synthesis of different elements. 'Hybridization,' he writes, 'is the making of global culture as a global mélange' (ibid.: 77). I return to this perspective in the following chapters.

If on the basis of cognitive, as well as grammatical logic, it seems inaccurate to speak of *a* or *the* global culture, this still allows Pieterse (1995) to refer to the 'creolization of global culture' or Appadurai to write of 'the politics of global culture' (1996: 37), that is, in reference to the many different cultures, or forms of culture, in the globe. In a similar sense, Hannerz (1996) refers to 'world culture'[12] and, in a neat grammatical manouevre, Galtung (1999) asserts that there is, indeed, a global culture but it is 'a multicultural global culture'.

GLOBAL CULTURE AS IDEOSCAPE

In a much-cited and influential paradigm, Appadurai suggests there are five dimensions of global cultural flows which move in non-isomorphic directions:

> *ethnoscapes* produced by flows of peoples: tourists, immigrants, refugees, exiles and guest workers. Second, there are *technoscapes*, the machinery and plant flows produced by multinational and national corporations and government agencies. Third, are *finanscapes*, produced by the rapid flows of money in the currency markets and stock exchanges. Fourth, *mediascapes*, consist of the repertoire of images of information, the flows of which are produced and distributed by newspapers, magazines, television and film. Fifth, *ideoscapes*, linked to flows of images which are associated with state or counter-state movement ideologies which are comprised of elements of freedom, welfare, rights, etc.
>
> (Appadurai 1990: 295–310, as paraphrased
> by Featherstone 1990: 6–7)

To these might be added *townscapes*, *builtscapes* and *landscapes*, produced by the common adoption of ideas, techniques, standards, design ideologies and the worldwide diffusion of information, images, professional cultures and sub-cultures (of architecture, city planning, urban design, conservation), and supported by international capital flows (King 1991a). In the context of our arguments above, there are also *religioscapes*, represented by a variety of religious fundamentalisms or more liberal movements, whether Islamic, Hindu, Christian, New Age or others. Lash and Urry suggest that what characterizes Appadurai's 'scapes' is the fact of their 'deterritorialization'. Yet in so far as one can experience, see and actually live in them, we might also refer to their 'reterritorialization'. None-theless, Appadurai's ideas 'challenge the simple notions of a cultural center and a subordinate periphery' (Lash and Urry 1994: 306–7; Gupta and Ferguson 1997). And as Urry writes elsewhere:

> globalization is never complete. It is disordered, full of paradox and the unexpected, and of irreversible and juxtaposed complexity . . . the linear metaphor of scales – such as those stretching from the micro level to the macro level, or from the local to the global – that has plagued social theory from its inception, should be replaced by a metaphor of complex mobile connections.
>
> (2002: 58)

GLOBAL CULTURE AS A CONSTRUCTION OF CULTURAL POLITICS

To provide some relief from what, so far, has been a completely theoretical discussion, I now turn to an instance of practice.

It would be difficult to find a better example of the discursively constructed nature of the concept than *The Dictionary of Global Culture* (1996) edited by Anthony Appiah and Henry Louis Gates Junior. The subtitle, 'The global citizen's guide to culture emphasizing the achievement of the non-Western world' reveals both the cultural politics behind the project and, in its reference to 'non-Western', its inherently Western (and specifically American) origins. The dust cover states, from the Introduction:

> We all participate, albeit from different cultural positions, in a global system of culture. That culture is increasingly less dominated by the West, less Eurocentric, if you like . . . Our idea in making this book was . . . to give people . . . a sampler of cultural contributions from around the world.
>
> (Appiah and Gates 1996)

This includes familiarizing the reader with what they assume will be lesser known cultural phenomena from Africa, Asia, the Middle East, and Latin America.

With some 1,260 entries in 717 pages provided by different contributors, the dictionary is an interesting, but also idiosyncratic compilation. 'Culture' is primarily understood in terms of the arts and politics, with some 60 percent of the entries providing biographical details of artists, writers, poets, painters, politicians, religious figures and intellectuals, and the remainder details of institutions, historical events, ideas, ethnic groups and religious groups, including the main world religions, though omitting Sikhism). Along with attention to prominent figures, texts and monuments of medieval Islamic or ancient Chinese culture, or political and cultural figures from Africa, or the African diaspora (Patrice Lumumba, Louis Armstrong), also included are contemporary phenomena from 'the West' (Henri Matisse, punk, Walt Disney, blues, gastarbeiter).

As what is included under 'high culture' as well as 'ordinary culture' does not specifically mention architecture and urbanism, the spaces, built forms and architectural cultures associated with 'global culture' are given short shrift. Entries in this category are mainly focused on the urban and architectural aspects of particular 'non-Western' cities: Tel el Armana, Angkor Wat, Babylon, Benin City, Chichen Itza, Delhi, Fatepur Sikri, the Forbidden City of Beijing, Katmandu,

Zimbabwe – well enough known from a list of UNESCO heritage sites. The only social and spatial categories addressed include: four building types (hammam, harem, mosque, synagogue) though not, for example, the shopping malls in Cairo (Abaza 2001); two forms of settlement (ghetto, kibbutz), though not the increasing number of gated communities worldwide; and two dwelling forms (Iroquois longhouse, Mesa Verde), though not the globally ubiquitous suburban villa (see Chapter 8), let alone the bungalow (King 1984). Some spectacular monuments get entries (Taj Mahal, Hoysola temples of southern India, Ziggurat pyramids of Egypt). Ironies include reference to adobe but not concrete.

The two sole entries specifically devoted to architecture include Bauhaus, which mentions Walter Gropius and Mies van der Rohe, but ignores the colonial and postcolonial penetration of the Modern Movement into the world outside 'the West' as well as its political and symbolic adoption (and adaptation) by nationalist agendas in Brazil, India, Indonesia and elsewhere (Holston 1989; Lang *et al.* 1998; Kusno 2000). The sole entry for an architect is that on Frank Lloyd Wright. As one reviewer wrote, this is 'an American book for American readers'.

Given the precapitalist context of many of the other entries on 'non-western' culture, this unproblematized focus on the individualized 'artistic identities' produced by modern capitalism serves to remind readers both of the 'anonymous' and collective forms of building/construction in the precapitalist 'non-Western' world as well as its transformation in places such as Shanghai (Olds 2001) of which the 'architectural star's' 'signature building' is the principal symbol.

Irrespective of its merits and weaknesses, *The Dictionary of Global Culture* is nevertheless important in demonstrating how very specific, politically motivated and culturally positioned discursive constructions of 'global culture' can be. Indeed, much of the value of the book is in the many critical reviews it has generated. As Howe (1998) asks, does the dictionary aim to give proportionate weight to all the world's major cultural traditions or only those whose own influence has spread culturally? The highest weightings, Howe suggests, are given to diasporic British and Jewish populations scattered across the globe, and especially their North American offshoots, presenting the reader with 'an export model of global culture'. As no mention is made of living writers writing in an Indian language (as opposed to those writing in English) it is also a postcolonial model. Francis Fukuyama (1996) suggests that, as most of the book is just a catalogue of cultural artefacts across the globe without regard to their influence on other parts of the world (or indeed, on each other), the transnational element of a different understanding of global culture is lacking. It is global culture from a particular perspective.

This is, perhaps, also the place to mention the publication *Global Architecture: An Encyclopaedia of Modern Architecture* (Futagawa 1997) produced from Japan and with Japanese and Korean subtitles. The contents list the names of some sixty architects and what are typically taken by the profession as their most 'famous' works. All are male, white and Western (e.g. Frank Lloyd Wright, Kevin Roche, Eiro Saarinen, Le Corbusier, Alvar Aalto, Paul Rudolph and others). The book aptly conveys, in an unproblematized way, the globally hegemonic sense in which some sectors of the architectural profession represent the practices of architecture as uninhibited by local, regional, national, class, ethnic, racial, gender or ecological constraints.

GLOBAL CONSUMER CULTURE

Franklin *et al.* (2000) suggest that 'Studies of global culture have tended to postu-late the emergence of a new set of universally shared images and practices and thus, *an altered condition of universality*' (2000: 2). Though this statement need not necessarily refer to 'a global consumer culture' this is apparently what the authors intend. They refer to the increasing growth of tourism, international migration and the homogenization of commodity consumption generally associated with globalization, and which implies 'an increased sense of proximity across national and international boundaries as a consequence of the pervasiveness of common cultures' (ibid.). In suggesting that 'this sense of global culture is typically associated with products, industries and technologies, including the growth of international tourism and the airline industries, multinational consumer brands such as Coca-Cola and Holiday Inn; popular media, such as television soaps or disco music . . . the Internet or satellite telecommunications', the authors subscribe to what is probably the most common understanding of global culture, associated with the worldwide spread of market capitalism (see also Sklair 2001 on the global consumerist culture). This is also the meaning stated, or implicit in accounts by Roche (2000), Bannerjee and Linstead (2001), Rieff (1993) and, to a lesser extent, Mathews (2000), each of which, raising different points, deserves some comment.

Roche (2000) traces the historical origins and development, from the nineteenth to the twentieth century, of what he terms an 'international public culture' focusing particularly on the contribution of 'mega-events', in the form of international expositions, sports events and, especially, the Olympics, to this process. Recognizing that the nature of the international world as a 'world of nations' strengthened and emphasized by this process will not disappear, he nonetheless argues that the variety of social, economic and cultural pro-cesses associated with mega-events makes them central to the emergence of the global consumer culture, particularly in the role they play in touristic consumerism (Roche 2000: 21–28). These contribute to 'understandings and experiences of "one world" through their capacity to carry universalistic mean-ings and ideals' (2000: 26). Typically, global culture is mediatized in cities, and especially, capital cities. In the new balance of power between cities and states, mega-events reflect 'not only a "world of nations" but also a "world of cities" (of localities and different identities) together with versions of a "one world" (an evolving singular and interconnected "global society") world view' (ibid.). This is a viewpoint that has much in common with Robertson's historical (though 'Western') account of emerging notions of globality (Robertson 1990; see also Hopkins 2002).

The impact of mega-events on the urban, spatial and architectural and built form of cities, including the construction of stadia and exhibition buildings, and the restructuring of space – including the negative impacts on the housing of the less well off which frequently occurs (as in Atlanta, Seoul, Beijing) – are obvious. Dovey (1999), for example, has discussed the pernicious impact on Melbourne's downtown of introducing Formula One car racing, with the new race track requiring the ripping up of part of the city, all part of Melbourne's strategy of becoming a 'global city' (a strategy which, according to Vladimir Putin, is to be adopted in Moscow).

The global consumer culture consumes both signs and symbols as well as products and services (Bannerjee and Linstead 2001, citing Lash and Urry 1994). This is what S. Hall (1991a: 7) refers to as 'global mass culture', one that is:

> dominated by the image which crosses and re-crosses linguistic frontiers much more rapidly and more easily, and which speaks across languages in a much more immediate way. It is dominated by all the ways in which the visual and graphic arts have entered directly into the reconstitution of popular life, of entertainment and of leisure. It is dominated by television and by film, and by the image, imagery and styles of mass advertising.
>
> (S. Hall 1991a: 27)

Lash and Urry, however, have a different view. Drawing on Appadurai's account, they deny that there is one global mass culture. Rather, 'transnational processes produce the globalization of culture as a multitude of cultural flows, not always consistent with nation state ideologies' (Lash and Urry 1994, in Bannerjee and Linstead 2001).

In this sense, globalization does not contradict the fact that cultural diversity continues to flourish. As different authors have suggested (Bannerjee and Linstead 2001; Robertson 1992) diversity can be seen not only as a pre-existing condition but as a consequence, an outcome of globalization. While the emergence of a global consumer culture is a homogenizing trend it simultaneously acknowledges and exploits distinct market niches based on cultural differences (Bannerjee and Linstead 2001: 698). The result of these processes of 'cross-cultural consumption' results in creolization, a term Howes (1996: 5) uses to describe the processes of 'recontextualization whereby foreign goods are assigned meanings and uses by the culture of reception'. Consumers select and adapt products according to their own desires, knowledge and interests, investing them with their own meanings.

GLOBAL CONSUMER CULTURE AS 'AMERICANIZATION'

Cruder versions of the 'global consumer' thesis suggest that 'cultural power moves with financial and industrial power' (Rieff 1993: 75) and ignore the question of meaning. In this context, they represent (often uncritically, if issuing from the US) the ensuing space of the global culture as simply reproducing 'America' (whatever this means). Thus, Rieff, a senior fellow at the World Policy Institute in the US writes:

> the fascination with diversity . . . should not obscure the fact that the general direction in the world is toward greater and greater similarity, at least on the level of material ambitions, architecture, food and ambient noise, a.k.a. music . . . [I]mmigration [to America] and global consumer culture are part of a larger uprooting, which is another way of saying a larger Americanization of the world.
>
> (Rieff 1993: 76–7)

As traditional societies cannot support 'traditional culture' in a period of rapid increases in world population, the cities to which their inhabitants move – Jakarta, Lagos, Mexico City – 'are as corrosive of tradition as Coca-Cola and the internal combustion engine'. In this event, 'global culture can, finally, only be American because only America has accommodated these new realities' (Rieff 1993: 77–8).

Some British commentators seem to agree with this. In a 'popular' reference to the term, journalist Jackie Ashley writes, in reference to the British monarchy, in an article titled 'Global culture has squeezed royalty from out of our hearts' (*The Guardian* April 3, 2002) that:

> an 'older' sense of national identity is being replaced by a global making-and-selling culture (that) has seized the imagination of people everywhere, but particularly perhaps in English-speaking places most open to American influence. My children are less British than I was as a child not just because they have Asian and black friends at school, or because of the Single European Act, but because their street culture is all American, culled from films, magazines, the net, music and advertising.
>
> (Ashley 2002)

Britain she refers to as 'today's Americanized, demotic, multiracial island' (ibid.).

What is apparent from many of these essentially *nationalistic* claims, whether by Americans themselves or by other hyper-nationally conscious subjects, is that they fail to address three simple issues. The first is what Harvey, many years ago, called 'cultural appraisal' (1973); that when traveling around the world, what tourists as well as more seasoned scholars most easily 'see' are phenomena which are immediately recognizable; that unfamiliar phenomena have less immediate impact on the eye (and brain) is equally true. Related to this is the phenomenon of the massively increased attention and meaning given to the visual in contemporary culture at the expense of the cognitive (Mirzoeff 2000). The third is the hubris of some American authors that, somehow, every cultural phenomenon, irrespective of its origin, provided that it is found within the bounded shores of the United States part of the North American continent, *must*, exclusively, solely and proprietorially, be appropriated and pressed into the service of the nationalistic project as 'American' even though the phenomenon may, in part or whole, have originated in any other part of the world. 'Americanization', in short, is the latest version of 'Westernization' (Pieterse 2004: 49) and pays insufficient attention to processes of indigenization.

Finally, too little attention has been paid, in the literature, to the question of language, particularly to the language of international English, in the competence to make acts of cultural appraisal. This is where Nabar's understanding of the concept is valuable. Writing in 1990 of the way in which global culture becomes (or does not become) part of the culture of the *English-educated class* in India, he defines global culture as 'one which has its regional, national or religious basis but is capable of assimilating anything culturally significant that has happened or is now happening in any part of the world' (Nabar 1990: 1). This highlights the anglophonic view of global culture assumed in much American and British discourse on the topic where, at most, only 10 to 20 percent of the world speak English of some kind (Crystal 1997). How far any idea of a common 'global culture' presupposes a common *linguistic* literacy, based on the world's major languages, or simply visual, or sonic literacy based on globally circulated images, signs or sounds (as in so-called 'world music')[13] is an issue too large to discuss here.

In the context of arguments over 'Americanization', not only do Pieterse (1994) and Appadurai emphasize the fact that cultural forces coming from other metropolises get very rapidly indigenized but the latter also alerts us to the idea that for Koreans, Japanization may be a more important cultural threat; for Sri Lankans, Indianization; and for the people of Irian Jaya, Indonesianization (1996: 32).

GLOBAL CORPORATE CULTURE

Robertson (1990), Spybey (1996), Appiah and Gates (1996) and others apparently assume that the initial territorial base of specific global cultures is in the West, and in some cases, more specifically in the US (a view that would not accord with the origins of particular world religions in what is now referred to as the Middle East). This is particularly the case with the notion of global corporate culture, a subcategory of the global consumerist or capitalist culture. For Dobson 'whatever ethnic, religious, or other cultural boundaries may have evolved through history' these are now being increasingly subsumed by a global corporate culture, characterized by 'multinational corporations, internationally-linked security markets and omnipresent communications networks' (1990: 41). The dynamics of such a culture rest on 'the intricate web of contractual relations between stakeholders' (ibid.). In his discussion, Dobson pinpoints three alternative mechanisms which enforce these contracts: 'the legal system, a generally accepted moral code and the stakeholders' desire to build and maintain their reputation' (ibid.: 41).

In his research on the 'World System of Culture', Swedish anthropologist, Ulf Hannerz, sees the transnational business class (who may be assumed to belong to and represent the global corporate culture), as one of the four categories of people who account for the transnational nature of contemporary world cities in the West, the other three being Third World migrants, tourists and people 'specializing in expressive activities' (Hannerz 1993). And the institutional and spatial forms, as well as the symbolic signs provided for the consumption of this class (whether in transnational headquarters, banks, corporate offices, transnational hotel chains, airport facilities or the construction and marketing of real estate) provides the rationale for much of one particular architectural culture (King 1995c: 225).

GLOBAL CULTURES AS CULTURES OF TRAVEL

Appiah and Gates' construction of 'global culture' is one of assemblage and accumulation; of collecting various cultural artefacts and practices of culture together but without any sense of transformation or change. This latter is a dimension specifically targeted in New Religions as Global Cultures (1997) where the co-authors, Hexham and Poewe, focus more on the process of persistent and continuous cultural transformation. It is a concept of global culture rooted in the culture of travel (Clifford 1998); of cultures developing, and coming into existence as an outcome of movement and mobility, whether this applies to people, ideas, media, technologies or particular religious traditions. 'One could say,' they suggest, 'that a global culture is a tradition that travels the world and takes on local color. It has both a global, or metacultural, and a local, or situationally distinct, cultural dimension' (Hexham and Poewe 1997: 41).

Citing other authors, Hexham and Poewe set out 'a general sense' of what a global culture might be:

> a transnational or trans societal network of cosmopolitan people who self-consciously cultivate 'an intellectual and aesthetic stance of openness toward divergent cultural experiences' (Featherstone 1990: 1, 239). As Ulf Hannerz points out, rather than being territorially defined, global cultures 'are carried as collective structures of meaning by networks' that are transnational. People who belong to new religions, for example, may be 'somewhat footloose': They are as ready to move on as they are to stay in order to immerse themselves temporarily within other cultures and religions. (Featherstone 1990: 239–241).
>
> (Hexham and Poewe 1997: 43)

Buddhism, Christianity and Islam, they maintain, have always been global cultures. 'The ideal of these religions, however, was to spread a religious *meta-culture* that was perfectly capable of remaining identifiable while being absorbed by local cultures' (Hexham and Poewe, 1997: 43; see also Pieterse 2004: 29).

However, not all new religions are local adaptations of some major tradition. Although one major tradition may predominate:

> all new religions incorporate, often indiscriminately, insights from other cultures and traditions . . . Global cultures transcend national, international, ethnic, racial and class boundaries to create a new whole. They are, then, in effect, local cultures because they always grow out of, and incorporate, local beliefs and practices, their participants self-consciously cultivating an openness to diverse cultures. Global cultures are, therefore, meaning networks or transnational webs of culture.
>
> (Hexham and Poewe 1997: 46, 57)[14]

Hexham and Poewe's observations could well be linked to Pieterse's (2004) comments on hybridization and used to apply to the way the spaces of buildings and architectural cultures are frequently transformed over both space and time (Brand 1994).

POLITICAL CULTURES OF THE GLOBAL

Smith (1990) suggests that recent imperialisms are ostensibly non-national – capitalism, socialism, and in a different sense, Europeanism. They are, by definition and intention, 'supranational' if not universal, and are supported by a technological infrastructure that is 'truly cosmopolitan'. This helps to create a global culture 'based on properties of the media themselves to which the message becomes incidental', a characteristic having analogies with contemporary architectural culture where the properties of the medium (materials, technologies, CAD, standards, legal requirements, design presuppositions) become more important than the 'design' of individual architects or firms.

Yet contrary to the majority of other views, Smith sees what he represents as 'the' emerging global culture as 'context less', 'tied to no place or period' but consisting of a 'true mélange of disparate components drawn from everywhere and nowhere, borne upon the modern, and postmodern chariots of global communication systems' (Smith 1990: 171–92).

Similarly, Lash and Urry tend to agree that, compared with 'national cultures', 'putative global cultures have, by contrast, no such collective memories, no succession of generations, no sacred landscapes and indeed, no Golden Age' on which to look back (Lash and Urry 1994: 305–13). This is arguable. Through transnational forms of communications, leisure travel, work-related international migration, exposure to transnational global imagery, the internet, new generations are growing up today, in different parts of the world, who have totally different cultural roots to previous generations. Mirzoeff, for example, writes of a shared visual culture, using the example of the worldwide televisual transmission of Princess Diana's funeral of 1997 which supposedly reached 2.5 billion viewers (2000: 253). To this can be added similar major spectacles, from the world of sport (Olympics and World Cup finals) to the global visual transmission of the repeated, slow-motion destruction of New York's World Trade Center in September 2001. It is the generations exposed to these images who would take issue with Lash and Urry's assertion that 'at the level of audiences it is inconceivable that there could be a global culture' (1994: 308). A simultaneous reception of transmitted images creates a collective experience, even though that experience may be invested with a myriad of different meanings. As members of those audiences, they are increasingly likely to see themselves as part of a global culture. The argument of Mathews (2000) that national identity is being eroded by the 'cultural supermarket' which permits 'national' subjects a greater choice of the values and ideas they wish to live by is relevant here.[15]

ARCHITECTURE AND GLOBAL CULTURE

Within these different conceptualizations of global culture, can we speak, historically, of the development of a global architectural culture, whether in terms of theory, design and/or practice? In the phrase architectural culture we might also subsume practices and theories of urban planning and design. Given the large scope of this question and the complexity of the issues, I explore only some of the key issues here.

We might begin by referring to some of the principal factors that have led to the internationalization of architectural culture. Here, probably the most important have been the changes throughout history in the various forces and social formations which, as patrons, have given distinctive identities to the products and forms of architecture (Gregotti 1996). In Europe, in medieval times, these were the church, monarchs, ducal courts, religious foundations and guilds of wealthy towns; in the nineteenth and early twentieth centuries, patronage lay with imperial, colonial and national governments, city corporations, newspaper and bank moguls, and the raw power of industry; in the early twenty-first century, the most powerful patrons are multinational corporations, banks, national and international organizations, and also the system of multinational franchises and the military and industrial knowledge complex. Changing forms and identities in architecture have as much to do with the disappearance of a particular type of patron as much as the appearance of others. And as Smith (1990) suggests, modes of production and ideologies, global in their scope, like capitalist consumerism, or socialism, have replaced the nation state as a major influence on architectural identity (not least, as the state, in public/private partnerships, either collaborates with the market or virtually withdraws altogether from the public sphere).

A cluster of developments has globalized the nature of architectural production (by which I refer to the highly capitalized rather than vernacular or domestic forms): the internationalization of images, trade, information, technology, recently accelerated by revolutionary communications facilities: facsimile transmission, internet, CADCAM design methods, the dispersal of design expertise worldwide and the increasing frequency of international competitions. Since the European Renaissance, architecture, like urban planning, has (not least in its colonial practice which has taken European classicism round the world) been understood as an international profession. In the twentieth century, it has had its own professional international union, and in the 1930s, developed its own, socially and ideologically informed understanding of 'internationalism'.[16] For a century at least, there has been an internationalization of theoretical debate (Gubler 1996).

Yet as the historical process of globalization is uneven, accelerating and decelerating at different points in time, other authors emphasize different critical periods (Robertson 1990; Held *et al.* 1999; Short 2001; Hopkins 2002). Ibelings, for example, reflecting the viewpoint that globalization is a very recent phenomenon, puts a much later date to this process, suggesting that it was only in the 1950s that 'there developed, for the first time, an international architectural practice' (1998: 34). Citing the names of Mies van der Rohe, Walter Gropius, Marcel Breuer and Skidmore, Owens and Merrill, he suggests that it was the big hotels which shot up in cities all round the world in the 1950s and 1960s which 'may have belonged to different companies; but which nevertheless could be seen as one big American chain'. As such, they were 'the first true examples of world architecture' (1998: 38).

These developments, according to Ibelings, were what sparked off the global 'architectural homogenization' thesis. As his interpretation may be taken as representative of widely held contemporary views, it is worth stating in more detail. In addition to the 'big hotels' and 'glass box' office buildings and housing blocks, 'uniformity also manifests itself in singular structures like conference halls, theaters, exhibition complexes, churches and stadiums'. This worldwide 'standardization', in his view, is to be explained in terms of 'economics, similar architectural principles as well as construction systems' (1998: 42). Globalization, according to Iberlings, affects architecture in that increased mobility and telecommunications alter the experience of time and space and therefore affect the way that architecture and urban planning are undertaken. Iberlings also cites the much-quoted book by French anthropologist, Marc Augé (1995), on 'non-places' – airports, hotels, supermarkets, shopping malls – all representing a growing proportion of space that lacks meaning in the classic anthropological sense because nobody feels any attachment to it' (1998: 65).

Despite the fact that Ibelings suggests that 'the strongest arguments' seem to favor the 'homogenization thesis' (1998: 67), earlier discussion in this chapter leads us to question this. On one hand, the architectural practices of the most prominent American, British, Japanese or other architectural firms can well be represented by Featherstone's (1996) conception of global culture as 'sets of practices, bodies of knowledge, conventions, and lifestyles which have developed in ways which have become increasingly independent of nation-states'. On the other hand, however, Iberlings ignores both the agency of the state, or the institution, as patron, to resist and transform the situation he describes. He equally ignores the question of the audience and the issues of reception (Crane *et al.* 2002). The views he expresses are those of a mobile globe-trotting elite, not least the architects and critics whose gaze is perpetually drawn to the objects of their primary concern. He also discounts both the environment and forms which his own cultural appraisal overlooks, and the infinitely varying contexts – historical, political, cultural, environmental, associational – in which the locations he describes are imagined, perceived and invested with meanings and memories by local others. Nor, as the privileged mobile viewer, does he address the gaze of the less or more mobile local subject who, familiar with images of environments and buildings which Ibelings describes as 'similar' and 'homogenous', none the less *prefers* for them to be as they are, perhaps because they represent 'modernity' or 'difference'. What is seen as 'globalization' looks very different from different points of view. Nor does Ibelings look at the phenomena he describes in a long-term as opposed to a short-term perspective, the period in which they are naturalized, indigenized. Nor does he allow for the unforeseen, the unexpected (see Urry 2002 above).

In terms of the public reception of a particular product, the 'global' meaning of a high rise tower, a public housing project, at any particular site in the world, will be de-coded and re-coded, invested with a myriad of different interpretations. It may be used to represent imagined discourses of 'modernity', civic and national pride, community vitality, ethnic identity, the triumph of the market or the paternalism of the state.

Ibelings' text, as well as the architecture and spaces he describes, are highly significant players in the script and discourse of globalization. They can be used to 'demonstrate', to a rich and influential mobile elite, arguments of 'standardization', 'homogenization' and the 'inter-relatedness and emergence of worldwide networks'. None of these developments, however, occur without agency. None of them are immune from decisions of cultural policy or popular resistance.

Yet as the emphasis of the studies mentioned in this chapter has been on stressing the importance of transnational forces, 'the practices of coding and recoding that disrupts the very identity of the global are not exposed'.[17] One realm of scholarly inquiry that aims to do this, namely, postcolonial criticism, is addressed in the following chapter.

NOTES

1 'Global: pertaining to or embracing the totality of a group of items, categories, or the like', *Oxford English Dictionary* (supplement) 1971; 'Global: pertaining to or embracing the totality of a number of items, categories, etc; comprehensive, all inclusive, unified, total. *Spec.* Pertaining to or involving the whole world; world-wide, universal', *Oxford English Dictionary* (1989).

2 'Receptiveness to (and understanding of) cultures other than one's own, often as part of an appreciation of world socio-economic and ecological issues (April 17, 1989, *Nation*, "One of the least pleasant characteristics of our era must surely be its transformation of global consciousness into a sales item")'. *The Oxford Dictionary of New Words. A Popular Guide to Words in the News* (1991: 133).

3   Both in this, and the questions below, I will assume that the questions can also be put in the plural, i.e. if there are global cultures, what are they?

4   Needless to say, not all authors who use the term define what they mean by it.

5   E.g. 'Global consumer culture' as the culture associated with worldwide capitalism (Ashley 2002; Cvetokovich and Kellner 1997; Roche 2000; Bannerjee and Linstead 2001); the same, but conceptually linked to 'Americanization' (S. Hall 1991a; Rieff 1993; Franklin *et al.* 2002); this in turn is linked to 'global corporate culture' (Dobson 1990). Other classes include global mass culture (S. Hall 1991a), global civic culture (Boulding 1989), global world culture, and world global culture (Cvetkovitch and Kellner 1997), global drug culture, etc. For reasons of space I do not address here the many political and economic instruments of globalization and global culture, e.g. the UN, World Bank, IMF, ILO, multinational corporations, international Marxist movements, terrorist networks, etc.

6   This is, of course, not the case with the various Indian writers I cite, as well as others.

7   Hopkins dates the debate on contemporary globalization to the 1990s. Though this may be correct in regard to its popularization in the general public, a significant academic literature on the topic, and particularly in regard to 'global cities', already existed from the early 1980s (see King 1990b: 3–4).

8   Some of the essays in Jameson and Miyoshi (1998) (e.g. Dussel, Kapur, Moreiras) and also Fisher (1995) (Kapur) address the eurocentricity of the discourse, as also does Pieterse (2004).

9   'The metaphor of a (smooth and spherical) "global city" . . . is too unitary, neutral and balanced for the fragmented, scarred and lopsided social and economic contradictions which the city contains' (King 1996a: 9).

10 Postcolonial globalization would equally be more appropriate for Olds' detailed and important study of 'Pacific Rim Megaprojects' in Shanghai and Vancouver, titled *Globalization and Urban Change* (2001).

11 Writing of the worldwide influence of different media, Crane *et al.* suggest that 'cultural globalization is sufficiently complex that no single theory can explain it adequately' (2002: 2) and offers four theoretical models of the process: (1) The cultural or media imperialism model (Tomlinson 1991) where 'the process of cultural transmission' is center–periphery, the principal actors and sites being global media conglomerates and the 'possible consequences', cultural homogenization. (2) The cultural flows/networks model (Appadurai 1990), envisaging two-way flows, the principal actors being regional and national conglomerates and corporations and the possible consequences, cultural hybridization. (3) Reception theory. The process of cultural transmission is both center–periphery and multidirectional. Principal actors are audiences, publics, and entrepreneurs who respond actively to globally disseminated culture and the possible consequences, resistance and negotiation. (4) The fourth model, advocated by Crane, is one of cultural policy strategies: of cultural preservation, resistance, reframing, glocalization, as adopted by national or regional organizations. These involve framing national [*sic*] cultures to counter, or also to promote, cultural globalization. Principal actors are global cities, museums, heritage sites, government ministries etc. Possible consequences are competition and negotiation in regard to cultural globalization (2002: 2–4). As far as urban, architectural and spatial realms are concerned, extensive literature exists on these policies of preservation, conservation and the 'reinvention' of 'tradition' (e.g. AlSayyad 2000, 2001; Crysler 2003; Logan 2002; see also Nasr and Volait 2003).

12 '(N)ot a replication of uniformity but an organization of diversity, an increasing interconnectedness of varied local cultures, as well as a development of cultures without a clear anchorage in any one territory' (Hannerz 1996: 102).

13 According to Tom Schnabel (*Rhythm Planet* 1998) 'world music' was invented as a marketing device by the record industry in 1978 to distinguish it from folk and ethnic categories (Interview with Renee Montaigne, National Public Radio, January 25, 1998). As a commercial invention of 'the West' it is, according to some, a genre premised on Western possessiveness of the Other. Thanks to David Brackett and Deryck Holdsworth for information here.

14 For an interpretation of Islam as an historically globalizing religion, see Bennison (2002: 74–97).

15 I have not included in the main text the views of sociologist, Roland Robertson, who has written extensively on globalization since the early 1980s. For Robertson, simply 'thinking about' the world is an aspect of global culture, as is the general rhetoric and discourse of globality, globalization and internationalism, 'a vital component of contemporary global culture' as also is thinking about 'the shifting and contested terms in which the world is "defined"'. The idea of a universal proletariat, the world-federalist movement or a distinct form of religion may also be said to represent the formation of global cultures as also is the shift towards a unified global time (Robertson 1991: 82–90).

There is some overlap here with Surin (1995: 1182) for whom a theory of global culture is not about culture/global culture, but about the concepts that culture generates. A theory of culture does not impinge directly on culture but on the concepts of culture. It is part of the process by which every culture generates for itself its own 'thinkability' (and 'unthinkability').

16 On the conventional architectural interpretation of the 'International Style', see Chapter 3.

17 I am indebted to Abidin Kusno for this phrase.

Chapter 3: Cultures and Spaces of Postcolonial Knowledges

Postcoloniality awaits consignment to oblivion.

Rukmini Bhaya Nair, *Lying on the Postcolonial Couch:*
The Idea of Indifference (2002: xi)

INTRODUCTION

In the obvious sense, postcolonial simply means 'after the colonial' and, until the early 1980s, was used 'to describe a condition referring to peoples, states and societies that have been through a process of formal decolonization' (Sidaway, 2000: 594). In the flurry of literature since that time, the scope of the term has widened. In 1990, Robert Young (1990: 11) suggested that the analysis of colonial discourse 'itself forms the point of questioning Western knowledge's categories and assumptions'; it demanded, in Mongia's words, 'a rethinking of the very terms by which knowledge has been constructed' (1995: 2).

These claims are reflected across the disciplines, including geography, which forms part of the focus of this chapter. Thus, Gregory (2000: 612) views 'postcolonialism' as 'a critical politico-intellectual formation that is centrally concerned with the impact of colonialism and its contestation on the cultures of both colonizing and colonized peoples in the past, and the reproduction and transformation of colonial relations, representations and practices in the present'. As 'there have been many colonialisms' the 'post' especially brings into conscious-ness those of the sixteenth to the twentieth centuries 'in such a way that our understanding of the present is transformed' (ibid.). Postcolonial approaches, according to Sidaway (2000: 594), in some accounts 'aim to transcend the cultural and broader ideological legacies and presences of imperialism' [*sic*]. Does this hint at an intellectual (or social) revolution from below?

In these conceptualizations, both Gregory and Sidaway implicitly connect a longer tradition of critical writings on colonialism with work more recently established as 'postcolonial studies' (Loomba 1998: xv). Given the proliferation of valuable accounts of postcolonial studies at the turn of the millennium,[1] my first aim will be to address certain key issues which, because of the failure to combine insights from different disciplines, have been neglected. Moreover, recognizing the need for postcolonial theory to engage with 'material practices, actual spaces and real politics' (Yeoh 2001: 457; Loomba 1998: 94) rather than simply analyses of representation and discourse, I also take up Driver's (1992: 25) suggestion to explore the 'relatively unexamined . . . role of space in a whole variety of modern aesthetic, cultural and political discourses beyond a narrow definition of social theory' though particularly, in relation to architecture, urban form and built and spatial environments, not least as these are critically impacted by such socially constructed notions as 'the tropics' as a climatic and natural environment. To do this adequately, attention must be paid to postcolonial studies and paradigm(s), undertaken prior to the publication of Edward Said's *Orientalism* (1978), frequently taken as the starting point of the current phase of postcolonial studies (e.g. Williams and Chrisman 1994; Ashcroft *et al.* 1998; Ashcroft 2001; Loomba 1998).[2]

The chapter also addresses perhaps the most neglected question in the literature, namely, why, when, where and by whom has this new knowledge paradigm developed? This suggests not only a particular spatialized history but also one inflected by issues of social and political power in the academy. Following some initial definitions the first section therefore begins by addressing questions in the geography (as well as history and sociology) of knowledge: what are the spatial, political and social *conditions* accounting for both the production and consumption of postcolonial studies? How have meanings and values that construct the world we know as postcolonial (including the intellectual practices, cultures and social networks that constitute 'postcolonial studies', if not actual postcolonial conditions) got established and institutionalized? Other than new electronic communication technologies, what do these social and intellectual movements have in common with, for example, the global indigeneity movements where worldwide connections have been made between what were once highly localized struggles of indigenous peoples?

TERMINOLOGY AND CONCEPTS

'Postcolonialism' is frequently used in the literature in a relatively loose way to refer to phenomena both in the postcolony and the postmetropolis. In this essay, I conform with Loomba's definition (1998: 6) and adopt a more precise spatial conception that highlights the distribution of power. Imperialism (or neo-imperialism) refers to a phenomenon that originates in the metropolis; what happens in the colonies, as a result of imperial domination and control, is colonialism, or neo-colonialism.

Similar variability exists in the literature concerning the term's periodization. Ashcroft *et al.* (1998: 186) state that 'post-colonialism deals with the effects of colonization [*sic*] on cultures and societies and has generally had a clearly chronological meaning designating the post-independence period', the meaning adopted here. However, 'post-colonialism as it has been employed in recent accounts has been primarily concerned to examine the processes and effects of, and reactions to, European colonialism from the sixteenth century up to and including the neo-colonialism of the present day' (Ashcroft *et al.* 1998: 188), that is, from the moment colonization began (see also Ashcroft 2001). The distinction between postcolonial and postimperial can also be ambivalent, according to the positionality and location of the author. Describing London as a (technically) postimperial city (King 1990b) foregrounds its earlier imperial role, without necessarily invoking imperial contexts. For postcolonial migrants from Jamaica who live in London, however, it may be seen as postcolonial. As Australian Jane Jacobs (1996: 37) points out, 'in settler dominions like Australia, it is the colonist who is imperialist' and historical references to the British Colonial Empire (Sabine 1943) are common.

As colonialism impacts the metropolitan society and culture as much as it does the colonial (if not in the same ways) it is clear that, while distinguishable, the phenomena (and their analysis) are inseparable. No discussion of the facts of race, space and place in the historically imperial, postimperial, or neo-imperial city, such as Paris or Brussels, is complete without reference to the colonial, postcolonial or neo-colonial city of Algiers or Kinshasa (Driver and Gilbert 1999; Jackson and Jacobs 1996; King 1990b; Yeoh 2001). Theories of the post-colonial, as also of globalization or the world-system, envisage the singular nation state as an inappropriate unit of analysis.

While the bulk of the literature restricts the scope of the paradigm to the impact of European imperialisms between the periods stated, Sidaway's (2000: 596) valuable essay reconsiders 'different and diverse demarcations' of the term, exploring the possibility of extending the scope to the 'multiplicity of postcolonial conditions', and investing a wider meaning in the oft-stated comment that 'post-colonialism doesn't describe a single condition' (McClintock 1992; Loomba 1998; Dirks 1992). As much of Europe has been subject to imperial rule, Sidaway considers the use of the analytical paradigm for Roman, Hapsburg, Ottoman, English, French and other empires in Europe as also for the Soviet successor states and ex-Yugoslav republics and develops a suggestive categorization of multiple *post*colonial conditions. These include: first, colonialisms, quasi-colonialisms and neo-colonialisms; second, internal colonialisms (see also McClintock 1992); and third, break-away settler colonialisms. Whether addressing issues of identity, the ethnic and racial composition of societies, political and spatial organisation, archi-tectural culture, language, or other cultural phenomena, these categories have obvious analytical utility.

CRITIQUES OF THE 'POSTCOLONIAL'

The most trenchant critique of the 'postcolonial' is probably that of McClintock (1992: 85) who argued that the term 're-orients the globe once more around a single, binary opposition: colonial/post-colonial . . . [such that] Colonialism returns at the moment of its disappearance' (1992: 86). For Boyce Davis (1994), among others, it is 'too premature, too totalizing', and 'recentering resistant discourses of women'. Robinson (1999: 210) has suggested that postcolonial studies 'has replaced the "other" and "other" places as the object of study of Western academics, simply replaying the same relations of domination which character-ized colonialism'. From a more conventionally Marxist perspective, James Blaut (1993) has argued that notions of the postcolonial misrepresent the realities of neo-colonialism which structure the contemporary world. Thus, in Dirlik's (1994: 336) terms, 'The global condition implied by postcoloniality appears at best as a projection onto the world of postcolonial subjectivity and epistemology – a discur-sive constitution of the world'. It is an analytical category that began, in his (only partially facetious) view, 'When Third World intellectuals . . . arrived in First World academe' (1994: 329). If postcolonial studies has become institutionalized in the anglophonic Western academy, especially as colonial discourse analysis, we need to know what, where and who are its political, social and cultural referents. And as implied in Dirlik's comments, we also need to know what the material and political implications, and real effects, of postcolonial studies actually are.

In this chapter I shall argue for postcolonial studies and criticism not only as relevant for understanding the contemporary world but, more especially, for the relevance of material, spatial, architectural and urban geographical studies for the development and strengthening of recent 'literary-based' postcolonial theory and criticism from which, with some few exceptions (Ashcroft 2001; Said 1993) it is conspicuously absent (e.g. Loomba 1998; R. Young 2001). Moreover, the neglect of the cultural realities and cultural politics of post-colonialism and colonialism in conceptualizations of 'globalization' or the 'world system', and in theories of 'development' over the last four decades, has been one of the most profound omissions in both the public, as well as academic study and understanding of the modern world. The most visible aspects of this omission are the inequities of economic, cultural and political power, both material and symbolic, manifest in both the territories and especially the cities of the supposedly 'postimperial' as well as 'postcolonial' world (as land and racial disputes in Zimbabwe, or North of England race riots demonstrated in the early twenty-first century).

UNDERSTANDING POSTCOLONIAL WORLDS: QUESTIONS OF KNOWLEDGE AND POWER

At the root of all postcolonial theory and criticism are questions of knowledge and power. It is essentially concerned with issues of agency, representation, and especially, the representation of culture(s) under asymmetrical political and social conditions. And as Dirlik (1994: 334), Chakrabarty (1992a) and others have stated, it takes 'the critique of Eurocentrism as its central task'.

In thinking about the representation and understanding of issues in the contemporary world, culture becomes important in two ways. First, theoretical and historical representations of imperialism, colonialism and the contemporary global condition, are culturally and historically constructed. In stating this we recognize that 'culture', used in the anthropological sense, is itself a particular and powerful construct that accompanied imperial expansion, a lens or container through which other peoples were known and delivered back to the West, as indicated in the previous chapter. The concept has nevertheless remained. Second, in their interpretations of social, political and spatial relations, different representations give greater or lesser attention to specific cultural phenomena such as language, religion, aesthetics or other symbolic and representational practices. In this context, the concept of the postcolonial has become of partic-ular significance in regard to issues of identity, meaning and agency and, not least, in regard to the material forms and spaces in which they are embedded (Yeoh 1996, 2001; Bishop *et al.* 2004). It is these which act as vehicles for the exercise of subaltern agency.

In the following sections where I explore explanations for the earlier rela-tive invisibility of postcolonial studies and then, from the 1980s, their subsequent explosion into view, I trace two traditions of 'postcolonial' scholarship, located broadly in the social sciences and in the humanities, but separated both in histor-ical time and by geographical and disciplinary space, whether in regard to production or consumption. The need to combine insights from both approaches is implicit in the account.

POSTCOLONIAL WORLDS: THE SOCIAL SCIENCES

Critical and theoretically informed studies of modern European colonialism as a political, economic, socio-spatial and cultural process, were produced in the final decades of, or just after, the formal ending of colonial rule by metropolitan sociologists, anthropologists, geographers and others, whether French (Balandier 1966), Dutch (Furnivall 1948; Wertheim 1964), American (Cohn 1987, including essays from 1960; Turner 1971), British (M. Smith 1965; McGee 1967; Langlands 1969) or others. Based on fieldwork in the colonial or postcolonial territory, their audience was presumed to be in that territory or the metropolis. Critical writings of Fanon (1967, 1968), Mannoni (1956) and Memmi (1965) remain the outstanding texts of the colonized, addressing, among other issues, the psychological traumas experienced by the colonially oppressed.

Significant here, however, are those studies which focused not on representations of the colonized but on the institutions and cultures of the colonizers themselves, particularly their forms of knowledge or particular *practices* which may, or may not, have had written texts to accompany them but which are, as Rabinow (1989) illustrates, all part of the system of discursive power: for example, medicine, cartography, agriculture, urban planning or architectural design. Subsequent to Said's use of Foucault's concept of discourse in *Orientalism* (1978), this has been termed 'colonial discourse' and refers to cultural forms and practices developed in the very specific context of the colonial situation with its particular distribution of power.[3] Ashcroft *et al.* (1998) write:

> Colonial discourse is greatly implicated in ideas of the centrality of Europe, and thus in assumptions that have become characteristic of modernity: assumptions about history, language, literature and 'technology' . . . It is the system of knowledge and beliefs about the world within which acts of colonization take place.
>
> (1998: 41–2)

I take up these issues again in the following chapter.

A prime example of such knowledge, and one having momentous influence on decisions about the location of settlements, the appropriation of space, socio-spatial forms, practices of urban development and architectural culture was the so-called 'miasmic' theory which perceived the origins of disease as determined by emanations from the ground, particularly in the so-called 'tropics'. Here, 'the tropics' are to be understood as perhaps the most foundational concept in the 'imagined geographies' of imperialism, a colonial construct of climate and nature. In this sense, making colonies was also about remaking nature, not just in terms of assessing and exploiting the economic value of colonized lands as resource value, but also in terms of other (scientific) values and risk (disease). Encountering 'the tropics' was about fear and the risk and threat of disease and madness, signs of not being in control. From this developed the myths and paranoias of the tropics, such as the notion of the 'white man's grave' or, in eighteenth century India, 'two monsoons' as the expectation of life. Combined at different times with various levels of racism and policies of colonial social control, this notion of 'the tropics' was to be a dominant factor influencing colonial social, spatial and political practices as well as relations.

The European construction of the concept of 'the tropics' and the 'tropical' has received attention from both geographers and others.[4] As Driver and Yeoh suggest, there is a need 'to raise questions about the multiple practices through which the tropics were known, by no means all of them articulated in discursive terms' (2000: 3). 'Identification of the northern temperate regions as the normal and the tropics as altogether other – climatically, geographically, and morally other – became an enduring imaginative geography which continues to shape the production and consumption of knowledge' (Arnold 2000: 7). In examining the history of ideas of tropical nature in general and tropical geography in particular Arnold emphasizes 'how important scientific ideas and academic authority were to the construction of the northern idea of the tropics' (2000: 3, 7). The discourse of tropicality, according to Arnold, is sufficiently important to parallel the idea of Orientalism as a cultural and political construction of the West, as discussed by Edward Said.

The material implications of these tropical discourses are best registered in relation to practices of medicine, housing, architecture, planning, dress and the body (that is, the specific construction of cultural knowledge and practice oriented to the habits of behavior of Europeans in 'the tropics'). In an age prior to the understanding of bacteriological theories of infection, or Ross's 1890s connection of malaria to the anopheles mosquito, miasmic theories dominated every colonial settlement and daily living decision. As polluted air was taken as the cause of disease, and 'native settlements' and 'habits' the origin of this, colonial settlements in India (and elsewhere in 'the tropics') were invariably located windward, in front of, at a distance from, and preferably at higher altitudes than the former. Throughout south and southeast Asia, as well as west Africa, massive local resources were expended on the construction of hill stations,[5] and road and rail access to them, at cooler, higher altitudes, distant from 'native towns' on the plains, primarily for the rest and recuperation of colonial military and administrative personnel, and later, the comfort of colonial wives. In cantonments, the extent of spatial appropriation, the design and orientation of colonial barrack rooms, the allotted space for each occupant, and the air-circulating design features were determined by reference to the temperature, flow and volume of air (King 1976). Special headgear and protection for the white, European body were the subject of extensive scientific research and Royal Commissions (Renbourne 1961; King 1976). 'The tropics', as Arnold states, 'were created as much as discovered' (2000: 10), not least with the help of the ideological and material apparatus disseminated by imperialism, including the two most globally recognized tropical symbols, the sola topee and the tropical bungalow. As forms of protection for the body, they shared an uncanny similarity of structure: the high, 'double-layered' crown and double-layered roof; the broad rim of the hat and the broad roof of the verandah, overhanging and shading the head or body; the ventilation holes in the crown or the high windows permitting cross-ventilating currents of fresh air; the raised crown, not touching the head or, using stilts or pilotis, the raised floor of the bungalow, high above the 'dangerous emanations' from the ground. All resulted from the same 'scientific' medical principles: protecting bodies from the sun's heat and encouraging the circulation of 'fresh air' (Renbourne 1961; King 1984).

Combined over decades with changing racial attitudes, cultural (and capitalist) notions of property and with planning principles based on colonialist rationalities, miasmic theories of disease structured the shape of colonial cities, and European sectors in them, in ways recognizable long after the end of colonial rule. The less densely developed, cleaner and greener, windward sector of the colonial city was to become the site for post-independence suburbs of the elite and multinational tourist hotels.

Notions of hybridity and mimicry which characterize colonial discourse (Bhabha 1994) also have their referents in spatial and building form. They also provide opportunities for thinking about hybridities in a cultural geographical sense, not least in relation to hybrid cartographies (Jacobs 1993) and different types of hybrid architectural forms (Jacobs *et al.* 2000). The concept of the bungalow, 'the one perfect house for all tropical countries' (King 1984: 200), the outcome, over time, of 'interactions with indigenous peoples and places' (Driver and Yeoh 2000), with the help of tropical discourses, moves into different regions of the globe.

The transformation of these tropical knowledge paradigms into the 'sanitary syndrome' of the twentieth century and subsequently into the 'scientific' basis of much contemporary urban planning worldwide is their bequest. That 'the tropics' 'continue[s] to shape the production and consumption of knowledge' (Arnold 2000: 10) is evident from southeast Asia to Brazil, where the concept of 'tropical architecture' or 'tropical modernism' is re-materialized through the lenses of 'regionalism', national culture and international capital (Kusno 2000; Tzonis *et al.* 2001, Yeang 1987). In this sense, the new 'tropical urbanisms' mark out newly developed regional or national identities while simultaneously permitting the urban elite to stay within the transnational space of modernism.

On the general topic of knowledge and power, in the context of colonialism, some of the most pioneering work was undertaken by anthropologist Bernard S. Cohn. In the words of Dirks:

> Long before the powerful theoretical proposals of Michel Foucault made knowledge a term that seemed irrevocably linked to power, and before Edward Said so provocatively opened up discussion of the relations between power and knowledge in colonial discourses and Orientalist scholarship, Bernard Cohn had begun to apply an anthropological perspective to the history of colonialism and its forms of knowledge in a series of essays written between the mid 1950s and early 1980s.
>
> (Dirks 1996: ix)[6]

If Cohn stands out as a pioneer in addressing questions of representation in colonial societies, there are other scholars whose ethnographic, descriptive, critical and theoretical explorations of colonial communities, colonial space and colonial cities between the 1950s and early 1970s laid essential foundations for any subsequent research in the field.[7] This raises important issues of whether a new knowledge paradigm only comes into existence when, like 'postcolonial theory', it is designated with a distinctive label. I suggest below the different social and spatial conditions under which the phenomenon of 'postcoloniality' became (belatedly) recognized and widely studied in the Western academy from the early 1980s.

To summarize: in what might be called (compared to the 1980s) the 'pre-global' 1960s and early 1970s, both the audience for, and interest in, such culturally oriented postcolonial studies in the metropolitan academy was restricted to specific disciplinary cells, whether in anthropology, development studies, or among those scholars with first hand experience of one-time colonies. From the late 1960s, radical movements in the West spurred a surge of interest in Marxism and, not least in urban and regional studies, the advent of a neo-Marxist urban political economy. Cultural issues, as understood in current post-colonial discourses, referring especially to issues of identity, cultural autonomy and subjectivity, were not part of these discourses. In David Slater's (1998: 71) retrospective view, 'the failure to theorize subjectivity and identity' was the major weakness of such Marxist accounts. We might say that in the 1960s and early to mid 1970s, compared to the situation in the 1990s, the social sciences were much less interested in culture, and the humanities (apart from an apolitical, 'Commonwealth Literature' discourse; Moore-Gilbert 1997: 2) much less inter-ested, if at all, in colonialism. One can search the geographical (and other) literature in vain at this time looking for research on issues of culture and iden-tity in 'postcolonial' or 'developing countries'. The surge of interest in these questions which surfaced in the early to mid 1980s appears overwhelmingly in the anglophone West, rather than the postcolonial societies themselves (see also R. Young 2001: 62). As I discuss below, it is the outcome of selective social and spatial processes of globalization.

POSTCOLONIAL WORLDS: THE HUMANITIES

What might be termed the 'second' or 'humanities' phase of postcolonial criti-cism seems, from the frequency of publication, to have taken off in the early 1980s,[8] its practitioners both metropolitan and 'Third World' intellectuals (Dirlik 1994). Compared to the earlier (social science) generation of 'colonialism' scholars who were generally male, European or North American, occasionally financed through 'aid' arrangements and 'displaced' from the metropole to the colony or postcolony, and with a research focus on the politics, culture, society and space of the colonial society, scholars associated with the second phase (specifically termed 'postcolonial studies') have generally been from the humanities, as likely to be female as male, Black (or non-White) as White, as likely to have their origins in the one-time colonies (either exploitative, e.g., India, Caribbean, or settler, e.g. Australia, New Zealand, South Africa) as the metropolis, and to have been displaced from the colony, or postcolony, to the metropolis. To various degrees, their critique is informed by cultural or literary theory, particularly feminism and poststructuralism, and the objects of analysis are primarily texts – literary (histories, travel writing, letters, diaries, manuals, etc.), as well as graphic, photographic or cartographic. As suggested above (see note 8) the direct or indirect starting point of this humanities phase of post-colonialism has, in many if not all cases, been Said's *Orientalism* (1978). While much, if not all, of the postcolonial geographical work dealing with 'empire' is in this mode of analyzing texts and representations, it is worth noting that, in terms of location, much of it is by 'postimperial' scholars rather than the one-time 'colonized indigenes' or 'settlers' suggested above. In geography, as well as other disciplines, it is also evident that the work from 'postimperial' as well as postcolonial (both previously colonized as well as settler) scholars has very different priorities, politics and agendas. Here, it is worth mentioning Western's work on Cape Town (1997, but first published in 1981) which, exceptionally for that time, deals with issues of identity and the politics of exclusion.

In recognizing that postcolonial theory and criticism comprise 'a variety of practices many of them pre-dating the period when the term "postcolonial" began to gain currency' (Dirlik 1994; see also Williams and Chrisman 1994, Moore-Gilbert 1997), both of the latter accounts begin their histories in the early years of the twentieth century with reference to the anti-racist, and/or anti-colonial writings of W. E. B. Dubois, Sol Platje and, subsequently, the Harlem Renaissance, C. L. R. James, Frantz Fanon and others. Moore-Gilbert (1997: 2) continues, 'While postcolonial criticism has apparently a long and complex history outside Europe and America, it arrived only belatedly in the Western academy and British university departments more particularly'. Here, Moore-Gilbert documents the development of the field in English studies, emerging from conferences held in the UK in the early 1980s (e.g. Literature and Imperialism, 1983; Europe and its Others, 1985), paying attention to the earlier, anglocentric and apolitical paradigm of 'Commonwealth Literature' whose sponsors had held their first conference in 1964.

Where Moore-Gilbert traces the chronology of the postcolonial paradigm in literary studies in the UK, less attention is given to the geography, sociology and demography of its development. No mention is made, for example, of the virtual absence, in British university populations in the 1970s, whether among humanities faculties or students, of non-White, British-born subjects. Moore-Gilbert is also silent in regard to his own origins (born in Tanzania, son of a game warden in colonial Tanganyika (Tanzania from 1961)) or his geographical location, like Paul Gilroy, the author of perhaps the earliest proto-postcolonial monograph in British cultural studies, *There Ain't No Black in the Union Jack* (1987),[9] also subsequently based in the University of London's Goldsmiths College in southeastern London, a major site of multiethnic communities, especially from the Caribbean and Africa, in the postimperial metropolis. In 1991, approximately one-fifth of London's 6.5 million inhabitants were classified as ethnic minorities, the large majority either born in, or descended from parents who were born in the one-time colonial Empire. Nearly half of Britain's ethnic minority population lived in London in 1991 (Storkey 1994: 24–5).[10]

While Dirlik (1994) is partly correct in maintaining that the postcolonial paradigm had resulted from a postcolonial, English (and native language) speaking diaspora from East to West, i.e. 'when Third World intellectuals have arrived in First World academe', it clearly also needed audiences, situated in appropriate locations. New forms of knowledge need receptive subjects and, where teaching relies on the publication of monographs, textbooks and journals to publish academic research, all three began to appear in the (postimperial?) global city of London, the major publishing center of the anglophone world in the late 1980s.[11] With minority populations predominantly formed, from the early 1960s, by immigration from the one-time colonial Empire (Ireland, India, Pakistan, Bangladesh, the Caribbean, eastern and western Africa, Hong Kong), the UK can more obviously be represented as 'postcolonial'. Conversely, the United States, with a much greater diversity in its ethnic minority origins (though with obvious colonial relationships with Puerto Rico and its indigenous Native American peoples), has been represented under this label in relation to its (internal) history of slavery and recent immigration. The widespread adoption of the paradigm in the United States academy from the late 1980s also rests on an increasing acknowledgment that most of America's 'ethnic minorities', Hispanics, Chicano/as, Asian Americans and others, are in the United States as the result of colonial wars (in the nineteenth century, with Spain and Mexico; and in the twentieth century, in Korea, Vietnam, El Salvador and Grenada among others). The adoption of the postcolonial paradigm is also associated with the Civil Rights movements from the 1960s and the resultant ideological construction of a multicultural society (Geyer 1993).

The growth of minority faculty numbers in the American academy, and an increasing audience of minority students in US higher education in the later 1980s and early 1990s, primarily in public institutions, also provided an educational market for postcolonial studies (Finkelstein *et al.* 1998).[12] The paradigm was also boosted by the increased internationalization of graduate education, not least, students from decolonized states. Under the category of the 'postcolonial', such students have acquired a framework with which to recognize their historic colonial connections with the US, with postcolonial confrères elsewhere, but also, an identity within 'the West' to contest both a Western, White (and as I discuss below, frequently male) cultural hegemony as well as the facts of social and academic racism. In this sense, postcolonialism has enabled an alliance between 'Third World' students and those of African-American, Latina/o, Asian-American or Native American US minorities. These material factors affecting the cultural politics of education also need to be seen alongside intellectual developments, including the emergence of 'an explicit theoretical sensibility (which was largely foreign to mainstream history); and second, an attempt to recover the political significance of culture and the epistemic violence of colonialism' (Gregory 2000: 613) if the rapid growth of postcolonial theory and criticism is to be understood.

It is evident from these accounts that different postcolonial critiques, irrespective of the geographical or disciplinary location in which they emerged, have shared a common objective in deconstructing epistemologies and reformulating the objectives and methodologies of knowledge production. Because they operate under different social, historical and geographical conditions, however, their referents, as well as their politics and agendas, are understandably not the same. This is apparent from the critical work that has been undertaken on interrogating and deconstructing 'imperial geographies'.

Geography, understood literally as 'a writing of the (surface of) the earth' (*Oxford English Dictionary*), is inherently a universalizing science, though developed within specific political and historical conditions. Can there ever be, therefore, a 'postcolonial geography' that allows people and places to represent themselves in their own terms? Such a question raises issues not only about the histories of geographical knowledge (Driver 1992) but also about its geographies – an issue which, in academic and popular imaginations, is more frequently grasped through their varied cartographies (Harley 1988) and the different world views they represent. In examining 'the interplay between colonial power and modern geography during the "age of empire" ', Driver (1992: 27) cites Hudson's (1977) pioneering account tracing the close correlation between the birth of modern geography and the emergence of a new phase of capitalist imperialism in the 1870s. Geography developed, in Hudson's view, 'to serve the interests of imperialism . . . including territorial acquisition, economic exploitation, militarism and the practice of race and class domination'. This radical, and also empirical geographical tradition is also manifest in *The Geography of Empire* (1972) where Buchanan suggests that the material impoverishment wrought by European and US imperialism 'may well prove to be of less significance than the undermining of indigenous cultures' through 'the pillage of brains', the 'infiltration of Third World education systems' and similar cultural practices (1972: 19).

However, as Driver is at pains to point out:

> (G)eography during the 'age of empire' was more than simply a tool of capitalism, if only because imperialism was never merely about economic exploitation. There are significant aspects of the culture of imperialism . . . which deserve much more attention from the historians of modern geography than they have yet received.
>
> (1992: 27)

Many of these issues are addressed in the essays in Godlewska and Smith's collection, *Geography and Empire* (1994) the major merits of which are not only its wide geographical scope, addressing the origins and intellectual and material implications of imperial geographies in the main European imperial societies, as well as Japan, the US and elsewhere but also the fact that it draws attention to a critical postcolonial geographical tradition, largely independent (with the exception of the introduction and the chapter by Crush) of work developed in the light of the postcolonial theory of the late 1980s. The editors none the less fully recognize the contribution of Said's important works, *Orientalism* (1978) and *Culture and Imperialism* (1993). In highlighting Said's 'vivid geographical sensibility' they draw attention to his discussions of 'imagined political geographies' and particularly how literary scholars have 'failed to remark geographical notation, the theoretical mapping and charting of territory that underlies Western fiction, historical writing and philosophical discourses of the time' (Said 1993, cited by Godlewska and Smith 1994). Yet in recognizing the 'brilliant vista' of Said's work they also draw attention to its ambivalence 'towards geographies more physical than imagined, a reluctance to transgress the boundaries of discourse and to feel the tangible historical, political and cultural geographies he evokes' (1994: 6–7). This last is an important point and one to which I return below. However, irrespective of the objects, methods, scope, and not least, the possibilities of a reformed and critical geographical knowledge in a Western-oriented world of scholarship where English has, for better or worse, become the commonly accepted international language there exists the barrier (or facility?) of what I shall call the 'postcoloniality of English'.

THE POSTCOLONIALITY OF ENGLISH

The extent to which contemporary (anglophonic) human geography is still (unwittingly) a postcolonial project is manifest in a paper by two Madrid-based Spanish geographers, researching 'the extent to which international journals of human geography are really international'.[13] Language is probably the most basic constitutive feature of culture, occasionally used as a metaphor for culture itself. In postcolonial literature, not least in geography, only very recently has attention begun to be devoted to its most fundamental and constitutive feature, namely, the anglophonic nature of the discourse itself (see also Hopkins 2002).

On the assumption that English is the common language of communication of international journals, the study examines the national origins (by institutional affiliation) of papers published, the composition of editorial boards according to national locations, and related indices, of 19 prominent English language geography journals. The authors show, among other results, that over 86 percent of articles come from either the one time metropolitan country (UK) or countries of what they refer to as the 'Anglo-Saxon world' (largely, the US, and also Canada, Australia, New Zealand); similarly, the editorial boards are made up of scholars, over 80 percent of whom are from these countries. Either curiously or expectedly, in stating their conclusions, first, that such journals 'are not, in fact, very international' and also that 'human geography is still fragmented into national or linguistic communities' (Gutierrez and Lopez-Nieva 2001: 67), the authors neither refer to these findings as an outcome of politically, geographically, and culturally influenced colonial and 'postcolonial' histories, nor do they make any use of that term in their analysis. Yet combining this information with what is common knowledge about the extensive circulation of anglophone geographers (as well, of course, as many other disciplinary academics) between appointments in Australia, Canada, the UK, the US, Singapore, the Caribbean and elsewhere, the stereotypically weak language skills of (especially British, American and Australian) academics, and the relative lack of familiarity with developments in, for example, German, Russian, let alone Chinese or Arabic scholarship, would seem to confirm the persistently postcolonial nature of anglophone scholarship, from which the structural impediments of language (and the lack of it) offer little escape. This naturally leads to the question of academic diasporas.[14]

Unlike other major modern migrations, such as that of European Jewish intellectuals at the turn of the twentieth century, and subsequently in the face of Nazi persecution in the 1930s, the migration and transmigration of postcolonial anglophonic intellectuals within, and across, the space of the anglophonic world, have constructed what until recently may be characterized as disaggregated histories. Anglophone postcolonial intellectuals in New York are linked with those in India, the Middle East, Canada, South Africa, Australia, southeast Asia, the Caribbean and elsewhere. This creation of different postcolonial identities – a result of a 'technical' postimperialism – from nation states with widely differing standards of economic prosperity, even though (some) intellectuals within poorer states may be educationally and socially privileged, has constructed a cultural space linked across, and by means of, a particular anglophonic language world. It is this anglophonic postcolonial subjectivity which, as the opening quotes from Young and Mongia suggest, is behind the suggestion to transform the nature of established, metropolitan-based systems of knowledge.

An examination of at least some postcolonial texts can reveal a combination of citations drawn from authors originally from a vast array of postcolonial as well as other countries (see, for example, the extensive bibliographies in Williams and Chrisman 1994 or R. Young 2001). This (apparently) theoretically coherent assembly of diasporically related scholars, increasingly cutting across the disciplinary differences of the humanities and social sciences suggested above, would have been rare, at least on such a scale, as little as four or five decades ago. On the other hand, it would be necessary to recognize not only the dominance of English as the medium of this literature and the absence of other major world languages (Mandarin, Hindi, Spanish, Arabic), but also the metropolitan location where much of this knowledge is being produced, where it is being consumed, and by whom. What this indicates is how specifically postcolonial, and anglophonic, or perhaps, 'post' or 'neo-imperial', and very definitely not 'global', these particular discourses are.

POSTCOLONIAL GEOGRAPHIES: MATERIAL AND SYMBOLIC

Reference has already been made to the need 'to feel the tangible, historical, political and cultural geographies that Edward Said "evokes" rather than addresses' (Godlewska and Smith 1994 above) and suggestions have been made elsewhere as to why the current 'humanities' phase of postcolonial studies has, until the mid to late 1990s, largely ignored the realm of colonial urban, spatial, and built environment studies.[15] In ignoring the physical, spatial, architectural, urban and landscape realities in which many of these various colonial discourses developed, these accounts erase (by ignoring) the essential *material* conditions, and mental referents, without which other cultural practices and forms of representation (in addition to architecture, planning and urban design) – writing, mapping, ethnography, film, photography, painting – would have been impossible. In an analogy with Said's comment (cited above) that literary scholars 'have failed to remark the geographical notation, the theoretical mapping and charting of territory that underlies Western fiction, historical writing and philosophical discourses' we can also say that literary (and many other) scholars have failed to remark the physical, spatial, symbolic, visual and material environments in which everyday life actually occurs. Moreover, such spatial and built form arrangements are not simply signifiers of power and control, they also materially affect the life chances of those who live within them. As Brenda Yeoh has argued, they were also real spaces in which the authority of colonial power and control was effectively contested (Yeoh 1996). It is to the materialities, built forms and physical spaces of the city and how these affect, help to produce and reproduce social relations, identities, memories and subjectivities that I turn.

THE MATERIALITY OF THE URBAN

The real spaces of the city (whether seen primarily as representative of social relations of power or as the lived everyday space of socially, racially and ethnically differentiated populations) are essentially *dynamic*. As they change over time, they represent transformations (or reaffirmations) in the social distribution of power, in access to resources, not least in postcolonial times. One of the most frequently cited texts in postcolonial studies is Frantz Fanon's *The Wretched of the Earth* (1968: 37–40), particularly, his representation of the 'colonial world' as being epitomized by the racially and spatially segregated colonial city: 'The colonial world is a world divided into compartments . . . of native quarters and European quarters, or schools for natives and schools for Europeans, etc.'

This description would *seem* to provide both a clear benchmark from which to examine the extent to which such one-time divided colonial cities which fitted this description have been transformed in the decades since independence but also, the opportunity for an assessment of such transformations by postcolonial (and other) subjects (King 1976: 282; Yeoh 2001). However, as Yeoh, among others, points out, the situation is far more complex. In addressing criticism of the postcolonial paradigm, Moore-Gilbert writes:

> The objection of many (neo-Marxist) critics to postcolonialism rests on the assumption that material forms of oppression are the only ones worth bothering about and that postcolonialism's characteristic focus on the cultural or textual levels of the West's relationship with the 'Rest' is a sympton of its ignorance or inadequate attention to the 'real' dynamics of that relationship.
>
> (1997: 64)

The opposition which Moore-Gilbert suggests here between the 'material' and the cultural, or textual levels of oppression is a false dichotomy and one resulting from the unfortunate hiatus between what I have characterized as the earlier, 'social science' scholarship on colonialism and this second 'humanities' phase. Most obviously it is the absence, in the latter, of attention to the phenomenon/a of *material space*, which allows Moore-Gilbert not to recognize, or perhaps, not to acknowledge, that material forms of oppression are also cultural and textual as well as vice versa. Here, it is not the metaphorical 'space' which 'historians, anthropologists and literary theorists of colonial discourse' frequently evoke, but real, material space that needs attention; 'many of their works barely touch on the real, physical consequence of colonialism's spatial tactics, or indigenous responses to them' (Myers 1999: 27; see also Cairns 1998).

Myers (1999: 50) refers to 'the vast and growing literature by geographers engaged in the critical analysis of interrelationships between colonialism, geography and "discourse" broadly inclusive of travel writings, map-making and academic representations of formerly colonized places'. An archaeology of geographical knowledges (Driver 1992) would map out not only the critical turning points in the development of geographical representations, but how such geographies have been mobilized to counter material oppression (e.g. Crush 1994; Jacobs 1993, 1996). In the remainder of this section I draw selectively on research in these various fields in order to illustrate some of the different ways in which studies on the materiality of space (including issues of land, territoriality, architectural cultures, the built environment, planning and urban design) have illuminated issues of identity, subjectivity and resistance in a variety of contexts.

A broad distinction might be made here between two types of research and writing. The most common, 'critical colonial histories', use colonial discourse analysis to interrogate historical archives in relation to spatial environments, the objective being to raise political and social awareness around issues of representation and equity for the postcolonial present, and including issues of gender and colonial space (Mills 1991). Included here is the now extensive body of scholarship addressed to the analysis and deconstruction of colonial travel writing, much of it, from a critical feminist perspective (Blunt 1994; Blunt and Rose 1994; Duncan and Gregory 1999; Mills 1991, 1994a and b; Pratt 1992). The second type addresses contemporary situations in *supposedly* postcolonial states, focusing on continuing inequities and injustices based on race, class and other markers of difference as part of an ongoing cultural politics of space. Illustrative of this second approach are case studies explored in *Edge of Empire: Post-colonialism and the City* (1996) in which Jane M. Jacobs traces ways in which 'the cultural politics of colonialism and postcolonialism continue to be articulated in the present' (1996: 10). Documenting City of London redevelopments in the 1980s, she demonstrates how the continuity of discourses over sites, seen as 'the economic center of Empire as well as the spiritual and otherworldly sense of Empire', were mobilized to influence subsequent decisions about urban design. 'Place,' she writes, 'plays an important role in which memories of Empire remain active' (1996: 40). Addressing the settlement of Bangladeshis in east London's Spitalfields, and highlighting the continuity between colonial and postcolonial situations, Jacobs writes, 'Many of the new labour arrangements of global cities like London (produced by postcolonial migrations) quite literally re-work people already categorized as available for exploitation under colonial economies' (1996: 71). In her native Australia, Jacobs speaks to a contemporary politics of space, demonstrating, for example, the inadequacy of the 'paradigmatic imperial technical instrument of "mapping"' to establish the authentic Aboriginal sacred, and charting, as an outcome of the 'map's' ineffectivity, a shift in the Australian national discourse from the secular to the sacred (1993).

What is crucially important to recognize here, however, is the degree of public acknowledgment in Australia of a multicultural and postcolonial *consciousness* and a cultural politics willing to act on it. The postcolonial paradigm here is not (as elsewhere) confined to cells within the academy but operates on the streets. What this reinforces is a point already made, namely, how a postcolonial critique operates, and what it does as a result, depends on local contingencies, that is, how it shapes people's thoughts and conditions as specifically postcolonial.

Essays in *Postcolonial Space(s)*, by an international group of architects and urbanists, bring yet another angle to an understanding of the postcolonial. In the words of the editors, 'Postcolonial space is a space of intervention into those architectural constructions that parade under a universalist guise and either exclude or repress different spatialities of often disadvantaged ethnicities, communities or peoples' (Nalbantoğlu and Wong 1997: 7). While representative chapters (e.g. Nalbantoğlu, on the carved dwelling in Turkey, or Cairns, on the traditional Javanese house) successfully contest the boundaries of what 'architecture' is usually taken to be, the commitment of contributors to exploring innovative poststructuralist, psychoanalytic, feminist and other approaches, characteristic of postcolonial theory, need also be read alongside accounts that acknowledge the persistent and powerful material factors of uneven development worldwide (Smith 1984) and the corporate *knowledge* influences of global capitalism.

Whether postcolonial criticism can have real political effects can be seen by comparing some of the Australian cases cited above with the account of Chatterjee and Kenny (1999) who argue that, despite five decades of independence, attempts to bridge the vast spatial, social, economic and infrastructural inequities, as well as religious, cultural and lifestyle differences, between old and new Delhi, the legacy of hegemonic colonial planning, and to create a single capital symbolizing the unity and identity of the nation, have yet to be resolved. In suggesting reasons for this, the authors point to the *ambiguities* of the postcolonial, the fact that 'the replacement of previous hierarchies of space, power and knowledge has not been complete'; 'Muslim, Hindu and western socio-cultural norms co-exist, albeit uneasily, in Delhi's built environment' (1999: 93). Multiple identities produce a multiplicity of spatialities. I return to this question in Chapter 10. The issue of dealing with space and identity in postcolonial (as well as other) cities deserves a monograph in itself, not least because the *recognition* of postcoloniality apparently agitates outside commentators more than indigenous governments and professionals. Again, this demonstrates how different local circumstances of materiality produce different conditions for the possibility of thinking and being postcolonial.

Yeoh's (2001) overview of geographers' research on postcolonial cities in the 1990s is organized around four themes: identity, encounters, heritage and an interrogation of the relevance of the postcolonial paradigm itself. A cluster of studies has addressed the different ways in which postcolonial states have endeavored to engage with, but also distance themselves from, their colonial pasts, hoping to cultivate new national citizen subjectivities in the process: new capitals (Holston 1989; Perera 1998) or capitol complexes (Vale 1992), toponymic reinscription (Yeoh 1996), spectacular towers (King 1996b; Chapter 1, this volume), transformative modernisms (Holston 1989; Kusno 2000), among others. In Kusno's telling phrase, the spatial reformulations result from what 'the colonial and postcolonial have done to each other' but under very different political regimes. Yet while, in Yeoh's words, 'architecture and space can . . . be interrogated for their embodiment of colonial constructions and categories in order to reveal the postcolonial condition' (2001: 459), attempting to read architectural meanings without the discourses that accompany them is a notoriously ambiguous project. As colonialism and imperialism are two sides of the same coin, also important here are the essays in Driver and Gilbert's *Imperial Cities* (1999). These address the architectural and urban spaces constructed by imperialism in Europe's imperial metropoles, Paris, London, Rome, Vienna, among others, demonstrating in the process the urbanistic competition between these capitals which European imperialisms generated.

In urban 'encounters', Yeoh also reviews some of the literature on the distinctive social, ethnic and racial characteristics of postcolonial cities, the opportunities they offer for newly emergent practices and social identities, echoing themes in the classic essay of Redfield and Singer (1954), yet also noting the resilience of older colonial representations. Such 'imagined pluralism . . . is drawn upon in positive ways to position the postcolonial nation as a cosmopolitan society' (Yeoh 2001: 460).

Issues of heritage in the postcolonial city are buffeted between the cultural politics of different regimes and cyclical shifts of the world economy; what were once symbols of colonial control or authority get demolished or refurbished according to the priorities tourism policy commands (see Bishop *et al.* 2004). The contested 'heritage' of various elements in the postcolonial city and their investment with symbolic capital is an important theme of this literature. But one-time residential areas (and houses) of the colonial elite can also become, in postcolonial times, a contested terrain for different social and ethnic populations, both materially, and in battles over nomenclature (see Chapter 9). Focusing on the postcolonial as conventionally understood, Yeoh (2001) also cites studies that show how, in the Pacific Asian region, old colonial 'core centres' of the global economy are being spatially transformed by new shifts in the spatial economy, not least in regard to the economic power of Japan (see also Perera 1998).

These issues of identity, encounters, and heritage which Yeoh highlights here, with their emphasis on indigenous agency, focus attention once more on the different meanings of 'postcolonial'. The questions which Yeoh addresses relate to the possibility and methods (however contested) of 'hearing or recovering the experience of the colonized' (Sidaway 2000: 594) during or after colonization. Not all postcolonial places or nation states permit this possibility. As Myers (1995: 1357) writes in relation to postcolonial urban planning in east Africa, '(a)lthough draped in the banners of socialism rather than imperialism, the post-colonial state inherited from the colonial regime an obsession with spatial order as an ideological tool and means of civic control'. The result is that projects are 'activated in the interests of powerful leaders more than in the interests of the people for whom (they) ostensibly were planned'.

What emerges from these studies, therefore, is the critical importance of the presence, or absence of *local*, indigenous perceptions of 'postcoloniality', what is implied by it, and who has the power of political control. The problem of postcolonial studies, according to Kusno (2000), has been a tendency to undertake a critique of colonial discourse around a broad, often undifferentiated critique of 'the West', without acknowledging that colonialisms come in many forms. Recognizing historical differences between various colonial states, Kusno argues that, until the demise of Suharto's 'New Order' in 1998, Indonesia in fact continued as a colonial regime in all but name. As Indonesians were encouraged by Dutch orientalist discourse to remain 'Indonesian', they never thought of themselves as part of a colonial legacy.

Where many previous studies of colonial urbanism have examined ways in which colonial power attempted to use spatial discourses to exert control over the indigenous population (e.g. Çelik 1997; Metcalf 1989; Mitchell 1988; Rabinow 1989; Wright 1991), more recent research has documented the role of indigenous agency in either resisting, accommodating or problematizing this control (Hosagrahar 2000; Raychaudhuri 2001; Yeoh 1996). Yeoh's innovative study of Singapore (1996), for example, demonstrates the extent to which indigenous inhabitants retained power over their own space. Also absent in most postcolonial urban and architectural studies are attempts to understand the connection between the built environment and the construction of the subject. In this context, Kusno (2000) explores how different spatial discourses and practices under Sukarno helped shape the national imagination and subjectivity; and under Suharto, how the making of two social and spatial categories (the underclass kampung and the middle class 'real estate' suburb) helped to create two divided national subjectivities in the capital city.

POSTCOLONIAL PROSPECTS

As an interpretive paradigm, the use of postcolonialism is surely destined to spread. The evidence lies not only in the ever-increasing literature, or the new and imaginative ways the concept is being used (Sidaway 2000) but also because the political, cultural, social, demographic and also religious conditions (King 2000a, 2000b) in which it has been established will certainly grow. The present (2003) and future situation in Iraq and the Middle East more generally have again, more violently, underlined the relevance of imperial and colonial paradigms. Briefly stated, its achievement has been to put colonial, postcolonial and neocolonial realities at the center of understandings of the contemporary global condition. As a way of giving voice to, and recognizing the agency and identities of subaltern others, it is increasingly being taken up across the disciplines, irrespective of geographical location and language (R. Young 2001: 62; Vacher 1997). Its value is in contesting or in cases, complementing other representations of the contemporary world – cultural or political economic theories of globalization, postmodernism, dependency or post-dependency theories and others (Featherstone *et al.* 1995; Simon 1998; Yeoh 2001). Each of these can be of value but in specific and limited contexts. The dangers are in attempting to use the concept in a totalizing fashion or, indeed, attempting to explain *everything* from a postcolonial framework or perspective.

As for the world of cities, we conclude by asking two questions: how persistent are postcolonial (imperial, or neo-imperial) forces in impacting urban space, not only in postcolonial, postimperial situations but in other cities elsewhere? And are these conceptual categories the most useful, valid, or appropriate to describe contemporary urban transformations? Some scholars have suggested that the 'postcolonial city' is an 'unusual and transitory experience' (Yeoh 2001: 462). Yeoh asks if, in this case, the 'postcolonial' can endure as a meaningful category (see also Simon 1998). Less frequently asked is whether new forms of the diasporic colonial city (i.e. a social and spatial formation ascribable to imperialism) are being re-established in the one-time metropole (Philo and Kearns 1993) or in urban settlements in other parts of the one-time colonial Empire, not least, the US, generated not only from European imperialisms but rather by American imperialism itself. This I return to in Chapter 6.

NOTES

1   See Ashcroft 2001; Gregory 2000; Loomba 1998; Robinson 1999; Sidaway 2000; Yeoh 2001; Young 2001.
2   'Postcolonialism' and 'postcolonial studies' are used here to cover different theoretical and methodological orientations including colonial discourse analysis, postcolonial theory and postcolonial criticism and the use of the hyphenated 'post-colonial' (see Moore-Gilbert 1997; Williams and Chrisman 1994; Ashcroft *et al.* 1998). The use of the hyphen is not consistent in the literature.
3   These are what I have referred to, drawing on the work of sociologist John Useem, as those of the colonial third culture (King 1976: 58–66).
4   See Arnold 2000; Driver and Yeoh 2000; Livingstone 1991, 1999, 2000.
5   See Spencer and Thomas 1948; Freeman 1999; Frenkel and Western 1988; Kenny 1995; Kennedy 1998; King 1976.
6   For other comments on Cohn's work and influence on the power/knowledge issue, see the preface in Rabinow (1989). Ranajit Guha, co-founder of the Subaltern Studies group, in his introduction to an earlier collection of Cohn's essays, cites a passage from one of them: 'Anthropological "others" are part of the colonial world. In the historical situation of colonialism, both white rulers and indigenous peoples were constantly involved in representing to each other what they were doing. Whites everywhere came into other people's worlds with models and logics, means of representation, forms of knowledge and action, with which they adapted to the construction of new environments, peoples, by new "others". By the same token those "others" had to restructure their worlds to encompass the fact of white domination and their own powerlessness.' Guha goes on to comment, 'It follows, therefore, that according

to this approach, the interpenetration of knowledge and power constitutes the very fabric of colonialism' (Guha 1987, xx). This is a key to the main point of this chapter.

7 I list some forty of these in the twenty years following 1954. See King (1976: 22)

8 Homi Bhabha, 'The Other Question: Stereotype and Colonial Discourse', *Screen* 1983; an earlier reference reflecting Foucaultian influences is Peter Hulme, 'Hurricanes in the Caribee: The Constitution of the Discourse of English Colonialism', in Barker *et al.* (1981). In the humanities, Edward Said's utilization of Foucault's notion of discourse in his *Orientalism* (1978) is used by a number of authors to suggest this title as the foundational text in the analysis of 'colonial discourse'. Williams and Chrisman (1994: 5) state, for example, that 'it is perhaps no exaggeration to say that Edward Said's *Orientalism*, published in 1978, single-handedly [*sic*] inaugurates a new area of academic inquiry, colonial discourse, also referred to as colonial discourse theory or colonial discourse analysis', though see my earlier comment on Cohn and other writing on the postcolonial prior to 1978. The works of Gayatri Spivak (e.g. 1985, 1988, 1990) are central to the canon. On early precursors of postcolonial theory, see also Wolfe 1997.

9 The primary aim of Gilroy's book is to address the representation of the black presence in Britain and second, to provide 'a corrective to the more ethnocentric dimensions of (cultural studies)' (1987: 11–12). In a penultimate chapter on 'Diaspora, utopia and the critique of capitalism', Gilroy states: 'It is impossible to theorize black culture in Britain without developing a new perspective on British culture *as a whole*. This must be able to see behind contemporary manifestations into the cultural struggles which characterized the imperial and colonial period' (1987: 156). Gilroy's second major work, *The Black Atlantic*, setting out the space of cultural studies (especially Black music) delineated by his title, was published in 1993. Confirming his thesis, Gilroy subsequently crossed the Black Atlantic to a position in the American academy.

10 Storkey (1994: 24–5) gives figures of 20–7 percent Black African population, and of 10–12 percent Black Caribbean, for the boroughs of Lewisham and Southwark, the immediate environs of Goldsmiths College. Data on the percentage of non-white faculty in individual British universities has only become available in the 1990s. In 1998, 4.8 percent of female academics were Black (1.2 percent) or Asian (3.6 percent) and 6.1 percent of male academics (1.1 percent Black, 5.0 percent Asian). (L. Young, 1998: 17). In 2000, only 2.3 percent of (full) professorships were held by ethnic minorities (*Times Higher Education Supplement*, April 7, 2000: 18).

11 An early text, Bill Ashcroft *et al. The Empire Writes Back: Theory and Practice in Postcolonial Literature* (1989) was followed a few years later by two readers (Williams and Chrisman 1994 and Ashcroft *et al.* 1995), a minor marker in the institutionalization of new academic paradigms. Some conception of the extensive publication through the 1980s and 1990s is indicated in these texts, as well as the references list here.

12 Finkelstein *et al.* (1998) argue that the changing composition of new, full-time faculty, hired between 1988 and 1992, containing more women, minorities and foreign-born, is leading to a significant change in academia – even though many of the minority faculty are 'ghettoized' by discipline. The authors show that racial/minority representation in the American professoriate rose from about 6–7 percent (1970s) to about 10 percent (1987). In the cohort of new entrants (1988–92) they represent 17 percent (Asian/Pacific islander 7.7; Black/Not Hispanic 5.7; Hispanic 3.1; American Indian/ Alaskan native 0.5). The figures for the first three of these categories in the humanities are 6.0, 4.3, 4.5; in the social sciences, 4.3, 6.8, 3.4. See Finkelstein *et al.* 1998: 29, 125. Said (1993: 288) points out that 'few European or American universities devoted curricular attention to African literature in the early 1960s'.

13 Though I address geography here, the critique could apply to many disciplines.

14 For valuable critiques of the hegemony of Euro-American critical geography, see various guest editorials, 'Introduction: Tracking the Power Geometries of International Critical Geography', *Environment and Planning D: Society and Space* (2003) 21, 2: 131–68.

15 'The early exponents of postcolonial criticism focused on a critique of literary and historical writings and . . . were located in the humanities of the Western academy. Subsequently, the objects of the deconstructive postcolonial critique expanded to include film, video, television, photography, painting, all examples of cultural praxis that are portable, mobile, and circulating in the West . . . Why did it not address, in any significant way, the impact of imperialism on the design and spatial disciplines of architecture, planning and urban issues more generally, whether in the colony or, indeed, in the metropole? . . . not only because they are different disciplines (and difficult to handle) but because the cultural products on which imperial discourses are inscribed – the spaces of cities, landscapes, buildings – unlike literary texts, films, and photography, are, for these postcolonial critics and their Western audiences, not only absent and distant, they are also not mobile. Critics have to take their own post-colonial subjectivities halfway around the world to experience them' (King 1995a: 544).

It is appropriate here to mention Mark Crinson's book, *Modern Architecture and the End of Empire* (2003). Though not deconstructing notions of the Western 'modern', this interesting and valuable collection of historical case studies examines 'the interactions between modern architecture, imperialism and post-imperialism' in regard to the last years of the British Empire. As the book appeared only after this present work went to press, I have regrettably been unable to make use of it here.

Chapter 4: The Times and Spaces of Modernity

No-one living in the stone age would know he [*sic*] was living in the stone age.
He would believe he was living in the modern age. Today we believe we are living in the modern age. Time will tell.

Raymond Briggs, *UG. Boy Genius of the Stone Age*.
London: Jonathan Cape, 2001 (cover)

INTRODUCTION

In the previous chapter, my aim has been to spell out some of the key concerns of a postcolonial perspective, especially as they relate to the study and representation of the spatial and the urban. In addressing these concerns, I have also attempted to elaborate on and qualify some of the predominantly global concepts and discourses discussed in Chapter 2. While it is evident from the more geographically focused Chapter 3 that disciplinary discourses of the global can indeed be integrated with those of the postcolonial, this is the exception rather than the rule. It is not difficult, for example, to cite the titles of many recent texts in social and urban theory that address the topic of globalization but, irrespective of their significant contributions in the field, make either no or virtually no reference to the colonial or postcolonial. This is particularly true with recent work on the city.[1]

In this chapter, I address one of the foundational themes and analytical categories common to both social theory as well as the humanities and one that is central to an understanding of architecture and the city: the notion of the 'modern' and of 'modernity' and the dyadic categories of the 'modern' and 'the traditional'. In particular, I explore what has happened recently to the category of the modern as it has been confronted by notions of the global and particularly, the postcolonial.

THINKING MODERNITY

'Modern' must be one of the most common metaphors used to represent a myriad of aspects of contemporary life, not least the so-called 'modern city'. Let me start by looking at its taken-for-granted meaning given in contemporary dictionaries.

According to the *Oxford English Dictionary* (1989) (and also Webster's) 'modern' means 'characteristic of the present or recent times, as distinguished from the remote past'. We might distinguish it from 'contemporary' (which means 'right now') by saying that it 'pertains to the current age or period'. According to the *Oxford English Dictionary*, it is used in contradistinction to ancient, and medieval, as in 'Modern History', the period of history after the so-called 'Middle Ages' (e.g. the close of the fifteenth century to today, according to the 1864 source cited). We might remark in passing that this is an intriguing conceptualization of five centuries which – irrespective of *where* these 'Middle Ages' were – have sufficient coherence and commonality to be subsumed by one concept.

Just to destabilize our notions of the modern, we might note that its first recorded use in the sense indicated above is in 1585, and modernist, 1588; modernity, meaning the quality or character of being modern, is identified in 1627, and modernism, modernness, modernizer and modernize are all in use by the first half of the eighteenth century. For modernization, meaning to make modern, cause to conform to modern ideas, we have to wait a little longer, to 1770 though there are references to aristocrats 'modernizing' their ancient homes in the mid eighteenth century. Raymond Williams (1984) makes the point that for the earlier use of the terms, modern and modernize, the sense is un-favorable, i.e. that the alteration or change that was implied needed to be justified. Only in the nineteenth and twentieth centuries did modern acquire a positive connotation, meaning improved or efficient. Hence, whereas modern has generally positive connotations (though not always, as when we refer to modern problems) contemporary is a more neutral term. It goes without saying that all these citations from the *OED* are from English literature, presumably written in England (or Britain).

The etymology of modern suggests that it comes from the Latin modus, meaning measure. This is an interesting insight which turns our attention to both modish (fashionable), and à la mode. It also prompts a useful thought which I shall insert here though it will arise again later in the chapter: that is, if we adopt Williams' point that the contemporary connotations of modern are positive, by what and whose criteria is a positive notion of cultural modernity *measured*? How do we know which is a modern city? Or which is the most modern city? Who is doing the measuring? Are they female or male? Black, brown, or white? Is it the Population Crisis Committee in Washington (1991) with their 'livability' indices showing degrees of air pollution, murders per thousand population and telephones per head, or the late Ayatollah Khomenei?

The point I wish to emphasize, however, is that the criterial attributes of modern in the sense in which it has been defined here are primarily temporal, not spatial. Its meaning is defined not just in relation to 'history' but to someone's very specific history. The question of space, of the place, location, society, country, nation state or life-space to which 'the present or recent' refers, is taken for granted and unproblematized, though it is evident from what is referred to as 'Modern History' (so capitalized, and in contradistinction to the 'Middle Ages') that that space is Western, if not European, and at least titularly Christian.

If we acknowledge that these are mainly 'anglophone' understandings, additional historical meanings of 'modern' and 'modernity', not least in Latin, German and French, can be derived from *Geschichtliche Grundbegriffe* by Brunner *et al.* (1978), a 'historical lexicon of political-social speech in Germany', which extends Williams' historical comments back some few centuries.[2] Some of the more interesting insights include the following.

The authors suggest three possible meanings, over time, for 'modern': contemporary, now; new, as opposed to old; and transitory, as opposed to eternal (i.e. the past is the past of a future present). The earliest identified reference to the Latin 'modernus', used as an epochal boundary, is in 494/495, where 'modern counsels' are distinguished from old ones. In the twelfth century, 'Modernitas' ('modernity') is used to describe a new self-consciousness brought about by the twelfth century Renaissance, and is used, as was common in previous centuries, in contradistinction to classical antiquity which is seen as the norm by which the present is to be judged. In this sense 'modern' is viewed negatively, with the past as normative, and given a higher value. While this changes fundamentally during the Reformation, it is largely during the eighteenth-century Enlightenment that the meaning of modernity is uncoupled from antiquity with a new sense developing of the superiority of the modern over the antique, and where the model of progress is linked to the secular, rather than the theological world. Similarly, it includes the notion of superiority in all contexts of arts and sciences. Following the French Revolution, the usage of modern becomes increasingly differentiated in relation to different realms of experience in different countries and, in the second half of the nineteenth century, Baudelaire's (familiar) notion of the modern as the 'transitory, fugitive and contingent' becomes established. From then, and increasingly towards the turn of the century, modernism also takes on the meaning as being the enemy of past orders and values (which might, in what I discuss below, be seen as 'tradition'). In this context, the orientation of the present is to the future, rather than the past, and where the force of tradition is replaced by the force of choice and selection. Modern is already used as a noun in 1902 to describe the most recent social, literary and artistic tendencies, though also about this time, 'avant-garde' comes to replace 'modern', in that sense.

Two or three comments are needed on this (lengthy) essay. First, the overall framework for the essay is largely provided, with some brief exception (see below), from the discourses of literature, philosophy, the arts, and second, it is – again – entirely situated in 'Western' (if not European) space and time (i.e. without reference to Asia or Africa, and only marginally to the Americas). The exception is the brief reference, in the final pages, to the realm of sociology where the authors state that 'modernization', since 1960, has been used to refer to various developments in the 'lands of the Third World'. While extending Williams' comments, therefore, these insights do not contradict him.

In short, because modern and modernity, understood to mean 'as of the present', are neither temporally nor geographically grounded, because they float in space, they are empty of meaning and hence, irrelevant for either description or analysis. Strictly speaking, a phrase such as 'the modern city' applies equally to Kabul, New York or Varanasi.

DISCIPLINARY MODERNITIES

It is also the case that, till quite recently, scholars operating within various disciplinary discourses used these terms both selectively and differently. Some, indeed, continue to do so and it is the gradually disappearing distinction between what I would broadly call 'humanities' conceptualizations of modernity and those of the social sciences which is an important theme of this chapter. Like Williams

(1984), I would suggest that conventionally, modern, and especially modernism, modernity and modernist, are terms and concepts especially used in the human-ities to refer to particular movements and tendencies in the arts, literature and architecture, largely between 1890 and 1940, which took place principally in Europe and the US and with very little (though some) reference to the world-system as a whole (to use another metaphor, also in the 1989 edition of the *OED*). Indeed, in many humanities disciplines, the very concepts of the modern and modernity can be taken as *foundational* to the extent that they determine the nature of the knowledge produced, the temporal, spatial and concep-tual boundaries which govern its construction, as well as the identity of its producers. In art history, for example, professional identities are principally defined in terms of 'periods', structured across Western concepts of time. Practi-tioners are either 'modernists' or 'pre-modernists', and if the latter, medievalists, or someone who 'does' 'ancient' or 'Baroque'.[3] It is this geographically limited use of modern which is the parent of the so-called postmodern which I shall make a digression to address.

In contemporary (sociological) usage, this particular understanding of the modern is grounded in a very distinctive, industrial and monopolistic phase in the development of the capitalist world-economy which took place in Europe and the US, principally in the nineteenth and first half of the twentieth century. If modernity and modernism in the humanities sense can be defined by refer-ence to the cultural practices of specific elites (which is an arguable proposition in itself) then, according to Harvey (1989), it was a cultural manifestation of early twentieth-century capitalism. This, though *premised* on relations within the world as a whole, and particularly on those of colonialism, was nonetheless largely restricted in its manifestations to Europe and North America. I write 'largely' because it is necessary to acknowledge what Pieterse refers to as the 'upsurge of non-Western influences' on 'modernism' which were experienced in Paris, which he appropriately calls 'the cultural center of the colonial age'. He refers here to *l'art negre*, 'via the cubism of Braque and Picasso, the fauvisme of Matisse, and the naive painting of Henri Rousseau' (1992: 371).

Yet these (humanities) concepts of modernity and modernism as they have been utilized in Europe and North America were never understood in this way (see, for example, the representative texts in *Modernism, 1890–1930* by Bradbury and McFarlane (1976), or Timms and Kelley's collection (1985) on *Urban Experience and Modern European Literature and Art*). Modernity was invariably defined only in relation to Europe and the US, and not within the world as a whole. It follows, therefore, that postmodernity operates with the same geographical restrictions, whether in terms of the Eurocentric intellectual sources on which it draws, the phenomena it purports to explain, or the areas of the world to which it supposedly relates. (Lyotard himself stated that 'the post-modern condition' (1984) was only a symptom of what he calls 'the most highly developed societies').

In contemporary Western (and probably also in certain 'non-Western', 'non critical') usage, modern refers to 'modern industrial – and now, post-industrial – societies' which are usually though not necessarily market/capitalist. The general discussion of modernity in these societies, in the humanities especially but also in the social sciences, has conceptualized the topic historically in relation to economic, technological, social and cultural changes either within Europe, or 'the West' as a whole, or in relation to a nationally defined society. The second and, as I shall discuss below, more recent referent for modern is the Enlightenment project in Europe, with its emphasis on rationality, order, the state, control and the belief in progress. In both of these particular, and essentially Eurocentric discourses, Paris, through spatial, technological, energy and architectural transformations, becomes the paradigmatic 'modern city' in the last third of the nineteenth century, with Vienna, London and Berlin following close behind (Benjamin 1978; Lash 1990; see also Frisby 2001). Though numerous titles could be cited in support of these propositions, particularly representative would be Marshall Bermann's *All That is Solid Melts into Air* (1988) and its citing of Baudelaire's dicta on modernity: 'By modernity, I mean the ephemeral, the contingent, the half of art whose other half is eternal and immutable' (1863: 133) and T. J. Clark's *The Painting of Modern Life: Paris in the Art of Manet and His Followers* (1984). The factor common to both is that despite nodding reference to the French Empire or to the appearance (in Clark's account) of the black subject, the world outside Europe (or even, in some sense, outside France) hardly exists.

In what is now a well-accepted argument, postcolonial historian Dipesh Chakrabarty has called for a 'provincializing' of Europe, recognizing that 'Europe's acquisition of the adjective *modern* for itself is a piece of global history of which an integral part is the story of European imperialism' and that 'the understanding that this equating of a certain version of Europe with "modernity" is not the work of Europeans alone' (1992a: 20–1). 'Third World historians' he writes, 'feel a need to refer to works in European history; historians of Europe do not feel any need to reciprocate' (1992a: 2).

These comments are particularly pertinent to the representation of the 'modern metropolis' which, in the most recent, and otherwise well-researched book on that topic, is seen as an *exclusively* European phenomenon and one having no connection with the rest of the world, particularly, the world outside Europe (Frisby 2001).[4] Chakrabarty's comments are even more relevant in the case of those imperial capitals such as Paris or Amsterdam, or major industrial cities such as Manchester. Thus, Benjamin's well-known essay on 'Paris, Capital of the Nineteenth Century' (Benjamin 1978), often cited as the classic representation of 'the modern city', despite its references to the Empire as being 'at the height of its power' and to the world economy, makes no mention of the extensive colonial exploitation intrinsically linked to the commodity production displayed in the arcades. Similarly, in the case of the Dutch overseas Empire where, over its 300-year history, a knowledge of economic, social, architectural and urban developments in the Netherlands is necessarily seen (in this case, by Dutch historians) as essential for understanding their impact on the colonies (Groll and Alphen 2002), the economic subsidy of the colonies to the early twentieth-century rebuilding of Amsterdam is ignored, somehow taken for granted (Stieber 1998). Manchester's economic (as well as social and cultural) development (P. Hall 1998) was to a very large extent dependent on the domination of colonially controlled markets by the city's manufactured cotton goods during much of the nineteenth century (Bose and Jalal 1998; Cain and Hopkins 2001; see also Chapter 11). Without making these connections, there is no explaining contemporary forms of social and cultural modernity stemming from the presence of tens of thousands of Algerians or Moroccans in Paris, of Surinamese and

Antilleans (in addition to the many Moroccans and Turks) in Amsterdam, nor residents from India, Pakistan and the West Indies in Manchester. These problems arise because modern and modernism have been defined only by reference to time and not by reference to space.

MODERNITY, TRADITION AND 'THE WEST'

In the words of anthropologist Michel-Rolphe Truillot:

> Modernity . . . belongs to a family of words we may label 'North Atlantic universals' . . . Words inherited from what we now call the West . . . that project the North Atlantic experience on a universal scale that they helped to create . . . words such as 'development', 'progress', 'democracy' and indeed, the 'West' itself are exemplary members of that which contracts or expands according to contexts and interlocutors . . . they come to us loaded with aesthetic and stylistic sensibilities from what it means to be a human being to the proper relationship between humans and the natural world . . . since they are projected as universals they deny their localization, the sensibilities and the history from which they spring.
>
> (Truillot 2002: 220)

'Tradition' can also be added to Truillot's list of words.

According to fellow anthropologist, Nelson Graburn:

> The concept of 'tradition' emerged along with 'modernity' during the Enlightenment [a European phenomenon] specifically to denote objects, ideas and ways of life which were threatened by the change to modernity, and that were seen as dying. Ever since then, tradition has come to mean anything that is threatened by change. Indeed, it is 'modernity' that 'invented' tradition, just as it invented Anthropology and Folklore to study traditions, and just as it continues to create traditions.
>
> (Graburn 1997: 61)

In everyday use the term tradition generally refers to that which is handed down, or transmitted – whether beliefs, rules, customs, practices or the like (*Oxford English Dictionary* 1989). But tradition, as used in anthropology, Graburn suggests, 'shares its origins in early modernity with a number of other latently ideological concepts that relate to it and our study of traditional environments in the modern world'. He includes the anthropological use of the term 'culture' (1871), 'folklore' (1846) and 'heritage' (before 1900). 'These originated as concepts in the discourse of Western analysts, expressing a particular historical world view that was used not only for thinking about the Western world but also about the newly-colonized non-Western world' (ibid.). Originally, in the European world, the concept of tradition was first negative, associated with the irrational and superstition. Later, tradition came to be seen as a reservoir for the construction of community and identity, drawn on by late nineteenth-century European nationalisms, something to be preserved or even invented (Hobsbawm and Ranger 1983). In the twentieth century tradition has equally been taken up by politicians and elites outside the West, largely as part of a nationalist rhetoric and practice (Graburn 1997). In postcolonial nations such as Sri Lanka, Kuwait and Papua New Guinea, the architecture of new capitol buildings has drawn on real, imagined or invented 'cultural traditions' taken from local building (Vale 1992).

Partly because of its linguistic origin in English (and later, American English) and the subsequent linguistic imperialism of colonial and international English (Pennycook 1998), 'modern' therefore has become unproblematically associated with 'the West', to use a spatial and geographical metaphor, though one that is also economic, political, moral and philosophical. It has been given a very distinct and particular materialization, not only in Western literature, music and the arts, but in architecture and urban design.

THE MODERN AND TRADITIONAL CITY

The so-called 'modern city' we are speaking of was not only characteristic of 'present or recent times' *anywhere* but only in Western Europe and North America. Nor, of course, did it take the same manifestation in the various countries of those two continents, or did its 'modern' forms occupy all of the space of the city which it touched. To speak of 'Western modernity', there-fore, or of 'the modern Western city' is something of an excess, a kind of Orientalism in reverse. Nonetheless, the notion of 'the modern' was firmly and powerfully fixed in 'the West' and then conveyed to other parts of the world through the uneven relationship of colonialism and global capitalism (see also Sardar 1992).

The role of colonialism in creating and legitimizing the dichotomy between 'modernity' and 'traditional' (and of anthropology in institutionalizing it) also provided ways of materializing, as well as visualizing the distinction in real, concrete terms. In the late nineteenth and early twentieth centuries, in various parts of the colonial world ('French North Africa', 'Indo-China', 'British India', the 'Dutch East Indies' and elsewhere) the political, social, spatial and cultural phenomenon of the so-called 'modern city' [*sic*] was introduced, from Europe, as an instrument of colonial control. Here, as Shirene Hamadah (1992) has pointed out, it was through the construction of the centered authority of the so-called 'modern city' that the original indigenous settlement came to be called:

> the traditional city . . . [T]he dichotomy between tradition and modernity [is] a
> derivative of the dichotomy between East and West . . . To talk of the traditional city is
> to suggest an entire mode of operation, life and mentality which can only be defined
> and understood in relation to the 'non-traditional city' . . . [it] only gains legitimacy by
> reference to something else.
>
> (Hamadeh 1992: 241)

Hamadeh also points out, interestingly, that the English phrase 'traditional city' or the French, 'ville traditionelle' has no equivalent in Arabic, the city being known simply as the 'old city' (ibid.: 258).[5] The 'modern city' at this time meant the city of the automobile, the railroad, the planned streets, boulevard and airport – Rabat, New Delhi, Pretoria. In this way, the conceptual abstractions of the 'traditional' and 'modern' are further invested with images of the visual, physical, architectural and spatial realities of the city.

While this dualistic classification can be found in many academic discourses – in sociology, anthropology, geography – it lies at the heart of 'vernacular archi-tecture' studies which have at least two sets of intellectual roots. One, as Graburn suggests, is in the late nineteenth-century nationalist cultural revivals in Europe.

Here industrial capitalism and its social and cultural effects provide the basis for notions of the 'modern'. Its preindustrial 'predecessor', the rural, the handmade and that which is disappearing, become the 'traditional'. These debates occur across, and help to form, the spaces and identity of the nation. In Western Europe, they lead, in the late nineteenth century, to 'vernacular revivals' in styles of architecture, the Arts and Crafts movements (Watkin 1980), the invention of 'heimatkunde' in Germany, the establishment (in Britain) of the Society for the Protection of Ancient Buildings, the collection of 'traditional' folk music and its dissemination to the nation's schools.

The second set of roots of 'vernacular architecture' can be found in the immediate postcolonial conditions of the 1950s or early 1960s. They take root across the *transnational* spaces of the metropole and the postcolony, with the 'discovery', by Western architects and 'development consultants', of 'traditional' forms of dwelling in countries of what, after the invention of the term in about 1953, were increasingly called the 'Third World' (Wolff-Phillips 1987). These are conceived as culturally more appropriate alternatives to meet the crisis in housing and urban development (Oliver 1969). Like other binary, dyadic concepts (East/West, male/female, urban/rural) 'modernity' and 'tradition' are essentially *defined in difference*, each located at either end of an epistemological spectrum. Each acts as the 'constitutive outside' of the other. Each makes the other possible (Roy 2001).

Irrespective of the *site* where this binary of traditionality/modernity developed, two factors are paramount. It was a discourse that emerged *relationally*, dialectically, and it always occurred within an uneven distribution of power. It was a teleological view of history which, following a given line, focused on a point of arrival. This dualistic narrative has been woven into much of social and cultural theory for most of the twentieth century (Roy 2001), perhaps only being effectively challenged from the 1970s.

With regard to the 'modern' city of colonialism, as a number of studies have shown (Holston 1989; King 1976, 1990a; Rabinow 1989; Wright 1991) the urban outcome was not simply the transplantation of a 'modern Western city' but was rather the product of a distinct colonial modernity. Though having some superficial resemblance to aspects of the city in the metropole, it was not only inherently different from it but was to a large extent politically, economically, administratively and spatially dependent on it.

Nowhere is this dependence better illustrated than in the architectural and spatial practices of what at first was called 'Modernism' and subsequently, with a similar degree of Western hubris, the 'International Style' (King 1990a: 61, 78, 98). As applied to urban and architectural form, the term 'International Style' was coined in the early 1930s to refer, initially in Europe and North America, to the high tech, high energy materials, and capital intensive building and design practices usually located in central city sites housing the institutions of monopoly capitalism (Hitchcock and Johnson 1966). This was an era when world economic and political relations were dominated by capitalist institutions and European as well as Japanese colonialisms were at their height. It was the political space of French colonialism in the 1930s that permitted the designs of Le Corbusier to be constructed in Algeria in the 1930s (Lamprakos 1992) and, in a fit of postcolonial euphoria, in India's Chandigarh. And with different architects, under different conditions, Brasilia in the 1950s (Holston 1989).

In this particular historical and urban thematic context, therefore, Mark Elvin's conceptualization of modernity proves useful. As a historian whose work focuses mainly on China, Elvin is concerned to find a definition of modernity that (1) 'is not based on chronology, and so escapes the confusion caused by continuous updating' and (2) one that enables him 'to see societies as varying combinations of "modern" and "non-modern" elements, sometimes mutually indifferent, sometimes mutually supportive, and sometimes mutually hostile. In this view, of course, neither present-day Western Europe nor present-day North America emerges as wholly "modern"' (1986: 209).

On these premises Elvin defines modernity as 'a complex of more or less effectively realized concerns with power'. It is a complex that contains at least three elements: (1) 'power over other human beings, whether states, groups or individuals, according to the system under consideration'; (2) 'practical power over nature in terms of the capacity for economic production'; and (3) 'intellectual power over nature in the form of the capacity for prediction' (1986: 210). To this, however, we also need to add the power, under imperialism, not only to construct knowledge but also the parameters and paradigms within which that knowledge is made legitimate. It is the power to name, classify and categorize. It is the historical situation which Spivak refers to as 'the history of the epistemic violence of imperialism' (1988: 172).

THE TIMES OF MODERNITY

So far, my argument has stressed the essential spatialization of the Eurocentric concept of modernity; but what about what Bhabha (1994) has called its 'ambivalent temporality'? Because modernity, if it means 'as of the present or recent times, as distinguished from the remote past', not only exists everywhere, even though it may take on different nuances dependent on linguistic and cultural differences, it exists at different times: 'each repetition of the sign of modernity is different, specific to its historical and cultural conditions of enunciation' (1994: 207).

Bhabha also questions both the conventional spatialization of modernity as well as its temporality. He writes, '[T]hrough Kant, Foucault traces the "ontology of the present" to the exemplary event of the French Revolution and it is there that he stages his sign of modernity . . . The Eurocentricity of Foucault's theory of cultural difference is revealed in his insistent spatializing of the time of modernity' (1994: 202).

Bhabha's particular criticism, however, is reserved for 'the ethnocentric limitations of Foucault's spatial sign of modernity [which] become[s] immediately apparent if we take our stand, in the immediate post-revolutionary period, in San Domingo with the Black Jacobins, rather than in Paris'. Here, in short, Bhabha is pointing to the sharp disjunction between a so-called 'modern disposition of mankind' (based on ideas of the Enlightenment) and the contradictory (and conveniently forgotten) colonial and slave histories.

Modernity, he suggests, is about 'the historical construction of a specific position of historical enunciation and address'. There is never a 'real' modern in itself as 'modernity' comes out of a temporarily continuous and spatially comparative relational perspective.

Like Bhabha, I have also argued (King 1991b: 8) that the real emergence of 'today's' modernity, as an ideology of beginning, of modernity as the new, is in colonial not metropolitan space. My own 'specific position of historical enunciation' for deciding what is modern – which has a location both in time as well as space – rests on the following two criteria.

To begin with, we take the present (rather than 1904 or 1954) as the 'now' of modernity. This is a modernity judged not by some elitist Eurocentric conceptions of 'modernism' grounded in literature, painting or architecture, notions which are now firmly historic and fixed in the cultural canons of the West, but by the present-day reality, in conditions of grossly uneven development, of the total internationalization of production, and of world interdependence in which, in theory at least, there are no Others (Giddens 1990).

Second, if modernity is to be judged from the present, by the existence, in a significant number of cities round the world, of ethnicities, races and peoples from virtually all parts of the planet. If we ask, on the basis of these two criteria, where the first historical occurrence was of what today we call the 'modern multi-cultural' city, the answer is certainly not in the European or North American 'core' cities of London, Los Angeles or New York, but probably in one-time 'peripheral' ones of Rio, Calcutta, Shanghai or Batavia (today, Jakarta). I write 'probably' because it is precisely due to the Eurocentric focus of much demographic as well as other social research, that we do not have an immediate answer to this highly important historical question. I also put quotation marks round 'core' and 'peripheral' as it is evident from what I am saying that, from a social and cultural (rather than an economic and political) perspective, the core would become the periphery and the periphery, the core.

Clearly, I am not speaking here of some kind of technological or architectural modernity but rather of a social and cultural modernity. For example, were we to take New York City as the epitome of what many scholars have frequently represented as the paradigmatic example of what, through immensely powerful cinematic and photographic representations, the 'modern' city of the 1950s and 1960s was supposed to be (see Wallock 1988, for example), and examine it by reference to what some (even US based) organizations see as appropriate contemporary criteria (Population Crisis Committee 1991) the city would present a dismal picture of congestion, astronomical costs, air pollution, massive energy use, crime, and social malaise, even though many observers might see it as having a high ranking on scales of ethnic, cultural and racial diversity.[6]

Definitions of cultural modernity which made reference to 'quality of life' criteria, questions of equity in regard to gender, race, ethnicity, to questions of access, affirmations of identity, ecologically progressive transportation systems, security, and employment, would give us a totally different set of criteria by which the world's cities could be judged as the 'most modern'.

The question therefore is not only *whose* version of modernity we are operating with, but *when* and *where* that version comes to be fixed as a dominant global paradigm. From then, and there, it is passively used as a reference point (a *measure* in fact, to return to the start of this chapter), from which all forms of contemporary cultural and historical critique take off. We need only imagine the intellectual and disciplinary chaos (not least in conventional interpretations of, for example, literature, or art and architectural history) were the categories of 'modernity' or 'modernism' to be withdrawn from the canon or declared obsolete. Despite this, a restructuring of categories is clearly needed. I shall return to these issues below.

'MODERNIZATION', 'POSTCOLONIALISM' AND THE 'POSTMODERN'

If modernism, modernist and modernity are the preferred terms, with preferred meanings, of the humanities, modernization, while not normally found in the vocabulary of the humanities, is nonetheless central to the social sciences. To make my argument, I shall focus on a particular sociological understanding of modernization, and modernization theory from the mid to late 1960s.

The principal distinction between the humanities understanding of modernism and that of the social sciences on modernization falls along the following lines. Where modernity/modernism are Euro-American concepts, grounded in a spatially restricted historical temporality, modernization is a (largely American) term, the criterial attributes of which are both spatial and geographical, as well as temporal and historical. The meaning of the term, and the mode in which it is used, rest on an assumption that the modern – according to 1960s modernization theory – is measured not only diachronically, in relation to the past of one's own (always Western, Northern) society, but synchronically, in relation to the present of someone else's (always Eastern, Southern) society. Where the humanities 'modern' has, till quite recently, ignored what today we might refer to as 'the global' or 'the world as a whole', the social sciences 'modernization' attempted to address these dimensions, though within the paradigms of internationalism available in the 1960s (more recent concepts such as 'world-systems', 'globalization' and 'postcolonial' paradigms, of course, emerging only from the 1970s and 1980s).

As an example of such 1960s theories we can note Cyril Black's, *The Dynamics of Modernization: A Study in Comparative History* (1966) where 'modernization' (including its gendered and geographical positioning) refers to:

> the process by which historically evolved institutions are adapted to the rapidly
> changing functions that reflect the unprecedented increase in man's knowledge,
> permitting control over his environment, that accompanied the scientific revolution.
> This process of adaptation had its origins and initial influences in the societies of
> Western Europe, but in the nineteenth and twentieth centuries these changes have
> been extended to all other societies and have resulted in a worldwide transformation
> affecting all human relationships.
>
> (Black 1966)

Another influential interpretation from the same period is Marion J. Levy's *Modernization and the Structure of Societies: A Setting for International Affairs* (1966). To illustrate his theme, Levy addresses questions about the spatial 'spread' of modernization:

> There are of course conspicuous differences in the level of modernization. England,
> France and at least West Germany represent high levels of modernization. . . . Nothing
> in Asia would fall on the relatively modernized side of the line save for Japan . . . No
> African country save South Africa and isolated portions of Algeria could qualify as
> being on the relatively modernized side of the line.
>
> (Levy 1966: 37)

Significantly, however, in Levy's 850-page book, reference to colonies and colonialism occurs only on four pages. A third example, Myron Weiner's *Modernization: The Dynamics of Growth* (1966) includes contributions from 24 of the leading proponents of modernization theory in the 1960s. The book is divided into three main sections, each dealing with the modernization of society and culture, politics and government, and the economy. The fact that none of the contributors are women, or speak from Third World positions, or with one exception, are non-White,[7] is a simple but telling commentary on Bhabha's point about the different repetitions of 'the sign of modernity'.

It is not my object here to enter into a critique of these particular versions of modernization theory. Rather, in resurrecting these almost 40-year-old extracts from a discourse on 'modernization', my aim is to demonstrate that globe-wide discourses about 'the modern', and the social science debates which both preceded and succeeded them, have a substantial history long before the relatively recent discovery in the 1980s, in the prism of the postmodern, of the world outside Europe and North America and the interconnectedness of these places with it. For at least one theme which proponents of postmodernism are (or better, were) concerned with, is a very *belated* recognition of the world outside themselves – and the decenterings, cultural relativizations and contradictions that this recognition has brought about.

One explanation for this development is to be found, first, in the migration, and subsequently, the voices of 'Third World' intellectuals often doubly displaced from their own space (especially India, Pakistan, eastern and northern Africa, the Caribbean, Palestine, each place subsequently reconceptualized, in the 1980s, as the postcolony), often via the postimperial metropole, to the still globally culturally hegemonic realm of the US. Here, the debates around multiculturalism, diversity, anti-racism and cultural identity have provided fertile ground for the seeds of a postcolonial critique to develop, hybridizing with the narratives of Black, Hispanic and Native American oppression. Ironically, therefore, it is the presence of postcolonial 'Third World' intellectuals in the academies of the English-speaking regions of the ideological 'West' (the US, Canada, UK, Australasia) which has brought, in the 1980s, a new consciousness of colonialism to these countries and also elsewhere. As a central theme of cultural politics, this relatively recent 'discovery' of colonialism, displacement and of cultural difference has, as discussed in the previous chapter, been effected by scholars in comparative literature, cultural studies, history and other disciplines on the territory of the postimperial metropole (UK), in Australia, Canada, or the still imperial hegemon of the US and subsequently on the terrain of the postcolony itself.[8]

In an influential book, *What Is Post-Modernism?* (1986), read widely in both architectural as well as other circles, architect Charles Jencks constructs a table delineating three types of society based on their 'major form of production': 'pre-modern 1000 BC–1450; modern 1450–1960; post-modern 1960–'. Here, the distinction between the 'modern' form of production (Industrial Revolution: factory, mass production, centralized) and its related society (capitalism: owning class of bourgeoisie, workers) and the 'postmodern' production form (Information Revolution: office, segmentation, decentralized) and its related society (global: para-class of cognitariat, office workers) provides an even better example for my argument. In designating 'postmodern' society as 'global' *only* from 1960, Jencks totally ignores the development of the capitalist world economy from the sixteenth century, as well as the emergence of global relations of production and colonialism prior to that date.

In addition to the international migration of postcolonial scholars to the US in the 1970s and 1980s, the other factor which has inserted postcolonialism into the discourse on the postmodern is the increased awareness, by academics in the metropole, of 'the globe as such', to use Robertson's phrase. Both movements may be seen as the outcome of what Hopkins (2002) has called 'postcolonial globalization'.

RECOGNIZING MULTIPLE MODERNITIES

For two centuries at least, prevailing definitions of modernity have been premised on a set of values which were, as I have suggested above, predominantly Western, male, white, oriented to the individual, and ecologically innocent (in fact, rapacious). The cultural de-centerings of the last decade are altering these criteria. In his introduction to *Critically Modern* (2002),[9] a series of essays that critique the notion that 'being or becoming modern betokens the global triumph of Euro-American economic, social or cultural development' and that look at processes of 'being or becoming different modern in different world areas', Knauft (2002: 3, 4) writes:

> the various strands of Western and colonial modernity braided together in powerful new ways during the late eighteenth and especially nineteenth and twentieth centuries. It was during this period that industrial capitalism most dramatically transformed life in European towns and cities . . . these processes were recursively linked to . . . the increasing activities of Europeans overseas; the exploitation of non-Western areas in a global network of exploitation and commodity production; disruption and movement of non-Western peoples; the growing development of creole populations, including in Europe; and the hybridization of Western values, sensibilities and institutions among subaltern populations.
>
> (ibid.: 8)[10]

These new ways of how we represent 'the world', and the societies within it, have developed from, at least, the mid to late 1970s. One set of theorizations, from the early to mid 1980s, are debates about globalization and 'time–space compression' (Harvey 1989).[11] The second is the increasing acceptance of a pluralist notion of modernity, of 'multiple modernities', treatments that 'problematize and diversify modernity across ranges of time, space and identity' (Knauft 2002: 17). That modernity is recognized in many different forms is reflected in a myriad of book titles that have appeared in the last decade: alternative modernities, colonial modernities, competing modernities, repressed modernities, Other modernities, global modernities, hybrid modernities, gendered modernities, indigenous modernities, vernacular modernities, constructed modernities and, not least, postmodern modernities. What they all share is a *de-centering*, and also a multiplication, of the notion of modernity itself. This clearly implies that we relativize our notions of modernity, accepting that it is not 'an a priori unity' but 'an outcome of diverse conjunctures' (2002: 178).

'(M)odernity always unfolds within a specific cultural and civilizational context, and different starting points for the transition to modernity lead to different outcomes' (Gaonkar 1999: 15). It is also the case, however, that these different modernities emerge, not separately, but from an inter-connected world characterized by histories of colonialism, exploitation and conditions of grossly uneven development. Power relations are at the center of the debate. Societies and individual subjects have different visions of the future, informed by different aspirations, values, social and political ideologies, different histories and different degrees of power or the lack of it, in dealing with other parts of the world. While we can agree that 'all societies create their own paths to modernity' (Featherstone and Lash 1995) they do not do so, to remember Marx, in conditions of their own choosing.

In the last two decades, scholars have identified particular forms of colonial, and also postcolonial, modernities – hybrid outcomes of colonialism, with their own views not only about what they want to keep but also what they want to leave behind. They also have their own distinctive spatial, architectural and urban forms, emerging from their own political cultures, and all of these require new categories of interpretation (Kusno 2000).

Moreover, different modernities in the West were and still are also marked by different cultural characteristics consisting of 'a constellation of understanding of person, nature, culture, reason and the good' (Gaonkar, 1999: 15). To identify these characteristics, specific cultural histories that make for necessarily 'other' modernities are required, not least from voices other than from 'the West'.[12]

RECLAIMING MODERNITY: THE CONTEMPORARY METROPOLIS

In the original version of this chapter (King 1995b), I had suggested a solution to this conundrum of 'different modernities' on the following lines, namely, that there should be a readjustment, a conscious chronological sliding of the terms, modern and modernity, and the conditions and places to which they refer, as follows.

First, we should take the 'global space' of the present as the 'now' of modernity. This would allow us to see that what until now has been called 'modern society', i.e. nineteenth- and twentieth-century industrial, often capitalist, societies characterized by technology, rational bureaucracies and the rest, was a concept applied entirely to the West with little recognition that this state of modernity was premised on the West's colonized Other. This phase we should reconceptualize as the *pre-modern*.

We might then take what Occidental, generally European and American, intellectuals have conceptualized as the postmodern (using, as I have indicated, the myopic Eurocentric views of modernity suggested above) and characterized by Jencks (1986) for example, by fragmentation and irony, and which belatedly recognizes the existence of a world beyond the Western hemisphere, and re-label this as the *modern*. As this might more accurately capture the economic, social and cultural totality characterizing emerging urban formations round the globe, particularly the so-called 'world cities', this would seem a logical proposition.

On further reflection, however, it is clear that the notion of 'premodern' is equally as redundant as 'postmodern', necessarily fixed, as both of those terms are, by geographically, historically and societally specific meanings which are fixed 'in the West'. As children's author Raymond Briggs well states in the epigraph, everyone has their own version of modernity. If we are to live in a global world, we can only operate with complex and different forms of modernity. It is this re-spatialization of the modern which leads me to my conclusion.

CONCLUSION

Cultural modernity can hardly be addressed in the abstract, without reference to a specific, objective place, or a particular subject (or set of subjectivities). As far as large Western metropolises are concerned, the burgeoning increase in the internationalization of capital, international labor migration and technological transformations, as well as increased dependence on tourism, are likely to lead to many of the structural characteristics identified for the so-called global city, though not necessarily to give rise to their particular functions. I refer to the growth of indigenous as well as multinational producer services, with their dependent component of low level service provision, a multiplicity of cultures, the expansion of the cultural economy, the proliferation of the economy of the sign and the exacerbation of ethnic, racial and social difference such that, as Abu-Lughod (1991) has argued, New York and Cairo begin to have more in common, if only on the surface, than New York and Chicago.

In this way, the characteristics of cities in the so-called 'most advanced' urban economies increasingly approximate to those of what were once called 'Third World' cities, at least in the degree of economic, social and spatial polarization, in the extent and complexity of their ethnic, social and racial mixes, and in the occupational structures of their de-industrialized, or non-industrialized populations. In this sphere, a variety of competing modes of production (global capitalism, local state socialism, new forms of feudalism) produce on one hand corporate office towers, luxury apartments and hotels, state hospitals alongside a variety of local vernaculars, shanties, cardboard cities, and street people warming shop corners and entrances to subways, manifesting not only deep economic fissures and contradictions, but also cultural and regional heterogeneities.

If these are the characteristics of what is now the 'modern city' in the West, as we have seen it develop in the last thirty years, then it is evident that cultural modernity, understood in terms of poverty as well as riches, was prefigured much earlier, in what is generally referred to as the 'Third World' city of the 1950s and 1960s. Indeed, as I have argued elsewhere (1991a), the Eurocentrically defined cultural conditions of a so-called postmodernity – irony, pastiche, the mixing of different histories, schizophrenia, cultural chasms, fragmentation, incoherence, disjunction of supposedly modern and premodern cultures (Harvey 1989) were characteristic of colonial societies, cultures and environments on the 'global periphery' (in Calcutta, Hong Kong, Rio de Janeiro, Shanghai or Batavia/Jakarta) decades, if not centuries, before they appeared in Europe or the US. How did the local Gujarati inhabitants read the text of 'modern' Bombay in the 1870s? Or the British colonials, that of the village settlements of the Gujaratis? The same question can be put in relation to the Dutch, British and Iroquois in what was to become New York in the mid to late seventeenth century.

What this suggests, therefore, is that what some have labeled 'postmodern' culture pre-dated what they have labeled 'modern' culture, but then that is only possible if we look at modernity in terms of space as well as time.

NOTES

1   This is not the case in Latin American literature where the postcolonial paradigm has become prominent: see Castro-Gomez, S. and Mendieta, E. (eds) (1998) *Teorias sin Disciplina. Latinamericanism, Postcolonialiadad y Globalizacion en Debate*, San Francisco: University of San Francisco; also, de Toro, A. and F. (eds) (1999) *El Debate de la Postcolonialidad en Latinoamerica*, Madrid/Frankfurt: Vervuert, IberoAmerica. Thanks to Celia Zambrando for these references. See also Thurner and Guerrero eds (2003).

2   Many thanks to Ursula King for help with translating some thirty pages of this article from German.

3   Announcements of vacancies in the American College Art Association's *Positions Listings* (December 2002) refer, for example, to 'Art Historian Nineteenth/Twentieth Centuries', 'Modern and Contemporary Art Historian' and [*sic*] 'African or Contemporary'. In all cases, the geography unproblematically assumed for these 'periods' is Euro-America or 'the West'.

4   Though the cover description states 'The modern metropolis has been one of the crucial sites for the exploration of modernity since at least the mid nineteenth century' the sources and treatment of the topic are entirely drawn from European (especially German and Austrian) and American sources. The brief mention of Cairo is simply a passing reference to its representation in international exhibitions.

5   In a similar way, Bengali residents of Calcutta in the nineteenth century did not – as is common in anglophone literature on the city – use, or refer to the city in terms of 'the white' and 'the black' or 'native city'. Personal communication, Swati Chatto-padhyay. For further critical discussion of the term 'traditional' in this sense, see Crysler (2003).

6   On a scale measuring public safety (murders per 100,000), food costs, living space per person, education, public health, clean air, peace and quiet, New York was listed 12th of the 14 largest metropolitan areas in the US (Seattle was the first) and 27th of the world's 100 largest cities (Melbourne was the first) (Population Crisis Committee 1991). As this organization has not updated this report, more recent (2003) data evaluating 215 cities round the world on 39 'quality of life' criteria is available at mercerHR.com. Rankings (March 2003) for 'personal safety' on a world scale placed three Swiss cities in the top position, and in North America, four Canadian cities at 25th, Houston and San Francisco at 40th, Chicago, Seattle, New York at 64th and Washington at 107th. See mercerHR.com for further details.

7   This is the only book I have on my shelves which has photographs of each author at the beginning of their chapters

8   The relation of these discourses to critiques of colonialism in the 1960s and earlier by, for example, Ranajit Guha, Romila Thapur, Syed Alatas, Susantha Goonatilike and the geography and history in which they take place is referred to in Chapter 3 (see also King 1999).

9   My thanks to Janet Wolff for bringing this book to my attention.

10   Though I reproduce Knauft's use of 'non-Western' here (a term in widespread use in the US academy) it is a term that, for most readers, would epitomize what Knauft and his contributors are criticizing.

11   While recognizing the positive aspects of Harvey's discussion on postmodernism (1989), Knauft also states that his 'characterization of contemporary space and time ultimately draws more from . . . Western intellectualism than . . . how time and space are in fact constructed and experienced in different parts of the world' (2002: 14)

12   To take two relatively recent books in sociology: In Malcolm Waters' three-volume collection on *Modernity: Critical Concepts* (1999), London and New York: Routledge, while three of the ninety-nine readings address China, Japan and East Asia, only two at most of the 110 authors or joint authors of the ninety-nine extracts are from countries other than Europe or North America. And while Goran Therborn's chapter on 'Modernization Discourses, their Limitations and their Alternatives' in *Paradigms of Social Change: Modernization, Development, Transformation, Evolution* (2000) refers to 'classical modernization theory's . . . almost unbelievable *lack of empathy*

with the objects of European colonialism and Western racism' (p. 64) only 1 of the 73 authors he refers to is apparently from outside the Euro-American world (and only one, incidentally, is female). The contrast with the literature on postcoloniality could not be more striking (see, for example, the bibliography in Williams and Chrisman (1994), with authors from many different countries, mostly in the world outside the West).

Chapter 5: Writing Transnational Planning Histories: The Dialectics of Dual Development

> The city now stretches across nations, just as migration and diasporic cultures extend nations beyond their geographic territories.
>
> C. Greig Crysler, *Writing Spaces* (2003: 202)

INTRODUCTION

In the thirty years between the 1960s and the 1990s, the study of the city (and town) in anglophone scholarship has gone through three overlapping phases which, in an over simplified way, can be characterized as the study of the city *qua* city, studied in relation to itself or to others similar to or different from it; from the 1970s, the city in relation to the society where it exists and, from the 1990s, the city in relation to the world.[1]

In this chapter, I want to address a particular kind of city that lies between the models of the 1970s and the 1990s: the city to be understood not in relation to one, but rather two or more societies, by which, in this context, I refer to territorially based 'nation states'. In the process my aim is to explore the relevance of some of the theoretical issues and frameworks discussed in the three previous chapters.

Such a phenomenon – of a city developed and directly influenced in its social, ethnic and cultural composition, in its architecture and spatial form, its political and geographical significance, not just by the territorial society where it exists but by others 'external' to it – has been common throughout history, though it is usually understood as part of a sequential as much as a synchronic process, and often the result of imperial conquest. Greek Byzantium became Roman Constantinople and subsequently, Ottoman Istanbul. Christian Cordoba was transformed into a center of Muslim Spain. After less than three decades, New Amsterdam under the Dutch became New York under the British; over a century later, a different New York was given a different form under a much more diverse population of Americans.

The most common historical conditions under which the economic, social, ethnic, religious, cultural and, not least, architectural and spatial characteristics of individual cities are ruptured and transformed by social formations external to them are those of war and conquest, or long-term colonization as part of someone's empire. Any of these processes can, to different degrees, eliminate an existing city (as with the Spanish conquest of what became Mexico City), modify its form or, as with many nineteenth- or twentieth-century colonial cities in northern Africa or southern and southeastern Asia, 'duplicate' the existing city by planting a 'modern' settlement alongside it (Abu-Lughod 1965; King 1990a: ch. 2). There are, however, many other historical conditions in which the physical and spatial form of cities, in relatively autonomous societies, have been transformed by 'external' forces, whether in whole or in part.

Revolutionary movements, inspired by culturally exogenous ideologies, have changed the spatial order of capital cities. Mao's Beijing or, in different circumstances, Nehru's Chandigarh, both owe their present spatial form to a combination of both 'external' and 'internal' ideas as well as the everyday activities of their inhabitants (Broudehoux 2001; Prakash 2002). State governments, making use of different conceptualizations of 'the modern', have introduced from other countries the latest technologies, energy systems, transportation modes and urban designs, and 'modernized' cities all over the world: St Petersburg in the early eighteenth century (Bater 1976), Cairo in the mid nineteenth (Abu-Lughod 1971) and Jakarta in the mid twentieth (Kusno 2000). Under the conditions of military occupation by two ideologically opposed regimes, Berlin during the Cold War became a site to simultaneously implement both free market as well as socialist forms of urban design, in each case a prosthetic extension of American and Soviet ideologies (Castillo 2001). Individual teams of planners, or even individual architects, invited from some societies to produce their designs for others, have often had immense impact on the form and shape of individual cities (P. Hall 1998). In more recent decades, influences on the form and development of major cities, from the World Bank, global corporations, international planning consultants, global tourism (Judd and Fainstein 1999) and, not least, global terrorists, make the idea of the city being the sole product of a single, geographically bounded 'society' enclosed behind the borders of the nation state, increasingly suspect (if, indeed, the idea ever had credibility before).

A myriad of issues are raised by such cities, produced under socially, politically and culturally plural conditions. Half a century ago, anthropologists Robert Redfield and Milton Singer (1954) proposed the classic categorical distinction between orthogenetic and heterogentic cities – 'the city of the moral order; the city of culture carried forward' on the one hand, and 'the city of the technical order' on the other. They included among the latter colonial cities ('the mixed cities on the periphery of an empire which carried the core culture to other peoples') providing as examples cities such as Calcutta and Singapore. Reading between the lines of Redfield and Singer's article, we may assume that they were thinking of the ways in which the political, social and spatial order (and reordering) of colonial cities, combined with new economic institutions, cultural values and codes, new migrant populations and forms of labour, and new relations of power and control, generate political change, economic growth and new forms of identity, consciousness and aspiration.

In the last three decades, research and scholarship on these themes has been provided, in part, by the extensive development of interest and research in the history of urban and regional planning and, not least, the international dimensions of this.[2] Many such studies, undertaken by anglophone (i.e. European and American) scholars have been published on these themes in the context of European colonial development in the world outside 'the West' (for a comprehensive bibliography see Home 1997; King 1990a; Wright 1991). As might be expected, however, many of these studies, often drawing on colonial archival material, and irrespective of the critical edge they may adopt towards it, as well as the material and social space of the city itself, have tended to represent an 'external' or European viewpoint, a point to which I return below.

Studies of colonial architecture and urbanism, which have probably provided the majority of case studies on the 'export of planning', might be broadly classified into two approaches according to their methodology. Some focus more on a sociological or anthropological analysis of spatial organization contrasting, for example, the spatial representation of indigenous cultural and social organization with the social and spatial organization of specific colonial communities, highlighting the different meanings invested in each, reflected in (and constituted through) spatial taxonomies and systems of nomenclature and toponymy (see Archer 2000; also Kuper 1972). Other studies give more attention to the built environment as a domain of visual culture, treating space and architecture more symbolically as a system of signs and signification. More historical studies (Home 1997) and those with an architectural focus (Irving 1981; Hopkins and Stamp 2002) accord more importance to individual agency in the form of individual architects and planners and the ideological and cultural politics within which they operate. In different places and at different times, particular colonial regimes have used their own architectural culture to symbolize their authority or, on the Foucaultian principle of power/knowledge, they have appropriated indigenous architectural knowledge, structural and semiotic forms to construct new, hybridized forms of design, hoping, in this way, to domesticate or naturalize power in the interests of their own regimes. This process has been well documented, whether in relation to the British in India (Metcalf 1989), the French in Indo-China (Wright 1991), the Dutch in Indonesia (Kusno 2000), or, in different, non-colonial circumstances, Americans in China (Broudehoux 2001).

What the growing number of studies suggest is that, throughout the last two centuries, the existence of an increasingly large body of professional knowledge and set of techniques of urban planning – part of a larger fund of 'imperial knowledge' accumulated especially from the eighteenth century (Ballantyne 2002), as well as a cadre of 'technicians of a general order' (to use Rabinow's (1989) phrase from Foucault), predominantly based in Europe and its colonies but also including indigenous knowledges – was selectively applied to the development of a rapidly growing system of increasingly linked port cities and towns worldwide (Home 1997; King 1984, 1990a). This not only comprised a knowledge of town 'planting' and planning drawn from the Americas, Europe and Asia, of engineering and medical science, of architectural draughtsmanship and design but also, from the mid nineteenth century, the use of photography as an almost instantaneous means for transmitting urban images worldwide, an essential tool for modernizing practices of urban design (Zandi-Sayek 2000).

In tracing the input of local, indigenous knowledge into urban planning practices introduced at the instance of external or foreign powers, certain questions need addressing: what evidence exists, in different contexts, regarding the extent of indigenous or exogenous inputs? And does such a binary model exclude searching for the presence or absence of contributions from other third or fourth parties? Of transported labor, as with African slave labor in the construction of American cities? Itinerant craftsmen? Freelance engineers or architects, working at an international scale? Is evidence of local contributions to be found in the space, built form or architectural culture of the city itself, or in archival texts? If the latter, by whom are they produced, in what form and what language, and under what political or cultural conditions? What linguistic skills, ideological or theoretical presuppositions will be brought to bear in the reading of particular texts?

The varying historical, political, cultural and geographical conditions under which ideas and practices of urban development have been exported and imported over time make generalizations neither easy not particularly wise. Different cities fulfill different roles and different functions, and in relation to various larger economic, political, cultural and, not least, spatial systems which change over time. The economic, social and cultural flows (Appadurai 1996) which cities channel and concentrate are represented in a variety of different human, social or physical forms; by the ethnic, racial and social composition of the city; the configuration of its spaces; its modes and nodes of transportation; its institutions and building forms; its architectural cultures and symbolic forms more generally. How, in a variety of political conditions, does a local, indigenous population respond to, modify, control or domesticate the urban development strategies of an external authority or power, be it a colonial state, a powerful commercial interest, or simply a firm of planning consultants?

SUBALTERN PERSPECTIVES

If we concentrate, for the present, on the category of the colonial city, and the way much of the literature has been been produced, and by whom, it is possible, drawing on Chapter 3, to make some generalizations. Here, I refer to critical writing on colonial urbanism, planning and architecture between the 1960s and the early 1990s, not necessarily *labeled* as 'postcolonial', even though it obviously is. With relatively few exceptions, it is largely the product of authors from the Anglo-American 'West' (usually, though not only, male and white) and, as might be expected, in the metropolitan language (mostly English, and its sources predominantly in English, though there is also considerable literature in French and Dutch (Coquery-Vidrovitch and Goerg 1996: Groll and Alphen 2002).[3] The theoretical and methodological framework(s) drawn on, where explicit, tend to be whatever were the influential theoretical paradigms and theoreticians (e.g. Marxism, world-systems, poststructuralism, Wallerstein, Foucault, etc.) in the Western academy when the books were written, though in these accounts 'colonialism' is not necessarily treated as 'one thing' (Dirks 1992). Particularly since the 1990s, however, work by scholars indigenous to the world outside the West has become increasingly visible and it is this which I explore in the following section.

In using the term 'indigenous' (by which I mean those originally native to the one-time colony or postcolony), I am not subscribing to some essentialist theory. As in all forms of research and scholarship, scholars from both 'inside' as well as 'outside' a particular culture (or indeed, a particular gender, ethnicity or discipline) can make equally profound and critical observations. Yet in the context of what I write about language, and especially English, later in the book, it is generally if not invariably the case that scholars indigenous to the country under discussion are more likely to have not only the necessary languages but also cultural and political sensibilities different from those outside. The combination of both 'internal' as well as 'external' accounts (together with those that cross that divide) is needed to place questions in productive tension.[4] Moreover, 'indigenous' scholars are in 'exogenous' locations as well as vice-versa, and the realities of transcultural experiences and positionalities undermine this simple binary division. Nonetheless, reviewing some of the now substantial published scholarship of the last twenty five years on colonial architecture and urbanism and its relation to social and political power, Indonesian architect and scholar Abidin Kusno writes:

> These studies have opened up important new approaches . . . [yet] [i]n generating new theoretical ideas on architecture and urbanism as being the outcome of social, political and cultural forces, to what extent have studies centered on European imperialism themselves 'colonized' ways of thinking about colonial and postcolonial space? Is the colony, as well as the postcolonial world, condemned to be a continual consumer of 'modernity' and 'coloniality'? . . . While providing theoretically-innovative and valuable accounts of colonial urban situations, inflected through the practices of a specific colonial power operating in different locales, the standpoint or focus from which these works are written, to appropriate a critique offered by Chakrabarty [1992a], still tends to be that of 'Europe'. In other words, the intellectual focus . . . is still on the 'problematic' power of the colonizer.
>
> (Kusno 2000: 6)

Here, Kusno refers to the focus, or what might be called the epistemological positionality, of the research. The question of the actual 'framework' for the research is something different, something that Indian sociologist, Yogesh Atal, questioned two decades earlier: how to move from 'iconoclastic talk of "domination" of alien models and theories and construct alternative frameworks and metatheories which reflect "indigenous worldviews and experiences"'' (Atal, 1981).[5] A third, related point is made by Dipesh Chakrabarty, who refers, not only implicitly, to questions of focus, as well as framework, but also to the *knowledge* that both the framework as well as the position actually produce. As I cite in Chapter 4, he writes: 'Third-world historians feel a need to refer to works in European history; historians of Europe do not feel any need to reciprocate' (1992a: 2). Partha Chatterjee takes this further: 'Europe and the Americas, the only true subjects of history, have thought out on our behalf not only the script of colonial enlightenment and exploitation but also our anti-colonial resistance and misery' (Chatterjee 1994: 216). In this context, Yeoh suggests that 'to imagine our cities differently', the first step would be 'for the once-colonized to claim "the freedom of imagination" to do so' (2001: 464).

We might, however, begin with those 'indigenous' scholars who have questioned, problematized (Kosambi 1990) or even rejected the concept of *the* or a 'colonial city' which, as far as modern industrial colonialism in Asia or Africa is concerned, gets an early mention in the Redfield and Singer (1954) article on 'The cultural role of cities' mentioned previously. Yet as no comprehensive, up to date, critical historiography on the concept of the 'colonial city' exists in relation to Asia, Africa, Australasia, let alone North and South America, as well as Europe, even though many scholars use the term, it becomes a slippery concept with which to operate. As both Kosambi (1990) and Hosagrahar (2000) have pointed out, any attempt to construct 'snapshot' categories, frozen in one point of time, conceals changes over both space *and* time. This applies equally to notions of 'the colonial city' or the less precise concept of 'colonial urbanism' which might extend from between ten to three hundred years. We should also note the equally important distinction between colonial capitals, colonial port cities and other locations such as hill stations and mobile bases. Yet given the enormous significance of 'colonial urban space' not just simply as providing the location for 'encounters' between different pre-given 'cultures', 'religions', 'races' or 'world views', but rather as the sites, in many instances, for actually *constructing* these concepts, such a historiography would certainly merit one doctoral dissertation, not least (recalling Kusno's comments above) as the bulk of 'colonial city' scholarship has so far been produced by European and American scholars. How do the colonial and postcolonial cities look from the indigenous viewpoint, and why? And given that the colonial cities of Asia, Africa and South America were, as suggested in the previous chapter, 'multi-racial' and 'multicultural' cities long before this term was invented to describe cities in Europe, or the early post-colonial 'white cities' of Australia or North America, these are topics deserving serious research.

As discussed elsewhere (King 2003), recent work by Indian scholars has problematized earlier formulaic models of colonial cities, prompting questions, for example, about the degree and nature of racial, social and spatial segregation. Studies of Calcutta (Chattopadhyay 2000, 2004; Chakravorty 2000) and Delhi (Hosagrahar 2000, 2004), show how the new colonial space often provided new opportunities to develop alternative lifestyles, either occasional or permanent, for the emerging indigenous bourgeoisie. Questions of representation – by whom, of whom, to whom – are at the heart of such studies, particularly British colonial representations of Calcutta, either as the 'second city of Empire' during colonial rule or the 'City of Dreadful Night' subsequently (Chattopadhyay 2004). In a dialectical sense, the construction of colonial space focused indigenous attention on local space, contributing not only to the formation of local but also national identities (ibid.).

Studies such as these have deconstructed 'colonizer/colonized' binaries which have often characterized earlier accounts. In her work on Singapore, Yeoh (1996) has shown not only how far colonial authority was both resisted and contained, but also the degree to which the local Chinese community maintained control over their own space. Arguing that the city 'has to be treated on its own terms', Yeoh demonstrates that the colonial urban landscape resulted from the input of both colonialist as well as colonized groups and one where the colonized 'must be seen as knowledgeable skilled agents with some awareness of the struggle for control, not just recipients of colonial rule' (ibid.). In her case study of twentieth century Ahmedabad, Raychauduri (2001) not only suggests (like Hosagrahar 2000) that the European scholarly obsession with the 'colonial city' has been at the expense of tracking the development of the indigenous city but extends her argument to suggest that this has much broader significance for understanding the social and spatial transformation of other cities in the world outside the West. Hosagrahar's forthcoming book on *Indigenous Modernities* (2004) demonstrates how the spaces of 'Old' Delhi were also transformed and modernized by the local population, simultaneously with the building of imperial New Delhi, though according to (quite different) criteria of the local inhabitants. In this she both challenges as well as relativizes prevailing concepts of 'urban modernity' which, for the most part, are still invariably associated (in urban and architectural terms) with the experience of the Euro-American West. Also relevant here is Perera's recent work on 'indigenizing the colonial city' (2002) in which he documents the ways in which the space of colonial Colombo, largely developed by the British as a colonial port city, was increasingly appropriated by the local population in the later nineteenth century.

These and related perspectives are central to the essays in Nasr and Volait's edited volume, *Urbanism – Imported or Exported? Native Aspirations and Foreign Plans* (2003). Emerging from a conference held in Beirut in 1998, and primarily containing accounts of cities around the Mediterranean basin, the book shifts attention from an earlier scholarly focus on the *exporting* of models and urban plans from the European 'center' to one which aims at understanding the ways in which, as *imports*, these were adapted and transformed by local populations.[6]

The shift of urban geographers' attention in recent years to examining the impact of globalization on cities worldwide has, in some cases, led to a fairly predictable formula for examining 'postcolonial' cities which might be characterized as a revised 'stages of economic growth' representation. Irrespective of whether these cities are in southeast Asia (Dick and Rimmer 1998), India (Chakravorty 2000) or western Africa (Grant and Yankson 2003), the 'exogenous' analysis tends to follow a more or less similar general pattern of a three-phase political economy frame of development: colonial economy, postcolonial or command economy during a nationalist period, and 'reform economy' during the most recent 'global' period. In the postcolonial Independence period, the native upper class (capital and land owners, political leaders, top government officials) occupy the space once inhabited by the colonizers. What were once racial divisions turn into class divisions. With the arrival of the 'new' global economy, one time low-density colonial spaces, windward of the city, become the new spaces of international tourism with hotels, transport nodes or space for multinational companies. Such political economy formulations, while useful at a general level, nonetheless tend to emphasize similarities rather than addressing questions of difference.[7]

Kusno's study of architecture, urban space and changing political cultures in Indonesia takes this genre of work in a completely new direction. Following on the comments cited earlier (Chapter 3), Kusno's agenda is to unlink postcolonial criticism from its customary focus on the 'East/West' axis, the colonized and the 'Western' colonizer. In this context, the forms of planning and urbanism the Dutch introduced could be treated as 'a gift' inherited by the postcolonial state (Kusno 2000). What has been often overlooked in postcolonial studies, in Kusno's view, is the substantial role played by subjects who are not quite 'the Other' but also, are not entirely 'the same'. Those who live side by side, within the region (in this case, the Japanese or Chinese), are also important in constituting postcolonial identities.

FRAMING IDENTITIES IN SPACE

At the beginning of the chapter I referred to the many new empirical studies on the international dimensions of planning history that have changed our views in the last twenty-five years. We also need to acknowledge a similar growth in 'macro theories' or frameworks, the object of which is to help interpret economic, political, social, cultural and spatial transformations in the modern world: competing or complementary theories of postmodernism, of the world-system, of globalization, post development, postcolonial theory and criticism, hybridization, and no doubt others.

Given the comments of Atal (1981), Chatterjee (1994), Chakrabarty (1992a and b), Kusno (2000) and Yeoh (2001) quoted earlier (as also comments in the previous chapters about the essentially 'Western' perspectives of most of these frameworks), what can be derived from these theories which might help us address questions of culture and identity, both in the contemporary as well as the future, twenty-first century city? Whatever their merits and failings, what is probably their most serious problem is the lack of attention to the local and historically specific; not just in relation to the 'global condition' of contemporary capitalism but rather, in relation to the global *urban* condition. As I have addressed notions of the postmodern in the previous chapter, I refer briefly to only three of these: world systems perspectives, and theories of globalization and postcolonialism, particularly as they relate to questions of urban identity. Before doing this, however, I want first to mention the kinds of issues which any theoretical framework has to accommodate in dealing with what I have called, in my title, writing the 'transnational' space of planning history.

The adoption, modification or refusal of ideas and practices of urban planning between different nation states, whether in colonial or non-colonial situations, requires a framework for spatial analysis which extends beyond a single, or even two or three nation states and also acknowledges the uneven distributions of power between them. It takes place as part of a more general process of the diffusion of modern urbanism, both in relation to the rapid growth of urbanization and, in Harvey's (1985) phrase, in the 'urbanization of capital', even though that phrase does not capture or encompass *all* that urbanization implies. We need a framework for understanding transnational economic and political processes in which some nation states, at different historical times, exercise some hegemonic influence within the system of states or territories as a whole. As examples, we can cite the dominant influence of the Dutch in the seventeenth century, the British in the nineteenth century, the US or the Soviet Union in the twentieth century, and, most prominently, the US today (Reynolds 2002).

We also need a framework, however, that, while acknowledging these economic and political processes, also recognizes the social and cultural dimensions of urban life and the way these, together, bring about spatial and material changes. For example, in relation to increased processes of urbanization, these might be the adoption of new communication technologies (such as steamships, railroads, telecommunications), the distribution of local resources, the transformation (or introduction) of social, cultural and political institutions with a concomitant introduction of new (or modified) building types and forms of spatial organization to contain such institutions in the urban fabric (Markus 1993).

Recognizing that these processes need to be seen as part of 'intertwined histories, overlapping territories' (Said 1993), such a framework also needs to acknowledge the nature, scale and degree of local inputs and influences, and the political and socio-economic forms of organisation they exhibit: as feudal kingdoms, empires, colonies, or modern socialist or market democracies.

It requires sensitivity to issues of historical and geographical difference, to the importance of human and social agency and to the time- and place-specific exchange of ideas and technologies which are transferred, by means of human agency, from one part of the world to another (as illustrated in Chapter 10). Where social and political power is inequitably distributed, we need to be conscious not simply of 'resistance', and often, violent resistance, as in Baghdad in 2003, to the implementation of colonial 'norms and forms' but also of processes of accommodation and imitation as well as 'cultural translation' in specific colonial situations.[8]

We also need a framework that recognizes the role that existing spatial, built, or even remembered environments play in the formation of identity, whether we think of this at the level of the individual, the community, the city, or any other larger or smaller unit, including the nation state. Some part of these identities may develop from socially progressive planning policies, making housing, education or social amenities available to all, irrespective of background. Other kinds of identity, however, may result from the unintended (and sometimes intended) social consequences of particular spatial and perceived environments which help to reinforce, in negative and exclusionary ways, ethnicized, racialized, gendered and other place-specific subjectivities. The obvious examples here are the role of spatial segregation in contributing to the (involuntary) construction of race, ethnic, caste or class consciousness; or the nature of, and access to, public space in the construction of gendered and sexualized subjects (Bingaman *et al.* 2002). We also need to know how such subjectivities become politically mobilized at particular historical moments, whether in demonstrations, social movements or riots. Much more needs to be known about how material and spatial environments help to construct human subjectivity and identity.[9]

MACRO THEORIES AND THEIR LIMITATIONS

What macro theoretical ideas provide us with an understanding of 'transnational space'? And is it possible to take an eclectic approach towards them? Without necessarily taking on board all the different dimensions of the world-system perspective, one of the earliest though still controversial ways of looking at the world beyond the state, we might nonetheless note some of Wallerstein's premises in a conceptualization that has the merit of being historical and also acknowledging issues of hegemony. The 'modern world-system', he writes:

> took the form of a capitalist world-economy that had its genesis in the long sixteenth
> century and . . . involved the transformation of a particular redistributive or tributary
> mode of production, that of feudal Europe . . . into a qualitatively different social
> system. Since that time, the capitalist world-economy has geographically expanded to
> cover the globe and manifested a cyclical pattern including technological advance,
> industrialization, proletarianization and the emergence of structured political resistance
> to the system – a process that is still going on today.
>
> (1980: 7–8)[10]

Though such a framework would suggest that the diffusion of modern urbanism can be related to the expansion of the capitalist world-economy, and that, at different times, particular hegemonic and imperialist states have generated powerful political, economic and ideological influences (including ideologies and practices of planning), it does not address the ways in which culturally different forms of capitalism work in different places. From a postcolonial perspective, Ashcroft *et al.* are critical of world systems theory in that it:

> does not explain, nor is it interested in, human subjectivity, the politics of colonization, the continued dominance of certain discursive forms of imperial rhetoric, nor the particular and abiding material consequences of colonialism in individual societies. It offers no place for individual political agency, nor is it concerned with the local dynamics of cultural change, nor even with the operation of 'societies', all these things being subsidiary to the broad structural forces of the world system.
>
> (1998: 240)[11]

Ashcroft *et al.*'s critique is informed by a postcolonial theory and criticism which, since the mid 1980s, has brought important new perspectives to a wide range of disciplines and which I have discussed in Chapter 3. Applied in the realm of the urban, postcolonial criticism, by foregrounding indigenous developments and perspectives, provides new insights on urban planning.

If the focus is on questions of *identity*, of constructing and maintaining individual as well as collective identities in relation to others, theories of globalization (defined by Robertson (1992) as 'the increasing consciousness of the world as a whole') also have something to offer. Robertson suggests that:

> [T]he contemporary concern with civilizational, societal (as well as ethnic) uniqueness – as expressed via such motifs as identity, tradition and indigenization largely rests on globally diffused ideas. In an increasingly globalized world . . . there is an exacerbation of civilizational, societal and ethnic self consciousness. Identity, tradition and indigenization only make sense contextually. . . .
>
> (ibid.: 130)

However, the context is too often seen as the system of states.

While it is true that identities are established contextually, it is only in a very general sense that the increased concern with identity and tradition is an outcome of 'globalization' which is a rather *indiscriminate* way of referring to 'the world as a whole'. Here, the more nuanced and historically specific notion, applied to the recent and contemporary world, of *modern* and subsequently, *postcolonial* globalization, of Hopkins (2002) and his collaborators, has the advantage of injecting a missing historical dimension into the debate. Identities (national as well as other) are also established relationally and within the space of quite small regions.

TOWARDS MORE MICRO THEORIZATIONS?

The difficulty with many of these theories of social, political and spatial change in the modern world is that they conceive of social and spatial units that are often too large to be relevant for understanding identities, or places, at the local level, whether city, settlement, neighborhood or dwelling. Identities are usually constructed in relation to much smaller, historical, social and spatial contexts. While nationality, ethnicity, class, region, caste, descent, health state, kinship, race, gender, occupation, age – the categories dependent on where people live – all contribute to the making of people's multiple identities, spaces and locations far smaller than the state, region, or city are mobilized in identity formation. Various spaces, at different scales, take on identities invested in them by their inhabitants: not just cities, but villages and neighborhoods; not just villages, but markets and festivals; not just streets, but lots and vehicles; not just dwellings, but rooms and clothes.

This is where current transnational theorizations are seriously underdeveloped. How do we address the spatial construction of identity, at a local 'micro' level, in a world increasingly characterized by mobility and interactive cultural flows? Recent essays discuss transnationalism and migrancy as phenomena that create fluid and multiple identities that cross multiple racial, national and ethnic lines (Cairns 2003). Transmigrants move between a family network abroad and back home, maintaining many different racial, national and ethnic identities. In this way, people both express their resistance to the global political and economic situations that engulf them but, at the same time, may also immerse themselves in them.

This is why it becomes difficult to actually speak about 'the local' because, in many ways, the local is not in contradistinction to the global as it is not always static. It moves around. Arjun Appadurai has defined 'locality' as a 'non-spatial term . . . a complex phenomenological quality constituted by a series of links between the sense of social immediacy, the technologies of interactivity and the relativity of contexts' (1996: 178).

In addition to the transnational, we also need to recognize the transurban, transurbanity, or even, as bizarre as it may sound, transuburbanization, not least as this is what I address in the following chapter. We need to rethink the real connectivities in the inter-city system. Continuing processes of hybridization take place at scales smaller than the city, not least, the suburb, block, apartment or individual dwelling. Chinese-American scholar Wei Li, writing on the 'anatomy of a new ethnic settlement in Los Angeles' has coined the term, 'Chinese ethnoburb' (Li Wei 1998). If this sounds unfamiliar, we might remember that just over a century ago (1895) when the term gradually came into use, no one had heard of 'suburbia'. In 2025, will anyone raise an eyebrow to learn of the globurbs (i.e. transmigrant housing of people from all over the world) around Paris, London or New York? These phenomena, discussed in the following chapters, are part of what AlSayyad (2001) has suggested is an increasingly 'hybrid urbanism'.

Nor have we developed a way to conceptualize the transnationalization of the dwelling, that is, the transcultural adaptation of residential forms in places other than their native habitus. What we might refer to as 'cut and paste' forms of shelter, are cut from the history, society and mode of production in one society and culture, and 'pasted' into those of another, though usually with a fair amount of editing in the process (Nasser 2003). For native English-speakers or those of other languages with Latin roots, we might refer to transdomification, or the transculturization of dwelling forms. In a subsequent chapter, dealing with the recent extensive introduction of the European villa into Beijing and other coastal cities in China, villafication seems the obvious term. The diversity of the twenty-first century metropolis will need to generate a much more diverse set of conceptualizations and theorizations before we can begin to understand it.

NOTES

1   Or more usually, the world-economy, illustrated, among various other titles, by H. J. Gans, *The Urban Villagers* (1962), P. Abrams and E. A. Wrigley, (eds) *Towns in Societies* (1978) and P. L. Knox and P. J. Taylor (eds) *World Cities in a World-System* (1995).

2   The UK Planning History Association was founded in 1974, the International Planning History Association in 1999.

3   Attention should be drawn to Norma Evenson's (1989) architectural and urban history, *The Indian Metropolis: A View Towards the West*, which, particularly for the post-Independence period, makes much use of Indian sources and also pays attention to questions of gender.

4   Sneja Gunew points out that indigeneity works differently in settler colonies (Canada, Australia, etc.) as compared to India or southeast Asia in that it is not usually associated with cities (with thanks for this personal communication).

5   These views have a long history, certainly back to the 1950s and 1960s, if not earlier, in the writings of Indian historian Romila Thapur, and Sri Lankan as well as Malaysian sociologists, S. Goonetilike and S. H. Alatas.

6   Other papers from this conference, dealing with Calcutta, Izmir, Algiers, Singapore and Doha are published in *City and Society* 12, 1 (2000): 5–18. The conference and its organizers, Joe Nasr and Mercedes Volait, also motivated much of the content of this chapter.

7   This is discussed at greater length in King (2003).

8   The interstitial space of 'accommodation' between 'colonial domination' and 'indigenous resistance' is well addressed by Garth Myers in his account of Ajit Singh's architecture in colonial Zanzibar. See Myers 1999, 2003.

9   For a discussion of the Jakarta kampung in the construction of Indonesian subjectivities, see Kusno 2000.

10 Janet Abu-Lughod (1989), among others, has suggested an earlier world system.

11 Ashcroft, Griffiths and Tiffin (1998: 280). However, it could also be pointed out that Ashcroft *et al.* pay virtually no attention to the role played by place, space, architecture or the built environment in the construction of 'human subjectivity', 'individual societies', 'individual political agency' or, indeed, the 'world-system,' and the identities associated with each.

PART TWO

Histories

In the first four chapters that follow my aim is to examine new cultural, architectural and spatial forms emerging at the intersection of local and global practices, not always as 'resistances' to, or even 'accommodation' of spatial and architectural influences stemming from 'elsewhere' but simply as material manifestations of the workings of global capitalism found at particular sites. I want to ask, in particular, about the local, national, and transnational conditions in which these developments take place. Within a worldwide climate of neo-liberalism, what are the *local* politics behind these new developments?

The particular cases addressed are located on 'the edge' of three major world capitals, Washington DC, Beijing, and in the following two chapters, New Delhi and other major cities in India. While the architectural phenomena discussed are each the direct outcome of global flows of ideas, people and capital, they are also distinct hybridized products of local actors and local culture. They are not the result of uniform or monolithic forces nor are they homoge-nous or deterritorialized. The cultural, geographical and historical specificity of these processes are central to my argument.

I also want to ask about the different ways, alternative to 'the global', in which we might conceptualize 'the world'; to ask, in Spivak's (i.e. Hegel's) phrase, how the world is actually 'worlded', how it comes to be 'the world' (and subse-quently, 're-worlded'). If we are to address the meanings that local subjects attach to the phenomena themselves, and the micro and macro cosmologies with which they make sense of the world, we also need a much more differen-tiated array of conceptualizations than those simply suggested by ideas such as the 'international', 'transnational' and the 'postmodern', let alone 'global' and 'globalization'. What are the conceptualizations available to us, and how can they recognize and take account of indigenous and local meanings? How far can new concepts and terminologies be identified in the spaces of different speech communities worldwide?

The three case studies also pose questions about the adequacy of our contemporary theoretical language to represent not only so-called 'global' processes operating *above* the level of the nation state (i.e. supranational, trans-national), or at that level (international, interstate) but, more especially, at the infranational level: the regional, the metropolitan, the urban and suburban, the neighborhood, household, dwelling or even that of the individual room. While a search for indigenous means and local cosmologies requires a different research agenda (and also another book), in this chapter, I explore certain neoligisms of my own, deliberately with tongue-in-cheek, to highlight the spatial scale at which cultural and spatial transformations are taking place and ask about the meanings they have, both for the local community as well as the outside observer.

Chapter 6: Suburb/Ethnoburb/Globurb: The Making of Contemporary Modernities

> It is not on overstatement to claim that the Western suburb is quintessentially an imperialist form of human settlement.
>
> Michael Leaf, 'The Suburbanization of Jakarta' (1994: 341)

'MODERN' AND 'TRADITIONAL' CITIES

As discussed in Chapter 4, the idea of tradition is a creation of modernity, a view also expressed by Giddens (2002: 39). He sees globalization as the worldwide spread of the idea of the modern in which public life is opened up from tradition as a result of the spread of a global cosmopolitan society. Where tradition retreats 'we are forced to live in a more open and reflective way ... (where) ... autonomy of action and freedom can replace the hidden power of tradition' (2002: 4).

If tradition is an invention of modernity, the idea of the 'traditional city' (in the world outside the West), as has been mentioned earlier, is the invention of the 'modern city' or, more frequently, the city of colonial modernity (which is very different). I refer here, of course, to 'ideal types': of Old Tunis in relation to modern Tunis, Old Delhi in comparison to New Delhi. Though all such cities named as 'traditional' vary significantly in their form, space and social organization, treated as an 'ideal type, we might say that they are often walled, are a 'walking city', in the Middle East, northern Africa, parts of China, or elsewhere, often with inward facing courtyard houses, occupied by multiple members of extended families, spatially dense, with transport originally dependent on animate energy, and so on (Crouch and Johnson 2001: Chapter 11). The 'ideal type' of a so-called 'modern', industrial or postindustrial city, on the other hand, is based on capitalist forms of land and property ownership, inanimate forms of energy, is automobile-oriented, and is planned, to a greater or lesser extent, according to some form of 'Western rationality'.

While accepting that these are 'ideal types' and also stereotypical models, I want to focus on one aspect of the so-called modern (as well as modernizing) city which, whether more or less 'socialist' or 'capitalist', more or less centrally planned or free market oriented, can today be found, with different cultural meanings and consequences, and to different degrees, in most cities worldwide. This is the *suburb*, as well as the economic, social, spatial, cultural and political characteristics supposedly associated with and often represented by the term 'suburbia' – both as a settlement form and lifestyle. I want first to briefly explore some aspects of the language and space of the Western (particularly British and American) suburb, largely based on nineteenth- and early twentieth-century experience; in the second part, mainly developed in the following chapters, I want to do the same, though for the late twentieth century, and bring in some examples from India and China, to speak about the globalized suburb, or what I shall call the 'globurb.' I am proposing this term as part of a new vocabulary which might allow us 'to name and discuss new forms of territoriality and new classes of city dwellers',[1] not only in Istanbul (and Turkey) to which this objective was directed but also elsewhere.

SUBURBAN MODERNITIES

Typically, we assume that the spatial, built form manifestations of globalization are in the Central Business District, the downtown, evidenced by the appearance of high rise office towers, international banks, regional or multinational corporation headquarters, or the pervasive sign of franchised global corporations, the golden M, perhaps in some sort of vernacular disguise. The reasons for this are probably connected to the focus of scholars in the West on the phenomenon of the 'world' or 'global city', most of the examples of which are, according to the literature, not surprisingly, *in* the West (Knox and Taylor 1995; Sassen 2001; Taylor *et al.* 2002). With some exceptions (Graham and Marvin 2001), what has received less attention is globalization (and postcolonialism) in the suburb, particularly in areas *outside* the West, both as a cultural process and especially, as a spatial and architectural form.

Both Silverstone, in *Visions of Suburbia* (1997b) and Taylor, in *Modernities* (1999), while focusing on the anglophone world of the United States, Australia and the UK, see the contemporary suburb as the paradigmatic embodiment of modernity, the classic modern suburb of single family houses in large gardens in tree lined roads. 'This landscape of consumer modernity,' Taylor writes, 'represents the culmination of four centuries of ordinary modernity.' Presumably conceiving the suburb in terms of the immense proportion of a society's resources invested in it, Taylor states that it is 'the modern equivalent of the great Gothic cathedrals of the high middle ages in feudal Europe' (1999: 58–9). With some license, he writes that, with the era of American hegemony, 'the middle class suburb has spread to cities across the world' (1999: 58).

From a similar, yet rather different perspective, Silverstone writes:

> Suburban culture is a consuming culture. Fueled by the increasing commoditization of everyday life, suburbia has become the crucible of a shopping economy. It is a culture of, and for, display. The shopping mall, all glass and glitter, all climate and quality control, is the latest manifestation of the dialectic of suburban consumption. The hybridity displayed in the shopping mall is a representation, a reflection and a revelation of the hybridity of suburbia. Suburbs are places for transforming class identities. The differences grounded in the differences of position in the system of production have gradually, as Bourdieu states, been overlaid and replaced by the differences grounded in the system of consumption.
>
> (1997a: 8–9)

The term 'suburb',[2] as well as the phenomenon it represents, has been around at least since the fourteenth century. However, the massive expansion of suburbs in modern Western cities was principally a nineteenth- and early twentieth-century occurrence. They resulted from a variety of factors – a capitalist conceptualization of property, free markets in land, developments in transportation (carriage, train, automobile, subway), the growth in the *size* of cities, and to varying degrees in different societies, the use of space as a system of social, ethnic and racial stratification (Walker 1981). The notion that the suburb generates a particular style of life has, however, been especially asserted from the late nineteenth century, a time (1895) when the word 'suburbia' is first identified by the *Oxford English Dictionary*.

In a perverse way, Silverstone's arguments can also be linked to those of Giddens which I cited at the beginning of this chapter. Giddens' notion of escaping tradition and living in a more open, reflective way, with an autonomy of action and freedom, can also be used to describe the abandonment of the 'traditional city' and an escape – to some kind of social mobility, 'freedom' and re-imagined social identity – in the suburbs.

'Suburbia', writes Silverstone:

> is creative. The standardization bemoaned by modernist critics is . . . quite superficial. Levittown [the typical postwar, Long Island mass suburb, conventionally invoked to stand for the American phenomenon] has now become a passable model of post-modern individuality . . . Spaces . . . are redesigned, reformed into expressions of personal taste and identity. The shared products of contemporary material and symbolic culture are . . . arranged . . . according to desire, itself structured by class or ethnicity . . . The overall patterns of suburban growth . . . were never less than sociologically and socially varied. The modern suburb is a social as well as cultural hybrid.
>
> (1997a: 6–8)

There are, however, two aspects of the development of the nineteenth- and twentieth-century Western suburb which are neglected in these accounts. The first is the nature and physical forms of its settlement space and built environment (particularly, its residential forms), and the second, the inherently, and constitutively international context in which it developed.

Though we can interpret the economic, political and social meaning of modern suburbs in many different ways, the essence of the modern suburb is physical, social and spatial separation. The suburb is spatially separated from the city and, more particularly, each household unit is spatially separated from the others. The 'modern' nuclear or single parent family, or household of 'singles', is, in typical anglophonic suburban fashion, physically and spatially separated in their own dwelling. These might be isolated from others or clustered in small groups, each on its own plot. These physical and spatial divisions are not just 'reflected' in language but are also constituted by the discourses that use that language, i.e. the 'single family home' in the United States, in Germany, the 'einzelhaus', in Britain, the 'detached' or 'semi-detached house', terms which clearly take as their (historical) referent more physically collective forms of urban industrial dwelling such as the row house, tenement or terrace; or, as an implicitly positive referent, the concept of the 'villa' (which I address below). Alternatively, households may be collectively accommodated in the 'apartment' house, a building designed for people, to quote Hancock (1980), who are 'living apart' – from (the norm of) the majority of single-family homes, or from each other, a dwelling practice neatly summed up by the title of Elizabeth Cromley's book on the social history of the New York apartment building, *Alone Together* (1990).

INTERNATIONALIZING THE SUBURB

Let me turn now to my second point, the inherently international context of Western suburban development. Neither Taylor nor Silverstone pay sufficient attention to the dependence of suburbanization, as a physical, spatial, cultural, social, architectural as well as *economic* phenomenon, on the internationalization of the economy, not least, through the processes of imperialism, colonialism and the workings of the world economy and international division of labor. As these issues have been discussed elsewhere (King 1990a) I only refer to the vast transfer of resources to, and accumulation of capital in the metropole that characterized imperialism, not only helping to fuel industrial urban development but simultaneously promoting the economic, social and spatial expansion of suburban development. Or, in British, French, Dutch and Portuguese colonies, the appropriation and planning of colonial urban space for the white, European population, whether in colonies that became Ghana, Indonesia, Morocco, India, Malaysia, Vietnam, southern Africa or elsewhere (Grant and Yankson 2003, Abeyasekare 1987, Abu-Lughod 1980, Archer 1997, King 1976, Goh 2002, Wright 1991). (The colonial analogy with the United States, Canada and Australia should also be evident.) This is the space that was subsequently to provide the spatial infrastructure for postcolonial kinds of suburban development, including the influx of foreign companies, tourist hotels and residential developments for the new indigenous as well as international elite (Chakravorty 2000, Grant and Yankson 2003). Along with these developments went the transculturation and hybridization of suburban spatial and architectural forms.

Imperialism, in short, not only had an impact on the shaping of space and built form in the colony but also on the metropole at home (Driver and Gilbert 1999; King 1976, 1984, 1990a). Home (1997), for example, addressing this issue in relation to Britain, points to other specifically urban influences of imperialism, including ideas about the 'Green Belt' round cities, the influence of ideas and policies in new town development corporations derived from colonial improvement trusts, the significance and influence of specific ex-colonial administrators as managers in new town developments and, most far-reaching of all (recalling the indentured labor policies which moved tens of thousands of south Asians to colonies across the world), the continued practice, immediately after the Second World War, of using colonies as sources of cheap labor, begun in earnest with labor migration from the West Indies in 1948, a policy which has had major impacts on the social and spatial structure of cities. 'Assisted migration' from Britain to Australia is another facet of the same cultural and political economic process of which many other examples might be cited.

The continuing spatial, urban and built form significance of these (postcolonial) connections is not, to make an obvious point in regard to Britain, the appearance over recent decades, in particular British cities, of Hindu temples, Muslim mosques, Sikh gurdwaras or the indispensible '8 to late' corner shop (e.g. Nasser 2003). It is rather that compared to the contemporary racial, ethnic, social and cultural composition of, for example, American, Dutch, French, German, Italian or any other European city whose migratory streams developed from different histories and geographies (and migratory policies and practices), completely different 'multicultural' societies and spaces have been formed in each location (King 2003). As far as the material development of the suburb is concerned, however, some more historical background is needed.

From the mid nineteenth century in Britain, if not earlier, the Empire had been inscribed, or written, onto the space of its capital. This was to be seen principally in its 'working parts' like the docks and the area of the Victorian 'military-industrial complex' (the military barracks, academy, hospitals and arms factories in the southeast). In the dockland there were (and are) streets which, in their names, connected both the dwellings and their inhabitants to the East and West Indies, to Jamaica, Trinidad and Tobago, as well as Malabar, Penang and the Chinese cities of Canton, Pekin and Nankin.[3] Britain's brief eighteenth-century hold over Cuba is remembered in streets named for Havana, as well as Cuba. Around the military industrial complex (in Woolwich, Charlton and Plumstead) a cluster of road names brought India into the metropolis: Benares, Dacca, Kashgar, Lucknow, Bombay, Kashmir, Sutlej, Indus, as also Grenada, Kenya and Nigeria. In Battersea, an earlier (imperial) Afghan War (1878–9) brought the names of Afghan, Cabul and Khyber onto the streets. As the imperial capital expanded from its center (in what is now N1, E1 or EC3, with Delhi, Cawnpore, Poonah, India, and bitter memories of 1857) to the north and west, Cyprus, Falkland, Ceylon, Singapore, Australia and Canada are inscribed on the capital's thoroughfares. Later, or in some cases earlier, Auckland, Borneo, Gambia, Gibraltar, Natal, Rhodesia, South Africa, Toronto, as well as Imperial Close, Drive, Street and Way keep the geography of empire fresh in the spaces of the city.[4]

Yet these were only names that conjured up memories, imaginations or aspirations. Other ideas changed the nature and form of the urban landscape. Quite early in the development of the spatialized social differentiation that became the suburb, three spatial and architectural forms (non-native to north-west Europe or North America) were appropriated from other cultures to give new meanings to suburban life: the villa, the verandah and the bungalow.

'Villa', both as term and architectural idea, came into the English language from the Italian as a response to a renewed interest in the classics in the seventeenth century. It entered into the fashion conscious urban and architectural vocabulary of England, however, only from the late eighteenth century during the first spurt of expansion of the bourgeois classes (du Prey 1982). It was also taken up in Germany about the same time (Tyack 1996). As Archer (1997: 41) suggests, the appearance of the villa marked a critical change in English modes of consciousness; 'a consciousness that began to identify primarily in the autonomous *self* rather than in a social hierarchy or collective'. The villa was instrumental in 'spatially differentiating private from public, by establishing the suburban plot as a site for cultivation of the self (e.g. through leisure pursuits) instead of commerce and politics'. Its broader significance was the contribution it made to the creation of a bourgeois consciousness (ibid.).

The villa's transplantation to the United States early in the nineteenth century was an outcome of similar conditions. 'A villa,' wrote architectural writer, A. J. Downing, 'is the country house of a person of competence or wealth sufficient to build it with taste and elegance.' Where a cottage could be looked after by a family, 'a villa requires the care of at least three or more servants' (Downing 1969 (originally 1850): 257) (Figure 6.1). The idea of the verandah, another exogenous term and space, imported via colonial routes from India, though originally from Spain and Portugal, and an extension of the bourgeois villa to space that was both indoors and out, came – like the villa – from warmer, 'more exotic', Mediterranean climes, and was equally a space for consuming 'free

DESIGN XXII

VILLA IN THE ITALIAN STYLE

Fig. 119

PRINCIPAL FLOOR

Fig. 120

Figure 6.1

time' (King 1984). In the later nineteenth century, the verandah – when large enough – was stuffed with new consumer goods imported from the eastern colonies: rattanware chairs from Malaya, bamboo tables from India, Chinese porcelain and knick-knacks from Hong Kong. The notion of the bungalow, the classic single-storey, exurban and suburban dwelling – in the country but not of the country – was, both in East and West, equally a hybridized product of imperialism, transplanted from India, by the first decades of the twentieth century becoming the suburban house of choice, first in California (Winter 1980), then throughout the United States and Canada, transplanted (as well as translated and transformed) to Australia and New Zealand, to appear in Britain, South Africa and elsewhere in the first half of the twentieth century (King 1984, 1997).[5]

I turn now from the late nineteenth- and twentieth-century suburbs in 'the West' to those of the East (and West) in the early twenty-first century.

OLD AND NEW NEOLIGISMS

Not much Latin is needed to know that *sub-urb* originally implied that the suburban settlement was 'sub' (i.e. under or below) the city – a generic growth out of the city. Today, however, in many cities round the world, there are not just *sub*-urbs but also *supra*urbs (*suprurbs*) or, alternatively, *globurbs*. By this I mean forms and settlements on the outskirts of the city, the origins of which – economic, social, cultural, architectural – are generated less by developments inside the city, or even inside the country, and more by external forces beyond its boundaries. The influences as well as the capital come from afar, either electronically, or physically, and not least through printed media. The patrons fly in, and touch down at the airport which, as Sudjic (1996) points out, is increasingly the new urban center, replacing the old town hall and town square. The new suburbs are nourished and supported by umbilical cords that are not only infinitely extendable but have no recognizable source where they begin – taking in imagery from films, TV and transnational travel. These are in some ways part of what Garreau (1991) has called 'edge cities' but they are sustained more from outside the state's boundaries than, as Garreau assumes, within them. Dependent on their location, many of such suprurbs, or globurbs, as with previous historical experience, continue to be generated not just by 'international' or 'global' forces but, more particularly, by those of imperialism, colonialism, nationalism, as well as the diasporic migratory cultures and capital flows of global capitalism.[6] Drawing on Hopkins' notion of postcolonial globalization (2002), these are the postcolonial globurbs.

My illustrations for these phenomena come, in this and the following chapters, from the United States, China and India. They suggest not only the very different conditions, or transnational, postcolonial or neo-imperial 'threads' of capital and culture, migration and urban and architectural design, but also *the particular dynamics of locality* that help account for them. As new terms are needed to address new phenomena, I begin with the notion of the suprurb or globurb.

SUPRURBS/GLOBURBS

South of the American capital, Washington DC, some of these new suprurbs have been created in the last two or three decades in northern Virginia, significantly, not far from the Pentagon and Dulles airport. The new migrations which have largely helped to form them, mostly, but not all, Asian (and later, Asian-American) 'were, and are, in different degrees, tied to American foreign policy as well as patterns of colonialism and nationalism. Asian Americans, as well as Latinos/as have arrived in the United States as a result of colonialism in the region and the ensuing colonial wars'.[7] In the nineteenth century, these were with Spain, or, later, in the twentieth century, in Korea, Vietnam, and more recently, with actions in El Salvador, Grenada and Somalia. Immigrants of Asian and Central American descent, with their local suburban economies and also their distinctive mall architectures, carry the traces of wars. For government, military and intelligence reasons, 'Pentagon connections are today highly significant for first wave refugees from a number of countries to North Virginia' (Wood 1997: 59). Here, close to the CIA Headquarters at Langley, across the Potomac River from Washington, is where specific refugees feel they are secure. By Seven Corners in Fairfax County, the mall at Eden Center/Plaza 7 'replicates a small Vietnamese marketing town' (ibid.), with its Saigon East store (Figure 6.2), typical gold jewelry shops and cultural entertainments. It is the main center of attraction for some 50,000 Vietnamese Americans in the metropolitan area.

In the mid 1990s, however, Vietnamese were 'second only to the Salvadoreans in the number of immigrants entering the Washington metropolitan area' (Wood 1997: 59), largely represented in restaurants, food stores and in the (inherently suburban) landscaping business. Koreans, another war-related community, are largely centered on Annandale, where they support a large suburban mall, grocery and distribution center for Korean goods and several restaurants. Other war-refugee groups from eastern Africa – Somalis, Eritreans, Ethiopians – refugees of some status, often educated in the US, are also to be found in this area (Wood 1997).[8]

Not related to America's overseas wars are the significant numbers of highly educated Indians in other Washington suburbs, linked mainly to the high tech industries in the region (including the headquarters of America On Line (AOL)

Figure 6.2

and other dot com companies), with their commercial and cultural centers, and the Bollywood movie house at Loehman's Plaza on Arlington Boulevard. Viewed in the long *duree*, this Indian presence must also be accounted for, however, by the long-term (colonial) anglophonic connection, with Indians (from India) in recent years taking up almost 50 percent of the 200,000 highly sought-after H1-B visas for professionals issued in 1999. However, the visible collective identity of these communities is primarily evident in the public landscape of malls, shops, temples, cinemas, wedding houses, festivals and the Asian-American subjects themselves rather than, externally, in the realm of their dwellings. But other representations of transnational spaces, conceived from a slightly different angle, are signaled by the notion of the ethnoburb.

ETHNOBURB

Ethnoburbs, according to geographer Wei Li who coined the term, are 'suburban ethnic clusters of residential areas and business districts in large American metropolitan areas. They are multi-ethnic communities in which one ethnic minority group has a significant concentration but does not necessarily comprise a majority' (Li Wei 1998: 479). Li uses the term to refer especially to San Gabriel Valley, in the eastern suburban area of Los Angeles County where, in 1990, there were more than 158,000 ethnic Chinese (from mainland China, Taiwan, Hong Kong and elsewhere), making it the largest suburban Chinese concentration in the US. The ethnoburb, 'a new outpost in the global economy', according to Li, is an outcome of the 'influence of international geopolitical and global economic restructuring'; it also results from changing national immigration and trade policies, local demographics, economic and political contexts. The processes of ethnic restructuring include, but are not limited to, 'the rise of post-Fordism, the deindustrialization of traditional manufacturing industries, reindustrialization of craft sectors, rapid expansion of service sector activities, foreign direct investment and growth in the scale and spatial reach of multinational corporations – creating the need for high skill professionals and low skill laborers. At the same time major geopolitical ruptures (the Vietnam War and the end of the Cold War) have generated enormous pressures among affected international populations to emigrate to the US and other industrialized countries' (ibid.: 499).

The ethnoburb of San Gabriel Valley is a place where 'Chinese immigrants make a living through their own networks, eat their own types of food and shop in Chinese supermarkets, speak their mother tongue, keep close ties to their countries of origin by reading newspapers in Chinese, listening to the radio and watching TV in Chinese dialects'. In other words, the ethnoburb 'makes them feel at home' (ibid.: 490).

Li's focus on the ethnoburb here is more on economic, commercial, social and ethnic features; unfortunately, he does not address the visual imagery, the spatial, architectural and built environment characteristics, essential elements in helping to constitute, 'internally', the identity of its inhabitants for themselves and 'externally', the identity of the ethnoburb to others. It is these which also help to constitute their sense of 'feeling at home'. This is also the case with studies of an even larger set of Canadian-Chinese ethnoburbs, namely those that, together, provide for the 392,000 ethnic Chinese in the Greater Metropolitan Toronto Area (Ma 1998) and others in Vancouver.

TECHNOBURBS

Although Li refers in his account to the practice of reading Chinese newspapers, listening to the Chinese language radio, and watching TV in Chinese dialects, the major significance of the media in constituting the suburb also gets lost in this account. Yet as Raymond Williams points out, suburbia has depended for its existence on media technologies – radio, television, telephone, and now email, video and the internet – to overcome the disadvantages of distance, to compensate for the loneliness of the suburb, to link it with significant communities (cited in Silverstone 1997b: 10). Silverstone also cites Robert Fishman (1987) who, writing on the 'new high technological post-suburbs growing along the edge of the old' draws our attention to 'the home-centered nature of both physical and symbolic environments, as 'technoburb' and television promote their mutual interests, in their dependence on, and encouragement of decentralization (Silverstone 1997a: 9). Television provides the instantaneous links of the ethnoburb to the 'countries of home', the 'imagined communities' of ethnic recognition round the world. It is also television and the media which act as engines of suburban hybridization, reproducing in the process the 'ambiguities of modernity' (Silverstone 1997a).

SUBURBAN FANTASIES

As a place apart, the suburb offers a space of freedom, imagination, escape and fantasy. A place for the consumption of the globally produced, locally assembled, supermalled, hypermarketed cornucopia of goods. The suburb is a place of imagined identities, the infrastructure created by developers who provide images with which they market model (suburban) homes. The secret of such marketing, according to Dovey, writing about Australia, is the coupling of 'nostalgia for a past offering certainty' with a 'desire for the freedom of modernity' (1999: 150). The distinct culturally specific parameters of the site, however, are set by the design and brand naming practices of the developers. It is these which, with the forms and spaces of the individual dwellings, give us some insight into the different worlds in which the suburban dwellers exist.

In giving names to the varying types of suburban model homes, 'detached' or 'single family homes' located, as with the traditional villa, in a plot devoted solely to one individual dwelling, Dovey shows how Australian developers create provinces of meaning with which new suburbanites can identify. The most dominant theme, matching the myth perennially linked with the suburb (Barthes 1973), is one of 'Nature'; names of homes are linked to types of trees, flowers, country landscapes, idyllic views. Themes of social status, evoking power, success and privilege, form another cluster: Diplomat, President, Statesman, Director, Elite, Supreme. Equally frequent in the naming of these Australian homes are historical, geographical and cultural signifiers evoking distinctive, place-specific identities and associations, postcolonial connections to socially privileged locations in Britain – Cambridge, Kensington, Mayfair, Dorchester, Beaufort.

Other signifiers reveal the persistence of powerful Eurocentric orientations, a preference – despite Australia's Pacific, peri-Asian location – for French, Spanish, Italian and Mediterranean geographies (Marseilles, Provence, Granada, Seville, Monaco, Riviera, Monte Carlo). Similarly Eurocentric are the links to (European) arts and culture (Monet, Renoir, Leonardo, Van Gogh) though also with (American) links to California and New York (Malibu, Hollywood, Great Gatsby). Minor concessions are made to distinctive local identities (Settler, Squatter, Colonial) (Dovey 1999: 149).

The obverse side of this postcolonial picture is seen back in once metropolitan Britain where, in semi-postindustrial Lancashire, 'a totally new village community in countryside to the south of Blackburn' has been built. The 'detached modern homes', vaguely neo-Victorian villas to blend with the local vernacular, are displaced by their names to an imaginary world of a benign antipodean Australian climate of warmth, sunshine and prosperity far from where the houses actually exist, yet long known through anglophone colonial and postcolonial links to Britain: Perth, Canberra, Cairns, Brisbane, Darwin, Sydney, Adelaide and, via New Zealand, Christchurch and Auckland.[9]

Yet suburbs, if found worldwide, are never the same. Their inhabitants never inhabit the same identities. Each location is formed from similar, yet also different processes. In the expansion of suburban real estate developments in Jakarta under the oppressive, neo-liberal regime of Suharto, transplanted model designs draw on a different universe of meaning – the model houses are referred to as Caravan Style, Japanese, Mediterranean and Cowboy. More recently, despite, or perhaps because of, the seriously deteriorating economic, social and physical conditions in the city, the developers' fantasy locates new private suburbs in different dreamworlds of design far removed from both the city as well as the country of Indonesia itself (Kusno 2000). New villa type suburban housing is set in variously named 'Taman' or gardens, the house types labeled (and designed in the imagined style of) Taman Nagoya (Japan), 'Andalusia' (Spain), 'Casablanca' (French colonial), 'Sierra Madre' (California), 'New Britannia' (England), 'Chateau' (France), 'Riviera' (Italy). Suburban centers are built with the names (and imagined architectural styles of) 'Trafalgar Square', 'San Francisco' and 'Piazza Venezia'. As is also the case in India, the colonial past is commodified, with a terrace of houses and shops named Holland Village, with steep-pitched roofs and Dutch gables. More classical villa models include the 'Ambassador', 'Senator', 'Independence', 'Congress', 'Philadelphia', 'Capitol' and 'White House'.[10] (See Figure 6.3.)

While for Silverstone (1997a: 6) this may simply be 'suburban hybridity', there are far more subtle explanations. In Jakarta, to cite only one illustrative case, the Chinese Indonesian interests behind one of these new suburban developments target the new rich, disproportionately of Chinese ethnic origin. Yet within the delicate state of public culture in Indonesia, the open display of 'Chineseness' is being 'de-ethnicized'. In this context, the 'internationalist' architectural culture is likely to be a manifestation of Chinese ethnic modernism (Hogan and Houston 2002: 259). This has also to be seen in the context of the suppression of public manifestations of 'Chineseness' under the Suharto regime when the private business initiative of an Indonesian Chinese developer 'makes the reproduction of the Euro-American suburb, with its transnational living style, its most defining feature' (Kusno 2000: 158).

Sociologist Ayşe Öncü has suggested that globalization brings 'a pastiche of styles and tastes, creating a world of movement and mixture' (1997: 59). Yet as these examples show, particular histories and cultures also construct particular spaces.

Figure 6.3

THE GROWTH OF GATED COMMUNITIES

Related to the developments discussed above is the accelerating growth world-wide over the last two decades of 'gated communities'. In an overview of newly published research on their 'global spread', Webster *et al.* write:

> One of the most striking features of recent urbanization is the rise in popularity of privately governed residential, industrial and commercial spaces. In many rapidly urbanizing countries, gates and guards appeared at a time of double-digit economic growth and generated little public or academic commentary – they were simply part of the surreal economic and spatial transformation that engulfed so many countries in the last two decades of the 20th century.
>
> (Webster *et al.* 2002: 315)

Yet the phenomenon is not new. Walls and gates characterized the cities of the Middle Ages; Indian cities such as Old Delhi had sectors walled around and a gate to the main road as also did Old Jakarta (Leisch 2002). Nineteenth-century London in addition to other cities in Britain had exclusive, gated (and guarded) residential enclaves. What has brought the recent examples to the fore is their newness, visibility, profusion and, not least, as I discuss in the following chapters, their high profile promotion.

The phenomenon, especially but not only characteristic of rapidly urban-izing countries, has generated a rash of questions about the implications of these gated enclaves for civil society: about social exclusion, fiscal solvency, the efficient delivery of transportation and other public services. The significance of these developments, according to the authors, is less 'the physical impact of gated developments, even though this might pose challenges to urban designers, but in their underlying sociology, politics and economics'. Citing the study by Blakely and Snyder (1997) which estimated that, in the US, by the mid 1990s, up to nine million US residents live in three million units in around 20,000 proprietary residential communities bounded by walls and entrance gates, they suggest that the new gated communities challenge 'the spatial, organizational and institutional order that has shaped modern cities' (1997: 315; see also Graham and Marvin 2001).

While the authors suggest that the global growth in these 'private communities' has been influenced by American experience, they also agree that there are, in each case, indigenous developments which also contribute to the global phenomenon. Nor are the reasons for the growth of these developments the same; *local* institutional, social, economic and cultural contexts need to be considered in each case. Lebanese gated developments emerged during the civil war; south African walled communities developed in a context of institutionalized racism, yet mixed race developments in Johannesburg are not simply housing for the rich. In Saudi Arabia, gated compounds are based on reasons of privacy and identity. Elsewhere, in Spain and France, walled and gated entrances secure the envied 'residences secondaire' of the rich (Webster *et al.* 2002: 316). In a detailed study of Indonesia, Leisch (2002: 349–50) suggests a number of reasons for their profusion: the rapid expansion of the middle and upper middle classes, ensuing socio-economic polarization and the consequent insecurity of the wealthy; the need for security among minority ethnic groups, particularly the Chinese (the main victims in the 1998 riots); for the new bourgeoisie, prestige and status factors encourage the symbolic display of wealth behind forbidding gates and large houses. In addition, new globalized, consumer-oriented lifestyles introduced into southeast Asia have also been encouraged by some of the major developers, particularly the Chinese conglomerates like Lipp, Salim and the Ciputra Group, the latter prominent in bringing architectural influences from the US and the moving force behind the 'transnationalized' developments discussed above.

In these studies of gated communities, however, the emphasis has mainly been on geography at the expense of architecture: the visual and textual signs, including the architectural typologies of the new suburban enclaves, and not least, the central importance in many of them – including the Chinese and Indian cases discussed in the following chapters – of the *villa*. This requires some familiarity with its earlier history in the West, and the ideological implications, semiotics and spatial characteristics the villa is thought to embody. It is this which forms the subject of the next chapter.

NOTES

1   The phrase is from Professor Ayşe Öncü's proposal for the conference 'Global Flows/Local Fissures: Urban Antagonism Revisited', held in Istanbul, April 1998 at which an earlier version of this chapter was presented.
2   'The country lying immediately outside a town or city; more particularly, those residential parts belonging to a town or city that lie immediately outside its walls or boundaries.' *Oxford English Dictionary* (1989). The *OED* provides uses by Wyclif (c. 1380) and Chaucer (1386).

3　Spellings are as indicated in the *London A–Z c.*1970.

4　See *London A–Z: Street Atlas and Index*: Edition 11 (E) *c.*1960, Sevenoaks: Geographers A–Z Map Co. See also Chapter 11, note 15.

5　A complete account of the economic, social, political, cultural and spatial impact of imperialism on cities in the UK in the era of postcolonial globalization (i.e. subsequent to the work of Driver and Gilbert 1999) is still to be written.

6　I use these neoligisms both with caution and also tongue-in-cheek.

7　Many thanks to Binghamton colleague, Professor Lisa Yun for this comment.

8　I am indebted to geographers Provost Joe Wood, University of Maine, for a tour of the area described and for much of this information, and also, Brad Hunter.

9　The details are taken from sales brochures for the 'Oakdale' development by McAlpine Homes, Bolton Road, Blackburn, July 2000.

10　Many thanks to Abidin Kusno for this promotional material on contemporary suburban housing in Jakarta.

Chapter 7: Villafication: The Transformation of Chinese Cities

> Located at the central part of Binhai Lu Road in Dalian, the Overseas Chinese Garden Villa Complex faces the sea and (is) backed by a green hill. Dotted with islands in the sea and surrounded by green hills and attractive beach. The scenery is picturesque and the air is extremely fresh. The European-American style villas are built along the hill with a broad view of the sea. This unique character distinguishes the villa complex from ordinary garden houses. The villas exist amidst the butterflies, singing cicadas, flowers and trees. This should absolutely be the best place by the sea in Dalian. The Overseas Chinese Garden Villa Complex is the first one of its kind along Binhai Lu. The fenced residential complex guarantees the safety of the residents.
>
> Advertisement in *China Daily*, August 22, 1994

THE VILLA IN THE WEST

In the previous chapter, I have explored some theoretical insights into the meaning of recent suburban developments in different parts of the world and their significance as signs and illustrations of contemporary modernities. Before addressing these developments in relation to China, I want to return to the topic of the villa and bring into the discussion some further insights into its architectural history and social meaning in the West. To do this, I draw on James Ackerman's classic text, *The Villa: Form and Ideology of Country Houses* (1990). What hypotheses does Ackerman offer to explain why the villa typology became so popular in the West, irrespective of its appearance elsewhere in the world?

Describing the villa as 'a building in the country designed for its owner's enjoyment and relaxation', Ackerman suggests that 'the basic program of the villa has remained unchanged for more than 2,000 years since it was first fixed by the patricians of ancient Rome'. Where other architectural types have changed both their form and purpose, 'the villa has remained substantially the same because it fills a need that never alters, a need which, because it is not material but psychological and ideological, is not subject to the influences of evolving societies and technologies. The villa accommodates a fantasy which is impervious to reality' (1990: 9). To what extent do Ackerman's transhistorical views apply elsewhere?

Referring to its pre-nineteenth century development, Ackerman writes: 'The villa cannot be understood apart from the city; it exists not to fulfil autonomous functions but to provide a counterbalance to urban values . . . and its economic situation is that of a satellite.' The ideology behind it refers especially to a myth that most hold as 'an incontrovertible truth . . . a concept which Marxists interpret as the means by which the dominant class reinforces and justifies the social and economic structure and its privileged position', a view also put forward in *The Villa as Hegemonic Architecture* (1970) by German Marxist historians, Reinhard Bentmann and Michael Muller. From the fifteenth century in Italy to Le Corbusier in the twentieth, according to Ackerman, each villa revival has also been accompanied by a revival of villa literature. In eighteenth-century England, this was represented by the essays of Shaftsbury and Alexander Pope; in the nineteenth century, by the early novels of Jane Austen, 'obsessed with the property and status problems of urban oriented country life' (Ackerman 1990: 11). While today's suburban villa exists only in shrunken form, the discourses and mythology attached to it apparently continue, whether in realtors' promotional pages on the web or, as in the epigraph above, advertisements in *China Daily*.

'The content of villa ideology is rooted in the contrast of country and city in that the virtues and delights of the one are presented as the antithesis of the vices and excesses of the other.' From an economic and social viewpoint, Ackerman suggests, the villa is 'necessarily the possession of the privileged and power class in society, though at certain times in history, as in the eighteenth century, the privilege has filtered down to those of modest financial means' (1990: 14). The 'most radical mutation' in its history, he suggests, occurred in the following century when, in Europe and America, 'the villa ideology became democratized and accessible to the growing body of lower middle class city dwellers'. 'Villa' came to be applied to 'any detached or semi-detached residence in the city, suburb or country, with a little more space around it than dwellings in the densely populated streets of the urban core' (1990: 17–18). Irrespective of size, however, the distinctive visual attributes remained paramount; 'one has not only to look at them but out from them'.

The villa, Ackerman suggests, is itself a sign. It 'inevitably expresses the mythology that causes it to be built: the attraction to nature, . . . the prerogatives of privilege and power, and national, regional or class pride'. It is a typology that 'is supremely conservative socially . . . and the ideology that sustains the type has changed little over millennia' (1990: 30, 34). Where the first villas of the Renaissance took over the 'expressions of power and class aspiration evident in the vocabulary of the medieval feudal castle', adopting towers, battlements and crenellations (1990: 32), contemporary villas of Chinese, Indian and Indonesian suburbs have iron gates, CCTV, perimeter walls and squads of security guards.

The idea of and implicit ideology behind the free-standing villa – even though it is transformed in each case of its repetition – provides a useful example of transnational *material* culture. Following its history in Italy, England, North America and Western Europe, the villa moved with European imperial diasporas to other parts of the world. In the Caribbean and the American south, the Palladian version became an infinitely flexible model for plantation houses. In India, its image informed the designs of colonial buildings of the British Raj, from the Residency at Hyderabad to a thousand official bungalows in Delhi (Davies 1985; Nilsson 1968). Elsewhere in the colonial world, from the Dutch East Indies to South Africa, the Classical villa, irrespective of size, though always located in its own grounds, became a statement of social privilege, of social power, and of both class as well as national or imperial identity. (That the term 'Colonial', used to describe a pervasive and popular style of contemporary domestic architecture in the United States is equated with the basic features of the Palladian villa is sufficient comment on the deep embeddedness of the equation in the collective national psyche.)

THE VILLA IN TURKEY

In the late nineteenth century, the villa was also introduced 'on the margins of Europe', in Ottoman Turkey, as part of the transformation of upper-class domestic culture 'along European models' (Bozdoğan 2001: 193). With Ataturk's political and social revolution and the wholesale introduction of a Western 'Modern Movement' architectural culture in the 1920s and 1930s, villa building, and the suburban developments to which it gave rise, began in earnest at a distance from the 'traditional city' in Istanbul. Adopting (and adapting) the Latin name, as well as different architectural designs, Turkish language advertisements for exogenous styled villas appeared in popular illustrated magazines (as 'Mosyo Jakin Asri villasi' ('The contemporary villa of M. Jacques') or 'Bir Amerikan villasi' ('new American villas')) and also in the main architectural journal of the time. As Bozdoğan points out, by the late 1920s and early 1930s, combined with the social changes under way in the new republic, the connotations prompted by these villas, single-storey houses with lawns, patios and garages, 'evoke a utopian vision of Turkey with suburban middle-class lives and single family dwellings' (2001: 206-9). The villa, by this time adopting a Modern Movement cubism, took on the role as a sign for the individuality of the family and a preference for the suburbs. 'The distaste for dense urban life, the idealization of the single-family dwelling within a garden, and the conspicuous absence of higher-density residential types such as apartments, row houses and multifamily blocks, are important clues to the prevailing ideological climate' at this time (ibid.: 210). Though relatively few modern houses were built, for economic reasons, custom designed villas and apartments, based on Western designs, were put up for a few of the new republican elites – bureaucrats, professionals and the military. As far as the architecture of the early republic was concerned, Bozdoğan concludes, the two standard types of accommodation were 'the single story house or villa in a garden' and the urban 'apartment building'. The ideal type was 'the detached, single family house or villa . . . celebrated for its closeness to nature, sunlight, and healthy living' (ibid.: 225).

REBUILDING BEIJING

> Huge swathes of Beijing are being cleared by real-estate developers to make way for high-rise apartments, office buildings and shopping centers. The familiar syndrome of urban renewal is drastically changing the face of an ancient city within a few years. Within a few years around 90 percent of the old neighborhoods will be cleared.
>
> *New York Times*, March 1, 1998

Recent writing on society and culture in China has addressed the difficulty of attributing various cultural developments in the contemporary period, particularly in terms of positioning and interpreting them in relation to a 'Western' analytical or interpretative framework constructed around ideas of the 'modern', 'post-modern' and the like (Liu Kang 1995; Dirlik and Zhang 2000; Zhang 2000). Jameson, for instance, struggling to interpret cultural transformations in China, has suggested that 'A global or geographical term is needed for the ways in which chronological nonsynchronicity manifests itself in a spatial and even national form' (cited in Liu Kang 1995: 167). And while the architectural references of the contemporary Chinese city are – like the skyscrapers, new luxury apartment houses, and the villa (discussed below) – apparently derived from a 'Western' repertoire, others have suggested that the framework of comparison is, in fact, more aptly constituted when these developments are seen in relation to other cities in Asia undergoing similar transformations.[1] While these are some of the particular building typologies chosen by China as a way of entering into the world of global capitalism,[2] I focus particularly in this chapter on developments in some of the new suburbs. In the following account, my aim is to show how the construction of transnational space in the Chinese city results not just from a response to the regime of global capitalism, but also from the Chinese state project of modernity in the Reform era. To grasp the full significance of these more recent developments, however, some familiarity is needed with the massive political and spatial transformations that have taken place in Beijing over the last half century. For this, I draw principally on accounts by Zha (1995) and Jiang and Cheek (2002).

POLITICS AND SPACE

In writing about Beijing as 'A City Without Walls', Jianying Zha (1995) refers to what she terms the 'unspeakable sense of loss' that the city has endured over the previous four decades, particularly in regard to the dismantling of the city walls under the communist regime in the 1950s. This was followed by the smashing and looting of the city's cultural monuments and treasures by the Red Guard during the Cultural Revolution and the subsequent building of factories across the face of the city. It was a time, she writes, when:

> buildings took on a faceless ascetic look, housing got crowded and urban planning became a perpetually amateurish experiment, subject to bad politics and poor management . . . For an ancient imperial city that used to set a unifying aesthetic standard for the whole nation the new Beijing has a radically splintered image.
>
> (ibid.: 59)

The significance, not only of the city walls, but also, the walls of the traditional courtyard houses had, for hundreds of years, given the city its distinctive character. 'In Old Beijing, there were more walls than houses . . . the social status of an inhabitant dictated the size of his house and the length of his walls.' The city was oriented by its walls, east/west and north/south, with streets 'laid out arrow straight on these axes' (ibid.: 60). The walls gave the inhabitants their 'strong sense of direction, space and class, their notion of privacy and their claustrophobic tendencies' (ibid.: 60). And while the walls were erased in the 1950s, the walls in the minds of the population, according to Zha, did not come down for a long time.

With the assistance of the Soviet Union, the Chinese then built hundreds of factories and factory yards across the city, along with satellite towns for the workers, transforming the city into a major industrial metropolis. Old temples, tea houses, gardens and places for leisure were eliminated, replaced along the streets by official monuments, government offices and low rise apartment buildings including, in the late 1950s, 'the symbolic monuments to the socialist state', the Great Hall of the People and the Museum of Revolutionary History. The city acquired, in Zha's terms, 'a certain austere virtue': clean streets, plain orderly buildings, people in uniform clothes (ibid.: 62). The buildings of Mao's era, function halls and cheap housing, were 'more to do with political symbolism than practical returns' (ibid.: 65).

Following Mao's demise, attention shifted during the era of Deng Xiaoping to urban development with a focus more on commercial activities and 'everyday life', and particularly, the building of residential apartments. In the interests of tourism promotion, attention was given to historical sites, such as The Great Wall, and the construction of huge joint-venture hotels. Yet in the space of a few decades, the highly sophisticated tradition of Chinese city design had, in Zha's account, been lost, the symbol of 'Chineseness' only partly preserved, following the introduction of postmodernism in 1980, in the huge pavilion roofs, often 'squatting over modernist buildings'.

At the core of Old Beijing were the traditional courtyard houses, built along the *hutongs*, alleys or lanes (Jiang and Cheek 2002: 1, from which the following account is taken). 'Hutong' comes from the Mongol word for 'well', indicating that people could live only where wells could be dug. The history of Beijing begins with the Yuan Dynasty in the thirteenth and fourteenth centuries with the city of Dadu, constructed in the form of a chessboard, with a mere 29 hutongs, oriented either south to north or east to west, the number growing to 459 in the Ming Dynasty (fourteenth to seventeenth centuries) and over 6,000 by 1949. Between the hutongs, the land was used for residential compounds, quadrangular and four sided, with rows of rooms in four directions round a square inner courtyard (Figure 7.1). A single wooden gate provided entry onto the hutong, ensuring a great deal of privacy for those behind the walls. Within them, three or four generations might live, not necessarily of one biological family in the case of poorer people. 'Such a closed compound structure reduced individual family privacy but naturally increased a strong sense of community and community identity among its residents' (Jiang and Cheek 2002). The main entrance to a residence, according to the principles of *feng shui*, was located either at the southwest or northwest corner. In terms of social space, the rooms around the courtyard were allocated according to age and status, the best rooms being retained for the most important family members, the grandparents. The hutongs and the *si he yuan* (quadrangle), the major architectural form in Beijing for hundreds of years, have 'profound cultural connotations and are carriers of the art of Chinese living' (ibid.: 4).

Given the significance I have lent, both in the previous chapter as well as those that follow, to the nomenclature and signifying practices in particular vernacular and modern housing forms, it is worth noting here that, until 1934, there were no hutong street signs in Beijing. The names of different hutongs were conveyed by word of mouth. Names were given which were acceptable to the majority of people who lived there and were often determined by the location or shape of the hutong: Broad Street, Narrow Lane, One Foot Alley, Bamboo Pole. Others took their names from nearby gates, temples, bridges or wells: Temple Alley, Sky Bridge. Yet others from famous people, names of residents or from local stores: Rice Market Lane, Duck Market Lane, Candle Alley. Particular hutongs have 'a sense of place as an ongoing local community' and 'a focus on community identity rather than individual identity' (ibid.: 10).

Figure 7.1
Hutong, Beijing, China, 2000

In the early 1950s, Chairman Mao, with the help of Soviet planners, had erased swathes of the ancient fabric round the Forbidden City to make way for a socialist 'people's space' of Tianaman Square. However, with the shift to new models of capitalist modernity in the 1990s and, not least, in preparing for (and winning) its bid for the 2008 Olympics, central Beijing has been transformed into an 'International Metropolis' (Li Rongxia 2000), including the installation of much of the apparatus of a global financial center (Short and Kim 1999). The developments described below, therefore, need to be seen in the context of a Beijing (population 12.5 million) where the urban fabric, consisting of the ancient Forbidden City at the center, masses of 6- to 8-storey walk-up apartment complexes from the socialist era, and a rapidly diminishing area of 'traditional' vernacular housing, the single-storey 'hutong' settlements, are all gradually being marginalized by masses of immense, expensive 30- to 35-storey private apartment buildings. The information in the following account comes, in the first instance, from the English-language paper *China Daily*, circulating widely in the United States. This is supplemented by brochures and developers' promotional material from a number of sites visited in July 2000 as well as discussions with realtors' representatives. In examining the spatial and cultural transformations taking place, both in the immensely complex urban settings of Beijing and other major metropolitan centers in China in the decades linking the twentieth and twenty-first centuries, two phenomena are key to any interpretation. The first are the 55 million overseas Chinese who live and work in different locations around the world, the second, the more than $30 billion in investment they bring into the country every year; 60 percent of it from, and through, Hong Kong, and 15 percent from Taiwan (Ramesh 2000).

VILLAFICATION AND THE SUBURBS: CONSTRUCTING SIMILITUDES

In 1998, *China Daily* reported that Beijing had a stock of 21,000 units of residential property especially 'designed for overseas buyers' either 'quality apartments' or 'single family houses'. The major clients for these were said to be foreign multinational firms (and their executives), overseas investors (not least, those from the diasporic Chinese community) and also the large number of local Chinese, increasingly wealthy with the shift to free market capitalism.[3] If the number of advertisements published in *China Daily* in the mid 1990s is any guide, luxury villas were a significant sector of the investment market aimed at overseas Chinese.[4] At Regent on the River, 17 kilometers west of the city center, a 19 acre estate of luxury suburban homes 'surrounded by lovely woodland, rivers and streams' was on offer, the names and designs of these 'European and US style houses' – 'The American, the Nordic, the Baroque, Mediterranean, Classic European, The Georgian' – apparently selected to reach a culturally diverse array of Euro-American-Chinese clientele. Another development, 'River Garden Villas and Phoenix Garden Villas' are located near 'the only world class 18 hole golf course, managed by Japan Golf Promotions'. Other villa developments include Garden Villas, King's Garden Villas, the Beijing Eurovillage. It is, however, the images and descriptive captions of the Beijing Dragon Villas ('beautiful American-Canadian residences') that provide more precise insight into the transcontinental interconnectivity of places.

Writing on the development of the (Eurocentric) idea of the nation state as the dominant form of governance, Mohammed Bamyeh draws attention to the fact that:

> sovereign governance . . . is governed by the idea of constructing a similitude . . . whereby (on each occasion of the creation of a new state) one constructs a globally legitimate player. With the rise of the state as the standard form of governance, standard structures of dominance and models of political behaviour were created. The rise of total politics in modernity cannot thus be separated from their obsessive attention to each other, an attention which is itself a feature of globalization.
>
> (Bamyeh 2001)

Just as Bamyeh suggests that 'one of the consequences of global modernity is that every state has to see itself in the contexts of other states' so, inherent in the same process, every 'real' or aspiring world city strives to define itself in the context of other world cities. Thus, in promoting new developments, the creation of a new commercial plaza in Beijing is compared to those at Ginza, Tokyo, Manhattan, New York and Canary Wharf, London (King and Kusno 2000). In a similar way, the new Beijing Dragon Villas are advertised as 'Just like Beverly Hills in California', 'Just like Long Island in New York', or 'Richmond in Vancouver' (Figure 7.2), aiming to create an equivalence between these two different sets of places. This latter is worth noting as, with the influx of (especially) Hong Kong migrants into Vancouver in the decade prior to the British handover of Hong Kong to China in 1997, residents of Chinese descent in this upmarket suburb of Richmond increased from 7 to 37 percent (Mitchell 2000: 13).[5]

Figure 7.2
Advertisement, *China Daily*,
April 1994

In the summer of 2000, visitors staying at major international hotels in Beijing could pick up a map of the city produced by realty consultants, Jones Lang LaSalle, showing the locations of over one hundred 'Beijing Luxury Residential' complexes. Mainly clustered in seven locations, predominantly round the outskirts of the built up area of the city, though with the main concentration around the Airport Expressway, the sites are mainly accessible from the Fourth Ring Road. Closest to the center (in Sanlitum and the 'second Diplomatic Area'), are some thirty mainly multi-storey luxury apartment complexes. The villa developments are (expectedly) further out, closer to the airport, or to the north, beyond the Asian Games Village. For their (mainly) transnational residents – employed, for example, by IKEA, Hoechst, BASF, BP, Siemens, Audi, NOKIA, PriceWaterhouseCoopers, Hewlett-Packard and others – they are within reach of (expatriate dependent) facilities such as the German School, Beijing International School, the Montessori Kindergarten, Family Hospital, in this case, in the 'third Diplomatic Area'. In these outlying areas, carefully located by the Beijing planning system in the middle of open country, far from the noise, pollution and what, to a non-local visitor, appears like intense crowding of the Chinese capital, are the large, meticulously planned estates, including the Purple Jade Villas, King's Garden Villas, Beijing Riviera Villas, Capital Paradise Villas, Silver Lake Villas, Legend Garden Villas, Regent on the River and Dynasty Gardens. Huge hoardings located at key sites and intersections along the otherwise building- and advertisement-free four lane highway to the airport promote the villas to the air travelling elite, flying in and out of the capital city. Large boards announcing 'INTERNATIONAL VILLAS' protrude through the greenery and vegetation of tree-lined roads, breaking the visual silence of the Airport Expressway running out of the city. All the developments have apparently appeared since the early 1990s.

The concept of 'luxury' is perhaps first conveyed by the price. In a city where average wages were, in 2000, in the region of 2,000 RMB per month ($200) villa prices in the Beijing Riviera complex range from $765,000 to $1.3 million (total floor area about 250 square meters for the lower range up to 464 square meters for the more expensive). Rentals (for a 400 square meter villa and above) range from $9,000 to $13,000 per month, plus a management fee (for owners and renters) of between $492 and $677 per month and a membership fee for the Club (providing a wealth of recreational and sporting facilities) of $120 per month. In its promotional literature, Beijing Riviera is marketed as 'North American style in the Beijing suburbs. Beijing Riviera has succeeded in replicating North American Life and Architecture'. The Capital Paradise Villas are 'a leading expatriate society in Beijing with 500 European style villas'. Over the last twenty years, according to the Beijing Riviera literature, 'Beijing has exerted itself as one of the world's greatest international capitals. With over 100,000 expatriates from over fifty countries, Beijing offers an opportunity for interaction unrivaled in most other Asian cities'. The complex, a walled and gated compound with 'electric sliding gates' (as with all these villa developments), houses 700 residents, 'ambassadors, embassy staff, executives of the world's leading companies', representing 28 countries, 30 percent of whom, according to the agent's publicity, are from the US, and from 4 to 7 percent from each of France, Australia, Germany, UK, Taiwan, Singapore, as well as China.[6] The latest American fittings (some made in China) complement the bathrooms, kitchens, home theater, gym and bar. A regular shuttle bus runs between each of these developments for the 20 minute journey to the city. The architects, developers and mortgage banks, are apparently Chinese firms in Hong Kong and Singapore.[7]

The major feature marketed by these developments is security. Dragon Villas, the most expensive of these luxury villas, 231 'residences fit for royalty' with 14 different designs (from 341 to 886 square meters) and 'utilizing North American style architecture' are 'behind carefully guarded stone gates' and originally, were built primarily for the American and European multinational executive market. The estate, 'a masterpiece of magical creation, is built on a 372 acre dreamland, offering unobstructed panoramic views and vast landscaped area'. Dragon Villas 'puts residents' safety first'. An infra-red alarm system seals the community's outer walls; at each villa, closed circuit TV and coded alarm systems 'ensure residents' safety and security'. The economic polarization between the wealth of the expatriate or local Chinese inhabitants who live in the villas and the guards who look after their security is evident in the wages (in Summer 2000, 800 RMB – $80 per month).[8]

Figure 7.3
'Beijing Dragon Villas',
China, August 2000

The design of the Dragon Villas 'utilizing North American style architecture' (by a Canadian architect) is basically Classical and 'Georgian', brick-built, with a massive one- or two-storey classical portico framing the front door (Figure 7.3). Quoined corners and a large double garage, like a snout, face the front. Publicity postcards feature groups of smiling European or American families standing around with bikes, a young (white) mum seeing her toddler off to the compound kindergarten, a young executive busy in his book-lined study, (caucasian) children chatting with security guards, lavishly spacious interiors and a club house as large as a mid-sized (French) hotel.

Apart from the non-Chinese residents, in Spring 2002, according to the *International Herald Tribune* (April 23), Beijing-area villas at 14 million RMB each ($1.7million) were drawing 'newly affluent locals.' These were located in 'Orange County [*sic*]', 30 kilometers from Beijing and 'a world apart from the living conditions of the vast majority of Chinese' where average annual income for city dwellers is 6,869 RMB, three times as much as for those in the country. According to the real-estate agent interviewed by the paper, 'the carpets are similar to ones in the White House', the red tapestry and crystal of the dining room giving the building 'a special French touch', also complemented by a wine cellar, gym and billiard room.

Though originally catering mainly for foreigners paying as much as 83,000 RMB per month for rent ($1,000), the villa developments were now 'focusing increasingly on China's own nouveau riche', business people 'who have made a fortune abroad'. Following Beijing's successful bid for the 2008 Olympics and the country's entry into the World Trade Organization in December 2001, 'vast amounts of money are pouring into expensive investments as the demand for villas is large and will continue to grow . . . as Chinese, but also foreigners, move from the center of the city to the suburbs'. Simultaneously 340,000 families are being required to leave their traditional homes over the next five years as the authorities clean up the city for the 2008 Games (ibid.: 2002).

GUANG DONG AND SHANGHAI VILLAS[9]

The degree to which villa developments have 'taken off' around the inner fringes of other major Chinese metropolises can be seen in two glossy collections of color plate images produced as books by Pace Publishing, a major business publisher, in 2002. The books, *Neighborhood Villas – Shanghai* and *Neighborhood Villas – Guang Dong* (Guan and Zhu 2002), consist solely of glossy images of upmarket villas (as well as townhouse and other residential typologies), with virtually no text, in the outer suburbs of China's leading 'World City' and in the province of Guang Dong, the latter developments, about two hours by shuttle bus from Hong Kong with its prohibitive land and property prices. Published partly as a promotional exercise (though also used to provide design models), the books provide some insight into the new property market for weekend, vacation or permanent housing (in any or all cases, as investment property) by China's new business classes as well as overseas Chinese.

Unlike the new exurban developments around major metropolises in India (see Chapter 8) signified through an anglophone postcolonial imaginary, the meaning of the names attached to these villa townships, given both in Chinese as well as English (and where each is not necessarily a translation of the other), pose some hermeneutic puzzles. Of those in Guang Dong province, richly landscaped with reference to what might be taken as traditional Chinese features – rocks, pools, extensive water features, traditional sculpture – all bear names that match their locale: Evergreen Villas, Glade Village, Summer Palace, Riverside Garden, Shangrila Villa Garden or draw on vernacular references (in English), such as Tian an Hung Kai Garden, or the Zhuhai Golf Villa Resort. Supplementary signifiers in English merely add a 'touch of (international) class' for the mainly Chinese-speaking buyers. Elsewhere, a more consciously international imagery is at work. For example, with 'Global Villas' where, in part of the development

Figure 7.4
'Global Villas', Guang Dong, China, 2002

at least, 'global' apparently signifies low density, 'detached' or (in American terminology) 'single family homes': the 'Victorian' timber-framed, pitched roof design and front porch might equally be seen in upstate New York or anywhere in the mid West (Figure 7.4). To suggest, however, that 'global', in this instance, translates as 'American', sidesteps the assumption that 'American' does not, in this particular instance (or indeed, in many others), describe some pre-given cultural essence but is rather an outcome of mainly north European constructional and architectural features as might be found, for example, in Scandinavia. As Robertson (2002: 37) points out, 'the US was itself born out of the globalization process'.

Of the villa developments round Shanghai, for well over a century and a half at least a richly cosmopolitan city with a history of housing (colonial) cultural diversity, villa names are mainly inspired by vernacular images – Tianma ('Skyhorse') Villas, Peony Garden, Sheshan Yinhu ('Silver Lake') Villas. Others, however, are targeted at a more culturally cosmopolitan clientele: Shanghai Venice Garden, with some 130 identical two- and three-storey villas, is laid out around a lake; waterside walkways and the odd boat conjure up an imagined Italian city. The featured design in Longisland [sic] Villas, is 'Modern Movement': flat roofed, all white and chrome, 'functional' and square meters of glass (Figure 7.5). Alternatively, Rose Garden designs are more Germanic with 'fachwerk' and steeply pitched roofs (Figure 7.6). Beverly Oasis Garden and, particularly, Fontainebleu Villas, are possibly aimed at the overseas Chinese or expatriate Euro-American market; the latter, classical, with ballustrades, ionic columns, rusticated stonework, suggestions of a mansard roof though relieved with a 'Modernistic' facade (Figure 7.7). Groups of 'Baroque' sculptures lend an air of Versailles to the gardens. Entrance to the Fontainebleu estate is through a massive 'Arc de Triomphe' gateway, heavily patrolled by security guards (Figure 7.8). Though glimpsed only occasionally in these images, perimeter fences abound.

What is particularly striking about these culturally hybridized and stylistically interesting developments outside different Chinese cities is the massive and rapid shift, over a period of less than one decade, from a state socialist to a market society, and from collective to individual forms of housing, represented by the individualized and increasingly globalized villa, as the epitome of the

Figure 7.5
'Longisland Villas', Shanghai, 2002

Figure 7.6
'Rose Garden Villas', Shanghai, 2002

Figure 7.7
'Fontainebleu Villas', Shanghai,
China, 2002

Figure 7.8
'Fontainebleu Villas', Entrance,
Shanghai, China, 2002

individualized, consumption-oriented suburb.[10] This is Smith's (1990) conceptualization of 'global culture' as a non-national, or better, supranational political
phenomenon where, if 'socialism' is equated with collective, multi-storey housing
blocks, 'capitalism' requires villas for a new bourgeoisie.

CONCLUSION

How do we interpret and give meaning to these recent developments in the
shape and form of luxury housing in China's capital as well as other coastal cities?
What is the significance to be attached to this new phase of transplantation and
translation, on such a scale, of what was originally the 'Western' concept of the
villa?

Does it, as Archer has suggested in relation to the introduction of the free-
standing villa into the late eighteenth-century English suburban landscape, herald
some form of social and psychological move to an idea of a 'more autonomous'
self in contemporary urban China? Or, collectively, an attempt to create such a
subject? Or, as Bozdoğan implies in her discussion of suburban villa developments in Ataturk's post-revolutionary Turkey, a more conscious move to link the
spatial manifestation of property ownership with the individualization of the
bourgeois family? Or, with the massive shift to the development of a free market
capitalism in China, by encouraging practices of spatial separation and individualized housing, the conscious construction of a spatially separate and
architecturally signified bourgeoisie, distinct from the bureaucratic leadership? Or
again, as Ackerman has suggested in relation to the West, the reordering of the
entire urban social order, constructing a power elite through the 'villa as hegemonic architecture', a new sign of privilege which demonstrates to the proletariat
to where, and to what, they should aspire?

As China's search for an alternative modernity is 'historically linked with
revolution; and ideological and political struggle . . . has always been explicit in
the symbolic sphere or the domains of culture' (Liu Kang 1995), what kind of
socialist modernity does this suggest, where luxury villas are being built and sold
at 250 times the average urban income in Beijing and over 700 times the average
income in rural areas? Research in the early 1990s showed that 'reform' in

housing in China was already reinforcing existing inequalities (Logan *et al.* 1999) though Deng Xioping's policy of 'Let one group of people be rich first so that we can march on the road to collective prosperity' might be a partial explanation to this major policy change after Mao.[11] However, no sociological or other research is available to answer the questions posed above.

In terms of cultural identity, the majority of the Beijing villa developments are no more perfectly mimetic of their generative models in 'the West' than were the houses in China's colonial port cities before them. And overall in China's modernizing cities, the number of villa developments is proportionately small compared to those with apartment houses. If it seems, on the basis of these examples, that Western 'Classicism' has become an architectural lingua franca to project the social status of the transnational bourgeoisie, there are a myriad of subtle differences to indicate that it is invariably both physically as well as semiotically transformed. Local norms and conditions are paramount. In most cases, the ratio of the building footprint to their plot size is very different, with the latter far smaller than would be the case in Europe or the United States, particularly considering the immense cost. High land costs may be an obvious explanation. Yet at the risk of stereotyped generalizations, Chinese house-owners, whether in China or Vancouver, tend to place higher value on having space within house walls than outside them. 'Wide open spaces' are American, not Asian longings. In many of the villa developments, high and formidable walls – an enduring feature of Chinese domestic architecture – separate the handkerchief sized plots securely from each other (Figure 7.9). Regimental security controls contrast with the serendipitous semi-neglect characteristic of private suburban property in the United States or Western Europe. And seen in the context of the cases discussed in the 'Indian' chapters that follow, the signifying nomenclature and landscaping, for the most part, remains 'traditionally Chinese'.

The question of whether these villa developments come from 'the West' or whether they are mediated via Hong Kong and Shanghai is also a relevant

Figure 7.9
'Beijing Dragon Villas', Beijing, China, 2002

question. Shanghai, as well as Hong Kong (as I discuss in Chapter 9) are both central to China's 'official' 'imagination of modernity'. In both these centers, innovations are 'culturally legitimate'. In this context, therefore, the reference group for the 'more traditional' national capital of Beijing may be its sister cities rather than cities in 'the West'.

Seen in the longer perspective of half a century of rapid transformations in the spatial and architectural form of the capital, there is also a sense, not least from Zha's (1995) account, that Beijing's inhabitants are losing their cognitive sense of the city, a phenomenon that is resulting in the playing out of memories of the past. Whether in plays (Li Longyun 2002) or in films, an increasing number of artists and directors choose the traditional courtyard house as their setting, a response to its decreasing presence in the city. Yet apart from representations in contemporary art forms, whether courtyard house or villa, how, in the reality of the newly owner-occupied apartments or the villas, are the social relations of the extended family being played out? The spatial recognition of patriarchy? Relations of gender?

Apart from these significant social issues, however, what I have also tried to demonstrate in this chapter is that, within a framework of an apparent 'globalization', historically *sub-global* processes, as well as the importance of the state, place and people, as 'constitutive of, and central to the functioning of 'global' (cultural as well as) economic circuits' (Mitchell 2000) demonstrate very clearly the myth of the 'global homogenization thesis'. When ideas, objects, institutions, images, practices, performances are transplanted to other places, other cultures, they both bear the marks of history as well as undergo a process of cultural translation and hybridization. This tends to happen in any or all of three ways.

Most simply, for material phenomena, they generally change their form, their social use, or function. Second, even though arriving in similar forms (whether material technology or images) they are invested with different cultural, social or ideological meanings. And finally, the different meanings with which material objects, ideas or images are invested, themselves depend on the highly varied *local* social, physical, spatial and also historical environments into which they are introduced and the equally varied local conditions under which they develop. Though as Pieterse (2004: 92) suggests, the 'local' should not be reified or made the subject of what he refers to as 'boundary fetishism'.

In the following chapter, I consider just one of the many possible contemporary ways in which ideas and imaginations about architecture and houses circulate between different places, cultures and agencies in the contemporary world.

NOTES

1   I am indebted to Abidin Kusno for this viewpoint. For a fuller account of these developments see King and Kusno (2000).
2   And not necessarily new, since high rise buildings were introduced into Shanghai, along the Bund, during the 1930s. Both here as well as in other European colonial settlements, such as Canton, villas were also introduced in Western colonial enclaves. The difference is in the rapid increase in the last decades.
3   I was informed in August 2000 by my Chinese guide, Virginia Wong (the wife of a developer in the outskirts of Beijing), as we visited some of the new outer villa developments, 'Before 1979, there was no rich class. Those with power were party officials – but they didn't have much money and, in any case, there was nothing to spend it on.'

4   In an advertising supplement to *China Daily* (August 22, 1994) headed 'Overseas Chinese Villas to provide comforts of home' the account refers to a joint venture between American South Pacific Technology Co Ltd and Dalian Municipal Utilities Industrial Development General Corporation as behind the developments indicated in the epigraph. 'Since the real estate market in Dalian opened, 590 domestic and foreign enterprises have been approved for property development, including 200 foreign-invested ones . . . as a result, more and more foreign investors are coming to Dalian to invest . . . Prospective business people from such countries and regions as the United States, Japan, South Korea, Hong Kong and Europe have come to Dalian to purchase villas'. Villa prices were from US$ 1,588 per square meter upwards and were located 12.5 kilometers from Dalian International Airport, 7 kilometers from the railway station, similar to Dalian Port, and 6.5 kilometers from the commercial center.

5   Mitchell (2000) and others have drawn attention to the interesting (and, for some local inhabitants, controversial) changes in the suburban housing landscape of Vancouver as a result of Hong Kong (and other Chinese) immigrants in the early 1990s reinvesting capital by buying and demolishing existing dwellings and rebuilding, on a considerably larger scale, houses that accommodate their extended families and provide space for additional uses.

6   According to a representative of Jones Lang LaSalle, Beijing, villas on the most expensive compounds are owned or rented by American and West European countries and companies, the less expensive by those from East European and less wealthy Asian countries.

7   On the globalization of property markets by Chinese construction companies, see Mitchell (2000) and Olds (2001).

8   According to Professor Jeff Cody of the Chinese University of Hong Kong, despite the massive security on these villa compounds, one German resident was brutally murdered in a messed-up burglary earlier in 2000 (personal communication). Entering and leaving the main gates of the compound, under the total surveillance of CCTV cameras and surrounded by guards with cell phones, conveys all the atmosphere of a high security prison, or army barracks, not least in regard to the military-style salute received on departure.

9   I am much indebted to Sam Liang for the documentation here.

10 Prior to the building of these developments, the (presumably much smaller numbers of) expatriates lived in hotels and apartments in the city.

11 My thanks to Sam Liang for this interpretation and suggestion. I am also grateful to Sam Liang for information that the National Land Resources Department had given notice to local government land bureaus on September 17, 2003 to 'stop issuing permits for villa developments' (*Jingji Ribao*, September 18, 2003, website), probably due to the over-development of these up-market houses.

Chapter 8: Imagining the World at Home: The Distant Spaces of the Indian City

You've seen the finest of luxuries, in foreign lands. And enjoyed the best life has to offer. Just for you, Celebration Homes. Perhaps the first concerted effort in India to create not just luxury homes but a complete luxury world for sophisticated people like you. Enriched with international luxuries and surrounded with advanced facilities, that have already attracted several important personalities – both Indians and NRIs – to . . . the elite neighborhood of Delhi . . . 10 minutes from the Indira Gandhi International Airport . . .

Real estate advertisement, *India Today (International)* 1997

INTRODUCTION

In his book, *Modernity at Large: Cultural Dimensions of Globalization*, anthropologist Arjun Appadurai explores the joint effects of 'media and migration' on 'the work of the imagination as a constitutive feature of modern subjectivity'. 'The media' he writes:

> offer new disciplines for the construction of imagined selves and imagined worlds . . . (they) are resources for experiments with self-making in all sorts of societies, for all sorts of persons . . . moving images meet deterritorialized viewers. These create diasporic public spheres, phenomena that confound theories that depend on the continued salience of the nation-state as the key arbiter of important social changes
>
> (1996: 3–4)

In this chapter, I want to extend Appadurai's valuable insights into the relationship between media, migration and imagination in the constitution of modern subjectivity. My aim is to show how the outcome of these inter-related phenomena is – with the help of other agencies and processes – currently influencing material developments in the architecture and suburban spaces of some of India's most rapidly developing cities, particularly Bangalore and New Delhi. However, I shall also take issue with Appadurai; not only does the nation state continue to be a major player in contributing to social change but it is critical to the construction of what he calls the 'diasporic public sphere'.

The chapter is in two parts. In the first, I address some of the presuppositions used in my framework before examining, in the second part, the particular instance of transnational cultures as represented in contemporary advertising, outside India, of suburban housing in specific Indian cities.

I use the term 'space' here in two senses: first, metaphorically, to refer to the discursive space in which notions of the transcultural are being constructed; but also, in a materialist, realist sense, to refer to those phenomena signified by these discourses – physical and spatial urban form, particular architectural cultures and the larger built environment. 'Space' here also implies the *production* of space – to use Lefebvre's (1991) phrase – and the economic, social, political and, especially, cultural conditions in which space is produced.

'Transnational cultures' is more problematic. If we can accept that transnational means literally 'extending beyond national bounds or frontiers', transnational *culture* perhaps implies not only that cultures are 'normally' 'national', that is, that they somehow belong to nations (that is, peoples, not nation states) but that they are also confined within the territorial boundaries of the nation state. Not only do cultures – by which I refer to issues of identity as well as socially organized systems of meaning and identity which are not necessarily coherent or even stable – exist far from their places of origin but, as Gupta and Ferguson (1997) have argued, cultures are not necessarily confined or situated in a particular space or place. Culture, and cultures, are constantly in process, being transformed as well as being created under very specific economic, political and historical conditions.

Here, I might revert back to the second chapter and the discussion about 'global culture', a concept which, as has been shown, has various inconsistencies. While people, ideas, memories, images or mobile material objects can be located (almost) anywhere and be moved around at will, immobile objects, such as real estate property or the spaces of city squares, are fixed in particular locations, frequently in cities, which are situated in nation states, though this, of course, in the context of some of the conceptualizations discussed in Chapter 2, does not stop them being represented as 'global'. My first assumption, however, is that transnational culture can only be understood when it is 'practiced', and becomes meaningful, when seen from a particular place.

The first component to my argument is the discursive, and imaginary, construction and representation of the spaces of transnational culture. This includes the concepts, images and visual representations, and the meanings attached to them by academics (Appadurai 1996; Hannerz 1996; Clifford 1998), media specialists, and – as is the case here – advertisers' copywriters and developers: ideas about the 'international', the 'global' and about what is 'modern' or 'world class'. These concepts, including notions of nationalism and cultural flows, are what people use to talk about transnational phenomena and, through these discourses, bring transnational spaces into representation.

The second component is what I have already hinted at, the 'fixed spaces' of transnational culture. These require that we give attention to the processes by which transnational cultures are constructed, whether these are political, economic, demographic, financial, technological and so on. I refer here to movements of both capital and people, migrations and transmigrations (Glick Schiller *et al.* 1995),[1] decisions and legislation of governments, the activities of the services industry such as legal or real estate professionals, the use of media technology (the press, television, fax, internet, the web). We can cite here Arjun Appadurai's notion of global cultural flows in their various dimensions – ethnoscapes, technoscapes, finanscapes, mediascapes (1990) and, as I have suggested in Chapter 2, extend these to the production of particular landscapes or builtscapes.

DIASPORIC DESIGNS: CONSTRUCTED DREAM CULTURES OF (AND FOR) THE NRI

To put some concrete substance into these ideas, we can take what might be described as a good example of a transnational culture, as outlined above. This is the diasporic culture (or better, cultures) of the 'NRI', the Non-Resident Indian, as it is (partly, but significantly) constituted by the policies of the Indian state. In addressing some of its characteristics, we can also consider some of the spaces produced in its name. These are some preliminary observations on this phenomenon as it manifests itself in a key institution of that culture, the international (US) edition of the magazine, *India Today*.[2]

Given my earlier definition of 'transnational', the category of the Non-Resident Indian is one that might be closely related to the idea of a transnational culture. On one hand, the legal status of the identity is established by the Government of India through various tax, citizenship and financial regulations in such a way that Indian subjectivity is firmly centered in a powerful sense of nation and culture, an essence where the notion of home (as residence from which Non-Resident takes its logic and meaning) is ultimately located in India. Non-Resident Indian refers to a *personal* identity as Indian (to be one, to be able to speak, feel and probably also look like one) but not, however, to reside like one.[3] The negation of this particular identity here is in the fact of residence; Indian residence is denied because, just like the definition of transnational, the NRI lives 'beyond national bounds and frontiers'.[4]

If living in the US, the NRI or, for that matter, the British expatriate (note the difference in terminology) can, of course, be a Resident Alien. This, however, is completely opposite to the status of the NRI, giving the right of residence, but only as an alien (defined in the *Oxford English Dictionary* as a subject of another country than in which he or she resides). Here, it is not residence that is denied but one's national, cultural, personal, and indeed, political (that is, voting) identity.[5]

Being resident in a country implies at least three conditions. We reside in a particular territorial nation state, as well as a particular part of that state (perhaps a city, town, and a neighborhood); we occupy some kind of accommodation or dwelling; and third, we are in some social and/or tenurial relationship – as tenant, paying guest, visitor or owner – to that dwelling, in which case the residence is also property.

As this dwelling or residence always involves different levels of choice, in terms of location, neighborhood, cost, size, typology, image, it is also part of our identity – whether that identity is professional, class, social, ethnic, cultural or, in particular places, racial. The location and dwelling where we live is one (important) way of how we either choose to, or are seen to, represent ourselves to others.

In the section that follows, I examine how some recent developments in domestic architectural culture in India are currently being imagined, represented, and globally transmitted in the pages of *India Today*. And, not least, how this is being done in the name of the NRI. First, however, some background.

ARCHITECTURE, PROPERTY AND CONSUMERISM IN
CONTEMPORARY INDIA

With the decline, if not the end, of over forty years of a predominantly state-regulated economy in the late 1980s, and the formal liberalization of India's economy and opening to foreign direct investment in 1991, the space of particular cities in India has been increasingly exposed to the winds of economic globalization – the speeding up of the denationalization of industry under Rajiv Gandhi was followed by the shift of multi- and transnational corporations into India (Breckenridge 1995), and the outward spread of the diasporic culture of the NRI.

After half a century of bureaucratic building by the state and a varying output of private enterprise, the last few years have witnessed vast changes in the production of domestic space. In terms of India's urban and architectural history, these have not only been of revolutionary proportions but also of revolutionary architectural design. The combination of India's booming economy and the much publicized growth in the size of its urban middle class (estimates range between 100 and 200 million significant new consumers in a total population of just over one billion) are two important factors. Two others have been the influx of investment capital from NRIs abroad and the establishment of multinational companies – especially in Delhi, Bangalore and Mumbai (Bombay). A further factor, despite the ups and downs in the economy, is the overall continuing rise in Indian real estate prices in what, from the mid 1980s, has become a global commercial and residential property market. According to the director of one Delhi development company, unlike in other parts of the world, real estate prices had not fallen in Indian cities in recent years whereas in the US (and the UK) values went down by 30–40 percent in the years after 1987 (*India Today*, June 15, 1995: 77). In Mumbai, Bangalore, Delhi and elsewhere they increased – in Delhi, by a factor of nine between 1985 and 1995. Since June 1994, following the relaxation of Government regulations, NRIs (including foreign citizens of Indian origin as well as non-residents holding Indian passports) have been allowed to repatriate the original investment of up to two houses in foreign exchange after a three year lock-in period. They have also been exempt from wealth tax for seven years. What this meant was that 'luxury living' had, by the mid 1990s, become the new buzz word in Delhi, according to correspondent, Monica Raina (May 15, 1995: 70), represented especially by the upmarket condominium – fully furnished, air-conditioned, high security, club, gym, pool and the rest. In mid 1995, according to Raina, over 50 percent of condominium buyers were said to be NRIs.

From one to two centuries ago, under the influences of capitalist imperialism and the historically distinctive forms of a bureaucratic colonial culture (Scriver 1994), local translations of European and especially British architectural paradigms, helped to shape the architecture of city centers and suburbs of both England as well as India, Egypt and elsewhere (Abel 1997; Crinson 1996; Evenson 1989; King 1976, 1995c; Metcalf 1989). From the 1990s – if the advertisements in *India Today* are a measure of the reality – the rapidly expanding suburbs of particular Indian cities are currently being transformed by an equally historically, culturally and geographically specific interpretation of transnational culture, though one in which local processes of adaptation translate different suburban models from Euro-America as well as elsewhere. We should, however, stress the specificities in the Indian case. Further discussion of these developments, though approached within a different framework, are explored in the following chapter.

THINKING ABOUT 'GLOBAL' CULTURES OF CONSUMPTION

The phenomenon I describe, namely, the international advertising and marketing of substantial suburban residential property apparently based on 'Western' styles, familiar to the residential locations of the Western-based NRIs has, over the last two decades, with other forms of property development, increasingly become a form of globalized practice (Olds 2001; Thrift 1986). Viewed through various theoretical optics, it has been addressed in places as far apart as Australia and California (Dovey 1999), Indonesia (Leaf 1994; Kusno 2000), Canada (Mitchell 2000), Turkey (Öncü 1997) as well as more generally (Graham and Marvin 2001). In Ayşe Öncü's account of how different segments of Istanbul's 'middle strata' were initiated into the fantasy world of the 'ideal home as the quintessential dream, symbol and embodiment of middle class identity . . . on the outskirts of the city' (1997: 58), she offers three potential ways of thinking about the phenomenon as 'a "global" culture of consumption'.[6]

The first is 'the universal language of money, interpenetrating . . . into an ever larger sphere of meanings, adding a new level of signification to "local" habits, standards, beliefs or practices, by attaching to them a monetary sign'. Money, she writes, 'establishes a universally valid equivalence, undermining a plethora of local logics by drawing them into the sphere of exchange, thus "commodifying" them'. She also draws on Bourdieu (1984) to address the symbolic significance of cultural practices. In this line of thinking 'it is possible to think of "globalization" as the erosion of referential hierarchies from which goods derive their meanings . . . consumption practices lose their anchoring in the class system, become footloose so to speak, ceasing to signify categorical differences'. In this sense, 'globalization . . . creates a world of movement and mixture, to evoke the "global ecumene" of Hannerz (1989) in which the global and the local are moments in the same process'.

Öncü also draws on Barthes (1973) to think about consumer culture as 'the realm of contemporary myth-making'. In this sense, 'a culture of consumption would mean a culture in which goods become the embodiment of desires, dreams, emotions; wherein subjective experiences of love, excitement, pleasure or freedom are objectified in goods . . . Such mythical properties of goods . . . are universalized in global culture'. These different ways of understanding consumer culture, Öncü suggests, 'need not be thought of as mutually exclusive' (1997: 58–9).

In discussing the conditions surrounding the marketing and introduction of the 'ideal home' into Istanbul's suburbs, Öncü emphasizes the internationalization (through joint ventures) of the advertising industry in the mid 1980s, which brings the same language and concepts into the process ('we are not selling a house, we're selling a lifestyle') and also the 'initiation into the global myth of the ideal home as the embodiment of a middle class way of life' (ibid.: 59).

Öncü's valuable account of the Turkish phenomenon also helps to point up the differences in the Indian case. As she writes 'consumer myths which circulate across the globe acquire facticity in response to different sets of circumstances in different, historically-specific sites' (ibid.: 70).

The most obvious difference in India is the existence of the NRI, a social, cultural, legal and financial category which seems to be specific to that country. This gives the new suburban phenomenon three historically distinctive characteristics: it secures a flow of investment which, in the context of changing exchange rates between India and other countries (especially the US and UK, and generally to the disadvantage of the rupee) encourages ever-higher investments of capital in ever-more luxurious and larger levels of construction; it helps to explain the culturally distinctive visual, spatial, typological, architectural and naming practices of new suburban developments and, not least, contrary to Appadurai's suggestion, it reaffirms the power of the state as a major contributor to the making of India's contemporary public culture.

It should, however, be noted that the NRI is not an economically nor socially 'unitary' category. By the nature of the different demands, worldwide, for different levels of skill and knowledge, more physicians, academics, IT engineers and similar highly paid professional personnel are to be found in the US (and to a lesser extent in the UK), whereas skilled manual workers, technicians and business entrepreneurs are more numerous in the Gulf states, for example. While all NRIs may invest money in property in India, the nature of that property, and its regional location, is (expectedly) different.[7] The following account, therefore, relates to the first of these categories.

WORLDS OF (AND FOR) THE NRI

The first issue concerns the way (local) Indian developers construct the relationship – and bridge the gap – between what they see as the world of the NRI and the world of India. As one advertiser suggests, 'You've seen the finest of luxuries, in foreign lands. And enjoyed the best life has to offer. [Selective Homes][8] [is] perhaps the first concerted effort in India to create not just luxury homes, but a complete luxury world for sophisticated people like you. Enriched with international luxuries and surrounded with advanced facilities that have already attracted several important personalities – both Indians and NRIs – to this address . . . the elite neighborhood of Delhi'. Or another, 'You've traveled across the world, acquiring a taste for the international while balancing it with the Indian . . . that's why all our complexes combine the very best world standards with values uniquely Indian'. For another, 'The world is an oyster for you. You breakfast in New York, lunch in London, and have dinner in Singapore. But your heart reaches out to India. Now [AB Projects] offers to fulfil that long-cherished dream with world-class apartments . . . minutes away from Delhi'.

In Bangalore, one developer announces, 'Live the way the world does . . . (We offer) International style houses . . . [and] exclusive locations in Asia's fastest growing city'. In Delhi, Palam Vihar apartments are built to 'global specifications'; other developments offer what they state are 'world class homes', 'exclusively for Non-Resident Indians'; in Pune, houses in a new project are of 'international quality and style' (*India Today* passim 1995, 1996). How is this sense of 'international style and standards', of 'global specifications' (not terms one normally sees, for example, in German, American or British real estate ads) constructed?

The first condition apparently is that one lives in a jet-set world, linked by global airways. Architectural critic Deyan Sudjic (1992) has suggested that the symbolic center of the contemporary metropolitan city has shifted from the city hall and market square to the airport plaza. In India, NRI favored properties are, for example, represented in Delhi as 'ten minutes drive from the India Gandhi International (IGI) Airport'; 'close to the international airport in Powaii' in Mumbai; 'near the planned new airport in Bangalore'. Manhattan apartments [sic] ('exclusively for non-resident Indians') are more specific about what they see as 'world class amenities', i.e. exclusive club-pool, sauna, jacuzzi, shopping complex, covered parking, remote controlled security systems or their 'international' features: paneled teakwood doors, powdered coated aluminum windows, colored fittings and single lever mixers in toilets. Other advertisers just offer 'western style amenities'.

Prominently featured facilities in the advertisements for these new developments include a greater or lesser selection from swimming pools (with spiral splashdowns) or 'Beverly Hills style pools', jogging tracks, dish antennae, supermarkets, vegetarian restaurants, party lawns, crèche facilities, libraries, tennis courts, croquet lawns, indoor badminton courts, putting greens, discothèques, boat clubs, 18-hole golf courses, private airstrips, shopping malls, multi-cuisine restaurants, laundromats, gyms, table tennis and billiard rooms, party rooms, health clubs, landscaped gardens, waterfalls; and inside, individual jacuzzis, video entry phone security systems, marble floors, teakwood floors, designer toilets and air conditioning.

The 'international' nature of facilities is matched by the 'international' (though mainly Euro-American) signifying nomenclature used to market the developments – Bel Air, La Hacienda, Villa Del Mar, Belvedere, Riviera, Manhattan, as well as a sprinkling of Anglicized pseudo-aristocratic names – Burlington, Somerville, Sinclair, Eden Gardens. On this evidence, 'international standards' are clearly *less than* 'international' and rather those of the 'First World's' wealthiest states and the most privileged class within them.

Though Indian names are also in evidence, the nomenclature is often less 'international' than post or neo-colonial, constructing a form of imperial nostalgia where colonial mimicry is strong. On the outskirts of Bangalore in a 'premier residential locale named Impero and signifying "The Imperial Revival", the essence of British architecture is about to make its presence felt, with Oxford Impero, with motifs and elements from different styles of early seventeenth century architecture spanning 350 years' (Figure 8.1). This 'mega project ... is sprawling across 13 prime acres of which 75 percent is devoted to traditional English style of landscape'. The 26 buildings (with 550 premium apartments) sport signifying labels designed to appeal to the specific social and spatial connections, or memories, of the diasporic NRI – in London's West End and inner as well as outer suburbs of South Asian London: Hampstead, Regent's Park, Royal Crescent House, Bedford, Dorset, but also Drayton, Shelburne and Bristol (though not Dubai, Dharan, Saudi Arabia).

The same company is also developing 'Oxford Hermitage' (with a club called The Scottish Glade), Oxford Suites, Oxford Studios, Oxford Chambers, Oxford Palazzo, Oxford Ambience, Oxford Manor and – expectedly – Oxford Spires. Transnational memory, or nostalgia, is used to spark the imagination of the NRI (though also other readers of *India Today*, possibly British and other

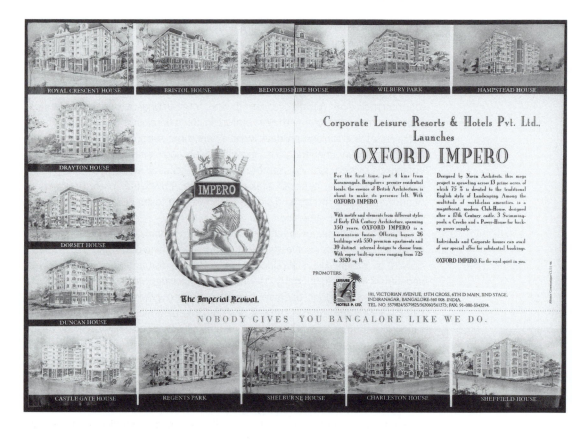

Figure 8.1

managers sent in with the multinational corporations). 'Come! Experience the
English splendor amidst the sprawling countryside' captions the second phase of
development for Oxford Hermitage. 'Doddaballapu might not sound as evoca-
tive of the English countryside as, say, Kent or Sussex. But it looks just as
picturesque'. Bangalore – developed as a cantonment city by the British in the
days of the Raj – offers, to the developers, the 'hypnotic beauty of a green
expanse' in which they build their 'English country houses'.

In the imaginary and symbolic construction of the 'international' with
which I began this section, presumably meaning *all* the world's nation states
including India (almost 200 in all) there is a noticeable disjuncture in that 'international' and 'India' are positioned as being mutually exclusive, rather than
inclusive of each other. Thus, advertisements for the Manhattan apartments in
Delhi suggest 'when you come home to India, you don't have to leave your international lifestyle behind'. 'International' here, therefore, is 'other' than, or
different from, India. Take, for example, 'Draw the curtains and you could be in
one of London's fashionable designer homes' (but not, apparently, in India), or
the Premier View apartments in Madras, 'that would easily belong in Park
Avenue, New York; Mayfair, London and Bel-Air, Los Angeles' (but again, apparently not in India). Or 'Men and women of the world may now [*sic*] feel perfectly
at home in India'.

Other appeals are to the social imaginary, linking architectural representation and personal status. For new, high rise apartments in Delhi's South City

('exclusively for NRIs'), buyers can 'Live above the Rest' in 'Homes the world will Look Up To'. In Mumbai, the Chesterfield apartments, stand 'Tall and proud, on a hill 100 feet above everybody else'. Also near Mumbai, a 'plush residential complex' is being developed, known as 'Milestone (to symbolize your success)'.

If height is one status indicator, distance from the city is another. 'As cities grow, become over-populated, polluted and real estate prices shoot up, more and more builders are shifting to the suburbs' according to the marketing manager of a major Indian developer, echoing the sentiments of two hundred years of suburban development in the West (Thompson 1982). 'Some things are just too good to be left to your imagination . . . Like a luxurious lifestyle finding expression in elegant surroundings . . . and the deep satisfaction of breathing in clean, unpolluted air as the breeze blows gently by you. . . . Yet knowing that you are just 15 minutes from New Delhi airport.'

Although most advertisements target NRIs, it is not evident to whom else they are addressed. Some demand for apartments with high specifications certainly comes from non-Indian representatives of multinational companies resident in India on corporate lease who, like NRI investors, seek large, high rise flats both for logistic convenience and security, though this clientele (unless Indian) is hardly likely to read *India Today*. Other potential buyers could be institutional or private investors, even drug lords. One might surmise that, whatever their nationality, they could belong to Sklair's 'transnational global elite' (Sklair 2001). Yet anecdotal evidence from India suggests the opposite, at least for some houses; space is bought by members of the new middle class and then split up according to family requirements. For many projects, the exotic specifications described in the advertisements are often not executed in the event. According to a local informant, it is largely for NRIs acquiring properties for their own occupation that projects provide all facilities prevalent in the West.[9]

Irrespective of ownership, however, where new developments of such 'international standards' are indeed built, they are likely to have a significant impact, as models of domestic consumption, on the new upper middle class. It is here where financial, economic, cultural, discursive, as well as spatial and architectural manifestations of globalization overlap. 'Liberalization' and 'globalization' have clearly brought many multinational companies into India. Indeed, multinational companies and NRIs are acknowledged, both in adverts and accompanying articles in *India Today*, as the principal forces giving 'a new impetus to building activity'; it is these who are associated with 'selling life-styles'. The association of MNC names provides added value, as well as esteem, to the project. In Chennai (Madras),[10] 'Spencer Plaza is already home to some of the best corporate names like Citibank, Cathay Pacific, American Express, Nestlé, etc.'. In Bangalore, 'the list' (of MNCs) 'is mind boggling: Nike, Reebok, Adidas, Sanyo, Samsung, Asea Brown Boveri, 3M, Motorola Siemens, Hewlett-Packard . . . IBM . . . AT&T, Compaq, British Aerospace, Rolls-Royce, Coats Viyella, Nestlé, Unilever' (*India Today* January 15, 1997). According to one property company in Delhi, 'the country is moving to the central stage of the world-economy. Ushering in an era of plenty and prosperity. Nurturing many new aspirations and many new dreams' which a newly built plaza, the 'international shopping-cum-office complex', is meant to symbolize.

Appeals to the collective diasporic imaginary fuse luxury with dreams. Delhi is represented as a 'dream city'; builders are said to be 'cashing in on the

NRI need to have dream houses and addresses in India' so they can 'come home to luxury'. In Chennai, another company suggests, 'We don't build apartments . . . We build dreams.'

Noticeable in these advertisements is the way that the space is gendered, that is, by the absence of reference to it. None refer to the domestic realm of eating, dining or cooking; none makes reference to kitchens, presumably because this is either not within the normal realm of the male owner or because it belongs to the space of servants.[11]

The principal dream, in fact, may simply be the accumulation of capital (Figure 8.2). These are 'Boom Times in Bangalore', Bombay/Mumbai, or Madras/Chennai, announce the developers. In Rosewood City, a 'luxurious 115 acre English township' [sic] in south Delhi, you can 'watch your money grow by leaps and bounds'; in nearby Charmwood Village, prices tripled in three years in the mid 1990s. In Bangalore, 'investment priorities have shifted from jewelry and stocks to real estate'. Throwing the gauntlet to the financial machismo of the NRI, another company challenges, 'The true measure of your success lies in how fast you can identify prime real estate opportunities in your homeland.'

Figure 8.2

These examples may suggest that the way this new architectural culture is being both imaged and imagined for the NRI diaspora is entirely exogenous, exhibiting little of 'traditional' indigenous values, and denying the identity from which it originates. This would be mistaken. Occasionally the plan of a house will reveal a puja room or, in regard to another Bangalore suburb, reference is made to a nearby temple. Other bungalow plots are 'developed with Vedic wisdom' according to the ancient principles of Vastu Shastra.

CONCLUSION

If we accept this advertising copy at face value, what meanings can we ascribe to these representations and the reality they purport to describe? My first inclination is to return to my comments at the start; to see these phenomena as the outcome of the inter-relationship between media, migration and imagination; between changing subjectivities and actions of the state and private capital. They represent a unique example of how spaces are socially produced (Lefebvre 1991) and the very historically, culturally and geographically specific conditions in which that takes place.

What these materials also tell us is that there is no singular phenomenon that can be categorized as an 'international' or 'transnational identity', any more than one can speak, in the singular, about a 'global culture'. International identi*ties*, in the plural, are formed and framed from socially constructed historical, cultural and spatially specific hybridizations. Nor, for obvious reasons, can there ever be 'global' or 'international standards', defined independently of the wealth, resources and power of the richest and most powerful states.

If we consider Breckenridge's (1995) view that it is 'the connection between public culture (in India) and global cultural flows that are at the heart of the matter', what we are seeing here is one dimension (though an important, spatial one) of an imagined transnational Indian diasporic culture. A significant determinant of this, on the evidence here, is clearly postcolonial: in the prominence of affluent English-speaking countries in determining the location of a large and influential number of NRIs (US, UK, Australia – but also other postcolonial sites such as Singapore, South Africa, Hong Kong, Malaysia) where English is the enabling language and where a level of reciprocity in regard to educational and professional qualifications persists. It is also these, principally 'First World', societies which provide the models for emulation and/or cultural translation: when copywriters exhort readers to 'Live the Way the World does' they no more refer to rural Bangladesh than they do to Ethiopia or indeed, rural India.

The assumption behind the advertisements – of the copywriters, developers, architects, or potential customers – is to create an equivalence between the developments and the wealthiest locations in the world. A similar logic explains the style of architectural and urban design – except that here, the distinctive historical connection to England privileges, for affluent NRIs who live there, their English associations. In this sense, not only is the economic, social and legal situation of the NRI historically and geographically unique but the Indian diaspora it supports is representative of no one but themselves.

When looked at 'internationally', and specifically in relation to the NRI community in either Britain or the United States, it is evident that Indian identities (and perhaps of others 'displaced' abroad) are apparently dependent on their cultural and spatial context, and formed in a dialectical relation (and reaction) to it. In the cultural space of 'the West', the objective is to look, and be, more 'Indian', signifying one's own difference in response to the difference of others; in India, on the other hand, the NRI's cultural identity is again signified by showing one's difference to others, though in this case, it is by being more 'Western'.[12]

This spatially split identity is especially evident when leafing through the pages of *India Today*. Cultural performances in the United States, when reported – traditional forms of dance, music, theater, as well as the Mumbai film – are 'typically' 'Indian' (expressed in one of its many regional forms). In India, on the other hand, the new domestic architecture of the NRI is typically 'inter-national'. Identities, social, spatial and cultural, are being remade not just from the 'outside' but from the inside and the outside each acting in reaction to the other.

The relative architectural uniformity which, for four decades of post-independence development, had spread over the built environment of new housing in Indian cities has, in the last two decades or so, become increasingly diversified. The combination of a state socialist agenda, the relative strangle-hold of the Public Works Department and the government ceiling on urban land holdings had, until the early 1980s, and with exceptions in wealthy sub-urban areas (Bhatia 1994), resulted in a typologically constrained culture of domestic architectural design. In Delhi and elsewhere, following independence, hierarchical government quarters, private flats, Public Works Department bunga-lows and private houses were the concrete (and pukka) building types which served to marginalize the makeshift dwellings (kutcha) of the poor. From the mid 1980s, however, the suburbs of such cities as Bangalore, Pune, Delhi, Mumbai, have been planted with a whole new array of market driven spaces of, and for, domestic consumption – four bedroom penthouses, luxury villas, garden homes, apartment blocks, duplex apartments, row houses, studio apartments, designer bungalows and, in Bangalore, if the advertisements are to be taken at face value, '100 aristocratic villas specially designed by an American architect'. With high rise towers and luxury villas come designs for ranch houses from the US, brick built English homes from Surrey, Canadian villas. As the habitus of the house and its environs establishes a particular kind of social, spatial and cultural order (Bourdieu 1977), the destabilization of old orders and the cultural imaginations of the new now create a totally new set of globally generated social, economic and political parameters.

These are the complex conditions under which new 'local' as well as traveling 'global' class identities are being formed. They result from the inter-actions between the 'real' as well as the imagined lifestyles of a globally dispersed, diasporic NRI, the local middle class, developers, entrepreneurs, and the urban policies of the state. And just as McDonald's has had to adjust to acceptable dietary norms,[13] exogenous spatial and architectural images have obviously been indigenized.

From a more political position, however, we can see that this expanding architectural culture emerges from a hybridization of historic (colonial) times and diasporic spaces, an imagination of exogenous standards and transnational lifestyles. The existence of developers' agencies in the US, UK, Australia, Bahrain, United Arab Emirates, Dubai and Kuwait suggests some of the locations from which ideas, finance and imaginations may arise. But property is also being sold to NRIs from the Sudan, China, Libya, Hong Kong, South Africa, Singapore, France – each group of potential investors and consumers responsible, if only in theory, for the expectations and standards of the lifestyle cultures.

In India, this internationalization of architectural space (whether in representation or reality) can be seen from many different perspectives. The obvious point to recognize in this chapter is the etic or 'external' subjectivity which has been given epistemological primacy in this interpretive account. From such a position, it can be said, for example, that the Indian city is becoming much more cosmopolitan, 'internationalized' by modified designs for suburban housing from America, Canada or Britain. It can also be said that these most recent developments are adding massively to the ways in which different forms of housing provision signal momentous social and economic, as well as shelter divisions, between the hyper rich and the utterly poor.[14] From this perspective, New Delhi, like many other cities in the contemporary world whether East or West, is fast becoming one of the most spatially re-feudalized cities in Asia, with new walled compounds sealing off luxury lifestyles from the surrounding poor.

NOTES

1   By transmigration, Glick Schiller *et al.* (1995) refer to the frequent and often regular movement between 'home' and destinations 'abroad'.

2   *India Today* was first published from India in 1975, its circulation rising from an initial 5,000 to 400,000 in December 1995. With regional and four international editions its total was estimated, in 1995, to reach 1.1 million (*India Today* December 31, 1995: 3). The international edition began in 1981, the American supplement to this (from which the information in this chapter is derived) in 1992, and the UK supplement, in 1995 (*India Today* April 15, 1995: 1). Since 1998, the magazine, previously bi-weekly, has appeared weekly.

3   According to Indian government regulations, NRIs can also be citizens of other countries.

4   Recent estimates (2002) put the total number of 'POIs' (People of Indian Origin, including NRIs, at 20 million and include 1.7 million Indian Americans in the US, 'whose average household income is far above the national average', of whom approximately 25 percent were born in the US, and approximately 1 million in the UK, 'with a per capita income of 15,860 pounds, among the highest earning groups in the UK'). The number of millionaires (as also billionaires) in each country is substantial. Some three million NRIs are in different Middle Eastern countries, of whom 20 percent are professional and 10 percent white collar (see *India Today International* January 15, 1997: 56c and March 13, 2002: n.p.).

In January 2002 the Government of India established a High Level Committee to address the issue of the Indian global diaspora, officially recognize the contribution of its most eminent members, establish procedures to resolve problems concerning 'overseas Indians', and ease bureaucratic issues regarding, for example, dual citizenship and financial investment in India. The Indian diaspora's annual remittances were estimated at about $10 billion and NRI deposits in Indian banks, about $23 billion. While the number of NRIs and POIs was not as large as the 55 million overseas Chinese, with their investment capital of $30 billion, the potential contribution of NRIs to India needed recognition. Especially in the US and the UK, the number and wealth of NRIs were sufficient to influence the policy of the country of domicile towards the country of origin (*India Today International*, 2002: 5). Since early 2002, *India Today International* has published a regular feature on 'The Global Indian', highlighting the business, financial, academic, scientific, cultural and other achievements of members of the diaspora. In January 2003, dual citizenship was recognized for

POIs in 'the West' (US, UK, Canada, Australia) and also Singapore, but not for those in the Gulf States who were (rightly) seen as being discriminated against.

5   As far as my own immigrant status is concerned, when in the US I have, technically, the same immigrant identity – as a British, Anglo-Saxon, white, UK citizen with a 'Green Card' – as the Indian Resident Alien.

6   For this phrase, and much of the following paragraphs, I am indebted to Ayşe Öncü (1997).

7   Thanks to Sanjiv Aundhe for drawing this point to my attention.

8   In the following I have replaced the original names of the developers with substitutes.

9   Many thanks to Bangalore realty consultant Lt. Col. C. B. Ramesh (retired) for some of the information here.

10 The irony of the mid 1990s Indianization of the (previously Anglicized) names of major cities – Chennai (Madras), Mumbai (Bombay), Kolkata (Calcutta) – and what I describe is not hard to grasp.

11 Local informants point out that 'design of kitchens and specific areas to meet ladies' demands are invariably incorporated', confirming the point that the advertisements are addressed to a male readership. For interesting insights into the shift in significance of bathrooms in relation to puja rooms and the underlying change in attitudes towards purity, pollution, cleanliness and hygiene in the modern, middle-class Hindu home in South India, see T. Srinivas, 'Flush with Success. Bathing, Defecation, Worship and Social Change in South India', *Space and Culture*, 5, 4, 2002: 368–86.

12 I am grateful to Abidin Kusno and Shery Ryan for this insight.

13 In January 2003 McDonald's paper place mats in their Saket restaurant in Delhi advertised their 'McVeggie Burgers', 'eggless mayonnaise', 'vegetarian cheddar cheese', '100 percent vegetable oil in all food items', 'separate equipments used to prepare vegetarian items' and 'visibly segregated cooking area for vegetarian items'.

14 Though I highlight here the growing gap between the rich and poor in India, it is important to recognize that inequality expressed in these terms is, according to UNDP figures, much greater in the UK and the US than in India (Pieterse 2002: 5).

Chapter 9: Transnational Delhi Revisited: The Spatial Language of Three Modernities

> . . . the 'real world' is to a large extent unconsciously built up on the language habits of the group. No two languages are ever sufficiently similar to be considered as representing the same social reality. The worlds in which different societies live are distinct worlds not merely the same world with different labels attached.
>
> Edward A. Sapir, *Selected Writings in Language, Culture and Personality* (1949: 42)[1]

INTRODUCTION

In their innovative collection on *Delhi: Urban Space and Human Destinies*, the editors introduce the varied essays by suggesting that 'the reality of India's vast capital is at once more diverse, more anarchic, and at times more intriguing than the semi-mythical Delhi of tourist book imagination' (Dupont *et al.* 2000: 15). To emphasize their point that there is 'no single way of grasping the complexity of a city like Delhi', they choose a range of contributors whose varied methodologies aim to overcome the editors' recognition that, whichever one is chosen – whether ethnography, photography or questionnaire – none can offer 'unmediated access to the truth. All are modes of representation with different strengths and weaknesses' (ibid.).

This chapter, addressing one aspect of Delhi in the early years of the twenty-first century, is written in the same vein. My focus is especially on recent architectural and spatial developments in the city but seen, initially at least, in the way they are represented in language.

Over half a century ago, the anthropologist Edward Sapir wrote the words which I cite in my epigraph above. Using this language-oriented approach, I want to focus on some recent major developments in the National Capital Territory (NCT), and in particular, on the ongoing construction of 'DLF City' in Gurgaon ('perhaps the largest private sector mega township in Asia' according to the developers),[2] to explore certain questions, not least those related to the theme of this book. For this, I draw on five 'field visits' to the city since 1985 (most recently in January 2003), and the recent research of other Delhi scholars.

To gauge the full significance of these new developments, however, we need to see them against a larger background, and in a longer historical setting. The first part of the chapter, therefore, provides a brief account of the two preceding cities in Delhi – Shahjahanabad and colonial New Delhi – reading the social organization of their space by means of a brief examination of the languages through which they have been constructed and represented. Irrespective of the many earlier Delhis, I shall argue that the most recent three have all been essentially 'transnational' settlements or, if not exactly trans*national*, at least – in the case of the first, Shahjahanabad, established in 1648 – trans-*cultural*, and like its comparable contemporaries, Lahore and Agra, the product of the Moghul Empire with its cultural origins partly on the other side of the Himalayas and partly in India. The second one, colonial New Delhi, established between 1911 and 1940, and like its comparable contemporaries, Pretoria and Canberra, colonial capitals of South Africa and Australia respectively, the product of the British Colonial Empire with its cultural origins partly in western Europe, particularly Britain, and again, partly in India (King 1976; Metcalf 1989). And finally, DLF City, or in its developers' phrase, 'Millennium City', a 'public/ private' township, currently under construction, and in many ways similar to other 'condominium complexes and master planned cities on the fringes of (Third World) megacities' (Graham and Marvin 2001: 271), the product of an anglo-phone empire of global capital and culture at the beginning of the twenty-first century, with its cultural origins partly in the US and partly in postcolonial India. The three types of modernity of my title, therefore, are indigenous Shahjahan-abad, colonial New Delhi and postcolonial DLF City.

STARTING WITH MAPS

One way of gaining some insights into this latest phase of transnational spatial development in Delhi is to begin by looking at any recent map of the city (International Publications 2001). Maps provide us, among other things, with representations of places, spaces, routes and locations on the ground. The graphic delineation of the shape, direction and width of thoroughfares gives the discerning reader insights into the eras when different parts of the urban fabric were built. Systems of nomenclature and, especially, toponymic inscription suggest clues about the different categories – social, cultural and spatial – into which units of urban space have been divided. Particular names, their etymolo-gies and histories, or their distribution across space, open windows on the past, providing information about the spatial distribution of social or political power. Which features are named or marked tell us what the producers of the map believe to be socially, politically or historically significant; just as what is omitted renders invisible what they assume is of little importance.

The space covered by the map is that of the National Capital Territory, an area extending in a rough radius of 40 kilometers from Connaught Place, the commercial centre of New Delhi. In 2001, the population of the city region was some 12.8 million having massively increased, since 1951, from 1.4 million.

Writing about the metropolis in southeast (rather than south) Asia, geog-raphers Dick and Rimmer (1998: 2318) have suggested that the 'postcolonial city' as a distinct type is 'an unusual and transitory experience', which will soon be eclipsed by the 'globalizing city'. They presumably imply, with this statement, that the spatial forms, racial, ethnic and socio-spatial divisions of the colonial (and in cases, postcolonial) city, its distinctive architectural imagery and its symbolic repre-sentation of imperial power, is likely to disappear. Whether this view is correct of other postcolonial cities in southeast Asia, it is hardly true of Delhi. Indeed, as I shall suggest below, it can also be argued that the inherently separationist structures of the colonial city and its asymmetrical power relations are being continuously re-invented, albeit in a new internal colonialist form.

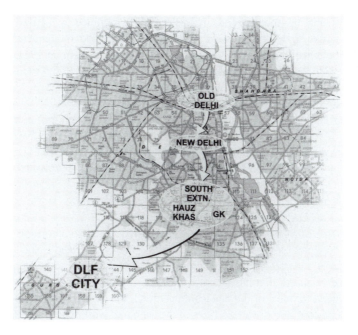

Figure 9.1

For the anglophone reader,[3] one feature of the map that is immediately apparent, is the hybrid Anglo-Hindi or Hindi-English (Hinglish) structure of many of the space and place names, particularly around the immediately post-colonial area of the city (e.g. *Greater* Kailash, Lodi *Colony*, Safdarjang *Enclave*). A second feature, equally apparent in the developers' map of the most recent, and as I shall argue, completely revolutionary transformation in the norms and forms of the city (Figure 9.1), is the continued thrust of planned, new city extensions towards the south, ever further from the commercially vibrant though also congested and increasingly decrepit city of Shahjahanabad. In the following section I look briefly at the spatial language(s) of each of the two earlier cities: the terminological systems used to describe, classify, represent, but also inherently to constitute, the spaces, built forms and architectural culture of the earlier though still extant and operative cities of Delhi. In this way, and in the context of Sapir's comment above, I want to draw attention to the spatially and culturally different forms – and implicitly, different lifestyles, status systems and social markers – as well as the way these are represented in the many different Delhis that both scholars as well as the local inhabitants recognize (Dupont *et al.* 2000: 15).

SHAHJAHANABAD

> Delhi . . . a celebrated city of Northern India, capital of the province and district of the same name . . . The *modern* city . . . was founded by Shah Jahan.
>
> *Chambers Encyclopaedia*, III, London and Edinburgh:
> W. A. Chambers (1862: 475, emphasis added)

Shahjahanabad, the city of Moghul Emperor Shah Jahan, founded in 1648, was the seat of the Moghul Empire until 1857 when he was deposed by the

British. After this time, the space of the city was drastically modified by the new rulers though subsequently, it continued to be transformed and modernized by its Indian inhabitants. Dominating the region until the establishment, in 1911, of the second transnational city of *New* Delhi as the new capital of British India (replacing Calcutta in that role), Shahjahanabad increasingly became known as *Old* Delhi, despite following its own indigenous path to modernization.

The spatial language of Shahjahanabad is originally that of Urdu, but also Hindi and even Marathi (such as 'wara' – neighborhood: Saha 1995). The two major institutions it describes, towering over the rest of the city, are *Lal Qila* (the Red Fort), built by Shah Jahan, and the massive *Jama Masjid* (the Great Mosque), the largest in India. The central public space of the tightly knit and originally, completely walled city, linking the crossing of a cluster of narrow lanes, is Chandni *Chowk*, an open area at crossroads. Unlike the space of New Delhi, produced by a series of axial roads linking widely separated points on an orthogonal plan, and designed for modern motorized traffic, the space of Old Delhi is formed by a tightly integrated conglomeration of buildings, internal courtyards and places, which assumes that movement is mainly on foot.[4]

Originally (and for most of the nineteenth century), the largest component of the urban fabric consisted of various types of dwelling and work space, differentiated in terms of size and form according to the status and wealth of their owner: the *havelis*, large courtyard houses or mansions named for the khans, nawabs or other nobility who owned them (*haveli Nawab Wazir Khan*), have now all been partitioned up into different sized *kothis* (courtyards); the *katras*, housing courts or market areas, again named for their owners (*katra Syaseed Khan*), the occupations of their inhabitants (*katra hakim*, house of the doctor), or more frequently these days, the specialized goods they sell; the *mahal*, or palace, originally for officials at the Moghul court, again, greatly redeveloped; *kucha*, a smaller courtyard dwelling or by-lane somewhat broader than a *katra*, perhaps occupied by low caste trades (*Kucha Chamar*, or leather workers), crammed up against the inner wall, and distanced from higher status areas; and *basti*, an area of informal or squatter housing. In various parts of the city, different religious-based institutions, such as the *dharmshala* and *sarai*, still exist to provide free accommodation for pilgrims (or at little cost); *madrasas* (religious schools) are located near the mosques; small workshops, *kharkana*, for metal working, tailoring or assembling spectacles, exist alongside various *katra* or up steeply angled staircases, on second floors; *bazaars* and *dukan*, markets and shops provide for specialized products and crafts, whether jewelers or cloth makers (many of them wholesalers); order is preserved by officials from the *kotwali* or *thana* (police station). Other spaces include the *hata* (compound), *dhabas* (makeshift stalls selling food) or, as with the *Bagh Begum*, a garden.

Moving around between these dense, tightly knit buildings and spaces of the city is made possible via *galis*, narrow, shaded lanes (the 'tortuous, labyrinthine passages' of colonial accounts), wide enough for an animal, scooter or two to three people walking abreast. Apart from the *mandirs* and *gurdwaras* (Hindu and Sikh temples), and some half dozen cinemas (their names, the Ritz, Novelty, Jubilee, Moti, Excelsior, Regal, Delite, providing clues as to when they were inserted into the city), few buildings rise more than three or four storeys. The whole city is divided into various different neighbourhoods, the *mohullas*, based on social, economic/commercial or craft associations. Even before the twentieth-century construction of New Delhi, the 'traditional' buildings of the 'Old' city such as the *kothi*, *havelis* and *mahals* have been divided up, remodeled for contemporary use and, partly in dialectical response to developments in the colonial city, continuously modernized by their merchant owners (Hosagrahar 2004).

With the departure of many Muslims to Pakistan in 1947, Hindu and Sikh religious, political and cultural influences on the city became much stronger. And despite the removal of large sections of the wall, the city is still circumscribed and held in by major roadways. Variously affected over the years by different municipal and government policies – in 1960 the Delhi Development Authority Master Plan designated it as a 'notified slum' though recent shifts of opinion in 2001 changed this to a 'Conservation Area' (Gupta 2000: 160, 164; King 1994)[5] – (and obligatory population removals to 'resettlement colonies' Tarlo 2000) – Old Delhi none the less buzzes with economic activity; industrial, commercial, and service. Despite its incredible congestion, overcrowding and municipal neglect, businesses are vibrant, thriving on national and international connections. Its intricate spaces are constantly adapted to contemporary global markets – not least, as a southern Asian center of a new 'copy culture', the production of non-legal (pirated) electronic media and goods (Sundaram 2001). In contradistinction to the 'colonial' and 'postcolonial modernities' of 'New Delhi' discussed below, 'Old' Delhi is a paradigmatic case of 'indigenous modernities' (Hosagrahar 2004).

COLONIAL NEW DELHI

In contrast to the *gulis*, *chowks*, *havelis*, *katris* and *kothis* of its urban predecessor to the north, the linguistic classification of New Delhi's spatial organization stems from a different cultural imaginary. The clues to this are found in a literal, as well as metaphorically different semantic field. It is defined, first and foremost, in and by the English language (though in its colonial mode), drawing on a one-time metropolitan terminological system of *roads*, *places*, *parks*, *gardens*, *markets*, as well as the language of imperial geometry that informed the original plan, *crescent*, *circle*, *square*, *circus*, *way*, *Central Vista*, the principal criterial attribute of these terms being visuality and spatial order. To these are added more specifically colonial (and postcolonial) terms of spatial appropriation, not found in the English metropole, such as *enclave*, *colony*, *quarters*, *complex* and *extension*. In this way, the imagined spaces in the head prompted by these terms match the formal hexagonal geometry depicted on the map. These include the precise and spacious directional axes springing from the key orientational nodes at Connaught Place or India Gate, as well as the rectangular formation and power-laden ritual crossing point of what were originally known as Kingsway and Queensway, but which are now nationalized and naturalized as Rajpath (Royal Way) and Janpath (People's Way). Here, at the heart (or perhaps, the brain) of the original colonial plan were placed a cluster of buildings which, as Narayani Gupta perceptively points out, 'house(d) the institutes which had explored, classified and documented India – the Archives, the Museum, the Oriental Institute, and the Library' (Gupta 1994: 259).

TOPONYMIC REINSCRIPTION

Prior to independence in 1947, the nomenclature of all these routes and spaces was entirely in English, stamping an indelibly English colonial identity on this control centre of the British Raj.[6] The most important road names commemorated royal and imperial personages (Kingsway, Queensway, King Edward, Queen Victoria, Queen Mary, Prince's Park). These names relocated the space of the city back to the imperial metropole or connected it up to other cities with similar regal nomenclature in Australia, Canada, Malaya, South Africa or elsewhere in the imperial domain (Driver and Gilbert 1999); the less important thoroughfares were stamped with the names of imperial viceroys or military leaders whose careers had been forged in India (Clive, Curzon, Elgin, Hardinge, Irwin, Kitchener, Metcalfe, Willingdon). Other road names were simply associational, descriptive or directional, pointing the way to new – not least, colonial – institutions (Race Course, Polo, The Mall, State Entry, Hotel, Factory, Central, Circular).

In the first quarter century following independence, the indigenization of Delhi's road names 'nationalized' the circulation system, making use of the names of national leaders from the realms of politics, culture and history (Jawaharlal Nehru, Mahatma Gandhi, Gokhale, Netaji Subhash, Tilak, Sardar Patel, Vivekanand, among others) or significant dates in the national calendar (Tees (or 30) January, the date of Gandhi's assassination). When the Hindi *marg* replaced the English *road* the space was semantically appropriated and seemingly given a new identity. But as the materiality of the length, width, surface, pathways, shade trees, verges and, not least, the PWD's continued colonial practice of painting the kerbs with whitewash, didn't change, it also had the opposite effect – conferring on the Indian national hero whose name it carried an anglicized and postcolonial identity. It was as if Aurungzeb took on the mantle and portly proportions of Edward VII. This is no doubt why Lutyens' huge baroque canopy at the end of what was previously Kingsway, keeping the sun and rain off the head and shoulders of a robed and crowned George V, once emptied of its occupant, has remained ever since as a prominent and very visible 'hole'. To have filled up this absence and replaced the imperial monarch by a stone replica of Mahatma Gandhi, as was once considered, diminutive yet noble, half-naked yet gracefully clothed, sitting cross-legged yet full of dignity, would have placed him in the same postcolonial light, especially when situated at the end of a 'British imperial vista' (Gupta 2000).[7]

After the 1960s, the municipal national imaginary began to extend to realms abroad: Keeling Road was replaced by Tolstoy Marg and the hitherto Outer Ring Road, as well as other avenues, were renamed after prominent nationalist leaders of other one-time British colonial territories, well beyond the boundaries of the Indian national state: Gamul Abdul Nasser, Nelson Mandela, Archbishop Makarios. Yet while erasing the memories of the names that were excised, linking India in this way with Egypt, South Africa and Cyprus, ironically evokes, in the postcolonial present, memories of a collective colonial past.

Though Lutyen's 'Vice-Regal Residence' or 'Viceroy's House' is now labelled Rashtrapati Bhavan, other prominent colonial landmarks retain, for the international tourist (as well as their indigenous) users, their English names: government administrative buildings, the 'North Block' and 'South Block', Delhi High

Court, National Museum, Delhi Race Course, Delhi Golf Club, Claridges Hotel, Connaught Place, Supreme Court, the Gymkhana Club.

When first completed, the main residential area of colonial New Delhi consisted of some 3,000 single-storey bungalows and quarters for 'officers, clerks and peons', designed in a formal classical idiom. The bungalows were located in huge square or rectangular compounds, the size of which, depending on the status of the 'gazetted officers' who occupied them, varied between two to three and a half acres (King 1976: 248). Like *chumries*, *gymkhana*, *verandah* and other terms in the Anglo-Indian colonial vocabulary (curry, dungarees, pajamas), *bungalow* and *compound* are paradigmatic examples of the distinctively hybrid colonial third culture (King 1976). The forms and spaces they describe (and help to constitute), were always historically, culturally and spatially unique. The subsequent transplantation of some of them – both in name and varying forms (particularly *bungalow*, *compound* and *verandah*), not only to the British metropole but, more extensively, to the rest of the world (King 1984) – is a major Indian contribution to the corpus of global culture.

In the last three decades high rise offices and hotels, from ten to fifteen storeys, have mushroomed in parts of Connaught Place, the main retail and commercial centre of the original colonial city, in many cases occupying the sites of demolished 'palatial bungalows'. Though architects and planners have occasionally tried to redevelop this 'bungalow zone', it was these low rise houses 'which made Delhi one of the greenest cities in the world' and 'which were coveted by senior officials and ministers' (Gupta 2000: 168).[8]

Adjoining the postcolonial residential space of Lutyens' Delhi, though now much more closely integrated with the city than previously, lies Delhi Cantonment (colloquially known as 'Delhi Cantt'). The regular grids of military accommodation, still designated with their colonial term as *lines*, commemorate the names of century-old campaigns and campaigners in Afghanistan and elsewhere – Khyber Lines, Kabul Lines, Kandahar Lines, along with Nicholson and Maude, even though the majority of labels are the later, Indian additions of Jai Jawan, Shumran, Malkan and others.

In his perceptive essay on 'The Contemporary Architecture of Delhi', A. G. Krishna Menon writes, 'The iconic power of Lutyens' Delhi (still referred to in municipal terminology as the *Delhi Imperial Zone* or the *DIZ area*) can be judged by the fact that it is the only urban ensemble in the city that is effectively protected against development – not Shahjahanabad (which) . . . until recently, was classified as a notified slum' (Menon 2000: 147). The reason for this, in Menon's view, and what makes Delhi distinctive among the world's cities, is 'the strong interventionist role of the state'. The preservation of the colonial buildings and layout of Lutyens' New Delhi is largely the result of the extent to which political and administrative elites continue to invest in this area (Gupta 2000). And as the state had total control over land (control that was inherited from the power of the colonial state, a critical historical factor that Menon omits to mention), land consolidation was never a problem. This allowed many large-scale building projects to take place to the south of the DIZ, all with large campuses, stretching the reach of the nature and quality of this 'garden city'; 'projects of this magnitude could rarely be matched or even conceived in other cities . . . The fact that they were commonplace in Delhi was entirely on account of the agency of the state and the imagination of the imported experts recruited by the Ford

Foundation to formulate the first Master Plan of Delhi' (Menon 2000: 155). This was to be another influence from 'abroad'.

Despite the new medium and occasionally high rise developments, the general shape and 'feel' of this entire area, south of the DIZ, as well as the extensions that push out to the city's perimeter, is of a low density, predominantly low rise *horizontal* city where transportation is provided by an ever-increasing number of cars, public and private buses, taxis, scooter-rickshaws, scooters (by the thousands), bicycles and simply on foot. A metro system is currently in the process of construction (though not due for completion till 2020). The four- and six-lane road system, jam-packed, polluting and congested for at least two three-hour commuting periods during the day, is none the less virtually empty at midnight when journeys to the airport can proceed at racing car speed. The massive investment in this road system (including the construction of huge flyovers) provides an immediate clue to the middle and upper middle class priorities of the city's planners. As Menon points out, the assumptions and policies implicit in Lutyens' and Baker's plans for the imperial capital have continued. 'After Independence, continuing the pursuit of these urban and architectural intentions became an article of faith with the planners of Delhi' (2000: 147). South and to the east and west of the postcolonial city where the colonial footprint was hardly placed, extensive new (private) housing developments have occurred. The 'state imposed austerity' characteristic of the first forty years after independence had the effect, according to Menon, of:

> trigger(ing) self indulgent and flamboyant architectural styles in the private sector – erzatz palazzos and Spanish villas with icing-like decorations, pompous ducal crests, baroque mouldings, curicued metal railings . . . the ascetic ideals of Nehruvian socialism may have inadvertently reinforced the allure of foreignness in architectural design.
>
> (ibid.: 151)

These are the developments – in the postcolonial spatial culture represented (in English) by 'Defence Colony' or 'South Extension' – that are captured, as Menon suggests, in the writings and expressions of Delhi architectural critic, Gautam Bhatia (1994): 'Punjabi Baroque', 'Marwari Mannerism', 'Banya Gothic'.

Further out from these postcolonial zones, new housing developments, public and private, have taken on the names of the villages which they have incorporated or displaced. As often as not these adopt the older indigenous names of *nagar* (city), *puram* (town), *gaon* (village), or in Urdu, *bad* (town) as in – moving clockwise round the outskirts of the city – Mustafabad, Shakapur, Malviya Nagar, Gurgaon, Uttam Nagar.

The pervasive language of the planning department with the ubiquitous 'enclave', 'colony' and 'extension', adds to these constructions, giving some insight into the development process. Dupont (2003), from whom the information in this paragraph is drawn, spells out the distinctive culture of the administrators and planners of the Delhi Development Authority (DDA) which makes itself felt both in the architecture and terminology of its activities. *DDA flats* are immediately identifiable as 'monotonous buildings in cement, three or four storeys high, that dot the urban landscape of the Capital' (Dupont 2003). *Urban villages* are those absorbed by the city's continuous expansion. Self-built, informal housing generally constructed by urban migrants on government-owned land over decades, are *slums*, *squatter settlements* as well as *jhuggi jhompries* (literally, huts in Hindi). *Resettlement colonies* have resulted in most cases from the forced displacement of thousands of squatters from the city centre (and Old Delhi), the majority during the Emergency (1975–7). In all cases, these were located on Delhi's distant periphery, far from the employment opportunities (as at the railway station) that had previous located them in town. As most of these 'irregular colonies' fall outside the regulatory framework of the Master Plan, they are *unauthorized colonies*, amongst other things signalling to their residents the risk of impermanence. 'Settlements of this kind provide shelter to almost one fourth of the Capital's population' (Dupont 2003: 6). Subsequently, however, some of these might become *regularized colonies*, particularly at the time of elections.

In recent years, houses in the wealthier suburbs (such as Hauz Khas Enclave, Defence Colony, Sundar Nagar) have been walled or fenced off and transformed into gated communities, the flamboyantly uniformed guards part of the burgeoning private security armies that now stand guard over South Delhi's richer suburbs.

These, then, are the spatial, architectural, as well as lexical forms of hybridized 'colonial' and 'postcolonial modernities', providing the material infrastructure in which forms of everyday life, social relations, as well as individual and group representation take place. While we can keep Shahjahanabad and colonial New Delhi as substantial case studies, they also enable us to better appreciate the significance of the new DLF City[9] under construction in Gurgaon, 25 kilometers from Connaught Place.

DLF CITY

> DLF City stands out as a unique experiment of public private sector partnership. Developed in accordance with the legal framework and Final Development Plan of Gurgaon, it has emerged as one of the finest suburban townships on the southern border of the capital city.
>
> (*DLF News* Winter 2001–2)

Begun in the early to mid 1980s with a modest 100 acre development at South City, by early 2002 the new development covered an area far larger than the size of colonial New Delhi. Part of the 'public' side of the public/private development is provided by the PWD nomenclature, the map indicating that the total area is divided into some forty *sectors* (named 'Sector 1', 'Sector 2', etc.), within which are various DLF *enclaves*, distinguished according to their phased development (*Phase* 1, *Phase* 2, etc.). Around the old village of Gurgaon, the new *colonies* (IOC colony, Friends Colony, Housing Board Colony) are outnumbered by the *nagars*, though supplemented by an intriguing 'Greenwoods City', to which I return below.

If the map suggests that the ordering of space has its roots in a colonial or postcolonial PWD system of categories, what is developing on the ground in Gurgaon is what the *DLF News* calls a 'Millennium City', presumably bringing a new sense of time, and history, to the vast satellite township of 2,800 acres consisting, by early 2002, of some forty vertically as well as horizontally massive,

Figure 9.2
DLF City: Towers. Gurgaon, National Capital Territory, India, 2002

Figure 9.3
DLF City: Apartments, 2001

high rise *towers* and *residential complexes* (Figure 9.2) containing over 5,000 *apartments*, as described in the *DLF News* (Figure 9.3). Spasmodically placed around the rocky scrub that forms the location, are three or four multistorey, *reflectively glazed* 'signature' buildings, the postmodern design of which would make them totally at home in downtown Chicago, Philadelphia or Seattle.

In contrast to the discursive Anglo-Indian colonial or postcolonial vocabulary of *quarters*, *lines*, *barracks*, *bungalows*, *compounds* or *chumries* of the colonial and postcolonial city – part of a distinctive language with its origins in colonial India (Yule and Burnell 1968) – the American-English capitalist terminology of these new developments is one that instinctively triggers images of exurban centres in Dallas, Los Angeles or Anywhere US: *condominiums, corporate towers, apartments, gallerias, megamalls, plazas, park-N-shop, supermarts, convention centers, executive homes, world class footplates* and the *Arnold Palmer Signature Golf Course*.[10]

The new city, according to the company Chairman, 'is set not only to replace Delhi as the Corporate Centre of the country but also (to) become the entertainment center of the nation' (*DLF News* Summer 2001–2).

Both the naming as well as the architectural form of the new condominium 'residential complexes', designed by prominent Mumbai architect, Hafeez Contractor, suggest that the developers (or their PR consultants and advertising executives) are working within whole new linguistic, cultural and geographical imaginaries. The names of the different complexes represent a subtly hybridized, anglophone realm of floating signifiers, some with postcolonial connotations of (especially) British royalty and aristocracy (Regency Park, Windsor Court, Wellington Estate, Carlton House), others with more pronounced American presidential, academic or corporate resonances (Beverly Park, Hamilton Court, Princeton Estate, Plaza Tower), yet others with more obvious socially prestigious (and for the potential buyers, implicitly masculine) overtones (Chancellor, Diplomat, Senator).[11] The rest, bucolic and rural, hint at the ex-urban aspirations of potential investors (Richmond Park, Belvedere Tower, Oakwood, Silverwood and Ridgewood Estates). All, in fact, belong to what is now a new global corporate corpus of signifiers used to label both upmarket real estate as well as five-star hotels, from Beijing to Berlin, in capital cities round the world.[12] 'Today, condominium culture is a way of life in DLF City on account of secure living in a landscaped environment', – the security apparently provided by the horizontal secessionary distance from the city, the elevated height of living off the ground in the 15- to 24-storey apartments and the bevy of security guards that will eventually control the walled and gated site. Security from electricity cuts is guaranteed by the '100 percent power back up', a not so subtle indication of the normal privations suffered frequently by the less privileged residents of the city.

The entrance to the extensive development (after passing by the fully glazed 12-storey office complex, 'Global Place') is marked by an 11-storey, postmodern 'DLF Gateway Tower' (Figure 9.4) in 'highly reflective, soft coated glass and clad in polished granite', the picture, captioned in the newsletter, 'Enter the Future' (though carefully excluding the crowd of huts and jhuggies clustered at the foot which a site visit makes visible). In the tower, according to the *DFL News*, Rolls Royce and other multinationals have already set up shop (Pepsico, Seagams, ICI, GE, Du Pont and Nestlé are other names scattered through DLF publicity).

Figure 9.4
DLF City: Gateway Tower,
March 2002

Another postmodern Corporate Tower offers a 'cost effective environment on its world class floorplates of 22,000 square feet' as well as 'parking for 1000 cars'. Close by is a new, custom built five-storey corporate headquarters building for Nestlé, 'nestl(ing) in exquisitely landscaped environment amongst fountains, falls and manicured lawns'. In DLF Square, another postmodern 14-storey office tower provides accommodation for the transnational – though mainly American – names of Xerox Corporation, New York Life Insurance, IBM, Deutsche Bank, Tata Telecom, as well as Fidelity Technology India Private Ltd, a wholly owned subsidiary of Fidelity International Ltd which 'enjoys a world class home in DLF Square'.

As with the Convergys Call Centre, housed in the adjacent DLF Atria, many of these new, multinational corporate spaces in Delhi, and also Mumbai, Bangalore and elsewhere, result from the rapidly growing transfer of information technology enabled services (ITES) jobs to India from the West. According to *India Today (International)*, between 1997 and late 2002, 336 call centers were established in India, employing over 100,000 operatives and generating $1.4 billion, making India the world leader in this sector, far ahead of Ireland and the Philippines. 'With over a quarter of Fortune 500 Companies such as General Electric, American Express, British Airways, HSBC, Citibank and AT&T shifting back office operations to India' where employees' wages can be (for the lowest) an eighth to a tenth of what they are in the West (and perhaps a quarter for those of higher status), call center and back office functions are expected to create two million jobs in India, earning $24 billion by 2008 (November 18, 2002: 10–16). The sector is also boosting the real estate market.

Apart from the lower comparative labor costs, it is, however, the specifically *postcolonial* factor of the widespread English language fluency amongst the university-educated Indian urban middle classes, as well as an equally *postcolonial* factor of a 'Western'-oriented (i.e. British and American) higher education system that has made the Indian graduate population the most globally appropriate and attractive market for what, in India, are comparatively lucrative and high status jobs (unlike in Britain where neither of these latter conditions apply) and where, for every vacancy, there are scores of applicants. Where the low end of this globalized employment sector includes customer service call centers, medical transcription, and billing and accounting services (processing six million General Electric worldwide invoices annually and saving the company $275 million), and major UK insurance companies paying Indian workers £2,500, some £10,000 less than workers in Britain; the high end might include risk analysis (with GE employing 600 PhD graduates in Bangalore), data mining and the remote maintenance of networks.

This shift of white collar and increasingly, middle class professional jobs from the United States and Britain to India (which different sources have variously estimated at between 3.3 million and 12 million jobs in the US by 2008), has been represented by *Guardian* correspondent, George Monbiot, as the return to India of jobs Britain stole from the country through the colonial control of its production and markets 200 years ago ('The Flight to India', October 2, 2003). The nature of the work, however, requiring Indian employees to mimic British (or American) accents, enthusiasms and tastes in order to convince callers that they are just 'round the corner' no doubt explains why, to some degree at least, the environments where they live and work are equally imitative.

As the development aims to be a self-sustaining township, with new service-oriented, computer literate jobs provided for those living on the development, a range of educational, entertainment, shopping, medical, beauty treatment, sports, leisure and commercial facilities are also in the course of development. The DLF Galleria, 'in the Mediterranean style', offers two tiers of shopping outlets and an office complex. Commercial complexes include the DLF Qutb Plaza, Shopping Mall, Central Arcade (housing the Hong Kong and Shanghai Banking Corporation), Supermarts, Pard in New York or LA, and the chef at Pizza Corner is careful to point out that 'we do not serve beef, pork or garlic to cater to the sensibility of our clients'. The restaurant, with its decorative theme of rugby, 'has a tie up with MTV and Cartoon Network' (*DLF News*, Spring 2001: 9).

As elsewhere in the postcolonial world (Singapore, Hong Kong, Kuala Lumpur, Macao), half a century after independence, politically inspired cultural animosity towards the architecture of the colonial past has long since disappeared. Colonial buildings are conserved, commodified, marketed for international

Figure 9.5
DLF City: Country Club,
2002

tourism, or occasionally (as in Singapore), if previously demolished, painstakingly rebuilt. 'Indian architects', writes architect and educator, Krishna Menon, 'did not revolt against the colonial order. Having always collaborated with the colonial architectural project, they had no reason to critically examine its legacy on achieving freedom' (Menon 2000: 149). Thus, in addition to the everyday textual as well as signifying language, we also need to be conscious of the architectural language. The *DLF News* image of the Golf and Country Club (Winter 2001–2: 17) depicts a superb replica of its model colonial predecessors, the long portico sporting a row of glistening white Doric columns, and lit with Victorian lamps (Figure 9.5). 'The sporting complex with its colonial architecture . . . comprises three floodlit astro turf tennis courts, two glass backed wooden floored squash courts . . . and a lagoon size swimming pool with a swim up bar.' 'Entertainment unlimited' is proposed at the new DLF Gymkhana Club (another revived colonial institution) with international events including St Valentine's carnival, beach parties and visits from Bollywood stars. The DLF Golf Academy, with its driving range, automated ball dispensing and 'the latest video technology that scrutinizes the golf swing and identifies flaws . . . has become the premier golf training facility in the country'.

THE VIEW FROM THE VILLAGE

> The exploitation of man and nature has not ended with the end of western colonialism. Urban-industrial enclaves in countries of the South are now ruthlessly colonising their own hinterlands, mostly settled by subsistence cultures. As in old style colonialism, displacement and dispossession continue to be justified and legitimized in the name of development and progress.
>
> Claude Alwares, *Science, Development and Violence: The Twilight of Modernity*, 1992: 21 (cited in Soni 2000: 93)

A different account of these developments is given by Anita Soni in her essay on 'The Urban Conquest of Outer Delhi' (Soni 2000) where she examines the impact of these developments on the livelihoods and futures of the farmers and rural poor of outlying villages. She writes:

> The direct colonization of Delhi's own hinterland has been motivated primarily by the quest of additional urban space. In this, the government has followed the example set by the British rulers who built New Delhi as their imperial capital, taking away the land of several historic villages in the process. During the British period, about 40 villages were incorporated within the urban limits. Since Independence, their number has risen to 185, the Land Acquisition Act serving as the legal instrument to enlarge urban space at the cost of agricultural land holdings and village commons.
>
> (ibid.: 80)

The 'urban invasion' was triggered off by the Delhi Land Finance company from the 1950s onwards:

> DLF agents swooped down on gujjar farmers, taking quick advantage of the difficulties they faced in the rain-dependent cultivation of their fields. The DLF carved cheaply purchased agricultural land into plots of assorted sizes, provided road connections and

electricity and auctioned land into plots of assorted sizes, provided road connections
and electricity and auctioned these developed estates to city-based, upper class buyers.

(ibid.: 84)

Power-operated tube wells provided water resources for the greening of their
farms 'cultivated and guarded by hired migrant labourers'. Here, Soni refers especially to the so-called *farmhouses*, 'arrogant complexes of palatial mansions with
gardens, enclosed behind tall boundary walls' which had begun to spring up in
the outer rural belt of Delhi which, from the early 1980s, was increasingly marked
by these 'prized fiefdoms of the urban gentry'. By the late 1990s, according to
Soni, there were some 1,800 of such 'farmhouses', used as weekend resorts,
and for 'lavish entertainment' by the urban elite. As commercial enterprises,
trading in floricultures, timber, nurseries – as well as being rented for wedding
parties – they were also used as tax write-offs. Apart from the immense social
polarization they represented, from an ecological point of view they were also a
disaster, the tube wells on which they depended leading to a depletion of the
groundwater table (Soni 2000: 76–77) and depriving local farmers of supplies.

An additional factor was to transform the rural economy. The 'long
distance colonization' was conditioned by the rapid growth of the urban
construction industry on a scale Delhi had never known before. The growing
demand for building materials like granite, sandstone, red sand, silica sand and
mica, gave rise to the emergence of a village-based quarrying industry (ibid.: 84).
Soni cites political activist Baljit Malik:

> What unfolds is a panorama of aggressive urbanism – a six lane highway with arterial
> roads cutting into farm building being bought out by property developers . . . You can
> see the bulldozers and trucks in their hundreds as they rip the Aravilli hills apart of
> their rock, soil and surviving vegetation. You can have your nostrils filled with smoke
> and dust as new industrial estates are carved out and trees and crops levelled to make
> way for air-conditioned country resorts and golf courses, greened with vicious
> chemicals . . . As the new high-tech homes, offices and recreation grounds expand into
> the countryside . . . an ancillary outcrop of *jhuggi-jhonpri* colonies comes into existence
> to service them. No planning, no infrastructre, no civic services . . . Here, then, is where
> our dispossessed villages find themselves.
>
> (Malik 1995)

The result has been a situation where the great majority of Delhi's rural population is either employed outside agriculture or is unemployed (Soni 2000: 8).

SOCIETY AND ECONOMY

The languages of space and architecture reflect, represent, and also help to
constitute, the new imaginary worlds in India which have developed since the
further opening up of the country to extensive foreign direct investment in 1991.
For the last decade or more, regular reference occurs in the Indian media to the
rapidly expanding size of the Indian urban middle class. Equally part of contemporary middle class urban lore are the American connections of many of these
middle class families with at least one son, brother, cousin, uncle or in-law apparently living, as an NRI, in the US, and generating regular visits between the two

countries. As discussed in the previous chapter, the NRI not only contributes to the material wherewithal for inward investment but also provides personal appraisals when rehousing parents, or other family members. In an *Indian Express* residential property supplement (March 31, 2002) appropriately titled 'Dream Merchants' and featuring new real estate projects in the surroundings of Delhi, 'Malibu Township' (drawing on the beach-related image of Malibu, to the north of Los Angeles), consisting of five 16-storey condominium towers, 'with manicured lawns on one side and the Malibu Country Club on the other' was credited as being 'the brainchild' of the developer 'who returned to India after spending fifteen years in the vibrant city of Los Angeles'. This at a time when 'NRIs started merrily investing a sizable amount in the NCT'. Featured are a retired army colonel and his physician wife, seeking accommodation similar to that of their army past. 'Army cantonments exist as isolated compact units. The awesome landscape of Malibu and its compact nature promised us the kind of life we were looking for . . . sparkling green fields and a place where we could breathe the fresh air'. Malibu Town was 'a township blessed with the luxury of American styled living . . . The majestic building was laced with marble flooring, brass fittings and fixtures'. Covering 180 acres, it offered 900 single family plots, 372 condominium apartments and 450 flats in three-storey row houses. According to the developer they have 'heavily drawn from the American pattern of home design', the housing, in the words of an ex-NRI, 'unequivocally designed to satisfy the growing needs of opulent accommodation for both domestic and Non Resident Indians'.

INTERNATIONAL VILLAS

As in China and other countries, the free standing villa has become another of the ultimate signs of status in the outer suburban areas of Delhi. As an individual entity set apart from its similar neighbours, it is also, collectively, set apart from other (high rise) developments. 'Greenwoods City' is something of a contradiction in terms: promoted as a clustering of some 165 villas set down in 30 acres at 'less than six homes to the acre', the 'International Villas (An Indo-American Creation)', 'conceptualized and designed' by a US company, aim to 'bring to India the American concept of living', not least, with their low, horizontal lines, flat angled roofs, projecting eaves and distinctive ironwork on windows and doors, in the image of Frank Lloyd Wright. Initially advertised to NRIs in 1997 in the pages of the international edition of *India Today* as providing 'within the perimeter wall', club house, health club and swimming pool, and offering 'chirping birds for an alarm clock', 'a fresh breeze for an airconditioner', five years later, in March 2002, the extent of the advertiser's vision had not quite materialized. Because of the market's resistance to the idea of the 'international' (absentee owners? foreign neighbours?), the name had been changed to 'Vista Villas'. Partly because of the absence of walls defining property boundaries the villas had been slow to sell.[13]

Yet the attraction of the villa in India must certainly be connected to its foreignness. In Palam Vihar, 'the elite neighbourhood of Delhi', advertisements for 'Continental Villas' (which continent?) and 'French villas' were common in the 1980s. The 'Continental Villa' was said to have 'a European touch of class about it', the 'French villa' a 'French flavour in every detail' (King 1994). Other villas, not least those with postcolonial geographical origins, such as the 'Scottish Villa', 'make use of the colonial style in their elevations' (Menon 2000: 152). In fact, in recent years, 'Neo-colonial architecture has become fashionable, as have colonial furniture, prints and even cuisine' (Gupta 2000: 169).

Other developments by different property companies advertised in the *Indian Express* included apartments and houses in Mayfair Tower, Charmwood Village (elsewhere described as in 'the English township of Gurgaon'), Royal Retreat and the state of the art office complex, Time Square.

THE REACH OF GLOBAL ENGLISH

It would be naive, though not entirely incorrect, to suggest that, simply because the language used to describe, to market and to sell these developments is 'English' that we are dealing here with a 'postcolonial' rather than, for example, an 'Indian', 'national' or even, simply, a 'global' phenomenon. In India, English is simply another Indian language and, as such, is as linked to Indian cultures as it is, in different ways, linked to English, Scottish, Welsh and Irish cultures as well as those in the United States, Australia, Canada, and as a second language, Malaysia and other postcolonial places in the world. In this sense, specific, and different, cultural identities can be represented by different varieties of English. In this case, however, the central corpus of the language, as well as the spatial and architectural forms it describes and helps to constitute, owes as much to American English and American culture, as it previously had done, in the colonial city of New Delhi, to (especially) 'colonial English'.

In their book, *The Words Between the Spaces*, Markus and Cameron have rightly suggested that 'the language used to speak and write about the built environment plays a significant role in shaping that environment and our responses to it' (2002: 2). It is, however, equally true that the built environment providing the context in which to speak and write the language plays a significant role in shaping that language. Indeed, much more than 'a significant role', for without the highly differentiated world of objects and spaces there would be little need to invent linguistic ways to describe them. Wherever they are, subjects live in, and are often described in relation to, the spatial categories which they occupy. This is one way in which they identify themselves as well as become identified by others (King 1994: 280).[14]

DISCOVERING DIFFERENCE

At the start of this chapter I drew attention to the fact that what I undertake in this language-oriented reading of the city comes essentially from my own anglophone perspective (in the context that my familiarity with Hindi is quite minimal). In India, of course, and especially in Delhi, where code-switching between Hindi and English (or Punjabi, or any other Indian language) occurs, for both speakers and listeners, quite imperceptibly and even unconsciously, such language consciousness would for the most part go unnoticed. In Britain or North America, who is aware (apart from those with linguistic expertise), in the course of everyday conversation, which words are of Anglo-Saxon, Celtic, or Latin origin? For most of the time, we take for granted, unquestioned, the language of our social surroundings just as we do the built forms, spaces, and architectural culture which it can also describe. The perception of what, in language or in space, we suddenly see as 'new', 'strange' or 'other' usually occurs as a result of one or more different conditions: for example, when, as members of a postimperial or postcolonial culture, we move to a different location (such as the one-time metropole) – yet using the same 'colonial language' – we see that what we have previously taken as 'familiar' and part of 'our' own culture, also exists some-where else. Or, as described here, if unfamiliar phenomena, whether in language or space, are suddenly introduced over a short period of time; or if others, more aware of the differences than ourselves, point them out to us. It is this phenom-enon, of seeing our own history and culture from the 'outside', as it were, defamiliarizing our knowledge in the process, which helps to explain why some culturally and politically sensitive travellers will return from living 'abroad' to become increasingly conscious about 'purifying' their mother tongue of 'foreign' expressions, or become conscious about preserving forgotten and neglected aspects of their native culture, whether 'vernacular architecture' or 'folk music', when arriving 'home'.

CONCLUSION

In their insightful monograph, *Splintering Urbanism* (2001), Graham and Marvin explore 'the scale and breadth of the global shift towards affluent, secessional living spaces' in the condominium complexes and master-planned communities on 'the fringes of megacities' in Indonesia, Turkey, the Phillipines and post-apartheid South Africa. They highlight various potential risks they see in these developments: the potential risk of collapse of the overarching municipal tax system, the secession of middle income groups from the central city with its poor infrastructure, pollution, perceived danger, contact with the poor, and traditional, street system (Jakarta), or in regard to Manila, with its gated communities, new developments and privatized, customized infrastructure networks. They also point to the construction of 'secure and exclusive islands of Europe or North America within the peripheries of Manila' (Graham and Marvin 2001: 271).

I have also referred briefly to the views of Anita Soni and others on 'internal colonialism' in Delhi, about the way in which the urban rich are colonizing the rural fringe, turning farmers into unemployed and casual labour and, from an ecological view, despoiling community resources by depleting groundwater tables. 'The agenda of development pursued by the rulers of India . . . in the recent era of "liberalization" has preserved the colonial legacy of asymmetrical power relations between the dominant urban elite and the vast mass of the rural population' (Soni 2000: 78).

It would be naive to suggest that just to 'balance' or 'complete' my earlier reference to 'indigenous' and 'postcolonial modernities', what I describe here is some kind of 'global modernity': naive, because – despite Graham and Marvin's valuable insights – what I describe here is not found 'all over the globe'. While some larger structural features may be common to other locations, the social, geographical, urban, demographic, cultural and administrative conditions in which these developments are taking place are unique to the DLF site in Delhi. The 'external' networks which are affecting these revolutionary new changes in Delhi's outer urban landscape, whether spatial, linguistic, socio-economic or cultural, are not just connected with 'anywhere' – Austria, Russia, Peru – but are apparently the outcome of the distinctive postcolonial connections between India and the US. They are, again, conditions of an 'indigenous modernity' but one significantly impacted by the geography of these particular linguistic and cultural flows.

While all of these issues are relevant to the above discussion, my main focus here, however, has been rather different. In drawing attention to the different social and cultural worlds constructed both in language and in space, and not least, in the new anglophone models of daily living introduced from the US, my aim is to ask how these different concepts and categories, imaginary as well as material, these different language as well as architectural and spatial worlds, are affecting processes of identity, as well as subject formation, as well, of course, as consumption. What difference do they make to the creation of social relationships, not simply within the city and the community, but also across oceans, and with other societies and cultures worldwide? In the space of half a century in India, the social and cultural links created through anglophonic post-colonial networks, whether in higher education, culture or commerce, have moved through glacial changes. In India today, the names of Princeton, Michigan or Berkeley have much more social and educational resonance than Oxford, Cambridge or London. PriceWaterhouseCoopers rings more bells than Tate & Lyle. Citibank is more familiar than Barclays. How do these new forms of 'Indo-American' space, buildings and behaviour relate to new patterns of consumption? To new forms of identity that are not only multiple but also flexible? And most importantly of all, how are these new forms of language, space and environment being transformed and indigenized?

Though only hints have been made in this chapter regarding the market to whom these developments are directed – returning NRIs, their relatives, non-Indian executives and employees of multinational companies – it appears that the members of the burgeoning Indian middle class are, with the huge growth in the mortgage industry in Delhi, likely to be the principal market. This is the new habitus for the bourgeoisification of India (Chatterjee 2003). But as the new occupants on the fifteenth storey in DLF's Princeton Apartments look across to distant Shahjahanabad, thinking of their nephew, son or daughter in California's Silicon Valley, or look down on the jhuggies and their occupants below – the women who sweep the floors, clean the bathrooms and remove the dross of paper and plasticized consumption – these are questions to address.

NOTES

1 Since first using this quotation as an epigraph in my first book on Delhi (1976: 68) I find it has lost none of its cogency.
2 www.dlf-group.com
3 By anglophone, I refer here to the reader whose primary, and also exclusive reading and speaking language is English. Further discussion of this is taken up towards the end of the chapter.
4 For the following information I draw on the maps and texts in Saha (1995).
5 See also Bharat Savak Samaj Delhi Pradash 1958; Jagmohan 1975.
6 A specifically English *colonial* identity, that of the hybrid colonial third culture (King 1976: 43 *et seq.*) because, not existing in the British metropolis itself, it was a distinctive product of the political and cultural conditions of colonialism.
7 This is not to imply that 'Lutyens' Delhi' has not been appropriated by independent Delhi. As Narayani Gupta writes in her insightful and well-documented essay,

while 'Rajpath remains a British imperial vista, the Central Vista has been fully democratized with the amazing ability of middle class Indians to create playgrounds and restaurants where neither had previously existed. Ice-cream carts, food stalls, street vendors, ball clubs, patronized by the large number of employees from the many postcolonially constructed offices located along Rajpath use the space in a way very different from what Lutyens intended' (Gupta 1994: 263).

8   'At least six Union ministers are still waiting to move into bungalows allotted to them in the tree-lined boulevards of Lutyens' bungalow zone. Saying enough is enough, the minister drew up a comprehensive "hit list" of 317 violators, including 100 VIPs belonging to various parties against whom eviction proceedings have already begun . . . Finance Minister Yashwant Singh, who has been allotted a ministerial bungalow on 8 Krishna Menon Marg has to make do with a two room apartment at V. P. house.' See Sayanta Chakravarty *India Today (International)* June 29, 1998: 18.

9   DLF stands for Delhi Land and Finance, the name of the developers' company.

10 In the following, unless otherwise stated, all the terminology and other information come from the developers' newsletters.

11 Dupont suggests, alternatively, that the referent for some of the names used in Delhi's new 'chic' suburban developments are either US towns and districts (Malibu, Riverdale, Manhattan Apartmansions, Beverly Park, Sun City), English towns (Windsor, Richmond), and even Singapore (Sentosa City, a mini-Singapore in India). This would suggest that the advertising copywriters may be drawing on models in these places.

12 Graham and Marvin (2001: 279) refer to the new Harvard Avenue, Greenhills, Brittany in Manila, places patronized by Sklair's global capitalist elite (Sklair 2001).

13 Information here comes from the selling agents for the project and other informants in Delhi.

14 Delhi social researchers classify residential environments into 'posh locality flats' or 'bungalow in the south, north or central areas' (see King 1994) just as in the US 'kids from the projects' or in the UK 'housing estate children' are commonplace signifiers.

Chapter 10: Imperialism, Colonialism and Architects of the Arts and Crafts in Britain

Culture, empire and modernity are historically linked in an inextricable way.

C. J. W-L. Wee, *Culture, Empire and the Question of Being Modern* (2003: 12)

INTRODUCTION

In the previous chapters my focus has principally been on the present and recent past and, in this second section of the book, on exploring how processes of postcolonialism and globalization, or postcolonial globalization, can be identified in spatial and architectural terms. Recent historical studies using the globalization paradigm mentioned in Chapter 2 (Held *et al.*, 1999; Hopkins 2002) have done much to remedy the earlier ahistorical theorizations which dominated discussion of the topic in the 1990s. They have also foregrounded the importance of imperialism, or rather imperialisms, as perhaps the principal form which globalization took between the eighteenth and twentieth centuries (Hopkins 2002). While much of the earlier treatment of the subject has concentrated particularly on an economic interpretation of imperialism, the 'cultural turn' marked by the development of postcolonial studies has unearthed a vast and, in many cases, still unexplored agenda, particularly in relation to architecture and urban studies.

It is part of this agenda I address in this specifically historical chapter. As suggested in Chapter 6, the economic and cultural influences of 'imperial globalization' can be read in the suburbs of both colony and metropole in the late nineteenth and early twentieth centuries, just as they can be read in major metropolises today. In this chapter I want to explore, through the use of a more conventional architectural history, how architectural and urban developments in the colonies were influenced by ideologies and practices in the metropole, and also vice versa. I also draw on the ideas expressed in Chapter 6 and focus particularly on the micro-processes of globalization by looking at the question of *agency*, examining particular subjects, with real names, dealing with real objects in real places.

IMPERIALISM AND THE COLONIES

In J. A. Hobson's classic text, *Imperialism*, first published in 1902, and to become a powerful influence on all later significant treatments of the subject, including that by Lenin (Siegelman 1988: v), the author leaves little doubt regarding the circumstances which had prompted him to write it: the massive expansion in Britain's colonial empire in the later nineteenth century. As Hobson points out, while one third of the British Empire (with its 400–420 million people) had been acquired since 1870, the movement:

> did not attain its full impetus until the middle of the eighties . . . The vast increase of territory and the method of wholesale partition which assigned to us great tracts of African land, may be dated from about 1884. Within fifteen years some three and three quarter millions of square miles were added to the British Empire.
>
> (Hobson 1938: 18–19)

In the early 1880s, to mention only the principal territories, the 'old empire' of colonies, dependencies and protectorates in Asia included India (1612, etc.), the Straits Settlements (Penang, Malacca, Singapore 1785, etc.), Ceylon (1796), Aden (1838), Hong Kong (1843, etc.), North Borneo (1881); in southern and western Africa, Gambia (1664), Sierra Leone (1787), Cape Colony (1815), Natal (1856), Lagos and protectorate (1861), Basutoland (1868), Gold Coast and protectorate (1868); in the Americas, the eight island colonies of the West Indies acquired between 1609 and 1797, and in South America, British Guiana (1803) and the Falklands (1833); in North America, Newfoundland (1583) and Canada (1623, etc.); in Australasia, the various colonial states established between 1787 and 1859 and formed into the Commonwealth of Australia in 1901, and New Zealand (1841). Following the collapse of Egypt's financial system in 1880 and the Khedive's abolition of the joint English and French control of the economy in 1883, the British had also occupied the country and taken control of its finances, even though the formal 'Protectorate' was not established till 1914 (Gill c.1901; Porter 1977: 242).

In the second half of the 1880s and up to 1900 – the years to which Hobson drew his readers' attention – British (and in many cases, 'native') troops and colonial officials, acting on behalf of the government, were to establish a whole new series of colonies or protectorates, principally in Africa, though also in Asia. Among others, these included the Somali Coast (1884–5), British Bechuanaland (1885), Tembuland (1885), Niger Coast (1885–98), Nigeria (1886), Zanzibar (1888), British Central Africa (1889), British South Africa Charter (Rhodesia) (1889), Uganda (1894–6), East Africa (1895), Transvaal (1900) and Orange River Colony (1900). In Asia, colonies or protectorates were established in the Malay Protected States (1883–95), Upper Burma (1887), North Borneo, Sarawak, Brunei, British New Guinea (all in 1888), Sikkim (1890) and the Hong Kong territories (1898) (Hobson 1938: 17).

Already from the 1870s, this huge expansion of empire on the outside of the nation state had been accompanied by administrative and political changes within it, including the construction of new buildings and architectural developments in the capital. At the heart of the imperial city, impressive new buildings for the Foreign Office, Colonial Office and India Office – ornamented with suitable imperial devices – were established in Whitehall (Port 1995). A decade or more later, the long-delayed symbolic recognition of the Empire was begun with the commencement, in 1887, of the Imperial Institute of the United Kingdom, the Colonies and India, laid out in South Kensington. Its objectives were to 'exhibit the Empire's products and raw materials, to collect and disseminate information on trades, industries and emigration and to promote technical and commercial education in the interests of Empire and further systematic colonization' (Beidecke 1896). While the overarching aim was to strengthen British imperial unity, not least in regard to other competing industrial nations, the Institute's symbolic role in promoting the imperial idea, and in commemorating the Queen's Jubilee, was also paramount (Bremner 2003: 50).

In recent years, scholars in history, geography, literature and sociology, as well as architecture, have looked into the ways in which cities in the metropolitan society, and especially imperial capitals, were transformed, spatially, socially, demographically and architecturally, from the eighteenth to the twentieth centuries, as a result of their imperial connections (Driver and Gilbert 1999; King 1990b; Crinson 2003). How imperialism (and postimperialism) inscribes itself on the culture and space of the metropole have been tracked in a variety of different ways; in London, banks and institutions catering primarily to the needs of the imperial economy and its governance (Black 1999); hints of orientalist and 'exotic' architectural influences; public facilities (museums, libraries, parks) or private ones (city or country residences) built by colonial plutocrats; or from boosts to the economy coming from colonial trade.[1] My aim in providing the list of colonial territories and protectorates acquired in the later nineteenth century relates, in the first instance, to the argument I set out below – but it also provides an insight into the geographical origins of a large proportion of the ethnic minority population of contemporary London which, in 2001, represented one fifth of the whole (Merriman 1993). In this chapter, however, I want particularly to look at the relationship of imperialism to the architects and, partly, the architecture of the Arts and Crafts movement in Britain.

IMPERIALISM AND THE ARTS AND CRAFTS

The architects of the Arts and Crafts movement have a twofold significance in this context. First, this was a generation of architects and planners whose professional careers coincided with the expansion and also the zenith of the British Empire in the early twentieth century. Second, because the ideology and principles of the Arts and Crafts, particularly its commitment to exploring and developing the 'local' and vernacular in building and architecture, would today be seen as 'best practice' by most (if not all) commentators for architects working in cultures other than their own. These two questions I explore in more detail below.

The dates of the rise of the Arts and Crafts movement in Britain – the significant markers being the founding of the Art Workers Guild in 1884 and the Arts and Crafts Exhibition Society in 1888, from which the movement took its name – uncannily coincide with the second major expansion in Britain's imperial domains. How, if at all, were the architect members of the movement affected by these developments?

According to the standard accounts, the basic aim of the Arts and Crafts was to revive handicrafts and reform architecture by using traditional building crafts and local materials (Fleming *et al.* 1991). Service has described their principles as 'simplicity, strength, and harmony with existing buildings and surrounding nature' (Service 1977: 37). Opposed to the machine-made products of industrialization, Arts and Crafts architects aimed to free their work from prevailing historical styles. Instead, the 'past art' of the vernacular could be used as a basis to develop a new architecture that was 'essentially national in style, British rather than imported' (ibid.: 21), a theme confirmed by Richardson (1983: 7, drawing on Watkin 1980: ch. 4): 'With the Arts and Crafts movement, went a strong love for England and things English.'[2] As part of the development of a discursively constructed 'national culture' in England in the second half of the nineteenth century, the Arts and Crafts movement was to become particularly influential on the European continent and especially in North America (Ogata 2001; Fleming et al. 1991).

Yet 'national cultures' do not develop in a vacuum. Rather than being *independent* of other nations they are dependent on them, as also on the inter-state system which enables members of such cultures to see themselves as different from others. In the late nineteenth century, the principal European states, as well as other large states, were also at the heart of vast empires, competing to appropriate what remained of the surface, as well as the resources and markets, of the world. As Hall suggests, the formation of English culture took place at a time when the world market 'was dominated by the economies and cultures of (other) powerful nation states'. This domination 'constituted the era within which the formation of English culture took its existing shape. Imperialism was the system in which the world was engulfed [providing a] framework . . . of world rivalries between imperial formations' (S. Hall 1991a: 20).[3]

In the first part of this chapter, therefore, I explore the connections between the growth of imperialism and the works of a number of prominent British Arts and Crafts architects whose careers, with the exception of two, Herbert Baker and Edwin Lutyens (Gradidge 2002; Ridley 1998, 2002; Stamp 2002), have usually been treated within a local and national, rather than imperial and transnational context. As these larger political conditions provided the opportunities as well as constraints in which they practiced, and hence influenced the nature and success of their designs, my aim here is to open up, if only in preliminary terms, the ways in which material facts of empire affected their careers as well as their designs. As members of a movement which, in the metropole, had a distinct political edge, how far were different architects sufficiently in sympathy with imperial expansion and the issues of race, culture and politics it presented, to undertake commissions in its various territories? As practitioners committed to exploring the vernacular, how far did they adhere to these principles or abandon them in favor of more ideologized imperial agendas?[4]

These are not simply 'academic' or historical questions. Half a century after independence, many postcolonial states today still struggle with the spatial and symbolic residue of imperialism. In his overview of heritage conservation in different cities in Asia, the holder of the UNESCO Chair in Heritage and Urbanism in Melbourne's Deakin University, William Logan, writes of those postcolonial societies where 'as time passes, memories of the colonial period fade'. In other societies, such as South Korea, the colonial impact 'continues to be rejected because of the intense bitterness still felt towards the colonizers who, significantly, were fellow Asians rather than Europeans' (Logan 2002: 72).

Important in these debates is not simply the visual, symbolic dimension of colonial architecture and planning which, in 1998, became the subject of the 'Shared Colonial Heritage Committee' of the UN's International Committee on Monuments and Sites,[5] but also the socially and ethnically segregated space in which it often exists. For the advocates of historic preservation, this space may seem essential to maintain the authenticity of the original imperial design. Yet from a social and political perspective, the persistence of 'imperial space', whether as built form or spatial distance – privileging social or ethnic elites, dividing the powerful from the powerless, inhibiting the more equitable distribution of space and the financial resources to service it[6] can be a perpetual affront to the egalitarian, democratic aspirations of postcolonial nations. Can architecture and urban design produced with the intention of conveying the messages of a supralocal imperial power – or separating ruler from ruled – ever become an indigenized postcolonial national heritage? In this context, therefore, whether the 'original' colonial architectural and spatial forms were sympathetic to the local vernacular or simply reproduced the norms and forms of an arrogant imperial power becomes a critical issue.[7]

In the second part of the chapter, I take up an interconnected issue; how do different visual and architectural cultures, originating in the colony and transplanted through the imperial connection, transform the built environment and architectural culture of the metropole? As suggested above, the early impact of empire in London was represented in buildings, the architectural style of which, though new, was both culturally and historically familiar. With few exceptions, only in relatively recent times, in Britain or elsewhere in Europe or Australasia, has the architectural representation of relatively unfamiliar cultures made itself visible, for example, in the converted or purpose built mosques, gurdwaras, Hindu temples, the ethnic emporium or shopping mall, the creative hybridization of architectural styles, or through the remodeling of local vernacular housing (see Cairns 2003; Nasser 2003).

In this context, I make use of new research (Hitchmough 1995) to revisit one of the major instances of the impact of imperialism on the metropolitan landscape, an instance in which culturally new and architecturally unfamiliar forms were introduced; the insertion of both the idea as well as the form of the new building type of the bungalow into the landscapes of the West and the connection of this to the architecture of the Arts and Crafts (King 1984).

As detailed historical research is needed on some of the architectural works mentioned in this chapter, a task beyond the scope of this book, I should state that my aim here is to raise issues which others may find sufficiently interesting to pursue.

THE ARTS AND CRAFTS OF IMPERIALISM

Few of the British Arts and Crafts architects who, in the 1880s and 1890s, were committed to the cultivation of English vernacular design, of creating buildings with an organic relationship to their local surroundings, would have envisaged that, somewhat later in their professional careers, these principles would be compromised or even abandoned. Such was the case, however, with a cohort of Arts and Crafts architects who, born within some fifteen years of each other (1854–69), were largely contemporaries. These were architects whose professional careers were in some cases benefited, or in others challenged – intellectually, politically, professionally – by working in the conflicted spaces of the overseas Empire in the early twentieth century.

Not all the architects I mention here[8] undertook imperial commissions overseas. In some cases, the commissions were at home and included the design of larger as well as smaller country houses that proliferated in the twenty years on either side of the turn of the century (King 1990a: 155). Most projects, however, were overseas, either in the new colonial capitals – New Delhi, Pretoria, Lusaka – or in the design of individual buildings which, like cathedrals and churches, resulted from the combined presence and power of colonial governments, the military and missionary activities.

Probably the most well known was Edwin Lutyens (1869–1944), prolific country house architect in England, and imperial architect par excellence, as the designer of Government House, New Delhi and other major monuments in that city,[9] following the transfer of the capital from Calcutta in 1911. Lutyens was also largely responsible for the city layout.[10] Over fifty years after independence, both Lutyens and the city he designed with Herbert Baker remain highly controversial. Of Government House, architectural critic Kenneth Frampton (1985: 49) writes, in 'this brilliant Neo-Classical monument, Lutyens ruthlessly renounced his Arts and Crafts heritage'. Jane Ridley (1998), however, suggests that Lutyens's background 'as an Arts and Crafts architect, taught him how to absorb the vernacular, how to analyze and recreate it' (1998: 67); and while 'Government House was, in fact, profoundly indebted to Indian architecture' (2002: 181) these comments might be taken to refer more to its detailing than the massive classically columned building itself, which elsewhere she cites as 'a statement of imperial despotism' (1988: 67). As for the architect himself, 'Lutyens was consistently dismissive of Indian architecture and indeed of Indians – small wonder that many Indians today dismiss him as an Imperialist and racist' (Ridley 2002: 181).

As in other architectural accounts of the city (Irving 1981; Stamp 2002), little if any attention is paid to the persisting spatial inequities and divisions in the residential area and the experience of the present day Indian government, as well as public, in coping with them. It was, and remains, a residential area carefully zoned for different classes and marked, in Lutyens's original drawings, for 'rich whites', 'thin whites' and 'thin blacks' (Ridley 1998: 73). The continuing controversy concerning the future of the postcolonial 'imperial city' is well represented by calls, on one side, for its total redevelopment and, on the other, by Lutyens-promotional literature, published in the one time metropole.[11]

Equally renowned in the annals of imperial architecture is Herbert Baker (1862–1946), unswerving admirer of empire-builder, Cecil Rhodes. Baker, having left England, placed himself at the service of Rhodes, at the time, Prime Minister of the self-governing Cape Colony and, in Baker's view, 'perceiving of himself as following in the footsteps of Pericles and Hadrian'. To educate his imperial sensibilities, Rhodes sent Baker on a tour of the classical sites of the Mediterranean. He returned 'no longer simply a craftsman in the Morris tradition but the architect of a new imperialism' (Metcalf 1989: 184). Baker's move from 'the vernacular to Imperial Classicism' (Gradidge 2002: 148), evident in the Rhodes Memorial and the monumental Government buildings in the new South African capital in Pretoria (1910–12), were the prelude to his arrival in New Delhi to work with Lutyens on the new capital. Here, he reproduced a similar set of imperial Secretariat buildings, as well as Parliament House and other buildings. The original plan of using the buildings in the new capital as an opportunity for Indian artisans to display their traditional crafts was abandoned (Metcalf 1989: 235).

Baker 'also contributed substantially to the shaping of imperial London', completing India House in 1925 and South Africa House in 1930, 'classicism providing the language of spatial order in which the dream of empire can be written' (Black 1999: 99). With his imperial experience from three continents, Baker was seen as the appropriate choice in the 1920s to remodel the Bank of England so that, in his own words, it contained 'the elements of architectural dignity commensurate with the Bank's position and destiny in the City and the Empire' (Black 1999: 100).

S. D. Adshead (1868–1946), another of many Arts and Crafts designers who, like Baker and Lutyens, had learnt their skills in the influential office of Sir Ernest George (Richardson 1983: 59), was to become, with the official development of the town planning profession, the first Professor of Town Planning at Liverpool University (1909–14) and subsequently (1914–18) at University College London. In 1931, the Crown, having taken over the responsibility of government from the British South Africa Company in 1924, decided to build a new capital city at Lusaka, previously a small agricultural service center on the main railway line carrying lead, zinc and copper from Northern Rhodesia (now Zambia) to the sea, for transport to England. The plan that Adshead produced was for 'a colonial capital of the New Delhi type' where the 'imported values of the colonial power were translated into the physical form of the city' (Collins 1980: 227). On the assumption that towns were primarily for Europeans (housed in colonial bungalows) and that rural areas were for Africans, Adshead – and the local colonial officers – laid out Lusaka on Garden City lines, making little provision for Africans (ibid.: 228). At the end of King George's Avenue, the principal thoroughfare running through the new city center, was a square with a market hall for the sale of native products. 'At the back of the square, invisible from the Avenue lie the native compounds. This neighborhood is to be entirely African' (anon. 1935: 29–30). For the Government buildings, Adshead worked with a pupil of Sir Herbert Baker, J. A. Hoogterp, who faithfully followed his mentor's imperial style. Government House was in the 'Old Colonial Georgian' manner, the entrance fronted by a semi-circular colonnade of columns, two storeys in height, in 'the style of an English country house' (ibid.: 40).[12]

Southern Rhodesia, established and run by the private British South Africa Company (receiving a royal charter in 1889), when eventually taken over by the British Government, provided Detmar Blow (1867–1939), another prominent Arts and Crafts architect, with the opportunity of designing the new Government House at Salisbury (now Harare, Zimbabwe).

Another architect, H. V. Lanchester (1869–1953) who, like Adshead, was to be a founding member of the town planning profession in Britain, was 'an active British architect-planning consultant during the interwar period' (Home 1997: 143). An enthusiastic supporter of Patrick Geddes (1854–1932), Lanchester made 11 visits to India between 1915 and 1937, advising on town planning and urban design schemes in many cities as well as undertaking similar work in Colombo (Ceylon), and the 'new colonies' of Burma and Zanzibar. Like Geddes, Lanchester was sympathetic to careful 'restorative surgery' and conservation in overcrowded Indian cities. Yet while he apparently favored the typical courtyard plan of much Indian domestic architecture, with its shade and protection from the climate, he was also inclined to the new suburban areas being developed by the British, concluding in 1947 that 'taking everything into account

... bungalows are healthier dwellings. A good many Indians are beginning to live in them' (Tyrwhitt 1947: 20).

Other Arts and Crafts designers were more sympathetic to preserving the indigenous vernacular. Britain's League of Nations mandate over Palestine, acquired in 1918, was to last for 'thirty turbulent years' during which Britain 'sent a succession of six town planners in an attempt to manage the intercommunal tensions' (Home 1997: 152). Prominent Arts and Crafts designer C. R. Ashbee (1863–1942) was Civic Adviser to the City of Jerusalem from 1919 to 1922 and for a time, professional adviser to the Town Planning Commission. 'The most pro-Arab and anti-Zionist' (ibid.: 153) of the six planners, Ashbee held on to his craft principles, personally supervising conservation and repair work in the city, and reviving craft industry to repair the damaged Dome of the Rock (ibid.: 155). Drawing on the resources and attitudes of the Arts and Crafts movement, Ashbee's view of Jerusalem 'was colored by a romantic sense of the vernacular ... the essence of the Holy City lay in its secular and traditional fabric' (Crawford 1985: 179, 181). Deploring 'commercialism' and 'industrialization', Ashbee aimed to protect this fabric and the Palestinian vernacular. In the words of Fuchs and Herbert, 'Medieval-looking Jerusalem was, for Ashbee, a heaven-sent opportunity to revive his notion of an Arts and Crafts utopia' (2001: 83, 89; see also Crawford 1985: 171–93).

Rather less is known of the architectural work of other Arts and Crafts designers, and space does not allow for much more than a brief mention. Churches and cathedrals were to be a major cultural export from Britain during these years. In the new colonies of east and west Africa, taken over from the late 1880s, the alliance between government, commerce and Anglican missionaries were to give a contemporary of (rather than a sympathizer with) Arts and Crafts architects, Leonard Martin (1869–1935), of the architectural partnership Treadwell and Martin (known primarily as designers of office buildings and public houses), the chance to design and build the Anglican Cathedral at Onitsha in Nigeria. Similar institutional connections provided A. Beresford Pite (1861–1934), an early member of the Art Workers Guild and prominent church architect in England, with the opportunity to design Namirembe Anglican Cathedral in Kampala, Uganda (1913–18). Following the British occupation of Egypt in 1883, the violent death of General Gordon at Khartoum and the subsequent defeat of the Mahdi revolt at Omdurman (1898), the British military commander, General Kitchener, had declared an Anglo-Egyptian 'condominium' over the Sudan. He laid out a new city at Khartoum 'on a pattern of Union Jacks in a symbolic statement of British dominance' (Home 1997: 41). Subsequently, Robert W. Schultz (1861–1951), 'a notable Arts and Crafts architect' (Service 1977), was to produce the design of All Saints Cathedral in that city.

Britain's control over the finances, and effectively, the government of Egypt from 1883 provides a partial clue towards solving what Durant, in his study of prominent Arts and Crafts designer, C. F. A. Voysey (1857–1941), states is 'a mystery as to how Voysey acquired th(e) unusual commission' of designing a house in Aswan for a British client in 1905 (Durant 1992: 87). Another clue might be found in the British firm contracted by the Government to construct the Aswan Dam between 1898 and 1902 (Joffe 1951: 154).

Apart from the Falkland Islands (1803), the principal colony in South America was British Guyana, taken from the Dutch and French in 1803 and assigned to the British by the Treaty of Paris in 1814 (Gill c.1901: 335). Here, a powerful missionary presence among a population of somewhat less than 300,000 at the end of the nineteenth century, including the descendants of African slaves, the indentured Indian 'coolies', as well as the small European presence including some 10,000 Portuguese (ibid.), had led to a sufficiently large Anglican population to merit the building of a cathedral in the capital of Georgetown. This was to be designed and built between 1914 and 1925 by Leonard Stokes (1858–1925), a prolific church and religious buildings architect, sympathetic to Arts and Crafts ideas (Service 1977).

Apart from the significance of such colonial ecclesiastical projects in contributing to the economic stability of various architectural firms, what can be said about their political and cultural significance? From the earliest times, religions, along with war, trade and migratory movements, have been one of the most powerful agents of cultural globalization. World religions such as Islam, Christianity, Hinduism and Buddhism, established partly through the visibility and materiality of their buildings, have, along with language and education, extended cultural as well as imperial links around the world (Held *et al.* 1999: 415–17). Cathedrals and their clerics have functioned, among other things, as part of the system of cultural and ideological control, of management of the population. At a symbolic level, cathedrals were major instruments in the establishment of a new social and religious order, a new hierarchy, a new disciplinary regime. The significance of when, and where, they were built, the architectural style they were given, its reference to what prevailed in the metropole or in the locality, have been critical in the complex process of establishing religious as well as cultural identities, whether for converts to the faith as well as those who remained outside it. In these contexts, a building which speaks in the local vernacular or one that bellows in high Gothic is of more than superficial importance.

The normal colonial logic behind railway construction was to move mineral or agricultural products from the interior to ports on the coast which, in turn, brought manufactured goods from the metropole. In India, it was linked to the system of colonial control, moving troops between centers of population as well as to and from the capital (Bose and Jalal 1998). In Calcutta, the design of the major railway station at Howra provided another 'leading figure in Arts and Crafts architecture' (Service 1977), Halsey Ricardo (1854–1928), with the opportunity to deploy his professional talents. In the Argentine, in what, controversially, were the 'informal colonies' of Latin America (Cain and Hopkins 2001: 243–44), the railways were largely capitalized and laid out by the British, providing Arnold B. Mitchell (1863–1944), a regular Arts and Crafts contributor to *The Studio*, among other architects, the opportunity to design and build three large railway stations, including the main Plaza Constitution station in Buenos Aires (Service 1977).

IMPERIAL BUILDING IN THE METROPOLE

There were also design projects to be undertaken at home, dependent, economically and politically, on imperial expansion abroad. In 1914–16, the huge offices of the Crown Agents for the Colonies on London's Millbank, were designed and built under the direction of architect John W. Simpson (1858–1933), in this case, a contemporary rather than a sympathizer with Arts and Crafts ideas. Of more significance in the annals of Arts and Crafts design was the Horniman

Free Museum in southeast London's Forest Hill, built between 1896 and 1906 to the designs of C. Harrison Townsend (1851–1928), 'the most successful of the English Free Style architects of larger buildings' (Service 1977). The museum housed the collection of curios and 'native' artefacts assembled by the globe-trotting collector, F. J. Horniman, scion of the wealthy tea-importing firm of H. J. Horniman whose extensive plantations in India and Ceylon had helped finance both the collection as well as the gift to the London public.

At its opening, *The Studio*, since its founding in 1893 an enthusiastic supporter of Arts and Crafts ideas, comparing the 'simple dignity of its strength' to the 'angular pretensions of the Natural History Museum', made a bold (and possibly unique) bid to appropriate Arts and Crafts design as a new imperial house-style for the capital. It found the Horniman's new Arts and Crafts style 'more in keeping with the immensity of London, the Empire-City' (*The Studio* 1902, vol. xxiv: 198). A large country house built at Frensham, Surrey ('Lowicks'), and designed by C. F. A. Voysey, was also for the Horniman family, presumably financed from the same source.

J. A. Hobson (1858–1940), an exact contemporary of all of the archi-tects discussed above, was 'a prodigious journalist and essayist for numerous English Liberal newspapers and periodicals, including *The Manchester Guardian*, *Progressive Review*, *Westminster Review* and the *Nation* . . . a teacher, university lecturer and participant in socialist, liberal, egalitarian, and ethical causes' (Siegelman 1988: v–vi). As such, his comments on the iniquities of imperialism, published in the same year as the opening of the Horniman Museum, provoke some serious questions. How far were his views shared by – amongst others – the more politically conscious Arts and Crafts architects? And if they were, how have they been dealt with in the pages of architectural history? To provide a context in which to address this question, Hobson's comments, cited only briefly in my original airing of this issue (King 1984: 262) are quoted here at greater length.

In a chapter on 'The Political Significance of Imperialism', Hobson wrote in searing terms about the character and habits of the colonially-returned. He states 'our despotically ruled dependencies' (as opposed to the 'free self-governing colonies' such as Australia and Canada):

> have served to damage the character of our people by feeding the habits of snobbish subservience, the admiration of wealth and rank. . . . This process began with the advent of the East Indian nabob and the West Indian planter into English society and politics, bringing back with his plunders of the slave trade and the gains of corruption and extortionate officialism the acts of vulgar ostentation, domineering demeanor and corrupting largesse to dazzle and degrade the life of our people . . .
>
> As the despotic portion of our Empire has grown in area, a larger and larger number of men, trained in the temper and methods of autocracy as soldiers and civil officials in our Crown colonies, protectorates and Indian Empire, reinforced by numbers of merchants, planters, engineers, and overseers, whose lives have been those of a superior caste living an artificial life removed from all the healthy restraints of ordinary European society, have returned to this country, bringing back the characteristics, sentiments, and ideas imposed by this foreign environment. The South and South West of England is richly sprinkled with these men, many of them wealthy, most of them endowed with leisure, men openly contemptuous of democracy, devoted to material

luxury, social display, and the shallower arts of intellectual life . . . Could the incomes expended in the Home Counties and other large districts of Southern Britain be traced to their sources, it would be found that they were in large measure wrung from the enforced toil of vast multitudes of black, brown, or yellow natives.

(Hobson 1938: 150–51)

Just how many of the myriad of country houses designed and built in 'the South and West' of England in the late nineteenth and early twentieth centuries were commissioned by clients who would fit Hobson's description is an important subject for research.

HIDDEN HISTORIES OF THE BUNGALOW

In earlier chapters I have discussed instances of suburban development, both historical and contemporary, in the US, China, India and elsewhere, as examples of contemporary modernities, each of them inextricably linked to transnational processes, including colonial, postcolonial and neo-colonial forces. Transnational influences are predominantly located in major metropolises, particularly capitals, even though the sites of economic and cultural flows (Castells 1996), as an outcome of individual agency, may occur on the periphery of such cities. This is also the case with the introduction of another, though earlier, transnational and eventually suburban innovation, namely, the idea as well as the form of the bungalow from India to the West, a development that occurred in the same thirty year period that Hobson saw as the height of imperial expansion (1870–1900).

The introduction of the bungalow at this time and its subsequent development in the twentieth century is probably the single, most geographically widespread illustration of the influence of imperialism – or the imperial phase of globalization – on the suburban as well as rural landscape of Britain. While the conditions of its introduction have been discussed elsewhere (King 1984), there are worthwhile reasons for revisiting this history, not least because the movement of the idea – unlike most of the cases discussed earlier – was from East to West rather than in the opposite direction.

Moreover, examining in detail the processes by which the idea, image and form of the building was introduced into England, under whose agency and at which historical conjunctures, provides us with an unusual opportunity to gain insights into the taken-for-granted processes in which cultural globalization occurs (Held *et al.* 1999: 327). And with its historically changing form worldwide, it also provides an excellent architectural illustration of processes of cultural hybridization (Pieterse 2004), translation (Bhabha 1994) and indigenization (Appadurai 1996) which I have discussed in Chapter 2. Any particular instance of what has increasingly been termed 'global culture' – whether the Trinidadian carnival (Nurse 1999) or spiritual beliefs and practices adopted from Eastern religions (Campbell 1999) – is invariably invested with new, and often controversial social meanings. So it was with the half-understood, partly familiar concept of the 'bungalow' as the idea moved, via various media and imaginations, from India to the West.

While terminologically, locationally, functionally, as well as structurally distinct (criteria which, in the early years of its introduction, were used to define

Figure 10.1

Figure 10.2

the term),[13] the first buildings to carry the name in Britain appeared on the north Kent coast, some two hours' train journey from London, at the end of the 1860s and early 1870s. Other than the name and single-storey form, however, these early models had more features in common with existing vernacular buildings and bore little resemblance to the descriptions and images of their Anglo-Indian referents circulating in Britain in these and previous decades (Figures 10.1, 10.2).

The inspired adoption, not only of the term but also the visual imagery of the Anglo-Indian bungalow and its architecturally defining elements – single, or predominantly single storey, often large hipped roof, small or larger verandah – by the architectural profession was to occur from the mid to later 1880s. While the development is usually associated with Arts and Crafts architect, Robert A. Briggs (1858–1916), the architectural idea of the bungalow was also, as I shall argue here, to be particularly significant in the work of his immediate contemporary, C. F. A. Voysey (1857–1941). In quite different ways, one directly and the other indirectly, these two architects were to play significant roles in translating and adapting both the bungalow idea, as well as some of its formal features, in Britain.

As discussed elsewhere, for Briggs, the main theorist of this early, experimental phase of the idea, Indian imagery and the consciousness of empire and colonies was to be a major source of his ideas (see King 1984, 1997). These images of what he described as 'low, squat, rambling, one-storied houses, with wide verandahs' were not, however, in Briggs' view, ' the kind of Bungalow suitable for our climate, neither is it necessary that it should be a one-storied building'. In his own designs, Briggs made a distinction between a 'Bungalow' (Figure 10.3), generally of one storey though also – for reasons of economy – sometimes with bedrooms in the roof space, and a 'Bungalow-House', the latter with more extensive accommodation under a Mansard roof, balconies, occasionally verandahs, and an informal architectural style (Figure 10.4). As a leading architectural journal was to comment at the time:

> No doubt any one is free to call his house a bungalow if it pleases him but the word . . . was, we believe, originally applied by Europeans living in India to the typical wide-spaced, and low-verandahed house all on one floor . . . and we think it might as well be kept to its original meaning. A house may, however, conform to the bungalow type architecturally without being literally of one story.
>
> (*The Builder* 1891: 33)

With other architects, Briggs had been instrumental in the development of a countryside retreat in Surrey, some thirty miles by train from London, called Bellagio (after the lake-side haven in Italy), not far from East Grinstead, and established by 1887.[14] By 1891, some forty 'bungalow residences' were 'dotted about the copse-clad slopes'.

C. F. A. VOYSEY AND THE ARTS AND CRAFTS BUNGALOW

So far in this chapter, and also in earlier work (King 1980, 1984), I have adopted a broadly structuralist perspective, arguing that 'larger' social and also global conditions have been influential, if not determinant, in the activities and lives of individual architectural subjects.[15] Without abandoning this perspective, I want

Figure 10.3
Design for a 'Bungalow', UK
(R. A. Briggs 1891)

now to give more attention to the question of agency, looking at the ways individual architectural subjects influence, and are influenced by, the work of their peers as well as other sources. In this, I also adopt a formalistic analysis, a method common to much work in architectural history not least because this allows me to show how processes of hybridization occur in practices of architectural design.

According to Hitchmough (1995: 7), at the turn of the nineteenth century (1900) C. F. A. Voysey (1857–1940) was 'the most influential designer in Britain, with a reputation that spread across Europe and as far afield as the United States of America' (see also Ogata 2001). He was 'a vital link between the Arts and

Figure 10.4
Design for a 'Bungalow-House',
UK (R. A. Briggs 1897)

Crafts and Modern Movements' in architecture, an architect, the extent of whose influence 'is conspicuous today in Britain's suburbs' (ibid.: 217).

Among Arts and Crafts architects, Voysey was probably far more familiar than others not only with the architectural idea of the bungalow as first introduced in England, but also with the first experimental phase of its development. After school, he had for five years first been articled (from 1874) and then spent an additional year with the firm of J. P. Seddon, the architect of the second phase of bungalow developments on the Kent coast between 1881 and 1882.[16] Voysey had also worked for some time in the office of an architect specializing in the 'design of substantial country houses for the aristocracy and wealthy landed gentry', when 'trips into the depths of Surrey, Sussex and Kent were common practice with young Arts and Crafts architects' (Hitchmough 1995: 22). With these connections, it seems likely that, in the mid to late 1880s, he was well acquainted with the experimental bungalow architecture being developed at Bellagio.

In 1889 or possibly earlier (Kornwolf 1972: 54–56; Hitchmough 1995: 225 note 8), Voysey was commissioned to produce a design for a house on the Bellagio estate, one subsequently published in the *British Architect* (June 10, 1898) captioned 'A design for a Bungalow at Bellagio' (Figure 10.5). Voysey's design is evidently based on the main defining features of what, in the mid to late 1880s, was understood as the image of an 'Anglo-Indian' bungalow, namely, a dwelling predominantly of one storey, probably with a verandah, and with an all-encompassing roof allowing for bedrooms in the roof space. As with other Voysey designs for artists' country houses, the ground floor studio necessitated additional light which, in this case, was provided by the large Jacobean bay at the corner. In terms of the flexible meaning attached to the still very new, architecturally experimental concept of the bungalow at this time, the 'two and a half storey Shavian gable' (Kornwolf 1972: 56) would be easily accommodated within the meaning of the term.

Two or three motivations for this design are possible: other bungalow developments in Bellagio at this time; the client, a Mr W. Allport, who commissioned it for the estate; or possible contacts with his contemporary, architect Robert Briggs.[17] Whatever the source, the bungalow idea represented by this drawing seems to have had a noticeable impact on his design thinking. The question of the terms Voysey used to describe his house designs I address below.

Prior to 1889 (or possibly earlier), of Voysey's few known designs, none are of single-storey (or, like the bungalow design), of predominantly single-storey buildings. Quite apart from other innovative aspects, all are of two or more storeys and with conventional hipped or side-gabled roofs. The exception is the design for an Artist's House where, perhaps a year earlier, and again, possibly motivated by the bungalow idea, he had experimented with a large, low-slung roof sweeping over the ground floor to cover a small verandah in a house with an asymmetrical elevation (Figure 10.6). Perhaps prompted by Briggs' notion of the bungalow as a two-storeyed house with bedrooms in the roof space, Voysey was to develop this idea of a house with walls of predominantly one storey in a number of his projects. His 1896 design for another 'studio-house', Hill Close, at Swanage, Dorset, was, by the 'style criteria' of the time, clearly a bungalow: a massive hipped roof incorporating the few upper storey rooms and lit by characteristic small dormers, swept down to the top of the ground floor windows

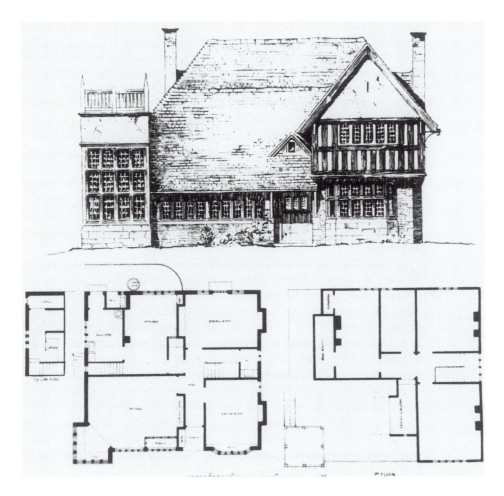

Figure 10.5
'Design for a Bungalow
at Bellagio', C. F. A. Voysey
1888

(Figure 10.7). Although Voysey chose function or 'use' criteria to call this a 'studio-house', as can be seen from the captioned illustrations here (Figures 10.8, 10.10, 10.11), others were using the term 'bungalow' to describe this style during these years. As discussed below, there may well be genuine reasons why Voysey eschewed the term.

The sweeping hipped roof, running down to the height of the first floor walls and giving at least one facade of the house design the appearance of a single storey, was to become a major feature of Voysey's personal style – most markedly seen in the rear elevation of the 1898 design of one of his most publicized houses, Moorcrag, on the edge of Lake Windermere, and incorporating a verandah – a feature (and word) long associated with the Indian bungalow (Figure 10.9). Not only did this have a profoundly 'bungalow look' but when fellow Arts and Crafts designer, G. H. Brewerton 'borrowed' the design some time later, both he, as well as the owner, clearly assumed that this was a bungalow and named it as such (Figure 10.8).

Brewerton's design confirms the view of Service, that the influence of Voysey 'can be seen in the work of countless other architects' (1977: 28), not least in 'the roof which swept up from near the ground'. According to

Figure 10.6
'Design for an Artist's House',
C. F. A. Voysey c. 1889

Figure 10.7
'A House at Swanage',
C. F. A. Voysey 1898

DR. EMERSON'S BUNGALOW AT SOUTHBOURNE
Designed by G. H. Brewerton.   From the south-west (Page 149)

Figure 10.8

Figure 10.9

Richardson, Voysey had impressed Edwin Lutyens with what he (Lutyens) termed 'the long sloping, slate clad roofs, the white walls clear and clean' (1983: 104). Part of Voysey's philosophy, in his own words, was 'to collect the rooms in such sequence that will enable you to cover them with one roof' (ibid.: 105). This key feature of the Anglo-Indian bungalow was in the design for a bungalow produced for his Bellagio client and, though never executed, it was the first occasion when Voysey had used this. The innovative practice of putting bedrooms in the roof space, as Briggs had argued, was an economizing measure that also appealed to Voysey. Were these, some of the most characteristic design features of probably the best known Arts and Crafts designer and 'Modern Movement' pioneer, C. F. A. Voysey, and one with the greatest influence on popular suburban architecture, imperial, Indian bungalow-inspired ideas?

CULTURE AND IMPERIALISM

I began this chapter by arguing that the Arts and Crafts movement in Britain, often represented as a phenomenon of national culture, developed at a time when the world was embedded in a system of imperialism, and cannot be understood apart from this. Edward Said has discussed at length the construction of what he calls an imperial culture in the metropole, especially in relation to the novel. It is, he suggests, at the end of the nineteenth century when 'scarcely a corner of life was untouched by the facts of empire' when 'British rule in the Indian subcontinent (was) at its height (that) empire was a universal concern' (1993: 7, 76), a time when 'all cultures are involved in one another; none is single and pure, all are hybrid, heterogenous, extraordinarily differentiated, and unmonolithic' (1993: xxix).

The year when Voysey was working on his bungalow design, a three-act comedy, titled simply *The Bungalow*, opened on October 7, 1889 in a West End theater, off the Strand. The play, a combination of farce and satire, involved an artist, Frederick Leighton-Buzzard (a hardly veiled reference to eminent Victorian painter, Sir Frederick Leighton, soon President of the Royal Academy), the artist's model, his friends, future in-laws and a 'Hindoo' housekeeper. The play revolves around the ambiguous, Bohemian, and occasionally sexually suggestive social spaces connoted by the play's title (King 1997). It was to run, uninterruptedly, for three hundred performances. The *double-entendres* suggested by the word at this time may well have made some architects shy of using it.[18]

Between 1891 and 1898, the *Building News* held three design competitions: for a countryside, hillside and riverside bungalow, sufficient evidence of both the novelty and experimental design potential of the idea as well as the economic and social conditions that were behind it. The winning designs, most

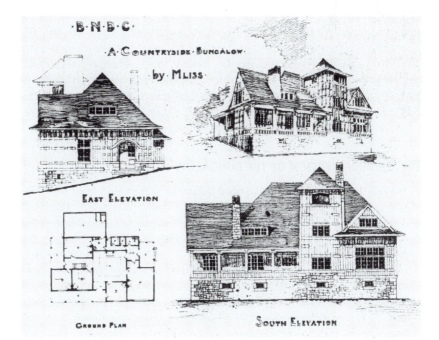

Figure 10.10

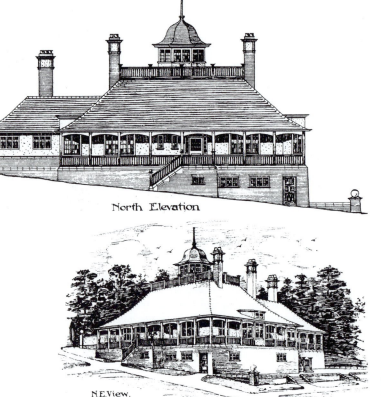

North Elevation

N.E.View.

April/98.

Figure 10.11
'A Hill-side Bungalow . . .
for a Gentleman', 1898

showing strong Arts and Crafts stylistic characteristics, all suggest not only the essentially recreational and leisure functions of the bungalow, with time consuming spaces represented in the billiard room, encircling verandahs, belvedere towers and accommodation for golf irons and bicycles, but also, in their size and accommodation for servants and guests, Briggs' notion of the bungalow as 'a little country house' (Figures 10.10, 10.11). Most were for occasional weekend or summer use, as Briggs had suggested (Briggs 1894).

THE SUBURBANIZATION OF THE BUNGALOW

By the late 1890s, the architect-designed bungalow was moving from the countryside to the new spacious suburbs of cities and towns. In the 1897 edition of his well known book *Bungalows and Country Residences*, Briggs refers to the desire not only for artistic but also for 'appropriate dwellings . . . among the larger number of persons of moderate income . . . hitherto content to reside in the *ordinary suburban villa* of a stereotype pattern' (emphasis added). His interpretation of the bungalow idea for one built in Surrey in 1897 includes dining and drawing rooms and three bedrooms and bathroom all on the ground floor (Figure 10.12). In the commuter belt of southeast London, architect A. Jessop Hardwick, more faithfully adapting and indigenizing the Anglo-Indian idea, lent

Figure 10.12
Bungalow design for the
suburbs, 'lately built in Sussex'
(R. A. Briggs 1897)

a neo-vernacular, half-timbered touch to a design for a client at Tunbridge Wells
(Figure 10.13).

By the turn of the century, Briggs' influence and the popularity of the
bungalow idea had spread beyond the Home Counties. In the new, prosperous,
merchant and professional suburb of Roundhay in Leeds, 'The Bungalow'
appeared in 1900 (Figure 10.14), its features closely following Briggs' prescrip-
tion for an 'artistic little dwelling with verandahs, oriels and bay windows'. On
the ground floor, three bedrooms, bathroom and dining and sitting room, with
four further bedrooms and bathroom in the roof space and a billiard or smoking
room in the gable.

Figure 10.13
'Proposed bungalow at
Tunbridge Wells, Kent.
Architect A. Jessop Hardwick'
(*Builders' Journal* 1903)

Figure 10.14
The Bungalow, Oakwood,
Roundhay, Leeds (built 1900)

Like other Arts and Crafts designs of this period (Kornwolf 1972: 57, 103), the symmetrical facade is balanced between the long slope of the roof line on the left of the elevation and the M-shaped gable on the right.[19] As is evident from all the discourse spelling out the variety of alternative lifestyles and social meanings invested in the bungalow at this time (King 1984) the symbolic dimensions of its architecture were meant to signify everything that the new, neo-classical Edwardian city architecture was not; to be informal rather than formal; vernacular (despite its origin) rather than classical; artistic, free and easy, rather than rigid, grandiose and uptight. As the space under the vast roof melted away to flow down and settle around the ground floor, the lines of the bungalow spread out horizontally at the base, like a huge A, closing in at the top, all in striking contrast to the right-angled, H-like verticality which had governed urban classicism from the Renaissance. These were all characteristics associated with English Arts and Crafts architecture – but in this case, inspired through the cultural channels of imperialism from Anglo-India and embodied in the indigenized bungalow.

Though the flattened 'pyramidal' nature of the lines may well have helped the form of these buildings adopt a particular Arts and Crafts characteristic, clinging closer to the landscape, the horizontality of the bungalow was also a response to the 'servant problem' and the need to cut down on unnecessary labor.[20] Other regional Arts and Crafts versions of the bungalow, both for permanent as well as weekend use, and literally embodying the time and space-consuming function associated with the term, frequented the pages of the twentieth century architectural press (King 1984: 121).

CONCLUSION

What I have aimed to show in this chapter is how the architecture of the Arts and Crafts movement, long associated with the development of a national culture in England, and in Voysey's case, with the origins of 'modernism' in architecture, is inextricably connected to the history of imperialism, both in the professional practices of its members in the colonies and in the development of its architecture 'at home'. Just as 'culture, empire and modernity are historically linked in an inextricable way' in the realm of literature (Wee 2003), this is equally the case in the realm of architecture. In pursuing this formalistic analysis, my aim has been to expose the connection between what is usually represented as a culturally 'autonomous', neo-vernacular design tradition and the imperatives of imperialism, a 'national' discourse which is only made possible by transnational and imperial contexts.

In the years when architects were preparing their entries for the various weekend, hillside and riverside bungalow competitions – creating, for their owners, a *second* or additional dwelling – used when bourgeois city lifestyles had filled up the first with a surfeit of goods – J. A. Hobson was reading as well as writing about India, the place from which the name, as well as the indigenous form had originated:

> There are some who maintain that the British government is draining the economic life-blood of India and dragging her population in lower and more hopeless poverty. They point to the fact that one of the poorest countries in the world is made to bear the cost of a government which . . . is very expensive; that one third of the money raised by taxation flows out of the country without return.
>
> (Hobson 1938: 288–9)

The erasure, or suppression, of the bungalow from the history of Arts and Crafts architecture has not only erased some of the movement's most prominent architects from the development of what, in retrospect, has become one of the most socially significant housing innovations in both Britain and North America, if not wider afield,[21] it has also constructed a history of 'national culture' haunted by the specter of its imperial connections. And as the figures here illustrate, it has also deprived us of insights into a process of architectural hybridization that is in a state of continuous change.

NOTES

1 An obvious example here is Castle Drogo, Devon, designed by Edwin Lutyens and built, 1910–30, for the Co-Founder and Chairman of the Home and Colonial Stores. See also King 1990b: 155.

2 In both these quotations, the supralocal assumption that the local, as well as the regional, is 'essentially national' might be noted.

3 Hopkins (2002: 25) points out how, in Britain 'a developing sense of nationality was spurred on both by conflict with the great continental Other – France – and by the extension of international and imperial ties'.

   Hobson lists the principal empires at the time according to the number of colonies: i.e. UK 50, France 33, Germany 13, Portugal 9, Netherlands 3, Spain 3, Italy 2, Austria-Hungary 2, Denmark 3, Russia 3, Turkey 5, China 5, US 6. The complete table also includes population and area figures (1938: 23).

4 Though the emphasis is on the national and supranational rather than the local or regional, some of the alternative intellectual, political-economic and cultural spaces available for such architects to occupy are well represented in a phrase which one imperial architect (Herbert Baker) wrote to another (Edwin Lutyens) concerning the proposed design for New Delhi: 'Delhi must not be Indian, nor English, nor Roman, but it must be Imperial' (cited in Metcalf 1989: 222).

5   See www.international.icomos.org/risk/2001/colonial2001.htm/
6   See Chapter 9. For example, Patwant Singh (2002) provides a sophisticated assessment of Lutyens' design for New Delhi but one positioned from an aesthetic rather than a social or political perspective. I am grateful to Professor Narayani Gupta for sending me this article.
7   As, for example, through the work of ICS officer, F. S. Growse, the vernacular-styled market buildings in Bulandshar, India, in the early 1880s. For this and other interesting insights into Arts and Crafts architecture in India, see Metcalf 1989, Chapter 5.
8   The names and dates of the architects that follow are taken from Service (1977).
9   Including India Gate and the princely houses of Hyderabad and Baroda. See Hopkins and Stamp (2002: 233–4) for a complete listing.
10 According to Service (1977: 204) 'the most famous British architect of the first half of the twentieth century, his achievements were of outstanding quality from the Arts and Crafts Free Style of his domestic work before 1903 to the originality of his later Classicism'.
11 Calls for redevelopment were expressed at the 'City One: South Asian Conference on the Urban Experience', Delhi, January, 2003; for its conservation, see the essays in Hopkins and Stamp, *Lutyens Abroad* (2002) with their nostalgic early 1930s photographs, voided of virtually any human being (irrespective of the 14 million Indian inhabitants of the city today). The hundred item bibliography consciously excludes any book or article on the city or its architecture by an Indian author. For discussion of alternative development strategies for the 'Lutyens Bungalow Zone' and the recommendations of the 1998 Ministry of Urban Development to consider these, see the special issue ('Delhi Debate') of *Architecture + Design*, xvi: 6 (November–December 1999), especially articles by M. N. Ashish Ganju, Ranjana Mital, Supendu Biswas, Anupam Kashyap.
12 'Government House is essentially something more than the residence of a Governor . . . It is not only a house but, as the residence of the King's representative, a national treasure, the evidence that a Colony gives to the world of that state of civilization which it has achieved' (anon. 1935: 44). The African population were accommodated in compounds on the 'traditional plan of the African village with circular huts, in effect, 'an improved type of African village'. 'It is hoped that the inhabitants, and particularly the women, will take away with them to their homes a determination to build a better and brighter Africa' (ibid.: 45, author is K. Bradley). For a more recent and detailed account of colonial Lusaka, see Myers (2003).
13 The following definitions were published between 1878 and 1906. 1878: While in India, the term was used 'for a country house of one floor only, in this country, the term is similarly applied to single dwellings on one floor, the general characteristics of them being a square plan with the entrance at the side or in the center a high-pitched pyramidal roof with sometimes the chimney made the central feature' (*Building News* 1878: 685). To date, no graphic evidence of this particular definition (in England) has come to light prior to the early twentieth century. 1891: 'a house for a special locality' (*The Architect* 1891: 215). 1906: 'distinguished from ordinary houses by being generally of one storey only and covered with a roof of one span from front to back' (*Building News* 1906: 904). Prior to the later 1880s, these definitional descriptions, together with drawings of the bungalows built at Birchington, in all probability account for the similar conceptualization of the term which circulated in the US after 1880 and account for the form, location and image of the two known examples of images of 'bungalows' published in 1880 and 1884. See King 1984, ch. 4 and Lancaster 1985, ch. 1.
14 The closest railway station of what is today Dorman's Park opened in 1884. Briggs had already published a design for a thatched roof bungalow at Bellagio in *Academy Architecture*, 1889 (see Kornwolf 1972) two years before his book appeared. The reference to 'bungalow residences' is evidence of the flexible use of the term at this date.
15 I refer here to the issue in social theory commonly referred to as the structure/agency problem. 'The debate revolves round the problem of how structures determine what individuals do, how structures are created and what are the limits, in other words, on human agency, on which there are varying views.' For a discussion of various perspectives on this issue see Abercrombie *et al.* (1988).

Figure 10.15

16 For early influences on Voysey's work, including his time in Seddon's office, see Hitchmough 1995: 18.

17 Hitchmough (1995: 54, note 119) states that the design, although never built, was for a W. Allport in 1889. Voysey's client was possibly from the Allport family, running the Wire Wove Company with their newly developed construction technology for inexpensive bungalows advertised in 1905. See 'Home Counties' (1905: 140). Voysey was also to produce a design for a 'lodge for a Manchester suburb' uncannily similar, in form and roof pitch, to one of Briggs' bungalow designs (Figure 10.15).

18 See King 1997. Abidin Kusno informs me that in Jakarta, the term 'villa' can have similar connotations. To say the Regional Governor 'has a villa' is a metaphor for other liaisons. As I have written elsewhere (1984: vii; 1997: 57), the social taboos associated with the term bungalow in England among some architectural historians may stem from the disrepute which the word (and the phenomenon it describes) gained in some upper and middle class circles in the inter war years in Britain as well, possibly, as its social class associations. This has had interesting intellectual effects, not least on the topic discussed here. Despite the increasingly prominent status accorded to C. F. A. Voysey in architectural history in Britain in recent years and the growing number of monographs or more general studies discussing his work (e.g. Durant, Hitchmough, Simpson, Davey, etc.), to date, the 1889 design for the bungalow has been carefully excluded from any British-authored book. With one exception (Hitchmough 1995) it has not been mentioned or listed in Voysey's works. The only text in which it appears is that by the American architectural historian, James D. Kornwolf (1972). In the US, where the bungalow is closely connected with the Arts and Crafts movement, the term has only positive connotations (see Cumming and Kaplan 1991).

19 That the house on the left was named 'The Bungalow' when built, and on the right, 'The Gables' provides some additional confirmation of the bungalow inspired design origins of the left side of the elevation of Voysey's Artist's House of c.1888 (see Figure 10.6).

20 This was a feature influencing its introduction into the US. In A. F. Oakey's *Building a Home*, published in New York in 1883, one of the advantages of the bungalow 'so-called from the East Indian name for a one-story house, "bangla" ', was that it simplifies service, making life easier for both servant and mistress (p. 29).

21 According to a report in *The Guardian* newspaper (February 10, 2001), based on a building society survey, 'almost one in three' people in the UK would rather live in a bungalow than other types of housing. The proportion in Scotland was 40 percent and in Yorkshire, specifically, 35 percent; elsewhere, it was 29 percent. In the United States, where the term invariably has positive connotations, the popularity of the bungalow is evident in a *New York Times* heading: 'Small But Sufficient: the Cozy Charm of the Bungalow' (*New York Times* March 21, 2003: D5). The prices of six 2-bedroom bungalows, similar in size and accommodation and built between the 1920s and 1950s, ranged from $69,900 in Fargo, North Dakota, through $139,800 in Dearborn Heights, Michigan to $545,000 in Santa Monica, California (the latter, remodeled and still 'with its original 1920s claw footed tub'). The contemporary ranch house was to develop from the bungalow, especially following the Second World War. Many thanks to Frances King and Janet Wolff for sending me these articles.

PART THREE

Pasts/Presents/Futures

Chapter 11: Ways of Seeing: Serendipity, Visuality, Experience

Serendipity: an apparent aptitude for making fortunate discoveries accidentally.

Webster's New Universal Unabridged Dictionary (1984)

INTRODUCTION

Writing cannot be anything but a personal experience. Yet in much academic writing the author usually keeps well out of the text. Paradoxically, however, 'personal experience' always takes place in conditions over which, at some level, we have little control: we have free will yet are always subject to larger determinations. As Marx famously said (though I cite him here as interpreted by Stuart Hall) men – and these days we would include women – make their own histories, 'but under conditions which are not of their own choosing' (S. Hall 1991b: 43). In this chapter I want to explore and also illustrate these and other propositions: how personal histories are embedded in larger histories, personal geographies in larger geographies. What may, at the time, seem to be the 'smaller' histories, geographies and sociologies of, for example, individual families, households or communities, are also part of 'larger' histories of regions, nation states, and empires. We are products of our circumstances.

Personal histories are also, of course, part of the histories of genders, ethnicities, classes, religions, castes and 'races', all socially constructed groupings that may exist inside and outside the boundaries of the larger spaces mentioned above. Depending on the pasts, presents and futures of the places and societies in which we live, of the languages (and accents) we learn and speak, we are presented with opportunities as well as constraints, opening up as well as closing off our options. And living in some parts of the world rather than others, and at particular historical conjunctures is, for most of its people, probably the factor which most governs what these options are.

These histories and geographies, large and small, are instrumental in forming the kind of people we become. They help construct our subjectivities, our multiple identities, both social and intellectual. The circumstances and location of our personal lives are therefore important in helping to explain what, as academics, we investigate and decide to pursue. In writing of the relevance of personal experience to cultural history, sociologist Janet Wolff states her interest in 'the role of culture in the formation of identity: the ways in which we use certain cultural events, practices, objects, in the continual process of our own production of self' and also, in the idea of 'memoir as cultural history, and in using the personal and subjective as access to social phenomena' (Wolff 1995: 28).

Though sharing something of these concerns, my objectives in this chapter are rather different. While not making the standard case of seeing autobiography and memoir as 'mere reflection' of a larger social or political history (Steedman 1992: 44), though any memoir writing does that to some extent, my concerns are with how our own interests and perceptions are affected by personal experience and how they enter into (or are deliberately kept out of) our narratives of interpretation.

In this context, I also want to pay particular attention to *visual* interests and experience and the importance of visual imagery in making connections not only between 'little' and 'larger' histories, but also between larger histories themselves. This is why I take John Berger's *Ways of Seeing* (1972) as the main title of my essay. It is a commonplace to note that, in the second half of the twentieth century, visuality and images have become increasingly dominant in people's lives: through television, video, films, photography, print media, advertising, surveillance through CCTV, or their personal production by video recorder or camera. Part of twentieth century subjectivity results not only from our being influenced by the mechanical and electronic reproduction of images but also of often seeing 'the world' through a frame with four sides. In the following, the visual constantly intersects with the text; in life, the visual confirms what is imagined.

For writers whose professional lives are largely spent in academic environments, their subjectivities, as Shermer-Smith writes, are distinctively marked by the experience:

Of all the lands a geographer may visit, there is, perhaps, none so strange as Academia. Academics the world over recognize one another and even if they do not speak the same surface language (French, Polish, Hindi) or even the same middle language (Physics, History, Lit. Crit.), they usually think, feel and communicate in the same deep academic language. All of the residents of Academia are naturalized citizens, none was born there, all are refugees from somewhere else, and, like most refugees, they have a simultaneous love and loathing for their new home, a place where their foreignness can suddenly confront them, just as they were feeling settled.

(Shermer-Smith 2000: 154)

While Shermer-Smith's insight is both witty and perceptive it is also quite generous. What is equally true is that, as adherents of different 'disciplines' in the academic division of labor, powerful – and often limiting – identities are formed not only by the different 'surface' as well as 'middle languages' we speak but also by the many languages – of both kinds – we do not know. Nonetheless, as inhabitants of Academia, if we are lucky, we might occasionally travel through different intellectual and disciplinary territories, and even different geographical terrains, learning, as we go, a little of the particularly distinctive argot of other natives.

In these travels, the *places* from where we originate, or where we settle, help to make us who we are, as well as who we are not (Haggett 1990: 126; Hagerstrand 1983). We are influenced by the institutions where we work, by the communities where we live, by the social relationships they help to construct; the array of cultural, political, climatic, historical or architectural experiences they provide; the memories they create, the sounds, smells and especially, the images they register on our minds (Urry 2000). What we *see*, and how we understand what we see, are important influences on what we know.

Here, the towns and cities we live in and the domestic space we occupy – homes, houses, apartments, flats, both internally and externally – become instrumental in shaping whom we become. What neighborhoods we choose (or avoid) to inhabit; what layers of associations and memories they leave behind; the homes where we live, and with whom, are not only associated with questions of memory, or markers of social position and status, they are also, in many industrial market societies, for those who can afford them, vehicles for storing wealth. And for others who cannot, they are a massive mechanism for keeping them poor. In my own case, having spent many years working at home and, for relaxation, walking around the neighborhood, especially when our children were young, domestic space assumed increased importance in my life (as is more usually the case for women). The actual dwellings where we live, therefore, can be seen as a way of 'grounding' what is called 'the local' even though, as I have argued in earlier pages, seen from different perspectives and in other frameworks, they can also be represented as 'global'.

As researchers and scholars, we work to construct the larger histories (and theories), browsing the web, searching archives. But how do these 'larger' histories and theories articulate with the personal experience of everyday? As Massey (1988) has suggested, earlier divisions of labor leave strata-like deposits, residual traces not only on the landscape but also on people's lives. The visual clues to these developments are all around us, evidence not just of some monolithic 'past' but of very distinctive and different pasts. While many of our ideas and arguments come from reading, consciously chosen and directed, from discussion, searching sources, or assembling sets of data, they also occur to us serendipitously. And moving between different towns and cities, or different countries, especially within today's increasingly compressed sense of time and space, we read one place through our latent memories of the other (Halbwachs 1992). We take our ideas with us, on our travels, and bring them back enhanced. And as with the dots in a children's puzzle, joining our experiences together forms a picture – even though everyone's picture will be different. Over time, isolated phenomena – remembered texts, phrases or images which we may have been vaguely aware of for years but considered of little or no importance, when seen through a different lens, or as part of a larger historical picture – take on much greater importance and meaning. What we see becomes informed by our theoretical knowledge, but the reverse is equally true.

These, then, are some of the ideas which prompted the writing of this essay. It is not meant to be a structured argument but rather, like life itself, a series of disconnected fragments – moments or, in some cases (literally) snapshots – which can be read as illustrations of themes encountered in the preceding chapters. What it relates is my own experience in (serendipitously) excavating and uncovering the often hidden, taken-for-granted presences of colonial, postcolonial as well as neocolonial traces, of places, objects and texts seen, sometimes literally, through the lens of my own experience.

BINGHAMTON NY

In November 1986 there were other academic positions in the postcolonial, anglophone world advertised in the *Times Higher Education Supplement* which,

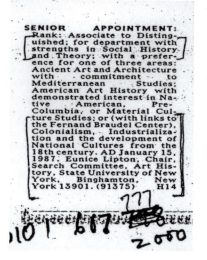

as I sat at home in the north of England, also caught my eye. Looking again at the *THES* over a decade and a half later, I found job ads that, had I been appropriately qualified, might have been of interest: in Botany, University of Natal, Statistics, University of the West Indies, Trinidad, Marketing at the Chinese University of Hong Kong, Psychology in the University of Queensland, Religious Studies and Classics in the University of Zimbabwe, and many more. At least fourteen posts were advertised in Australia.

Eventually taking up the new position at the State University of New York at Binghamton in January 1988, I was struck, among others things, not just by the challenge of developing courses and research relating to 'colonialism, industrialization and the development of national cultures' but what seemed to be the colonial landscape itself. New York was, of course, the 'Empire State'.[1] Near the campus entrance was an opticians, 'Empire Vision'. Across the road, Colonial Budget Rooms were being let (Figure 11.1). A sign over the clothing section in the university book store announced the presence of a Colonial Shoppe. The university basketball team, the Binghamton Colonials, proudly displayed their name on a green banner in the gym; their logo, the image of a Revolutionary War musketeer, white, male, and dressed in long uniform coat and matching tricorn hat[2] (Figure 11.2).

New to the city, I bought a map. At first glance, the only trace of the original indigenous, Iroquois inhabitants of the area were the names of the two rivers at the confluence of which the city had been built: the long meandering Susquehanna flowing east to west, and the Chenango, running in from the north. Along these, from the opening year of the nineteenth century, the white colonial settlers had laid out the first streets, and later, a series of grids, juxtaposed irregularly along the main banks. The Anglo names appropriated the territory, leaving only the rivers to the names of the Iroquois (Figure 11.3). Culture was the colonial, nature, the indigenous. As in colonial Australia, the land was treated as 'terra nullius'. The different native 'Indian' peoples who had lived here previously had already been driven out during the Revolutionary War, their villages burned, in some cases, as the price for fighting on the wrong (British) side.

Figure 11.1

William Bingham (1752–1804), after whom the city was named, was a wealthy Philadelphia banker, socialite and land speculator (G. Smith 1988: 22) who, following the end of the Revolutionary War, like many of his contemporaries, saw the capital that could be raised from land and purchased over 10,000 acres in the area. In 1798 he sent his land agent to lay down the grid, carve out the lots and either sell them off or rent them. Bingham himself, like the absentee landowners in Ireland, never managed to make the trip to the place named after him but stayed in Philadelphia; that is, when he was not traveling abroad. It was a year or two after I had arrived in Binghamton, and with my wife, Ursula, had moved our household in the UK from Leeds to Bristol (where she had a new appointment), that I discovered, when back in Britain and visiting Bath (30 minutes drive), that William Bingham was buried in Bath Abbey. Following the death of his wife in 1801, Bingham had moved to England and taken up residence in this, the most fashionable of English spas, the social

Figure 11.2

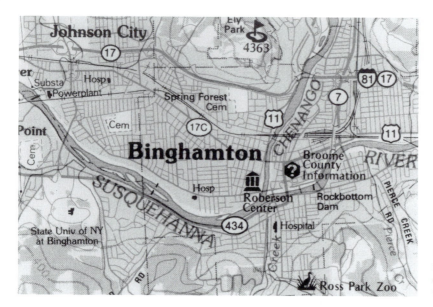

Figure 11.3
Binghamton, NY. Central area
© DeLorme, Yarmouth, Maine,
1988

meeting place of the transnational colonial elite, but had died in 1804. Along with the generals, admirals, sea captains, East India Company directors, West Indian planters and colonial governors whose commemorative tablets cover the walls is William Bingham's richly carved memorial, the work of John Flaxman (1755–1826), Britain's most prominent sculptor at the time.[3] Bingham's wife, Anne (1764–1801), had been the daughter of a wealthy Philadelphia merchant and had died while she and her husband were sailing to Britain's oldest (1612) colony, Bermuda, 'where the Binghams spent much of their time in the late 1790s and early 1800s' (G. Smith 1988: 23).

Today, the cultural geography of Binghamton has a good deal in common with other colonial places. In addition to the grids – the characteristic mark of many colonial settlements – of the 520 names which the city fathers have bestowed on the different streets, the vast majority are of (American) English origin. The main exceptions, on the West Side, are those of the 'German settlement' where these early twentieth-century newcomers, more conscious of their Germanic culture than other immigrants to the city, bequeathed a whole literary and musical aura on a cluster of streets with the names of Beethoven, Mozart, Schiller, Schubert, Goethe, Handel, Haydn, Mendelsohn. Hardly 1 percent of all the street names – scattered as they are in different locations throughout the city – commemorate the places or names of the indigenous peoples who, for centuries prior to their removal in the late eighteenth century, had inhabited the area: Mohawk, Genesee, Otsiningo, Oneonta, Unadilla, Nanticoke. Neither the culture, nor the visual signs of the colonized, are anywhere to be found in the city. The original city library, in Classical style, appropriately occupying a central place downtown and built around the early twentieth century, displays around the facade the names of cultural heroes[4] whose European and American origins no doubt reflected the inspirations and aspirations of the early city fathers who commissioned it: Plato, Homer, Dante, Shakespeare, Hugo, Schiller, Lowell, Emerson, Hawthorne. In addition to the downtown public sculpture which, most

Figure 11.4

prominently, commemorates (almost entirely in masculine form) the Revolutionary War, the American Civil War, the Spanish American War, the other major cultural marker, the Martin Luther King memorial arch on the side of the Chenango River, celebrates, if indirectly, the triumph of Black Americans over the (slave) history of the colonial past. In 1992, a bronze head of Christopher Columbus was added to the display, captioned by the 'Quincentennial Committee' of the County (but with no quotation marks), 'Discoverer' of America. Public markers or memorials to the indigenous inhabitants who once occupied and lived in the area are conspicuous by their absence.[5] The 'American Indians' are present only through their invisibility (Durham 1992).

The main exception to this absence can be seen along Interstate 17, the 'Southern Tier Expressway' which runs across the south of the state. Here, at regular intervals, for the occupants of automobiles speeding along at 65 mph, a profiled image of a 'native American' pays cursory respect to those that have 'disappeared'[6] (Figure 11.4).

The actual cultural and ethnic diversity in the city's population is less evident in the domestic architecture than it is in the different restaurants and food shops, and especially the religious buildings in and around the city, particularly the gold-leafed domes of a dozen Eastern Orthodox Christian churches, or the striking wooden architecture of the Ukrainian Catholic church, reproducing the vernacular style of its place of origin. In addition to the three Jewish synagogues, a mosque, and the numerous Roman Catholic and Protestant churches, those of particular ethnicities – African Methodist Episcopal Church of Zion, Polish National Catholic, Armenian, Lithuanian, Carpathian Russian Orthodox, Greek Catholic, Ukrainian Orthodox – give some insight into the ethnic and cultural profile of the city.[7]

After eighteen months, I bought a house on the West Side. Quite apart from the question of price, I preferred the older, 'walking city' with its sidewalks, and bus service, to the newer, post 1960 car-based suburbs, without them.

(Innocently, I assumed at the time that the absence of sidewalks in the newer suburbs in the United States was simply a matter of economy. Only later did I discover it was also a security device, a way of spatially marking unfamiliar 'pedestrians' – a word infrequently heard in the suburbs).

Binghamton was obviously booming in the early part of the twentieth century. The vast majority of West Side houses, timber-framed, and constructed from kits, each one slightly different from the next, tend to be one of two different architectural styles: most prominent are those with Classical features: porches (verandahs in 'English' terminology) supported by white Doric or Ionic columns, the product of the Colonial Revival style which swept across the US in the early twentieth century. Replacements are available from local suppliers. The other style displays the shallow angles and overhanging barge boards of the Arts and Crafts movement, influenced by the workshop of Gustav Stickley fifty miles north near Syracuse (Figure 11.5). The house I bought, built in 1910, is located in what might be seen as a Euro-American cultural space, the Beethoven end of Lincoln Avenue. The view from the porch takes in an avenue of colonial colonnades (Figure 11.6); from inside the hall, Doric columns: a cliché of colonial visuality (Figure 11.7).

The association, worldwide, of European colonialism, predominantly but not only British, in the eighteenth, nineteenth and twentieth century with the architecture of (earlier) colonial empires, Greek and Roman, is so taken for granted that in visual and architectural terms, 'colonial' is simply a synonym for 'Classical' which, in turn, is a synonym for the architecture of the (European) ancient world. In the United States where, like Australia, New Zealand, Canada and Ireland, white colonists settled permanently and to various degrees erased or subdued the indigenous colonized population, 'colonial' became a term, for the hegemonic white majority, with positive connotations; the eighteenth century 'Georgian' Classicism for ever a permanent visual sign that stood for the colonial

Figure 11.5

Figure 11.6

Figure 11.7

project: for European notions of Order, civilization and, above all, for control over the Native Other. In eastern, western and southern Africa, India, or southeast Asia on the other hand, where the colonists were obliged to leave, 'colonial' connotes foreign oppression. In upstate New York, following their secession from the metropolitan tyranny of Britain, the (American) colonial settlers, commemorating the culture and democratic ideas (plus the slavery) of (Classical) Greece and Rome, named a cluster of Classical settlements Ithaca, Syracuse, Utica, Rome, Marathon, Homer, Ovid.[8] Their mansions, churches, town halls and other public buildings ideally followed the style of the Greek Revival (Figure 11.8). 'Colonial Hotels' and 'Colonial Plazas' point back to this earlier history (Figure 11.9). 'Colonial', therefore, in the eastern regions of the US at least, is still for the dominant 'Anglo' or at least, 'Euro-American' culture, a positive term. It is an essentially Eurocentric identity and cultural preference, one which not only pervades the domain of popular domestic architecture but is the characteristic style of the plantation mansions in the American South, with all their connotations of (African) slavery. For people of African descent, European 'Classicism' conveys ambiguous meanings at best.[9] A few months after I arrived I visited the Immigration and Naturalization Service office in the Federal Post Office Building at Albany, the New York state capital, to change my status to Resident Alien. Somewhat in the manner of Michelangelo's Sistine Chapel, the ceiling had been decorated in 1935 by a Works Project Administration artist, Ethel M. Parsons, but in this case, displaying a map of the (European) colonial world (Figure 11.10) suggesting an interesting cultural link between, at this time, the white European (colonial) world of New York state with a larger world of similar continental and racial origins elsewhere.

From the point in time when the continents became known, in Europe, as 'the Americas', the indigenous population, for well-known reasons, became

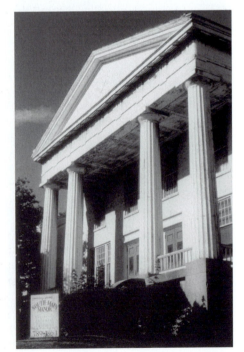

Figure 11.8

Figure 11.9

known as 'Indians', whether in the northern or southern continent, alternatively referred to today, naturalized and nationalized, in the language of colonial America as 'Native *Americans*' [*sic*]. While the material signs of these indigenous 'Indians' have effectively been erased[10] the material reminders of the *geographical*, South Asian India, while culturally translated, are clearly visible in selected spots all over the city. The stylish bungalows that exist, either singly, or in small clusters along the streets and avenues of Binghamton (and its two adjoining settlements of Endicott and Johnson City) bring to the domestic architecture of this otherwise Euro-American looking city – with its mainly 'single family homes' and 'duplexes' (detached and semi-detached), two-storied and 'vertical' dwellings, with their predominantly Classical features, semi-Georgian windows and references drawn from Greece and Rome – not only the more global resonances that the bungalow suggests (King 1984) but also, with their low-pitched sloping roofs, overhanging eaves, extended rafter ends, horizontal lines, broad verandahs and occasional Oriental (i.e. Japanesque) roof-line, references to a tropical elsewhere, whether California as well as India (Figure 11.11). Apart from the other colonial attributes I recognized, the presence of the American bungalows made me immediately feel at home, connecting me, via India, back to England and then to other bungalow locations round the world.

However, in the favorite phrase of British film actor, Michael Caine, 'Not many people know that'. That the bungalows of Binghamton – like those elsewhere in the United States – are seen (if, indeed, they are 'seen' at all) by the local population as part of a *national*, sometimes *regional*, rather than an international or global culture, and their connections to India as tenuous, should not only not surprise us but rather confirm what is known about cultural globalization: namely, that ideas, products and processes transplanted from one part of the world to another invariably undergo a process of 'cultural translation'. Words, ideas, material artefacts are used for different purposes, get adapted for different functions, become invested with different meanings and, in many cases, simply

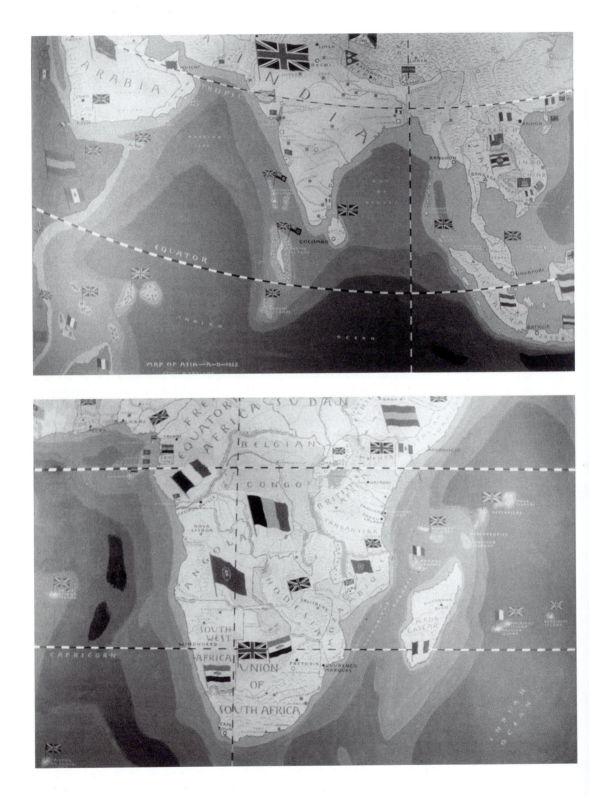

Figure 11.10

Figure 11.11

become attached to already existing forms or ideas to become both hybridized and indigenized.

So it was with the idea of the bungalow which, while originating in India, produced by Indians for Indians, was subsequently adopted and adapted by the British for themselves. After two decades of cultural translation following its introduction into Britain (1869), the idea then appeared (1880) in the US, apparently via England, again to go through a similar process of translation.

In the US, the bungalow lived a different kind of life. While generally retaining its 'generic' bungalow features, as a freestanding, one to one and a half-storey dwelling with bedrooms in the roof space, a porch or verandah, its local cultivation in the first two decades of the twentieth century by Arts and Crafts designers and its subsequent spread around the country (especially from California) were to make it the first 'nationwide domestic style' (King 1984: 152).[11]

South Asian Indians, though not very visible in the census – combined as they are with Chinese, Vietnamese, Japanese and others in a general category of 'Asian' (about 3 percent of the City population) – are nonetheless prominent in professional spheres, whether as physicians, high-tech engineers or academics, as well as running the odd gas station-cum-store or restaurant.[12] This disguising of the substantial Indian (but also Pakistani, Bangladeshi and Sri Lankan) population under the overall geographical category of 'Asian' in the US census erases, in some sectors of the American scholarly imagination, the continuing contribution of imperial and colonial histories to shaping contemporary American culture. In Abu-Lughod's excellent and critically comparative study of *America's Global Cities* (1999a), New York, Los Angeles and Chicago, this postcolonial English-speaking factor, however, tends to be underplayed. As the 'age of imperialism' ended around the mid-twentieth century, barriers to travel were removed from more than eighty states in Africa, southern and southeastern Asia, eastern

Asia and the Middle East, permitting massive diasporic populations to move to cities around the world (not least in the UK and US). Although Abu-Lughod highlights especially the presence of Jamaicans in New York, the over 1.5 million anglophone Indians in the United States (out of a global diaspora of some 20 million), representing a substantial proportion of the medical and information technology professions in America's cities (to say nothing of New York city taxi drivers, some half of whom are from south Asia), do not register as a highly important component of 'America's global cities', represented as they are under the 'Asian' census label. Focusing on the numerical strength of immigrant cohorts can elide the disproportional influence that specific groups can have. The immense intellectual influence in the academy, for instance, which particular 'postcolonial' southern Asian scholars have had throughout a wide range of the humanities and social sciences has been out of all proportion to their numbers.[13]

DELHI

These colonial readings of the architecture and space of Binghamton, visual, spatial, textual, lead back, through memory, to the five years we had spent in Delhi, India, some twenty years before (1965–70) and to travels to other Indian cities, occasionally manifesting the classic colonial pattern of the divided (European) 'Civil Station' and (also in the colonizer's language), 'Native City'. More particularly they relate to the social, urban and architectural manifestations of European colonialism I explored in *Colonial Urban Development* (1976) and subsequently, in *Urbanism, Colonialism and the World-Economy* (1990a) which had addressed the social and spatial segregation of colonial (and postcolonial) cities, the issues of equity and identity these posed, and the impact of their symbolic and spatial forms on the formation of subjectivity.

The more important lesson I had learnt from these studies, however, in the early 1970s, was the irrelevance of the nation state as an appropriate or adequate unit of analysis, whether social or spatial: the realization that neither metropolitan nor colonial space could be treated independently of the other. I also learned that what, for want of a better, less conflicted term, I would call a (technically) 'postimperial space', however contested, is a highly significant cultural space within which postcolonial subjects live and work, not least when it includes the US, the most economically privileged state in the world. Such a space is also one of postcolonial knowledges (see King 1976: 27) which, with other historically postcolonial languages – Spanish, Portuguese, French, Arabic, Chinese – forms an extensive, though sub-global space of transnational culture.[14]

LONDON

It was on our return from India that I increasingly became aware of how deeply the traces of colonialism, and particularly, the colonial connection with India, were inscribed on the culture and identity of Britain, less through reading books and more through everyday experience. Scratching below the 'national' surface there was always a surprise. Returning in 1970, we had eventually bought a house in south London's West Dulwich (where we had previously rented a flat). The previous owner was a retired police constable who had once served as a soldier in India. He became an important informant on the topic and space of army cantonments. One of our nearest parks had earlier been the London estate of the founder of the Peninsular and Orient Shipping Lines. Our closest public reference library, in Brixton, had been established through the benevolence of colonial sugar magnate, Sir John Tate (benefactor of the Tate Gallery). I subsequently learnt that the schools for which the area has long been noted had also relied for much of their patronage on colonial populations abroad. The vicar of a West Dulwich church, noting that the shift of imperial plutocrats to wealthier London suburbs to the south was seriously impacting on the class of housing built on Dulwich College estates, had written in 1900: 'The richer people are moving out to Beckenham and Bromley. There has been a complete change of character in the last fourteen years [i.e. 1886–1900]; then everyone had something to do with India . . . drawn by the nearness of Dulwich College (and the Girls Public Day School at Sydenham). These have almost gone now' (Nurse 1999). Of almost 40,000 different names listed in the *London A–Z Street Atlas* in 1970, the one called 'Bungalow Road' was just ten minutes away, near the site of the Crystal Palace (after a house, 'The Bungalow', built by an India-returned official/officer in the 1860s).[15] The road on which our house stood was the boundary between our own borough, Lambeth, and the adjacent one of Southwark, each one becoming increasingly significant in the 1970s as multicultural, multiracial, and largely postcolonial communities, their residents principally from the Caribbean, Africa and south Asia. In the census of 2001, some 37 percent of the population of each was described as 'non-white' (*The Guardian* February 2003).

We became friends with an east African south Asian family, recently expelled (along with over 30,000 others) from Uganda by dictator Idi Amin in what today would be called 'ethnic cleansing'. Our friends eventually moved up to join other members of their family in Leicester which, with a third of its population originating from south Asia in 2001 (and 25 percent of the whole of Indian descent), became known as Europe's largest Indian city.

On the walk from home to Gipsy Hill railway station was a house bearing a 'blue plaque' of the Greater London Council, indicating that it had once been the home of Annie Besant (1847–1933), socialist, theosophist, pioneering trade unionist, and a founding member and subsequently President (1918) of the Indian National Congress. In a school at the bottom of Gipsy Hill, one Saturday afternoon, I had bought, at a used book sale (for 25 pence/40 cents), the Oxford and Cambridge edition of *The British Colonies, Dependencies and Protectorates: Being a Geographical Treatise upon the Physical, Commercial, Political, Social, and Historical Features of the British Empire Beyond the Seas* by George Gill FRGS (no date but about 1901–2). On the title page is written, in a carefully schooled hand and a typically abbreviated military style, 'Garrn Sch B/dos 14/5/04'. An official government stamp, 'Supplied by the Public Service' indicates its official pedagogic function. As a reference guide to the British colonial world at the height of the Empire, it has proved indispensable.[16] As many others who migrate to London (in this case, from Lancashire, 'the north'), our location in the southeast resulted from my previously having had a flat (bedsitter) in the area: in this case, in a rambling early Victorian house (later demolished) immediately behind Horniman Gardens, in which stood the Horniman Museum containing the collection of musical instruments and curios made by F. J. Horniman (1835–1906), chairman of W. H. and J. Horniman, and ultimately sponsored by the coolie labor in the vast tea plantations in India, Ceylon and elsewhere.

LEEDS/LONDON

We did not stay in London for long. It was not a convenient location from which to commute the 100 miles to Leicester where, for two years (1970–2), I held a Fellowship, and even less convenient when, in 1971, Ursula took a position 200 miles north at the University of Leeds. As Ursula stayed during the week in Leeds, it fell to her lot to do the house-hunting while I (with help) stayed with the children in London. The house she found and that we eventually bought (1974) had been built in 1900 – brick, detached and with enough space for two commuting academics and four small children between 2 and 10. Looking through the deeds after receiving them from the solicitors, I discovered that one of the earlier owners had been a barrack-master and sergeant in the Indian Army.

With the exception of one year (1976–7) when Ursula had a Fellowship at the University of Cambridge (where I first came across Immanuel Wallerstein's *The Modern World System* (1974) and learnt of the Fernand Braudel Center at Binghamton) we lived in Leeds. For most of this time, I taught, part-time, first one and then two days a week at Brunel University, on the northwest outskirts of London, first in the sociology department and subsequently in a highly innovatory Department of Building, established under the genial and imaginative headship of the late Syd Urry, jazz pianist and pedagogical entrepreneur. For the remainder of the week, I worked at home. The new degree course at Brunel, aimed at bridging the professional and pedagogical gap between construction and architecture, was run by an interdisciplinary team that included courses in vernacular architecture and sociology. Serious research into the interface between sociology (particularly social theory) and built form, whether pursued as a theoretical project or more empirically, as social and cultural history, despite the fascinating intellectual challenge it poses and its undoubted social importance, is still a relatively rare pursuit, though some valuable studies have been published in the last two decades. One important reason for this is the absence of the necessarily interdisciplinary and intellectual research and teaching environments where it can happen. As stated elsewhere, buildings are not – as they are still often represented in architectural discourse – simply technical or art objects ('big sculpture'), but are, in the first place, socially and culturally produced, existing as social and cultural objects, invested with social meaning and shaping social relations.[17]

My teaching at Brunel provided as good a base as any to explore some of these issues around the social production of building form, as well as its consumption. The edited book, *Buildings and Society* (1980, 1984), was a serendipitous by-product of the project I had begun on the social, economic, spatial and historical conditions surrounding the production and social meaning of the bungalow, begun in a semi-serious way in the 1970s. By the early 1980s, when it became evident that a particular building type, carrying the name 'bungalow', varying in its form but having certain common functions, could be found in all five continents of the world, the study had become more serious.

For 13 years (1974–87), during term time, I commuted each week, by rail, the two hundred miles between Leeds and London, continuing by underground across the big city to stay overnight with a friend in Herne Hill (near Brixton). Early next morning, my journey continued, with two or three changes, all the way to Uxbridge, the last stop on the Piccadilly line, and a brisk 15 minute walk to the university. Returning home was easier: the underground to King's Cross station and a fast train back to Leeds.

Apart from providing the opportunity to read books and grade students' papers, the commuting provided a fascinating, as well as painless, way to supplement my urban fieldwork. What we see is informed by our theoretical knowledge, and our theoretical knowledge by what we see. The contributors to *Buildings and Society* had deepened my interest in the social production of prisons, hospitals, asylums and other institutional buildings. A short journey from Leeds, the train comes slowly to a halt on an elevated embankment above the high security prison at Wakefield, just long enough to catch a view (though only in winter when the trees are bare), of a mass of barbed wire, inward-extruded parapets and sombre barred windows to the rear. As I returned home in late Spring, the grim castellated image of the (equally Victorian) silhouette of Leeds Prison, outlined against the evening sky, occupied a carefully chosen and visible site, on rising ground, to the left as the train approaches the station. After moving to Binghamton and – in the UK – to Bristol (as I describe below), I was intrigued by the fact that the city fathers, in both places, almost 4,000 miles apart, though in the early nineteenth century probably ideologically quite close, had each located a castellated institutional building on prominent hill tops, a few miles outside the city. Of the Victorian categories of 'the sad, the mad, and the bad' (Markus 1993), it was in each case both to simultaneously accommodate but also to socially exclude the first; inebriates in Binghamton and orphans in Bristol.

Traveling these thousands of miles over the years consciously and subconsciously extended my historical, geographical and architectural knowledge, both of the urban vernacular in the cities, as well as, in London, the districts through which I traveled.[18] Not least important were the historical sites, locations, designs, appearances and spatial and social contexts of innumerable bungalows noted on the way.

Apart from my part-time teaching in London and Ursula's full-time job in Leeds, our travels were also determined by what sociology, in its ponderous way, describes as 'stages in the life course'. Especially in summer, with the children, we would make trips from Leeds, eastwards to the seaside, to Whitby, the site of a fine museum dedicated to the life of sea captain, explorer, navigator and scientist, James Cook (1728–1779), who started his seagoing apprenticeship there. Alternatively we drove to Scarborough, Hornsea or into the Yorkshire Dales. For seven years after we arrived in Leeds, we also traveled westwards once a month, making the one and a half hour journey past Ilkley Moor to Skipton, then into Lancashire via Clitheroe and Pendle Hill, to spend the day with my mother who lived in a small village (but a large house) near the Ribble Valley. Where journeys to the capital brought me into contact with imperial architecture and postcolonial populations, travels into the country and to the seaside enabled me to discover just how far the influence of India, and the Empire, had penetrated, in the form and ubiquity of the bungalow, into the metropole's deepest heartlands. In 1981, however, a minor earthquake was to upset our (and many other people's) lives.

Harold Macmillan, British Conservative Prime Minister in the late 1950s, was once asked what had been the most important factor in his political career; he replied, 'Events, my boy, events.' Margaret Thatcher had become Prime Minister of the Tory government in Britain in May 1979. Within two years, the transatlantic axis of evil, Reaganomics and Thatcherism, was in full swing: deregulation, privatization and the onslaught on public services, including universities. In 1981, Thatcher's axe struck university budgets, some of them (including Brunel), cut by 30 to 40 percent.

Earlier that year, my mother had died, leaving my two brothers and me with a large, early Victorian house in the country which she had encouraged my father to buy on his retirement. For long uninhabited, neglected and run down, the roof caved in and with an acre of overgrown land, the house had initially been seen by my mother as a 'retirement project': to restore the house, tame the land and, as both were enthusiastic gardeners, to encourage flowers to bloom where they had not bloomed before. But as the largest house in the village, with prominent gateposts and a sweeping driveway, it also sent social messages which were not in tune with my father's modest origins and views on life. The sale of the house, however, and the investment of the proceeds in two projects, one large, one small, was to have a major impact on our family's lives.

LEEDS

Despite loud protests from inside and outside the university, our innovatory department at Brunel was (unilaterally) closed by the Vice Chancellor, the existing students phased out over the next three years. Like other friends in the fields of architecture and building at the time, conscious of the rising property values, I moved, at least temporarily, from the world of books to the world of buildings. The large, architect-designed Edwardian bungalow in a leafy inner suburb of Leeds that we moved into in the summer of 1982 belonged to the early history of the Western genre of the type discussed in Chapter 10 (Figure 10.14), a period when prominent Arts and Crafts architects such as Robert A. Briggs saw the idea of the bungalow as a house mainly of one storey, as having immense economic and social relevance as well as aesthetic potential, a period before the negative, often class-associated connotations, began to be invested in the term in Britain.

There were more serious political protests in 1981. Urban riots in inner city areas – including Chapeltown (Leeds) and Brixton (London), in both cases close by where I stayed – erupted in the summer of that year. The causes were attributed to bad housing, racist policing, bad social conditions and, not least, bad politics, but it was almost entirely postcolonial, ethnic minority areas and people that suffered the damage. Overnight, the inner city urban landscape was transformed: shop fronts, previously simply glazed, were suddenly covered with wire mesh and steel bars.

MEXICO CITY

A smaller portion of the proceeds from the sale of my mother's house went on a return ticket to Mexico City and registration for the International Sociological

Association Conference scheduled for August 1982. As job chances were shrinking in Britain, I thought perhaps teaching opportunities would be better abroad. Listening to a paper on a hot, late summer afternoon, I was handed a note by John Friedmann, then Head of Urban and Regional Planning at UCLA. Would I be interested in participating in a project on 'world city formation'?

Having spent the previous few years working on the world-wide spread of one particular building type, and the conditions that had produced this, and convinced that 'studies of the urban environment, and no doubt many other topics, . . . need pursuing from a global perspective' (King 1984: ix) I found John Friedmann's invitation instantly appealing. As Friedmann has written elsewhere, ' "World city" was an idea waiting to be born' (Friedmann 2002: 145). The manuscript of his 'world city' paper arrived in Leeds just after I returned, the printed version shortly after (Friedmann and Wolff 1982).

'World City Formation: An Agenda for Research and Action', spelling out 'the spatial articulation of the emerging world system of production and markets through a global network of cities', was to have an immense (and still continuing) influence, not only on urban studies but also on the strategic development policies of major cities themselves, globally competing as they were increasingly doing for capital investment, cultural spectacles and both high and low cost labor. The particular focus of research studies 'would be the restructuring of economic, social and spatial relations and the ensuing political conflicts in world city formation' (1982: 329). In the last two decades, a flood of research has been undertaken and published, both on designating, according to specific criteria, which cities qualify as so-called 'world cities', the 'cotter pins of the world economy', but also others which, on the basis of quantified research (much of it related to the hosting of international quaternary services such as finance, insurance, real estate, advertising etc.) the move towards (or away from) 'world city' status (see Beaverstock et al. 1999, King 1990a, Knox and Taylor 1995, Sassen 2001, www.GandWC.com, etc.). So dominant, in fact, has the world city paradigm become, according to some accounts (King 2000b, Robinson 2002), that it has seriously distorted the amount of attention given in urban research to other topics and 'non world city' areas.

LONDON

Having finished the bungalow book, I started working on one of a number of case studies on London, as part of the 'World City Formation' project, helped by the continued (rail) commuting to and across London each week (reading more carefully the local and national press) and new part-time teaching positions with University College's Development Planning Unit and the International Housing Studies Programme at the Architectural Association School of Architecture. While the renovation of 'The Bungalow' slowed down, living in the house (not to all family members' tastes, as sylvan seclusion also had its drawbacks) fueled my curiosity about its architectural history.

Neglected in the research literature on the world city is its role and function in the production of knowledge. World cities (and particularly, one time imperial capitals) host vast archives, libraries, as well as museums filled with artefacts from all over the world, much of it, needless to say, appropriated from, and produced about, the colonies which they have at one time controlled. They also host what the United States refers to as 'world class' institutions of higher learning, again, with students and, increasingly, teachers from all over the world. Imperialism, and subsequently globalization, which in this case can be seen as a continuation of the former, has long required postcolonial scholars to come to the imperial center in order to consult their own archives as well as contest their own histories. As Appadurai has written, 'As an uneven economic process, globalization [a.k.a imperialism] creates a fragmented and uneven distribution of just those resources for learning, teaching and cultural criticism that are most vital for the formation of democratic research communities that could produce a global view of globalization' (2000: 4). Teaching courses during these years on various themes in the history and sociology of housing, planning and urbanism in Asia, Africa and Latin America not only resulted from these conditions of possibility but also was required by them.

Now that I was impregnated with the germ of the world city thesis it was also apparent to me that, with the restructuring of banking and financial services taking place during the 1980s, Leeds was increasingly being made into the 'financial center of the north' (King 1990b: viii–ix). This was also linked to developments in the world of entertainment and the media. With the first worldwide transmission of Bob Geldof's 'Live Aid' concert in 1984, it was only a matter of time before Leeds, like other major cities, was further incorporated into the global entertainment circuit. When the wind blew in the right direction, the sounds of Bruce Springsteen drifted into our garden one weekend from the nearby park. A year after my arrival in the United States, banner headlines blared across the free advertising paper in Leeds, 'International City of the Future'.[19]

As not infrequently happens in the academic and publishing world, the journal publication on 'World City Formation' envisaged by John Friedmann did not materialize as planned.[20] Yet by 1984–5, the privatized redevelopment of London's docklands, the deregulation of the securities industries and the shake up of the Stock Exchange (suitably named 'Big Bang') was well under way. By this time, it had become clear not only that the research deserved a book but also that, as far as London was concerned (and indeed, other one-time imperial cities), the phenomenon of the 'world city' was not entirely new, even though there were, of course, radical new elements. London's role in the world economy in the 1980s continued, in many ways, the historical role it had performed as an imperial capital. As far as many of its demographic, social, cultural, spatial and built form characteristics were concerned, it was essential to recognize its postcolonial and (technically) 'postimperial' characteristics (Driver and Gilbert 1999; Jacobs 1996; King 1990b).[21]

LEEDS

Shortly after I moved to the US, Ursula accepted an appointment at the University of Bristol. As our youngest daughter still had to finish high school and the eldest was working in the region, we decided, after the sale of 'The Bungalow', to buy an end-of-terrace, back-to-back house in the inner city, Harehills, an area favored by a South Asian (both Indian and Pakistani) population. Ursula, once more, had the task of finding the house, in this case, in Karnac Road (Figure 11.12). The name intrigued me. I subsequently learnt that this, as well as nearby Luxor Road, had been built about 1900 during Britain's colonial administration in Egypt.

Figure 11.12

Figure 11.13

The irony of these minimal 'back-to-backs' built for the (woollen) textile workers of Leeds at the height of the Empire being named after the spectacular Egyptian Middle Kingdom city of Karnak (3,500 years old) could not have escaped those who had financed their building. Occasionally visiting in the early 1990s, I watched from the upstairs windows the minarets of a large mosque rise up, high above the chimney tops. 'FREE KASHMIR', in large white letters five foot high, was daubed across the brick wall opposite (Figure 11.13).

Figure 11.14

Figure 11.15

BRISTOL

Before Britain's Industrial Revolution, Bristol was, in the middle of the eighteenth century, the second largest city in England (de Vries 1983: 270–1). Its fortunes were built especially in the second half of that century as the leading port engaged in transatlantic trade; the new colonial economy of tobacco, sugar, indigo, as well as slaves. Before being surpassed by Liverpool, it had the dubious role of being Britain's leading slave trading port. Additional to the many sites associated with the slave trade, a visible legacy of this history is one of the most well-known names in the history of tobacco in Britain, the family firm of W. D. and H. O. Wills. For much of the early twentieth century, 'Wills Woodbines', in familiar green packets, were the cheapest, most popular cigarettes among the working class.

Today, the name of Wills (and of Bristol) has disappeared from cigarette packets and advertising in Britain (though not from the business pages of the web). Yet around the sedate and leafier suburbs of the city, some of the large mansions previously owned by the family, donated to the University of Bristol as student residence halls, carry the family associations and one, the family name (Wills Hall) (Figure 11.14). This is also the case with the most prominent building of the University, the spectacular early twentieth century neo-Gothic 'Wills Memorial Tower', dominating the summit of one of the main roads from the city (Figure 11.15).

Figure 11.16

BOMBAY

Visiting Bombay for a conference some months after moving to Bristol, it was not the incredible Victorian Gothic architecture of the Municipal Building or the Victoria Railway Terminus, or even the double decker red ('London') buses that, instantly recognizable, established the postcolonial connection with India (as I had been to Bombay before), but rather – for me – the more 'local', and 'personal' signage for 'Wills' and 'Bristol' cigarettes all over the city centre. Even more than those of Coca-Cola or McDonald's, it seemed that 'Wills' saturated the visual environment (Figures 11.16, 11.17). These cultural linkings of space

Figure 11.17

Figure 11.18

and time were made even more poignant with the sight of Ashok Leyland (Figure 11.18) on the front of trucks and buses, an indigenized one-time British company, the name instantly displacing me to teenage bicycle rides to the Lancashire seaside, through Leyland (the location, at that time, of the country's major heavy vehicle manufacturer). Or even walking along Bombay's Juju Beach, to be suddenly confronted with the name of Annie Besant, spelt out in stained glass on the porch of a Theosophist Society home for the elderly.

MANCHESTER

In his outstanding 1,168 page opus, *Cities in Civilization* (1998), Sir Peter Hall begins Book II with 'The City as Innovative Milieu', opening with a chapter on 'The First Industrial City: Manchester 1760–1839':

> As all the world knows, the first industrial revolution happened in England [and] one industry above all came to dominate England's pioneering path to industrialization, and one city, above all, became the center and the symbol of the entire process, renowned worldwide and visited by inquiring pilgrims from every land. The industry was the manufacture of cotton and the city was the commercial heart of that industry, Manchester.
>
> (Hall 1998: 310)

In suggesting why Manchester and its region (of Lancashire) emerged as a leader and why, by 1830, over half the volume of British home-produced exports consisted of cottons, Hall addresses a number of complex, interlinking explanations, one of which was that Lancashire was already a 'proto-manufacturing seedbed' at the beginning of the seventeenth century, where the making of fustions, a combination of cotton and linen, had been introduced at that time 'in the hilly country between Bolton and Blackburn' (ibid.: 315). In 1700, these towns each had a population of about 2,000 to 3,000 (ibid.: 320).

Figure 11.19

Apart from four years away at university, the first twenty two years of my life were spent in a small industrial town (population 30,000) located 'in the hilly country between Bolton and Blackburn' the name of which does not figure in *Cities in Civilization*. With a number of other places in the area, it was known as a 'cotton town'. So important was this commodity that, along with an image of the river that flowed through the center, was the image of three sprigs of a cotton plant, reproduced not only on the town's coat-of-arms (approved in 1878) but also on the breast pocket of my Darwen Grammar School blazer which I wore, off and on, to school for over half a dozen years (Figure 11.19). The town, whose motto, also on the coat-of-arms, was 'Absque Labore Nihil' ('nothing without labor'), had, from the early nineteenth century if not before, prospered on the spinning and weaving of cotton.

Yet neither at that time, nor in the twentieth century had cotton ever grown in Britain, let alone in Lancashire. In the early part of the nineteenth century, much of it came, via the port of Liverpool, from the slave plantations of the American South. When that supply was interrupted during the American Civil War, it came increasingly from (colonial) India and sometimes Egypt.

DARWEN

The importance of India, both as a supplier of raw cotton, and much more significantly, as a market for Darwen's cotton goods, was symbolized in the late nineteenth century by the town's most spectacular monument. This was (and still is) the elaborately decorated, 303 feet high chimney of the India Mill, which stood out among all the others (Figure 11.20). As Mark Girouard writes in *The English Town* (1990):

The effect of the India Mill tower is still sensational – perhaps even more so than when it was first built since only a handful of the town's other factory chimneys survives. It soars out of the stone-built town, but itself, apart from its base, is built of purple engineering bricks. Like most of the more ambitious factory chimneys, it is modeled on Italian towers – not the domestic towers, however, which were mostly very plain, but church campaniles, such as that of St Mark's, Venice. The Darwen tower was built in 1867 by Eccles Shorrock, Brother and Co., the biggest mill owners in Darwen (until they failed in 1882). Its foundations rest on a stone said to be the largest block to have been quarried apart from that used for Cleopatra's Needle. Thirty five horses were needed to draw it from the quarry to its destination . . . it has a staircase running up it.

(Girouard 1990: 253–4)

Figure 11.20 India Mill and Darwen, c.1877

Yet while there was 'a special connection between Lancashire and India' (Hunt 1978: 207),[22] cheap British cotton cloth and the colonial connection had done immense damage to India, a major cause of the decline in her cottage

214 □

industries. Under colonial rule, tax policies in India favored British imports over India's own cotton production. As Mahatma Gandhi wrote in the early twentieth century, 'It is difficult to measure the harm Manchester has done to us' (cited in Hunt 1978: 207). These were the reasons behind the major boycott of British goods and institutions in India, beginning in 1905 and successively increased in the early 1920s (Bose and Jalal 1998: 141). The result of the boycott was extensive unemployment in Lancashire's 'cotton towns'.

It was his English friend, the missionary C. F. Andrews, who persuaded Gandhi, the promoter of the boycott, already scheduled to visit London for the 1931 Round Table Conference on future constitutional changes in India, to visit Lancashire and see for himself the deleterious effects that the boycott was having on working people. Darwen was chosen because, with Blackburn and Great Harwood, it manufactured cotton goods principally for India and was, therefore, more heavily affected by the boycott.[23] Gandhi agreed, though he had earlier written to Andrews:

Figure 11.21

Figure 11.22

The remedy for unemployment in England is not thoughtless generosity of India but a complete realization by England of the awfulness of exploitation of people, violently brought under subjection by her, and consequent radical changes in her conception of the standard of life and a return to simplicity.

(cited in Hunt 1978: 208)

Gandhi left London on Friday, September 25, arriving in Darwen in the evening, where he was hosted by local Quakers. On the following day, he visited Springfield Mill (Figure 11.21). In addition to speaking with the managers, he also met the workers. 'Everywhere his reception was friendly' (Hunt 1978: 210). One of the most well-known photographs of the visit depicts Gandhi surrounded by laughing and cheering mill workers, most of them women (Figure 11.22). Everywhere he explained that, if England faced unemployment, India experienced starvation. Indian poverty was the result of British policy in destroying the native cotton industry (Hunt 1978: 210).

I did not manage to see Mahatma Gandhi for a couple of reasons. First, some time before he arrived my parents had left the (social housing) of a terraced 'council house' not far from the mill which Gandhi visited and moved three miles across and away from the densely built terraced housing, to a semi-detached house in a 'nice' Edwardian suburb and hence, into a different 'class' of space. Though it never struck me till I was an adult, the fathers of my neighborhood friends (till the age of eleven) were to be managers of mills, banks, the gasworks and schoolteachers. The other reason, however, was probably more important. The weekend Mahatma Gandhi arrived, I was just five and a half months old.

The irony of Gandhi's visit, and the tumultuous reception he received, was that, with the continuing boycott, the cotton industry slumped even further into massive decline.[24] Unemployment was rife and, if William Woodruff's brilliant autobiography set in the adjoining town of Blackburn is any guide, there was also occasional starvation (Woodruff 1993). Fortunately for our family, my father was in a growth industry. Under 'Father's Occupation' on my birth certificate the entry reads, 'Staff Supervisor (glazed brick works)'. But Shaw's Glazed Brick Works was soon to change its name to Shaw's Faience (from Faenza, in Italy, which during the Renaissance had made the technique of glazed terracotta into an art form). It was a finish and cladding to buildings that, with the paradigm shift in design to the Modernism of the 1930s, took the architectural profession by storm. With the increasing penetration of the British retail economy as well as entertainment culture by influences from the United States (from F. W. Woolworth – their stores set up in every town and city beginning in 1926 – to Hollywood movies), it meant that 'moderne' and Art Deco facades of Woolworth's (and other) shop fronts as well as the new cinemas in many towns, the Odeons, Regals and Rialtos, were, as often as not, clad in the large cream, black or green slabs of Shaw's Faience.[25] Woolworth's new store in Blackpool, the most prominent and popular seaside resort in the country, was located immediately at the foot of what was then, at 518 feet/158 meters, the tallest structure in Britain, Blackpool Tower. The frequently reproduced images of Blackpool's most famous icon were simultaneously an advertisement for Shaw's Faience.

My parents had arrived in Darwen shortly after their marriage in 1921. After being discharged from the services at the end of the First World War, my father, like thousands of others at the time, had for long been unemployed. Having left school at fourteen (like my mother, who came from London), my father had first worked as a turner in a machine shop in his native Leicestershire. After the war, he began a correspondence course to learn to be a draughtsman. Their luck changed with the tip off by an uncle, already working at Shaw's, that there was a vacancy in the drawing office. As my father gradually rose up the ladder (architectural draughtsman in 1921, staff supervisor ten years later, then commercial manager) he was provided with a 'works car'. At a time when car ownership in England was limited to a relatively small middle class (perhaps 2 million cars in the country compared to some 26 million today), 'going out for a drive' in 'the countryside' at the weekend was, as I was subsequently to realize, a privileged recreation. Occasionally going 'for a look at the shops' in Blackburn or Bolton, or other (often run down) Lancashire towns (deserted on a Sunday), my father would occasionally punctuate the conversation with a nod from the wheel, and an approving comment, 'That's a Shaw's job!' If driving in the country, my mother or occasionally my father (since just before my arrival, members of the property-owning class), spying some (often overgrown) Victorian or Georgian villa in a cluster of trees, would say 'That's a nice house'. For my mother, who from early middle age was totally deaf, looking – vision – was her main access to information. Both were amateur artists as well as keen gardeners.

In Britain of the 1940s, these were leisure practices of a middle class that were suited to older, 'typically English', small-scale landscapes. In this context, this was doubtless a very socially and culturally specific pursuit which left its traces on my subconscious. As far as I can surmise, however, it is in this highly selective way that, from an age I can barely remember, I was introduced into a visual world of both 'looking', and of 'looking' at particular things, not least, buildings. What else we bring to our 'looking,' and what we actually 'see,' is a whole other story.

NOTES

1   'Empire State' possibly originated with George Washington in 1784 in the context of its rapid economic and industrial growth.

2   The name was changed to Binghamton Bearcats some years later, though the rationale for the change had nothing to do with the political and historical associations of the original 'colonial' term I highlight here. The Colonial Shoppe and Colonial Apartments have also disappeared.

3   Bingham shares this colonial space in the Abbey with, among others, Arthur Phillips, the first Governor of New South Wales, a governor of Bombay, another governor of Fort Marlborough, Sumatra, a Lieutenant Governor of Jamaica, the Governor of the Leeward and Charibee Islands, a member of the Committee of Barbado(e)s and various West Indian planters as well as their wives, especially from Barbado(e)s, Jamaica and Bermuda. Other parts of the colonial Empire represented include Australia, India, South Africa, Gibraltar, Ireland. Most of the memorials are from the period 1770–1830. I have not explored whether the health-giving spa waters of Bath were beneficial for treating the particular diseases of the tropics. As someone passing through two national identities, and managing his divided loyalties, William Bingham is an interesting figure. Having in colonial America served as British Consul at St Pierre, Martinique, in 1776 he agreed to serve the Continental Congress there.

During the American Revolution, he arranged for smuggled shipments of weapons to the army, recruiting privateers to prey on British shipping. This last task proved to be personally profitable, as Bingham was entitled to a portion of every British cargo appropriated. When he finished his stint in 1780, he returned to the new United States with a huge fortune; at the age of 28, one of the richest men in the new nation and soon to become a US Senator. His move to England was also to be with his daughters living there. (See http://chronicles.dickinson.edu/encyclo/b/ed_binghamW.html.)

4   These days referred to as 'DWM' – dead white males.

5   Otsiningo Park, the site of the most important indigenous settlement, occupied before the nineteenth century by the Onandagas, Nanticoke, Shawnee and other 'Indian' peoples, hosts an annual fair and pow-wow in the summer where indigenous people put on performances and sell indigenously-made crafts. At the entrance to the town of Owego, twenty miles up the Susquehanna, the official marker erected by the State Education Department in 1932 commemorates the burning of 'an Indian village' by the forces of American General Clinton en route to join General Sullivan, fighting in the Revolutionary War. The removal of the Iroquois from the territory would today be called 'ethnic cleansing'.

6   As one Native American woman student pointed out to me, the most common representation of a Native American woman is in the supermarket, used as a trademark for a particular brand of butter. Unlike in Australia, there is no 'Sorry' movement in the US to acknowledge earlier colonists' treatment of the indigenous inhabitants, although in recent years local tribes in New York State and elsewhere have made successful claims to regain previously lost lands.

7   The 2000 Census for Binghamton City gives the main categories (in percentages) as White 83.2, Afro-American/Black 8.4, Asian 3.3, Hispanic/Latino 3.9, American Indian 0.3. The principal 'ancestries' given (in percentages) are Irish 19.7, Italian 12.8, German 12.0, English 11.1, Polish 6.0, Slovak 3.6, Russian 2.7, Dutch 2.5, French 2.2. Within the city, the university population (of some 13,100 students, 60–65 percent from the NYC region), is more culturally diverse: White 51.5, Afro-American/Black 4.9, Asian 13.9, Hispanic Latino 4.9, American Indian 0.2, not known 15.9 percent; the remainder (8.4) are Non-Resident Aliens (international students). Of the total student population, about 8 percent are international students, coming from 113 countries. Of these, the largest number are from Asia (779) and the largest number (317) of these, from India, representing 29 percent of all international students. Other Asian students include those from China (16 percent) and Korea (12 percent). Other world regions represented include 41 countries in Europe (108 students in all), the Middle East (68, especially from Turkey, 57), Africa (65, especially from Kenya, 29), Central and South America (51) and Canada (25). About 21 percent of the total university student population consists of graduate students. Figures are for Fall 2002. The campus has 6,030 parking spaces.

8   Other classical names in upstate New York include Hannibal, Cato, Brutus, Aurelius, Romulus, Scipio, Ovid, Hector, Ulysses, Cicero, Pompey, Homer, Virgil. Many thanks to Deryck Holdsworth for this information.

9   This insight was conveyed to me by Ken Simmons, an African-American Professor of Architecture at U C Berkeley in 1991. In October 2003, the naming of a new Binghamton area restaurant as 'Plantation House' by its white owner was deemed by a group of black students to be racist. According to the Vice President of the University's Black Student Union, 'Just hearing it doesn't sound too appealing, but I'd have to see it. When you think of a plantation house you think of slaves, you think of indentured servitude, cotton picking. Historically, that's what "plantation house" has meant to black people.' See Rion A. Scott, 'Some find restaurant's name racist. Owner: Plantation House means "Elegant House".' *Binghamton Press and Sun*, October 25, 2003: IB.

10 I refer here to Binghamton. Some fifty miles north lies the Indian territory of the Onondaga Nation.

11 The point here about 'cultural translation', in particular, the transformation of existing forms of domestic architecture, first perhaps, only in the form of the name – i.e. a

shift from 'cottage' to 'bungalow' – and subsequently, by the adoption of more well-known Californian bungalow design features, is well illustrated in the recent study of the social meaning of the Chicago bungalow (used as a cultural sign to signal social mobility) by Joseph Bigott (2002). This point is, however, overlooked by the author who states that 'it was absurd to suggest that the Chicago bungalow derived in some way from the architecture of India' (2002: 228, note 79). As mentioned in Chapter 10, the first few bungalows in England were also based on already existing English house designs.

12 28 percent of motels in the United States are run by Gujarati Indians. Thanks to Deryck Holdsworth for this information. According to *India Today* correspondent, Arthur J. Pais, 'motels run by Patels are jocularly known as Potels'. Pais estimated a doubling in the number of Indian-run hotels in the US from 7,500 in 1995 to 14,000 in the late 1990s (*India Today* December 31, 1995: 72b).

13 I refer here, among others, to Arjun Appadurai, Homi Bhabha, Dipesh Chakrabarty, Partha Chatterjee, Gayatri Chakravorty Spivak, to say nothing of the influence in literary and cultural fields of writers such as Salman Rushdie, Vikram Seth, Amitava Ghosh, V. S. Naipal, Arundhati Roy, Hanif Kureishi, and others. The name of Palestinian Edward Said also obviously belongs to the important band of postcolonial scholars here.

14 The opportunity of working in India had occurred during Prime Minister Harold Wilson's first Labour Government (1964–70), and a new Ministry of Overseas Development with Barbara Castle as the Minister. Under the terms of the Colombo Plan, a number of British academics were paid to work at the newly established (1959) Indian Institute of Technology in Delhi. Five such IITs had been established in the immediate post-independence decades at the instigation of Prime Minister Jawaharlal Nehru, to meet India's needs for scientific and technological expertise. In order to benefit from the widest political and cultural spectrum of educational systems and knowledge, each of the institutes had been established with the collaboration of the leading industrial states at the time: in order of founding, Russia (Bombay), Germany (Madras), Kharagpur (through UNESCO assistance), the US (Kanpur) and UK (Delhi). The first Director of IIT Delhi, R. N. Dogra, was a civil engineer who had graduated from Imperial College London (founded 1907) with which the institute had a 'sisterhood relationship'. My own responsibilities were to assist in the establishment and development of an interdisciplinary Department of Humanities and Social Sciences.

15 I discovered London's Bungalow Road, serendipitously, when we lived in West Dulwich. Over thirty years later (2003), the *London A–Z* street guide tells me that the memory of particular Indian places and the historical events with which they were associated is inscribed on the spaces of the postimperial capital in interesting ways (see Chapter 6, note 4). India Way (W12), with Commonwealth Avenue, and Australia, Bloemfontein, Canada, New Zealand and South Africa Roads mark the site of the 1924 Imperial Exhibition at White City, though other explanations need to be found for Simla Close (SE14) and Poonah St (E1). Holding all these imaginary displaced sights and sounds of the East and West together, at the heart of the city, is the idea of empire itself. Yet signs of imperial consciousness are not in the city but rather the suburbs, spatially distributed around the inner fringes in the form of nine 'imperial' thoroughfares – including a Drive, Street, Road, Way, Mews and Close. A more advanced agenda might explain how and when the far flung territories of the Empire, through a consciousness of different events, came to be etched in the minds of thousands of residents in streets named Aden, Assam, Bangalore, Bengal, Burma, Canberra, Durban, Falkland, Gwalior, Hobart, Jeypore, Khartoum, Kidderpore, Kimberly (18), Malta, Mysore, Nile, Ontario, Ottawa, Pitcairn, Quebec, Tasmania, Toronto, Singapore, West India, Valetta, Vancouver, among others.

Between 1970 and 2003, numerous new streets appeared. With International Avenue (appropriately, near Heathrow Airport) I imagined a more global view on the world – until I discovered it sandwiched between Victory Way and Spitfire Way. However, a 10 minute walk from Imperial Street takes me to (a more) Global Approach (both in EC3).

16   Pages at the end of the book indicate that George Gill was a substantial educational publisher in the early twentieth century, producing a wide range of atlases and text books.

17   I take this sentence from the policy statement of Routledge's Archi*text* series, edited by Tom Markus and myself.

18   Architectural history buffs will know that Voysey's well known 'Tower House' design of 1889, can be seen in Bedford Park, in the winter, from the Piccadilly line.

19   On January 27, 1989, the Minister for Trade and Industry visited Leeds to launch its 'ambitious long-term inner-city plan . . . which aims to put Leeds on the international map alongside comparable cities such as Frankfurt, Milan, Toronto and Melbourne'. Proposals included the building of an international standard 5-star hotel, a conference and exhibition center, an entertainment, restaurant and night life district, plus road and rail investment to put Leeds 'firmly at the hub of the country's communication network'. *Yorkshire Advertiser* February 1989.

20   Following a further essay by John Friedmann, 'The World City Hypothesis' (1986: 69–84), a major conference was held on the topic in 1993 at the Center for Innovative Technology, adjacent to Dulles International Airport, Washington DC, papers from which were published as *World Cities in a World-System*, P. L. Knox and P. J. Taylor (eds), in 1995.

21   According to the 1991 Census, of people born outside England and living in London, 27 of the 36 national communities of over 10,000 were from postcolonial countries. With the exception of Germany and Italy, the 16 largest of these national communities (all over 23,000) were of postcolonial origin. These included, in numerical order of size: Irish Republic (over 200,000), India, Scotland (c.100,000–150,000), Jamaica, Wales, Kenya, Bangladesh, Cyprus (c.50,000–76,000), Pakistan, Northern Ireland, Nigeria, US (c.30,000–45,000) [Germany, Italy], Ghana, Uganda, Sri Lanka, Australia (c.23,000–27,000). Other postcolonial communities between 10,000 and 19,000 in 1991 included, in order of size, those from South Africa, Hong Kong, Malaysia, Tanzania, Guyana, Mauritius, Barbados, Trinidad and Tobago. These figures underestimate the true size of the ethnic minority communities as they do not include children born in the UK to parents born in the countries named. Nearly 350,000 people in London in 1991 belonged to the Indian ethnic group, while only 152,000 of them were born in India (not all of whom would necessarily be Indian) (see Storkey 1994: 15–16). Though my book was entitled 'Global Cities', the subtitle, 'Post-Imperialism and the Internationalization of London' reflected these interests.

22   I owe the following section of the story to a (serendipitous) phone call from a long time family friend, Professor Margaret Chatterjee of the University of Delhi. Following a visit to Bristol in Summer 2001 when we spoke about Gandhi's visit to Lancashire – which I had long known about but without being aware of either the date, the actual places he had visited, or the exact circumstances – Margaret told me of a recent BBC talk on 'Gandhi's Mill Tour', presented by Professor Biphu Parikh (BBC Bristol September 1, 2001). The talk included recordings of mill workers and managers, in their 80s and 90s, who had met Gandhi during the visit. On leaving Darwen later on the Saturday, Gandhi went to stay at a Quaker Guest House at West Bradford above the industrial town of Clitheroe. At the Quaker Meeting House, on the grass lawn, he played tennis with Edith Plaistage (?), a trainee teacher who recalled, seventy years later, 'He was a marvellous player . . . he made me look like a jelly fish' (from the BBC talk). On the following day, he met with delegations of the unemployed from the area, including Blackburn and Clitheroe. Later in the afternoon, he walked up Bowland Moor from which he could see Pendle Hill 'where the Quaker faith was born in George Fox's visionary experience' (Hunt 1978: 210). A detailed itinerary of the tour is given in Hunt's book. I am grateful to Frances King who had the talk taped for me at BBC Bristol.

23   Hunt's account (1978) here is supplemented by the oral accounts of both managers and workers included in the BBC talk indicated at note 22.

24   Bose and Jalal (1998) state that the importation of British cotton goods into India in 1939 was only one eighth of what it had been a decade before.

In Britain, the mill owners accused Gandhi of acting in the interests not of cottage industry but rather of Bombay mill owners. Gandhi, in turn, pointed out that India caused only a small portion of Lancashire's problems, and 'urged attention to the general worldwide economic crisis' (Hunt 1978: 210). On a subsequent conference visit to Bombay (then Mumbai) in March 2002, I was struck by the (cartographic) representational as well as real similarity between the abandoned cotton mills of Parel, Mumbai and those of Darwen which (with Blackburn), for the last three or more decades has had a substantial Indian (and also Pakistani) population. The Blackburn district of Bastwell has the highest percentage (73) of Muslims in Britain (*The Guardian* July 4, 2003).

25   The other main faience producer at this time was the Yorkshire firm of Leeds Fireclay. Swimming pools, hotels, the walls of school corridors, London underground stations and, not least, the interior of Battersea Power Station, taking 15,000 square yards of Shaws Faience tiles in 1931, were among other 'Modern' places providing opportunities for faience (Brochure, *Faience by Shaws during 1931*).

Afterword

During the two decades in which the interpretive concepts of 'globalization' and 'global culture' have come into use they have been invested with a much deeper, more sophisticated, more historical understanding, becoming the subject of an extensive empirical and theoretical literature. Though I have cited only a fraction of this literature, I have had two main aims in this book. First, I have argued that with the quickening pace of globalization, and especially increasing transnational migration, global media proliferation and cross-cultural exchange at all levels, consciousness of postcolonial experience and the critical perspectives on knowledge formation this has brought about, has become a major factor in understanding the contemporary world. It has pointed us to *different* globalizations, seen from outside 'the West', and also from below.

Though I have largely focused in this book on the postcolonial phenomenon in relation to issues of identity in both postcolonial and (technically) 'postimperial' anglophone cultures, developments in information technology enabled services have demonstrated the immense *economic* importance of the *cultural* phenomenon of language, especially the postcolonial anglophone connections between the US, India and Britain and also elsewhere. It is rarely, if ever, acknowledged that, outside the US, India has the largest number of English speakers and as the college educated urban middle class grows, their numbers increase. In the current globalized economy, postcolonial English combined with IT not only shifts services – and increasingly, professional – employment to India, Ireland and the Philippines but creates new spaces and built environments in the process. Despite its profound and completely taken-for-granted significance, tracking other dimensions of this postcolonial anglophone connection (including the so-called 'transatlantic alliance' between the US and Britain) would need another book. It may, therefore, take more than global mega-projects alone to bring investment to aspiring 'global cities' in Asia (Marshall 2002). Neglecting the significance of postcolonial languages (not only international English, but also other 'world languages') in studies of globalization and, especially, in distinguishing between the nature and language attributes of different 'global cities,' is a major lacuna in the literature.

Second, I have drawn attention to the ways in which building and architectural cultures are affected by transnational processes. Seeing and experiencing the spaces of the built environment in all their material, visual, urban and architectural dimensions, either directly or vicariously via the media, has become a primary form of 'evidence' which people use to 'confirm' ideas of globalization and global culture. However, I have argued against simplistic interpretations concerning the 'homogenization' of building and architectural forms worldwide, drawing attention to the socially exclusive conditions in which such interpretations are made and the very different circumstances in which buildings and environments are experienced by local people.

Understandings of globality and global culture are never static. What we think of as globalization changes from day to day according to different developments; political, technological, economic. The final drafts of this book were written in Spring 2003 against a news background of the invasion and occupation of Iraq by (mainly) US and also British forces and the subsequent 're-building' of Baghdad involving major American corporations (Bechtel, Haliburton and others) financially benefiting from the death and destruction wreaked by the American military. This has been on my mind especially when writing Chapter 5, on the transnational influences affecting contemporary urbanism. Like many other commentators I am increasingly aware that the discourse on 'globalization,' dominant in recent years, is now being increasingly overlaid by the consciousness of a new imperialism.

As my subtitle indicates, my main focus has been on the relation of architecture and urbanism to questions of cultural identity. Yet cultural identities can be understood from many perspectives, whether 'globally' or in relation to other spaces: the nation state, region, city or neighborhood, as well as social categories of gender, race, religion, ethnicity, class or caste to mention the most obvious. Cultural identity can also not be separated from questions of equity and inequity, issues both implicit and explicit in the preceding pages. Being impossibly rich or miserably poor, according to relative criteria, are also identities, as indeed, is any economic and social position. Global inequality, as a theme, goes back by and large to the mid twentieth century (Pieterse 2002: 2). It is usually measured in terms of per capita income and wealth and, as is well known, the differences in human inequality worldwide have been widening ever since the Industrial Revolution.[1] The growing differences, however, are equally visible in the way the global built environment has developed over these two centuries, in terms of scale, space, expenditure, cost and, not least, accessibility to the facilities and resources that buildings and urbanism provide, especially shelter, health, education and security. The most recent (2003) United Nations Habitat study of global urban conditions refers to a sixth of the world's population (640 million) living in squalid, unhealthy areas, mostly without access to water, sanitation, services, or legal security. These are also the spaces of global culture, a culture which today encompasses ideas of global citizenship, global equity and a global civil society.

NOTE

1   According to the UNDP, estimates of the income gap between the fifth of the world's people living in the richest country and the fifth in the poorest has grown from 3:1 in 1820, to 7:1 a century later, and to 74:1 in 1997 (UNDP 1999: 3).

References

Abaza, M. (2001) 'Shopping Malls, Consumer Culture and the Reshaping of Public Space in Egypt', *Theory, Culture and Society* 18, 5: 97–22.

Abel, C. (1997) *Architecture and Identity: Towards a Global Eco-Culture*, Boston: Architectural Press.

Abercrombie, N., Hill, S. and Turner, B. S. (1988) *Dictionary of Sociology*, London: Penguin.

Abeyasekare, S. (1987) *Jakarta: A History*, New York and Oxford: Oxford University Press.

Abu-Lughod, J. (1965) 'Tale of Two Cities: The Origins of Modern Cairo', *Comparative Studies in Society and History* 7, 4: 429–57.

—— (1971) *Cairo: 1001 Years of the City Victorious*, Princeton, NJ: Princeton University Press.

—— (1980) *Rabat: Urban Apartheid in Morocco*, Princeton, NJ: Princeton University Press.

—— (1989) *Before European Hegemony: The World System AD 1250–1350*, New York: Oxford University Press.

—— (1991) 'Going Beyond Global Babble' in King, A. (ed.) *Culture, Globalization and the World-System*, London: Macmillan and Binghamton: State University of New York at Binghamton: 31–8.

—— (1999a) *America's Global Cities: New York, Chicago, Los Angeles*, Minneapolis: University of Minnesota Press.

—— (1999b) 'New York and Cairo. A View from the Street', *International Social Science Journal* 125: 16–24.

Ackerman, J. (1990) *The Villa: Form and Ideology of Country Houses*, Cambridge, MA: Harvard University Press.

AlSayyad, N. (ed.) (1992) *Forms of Dominance: On the Architecture and Urbanism of the Colonial Enterprise*, Aldershot: Avebury.

—— (2000) *Hybrid Urbanism: On the Identity Discourse and the Built Environment*, Westport, CT: Praegar.

—— (2001) *Consuming Tradition, Manufacturing Heritage: Global Norms and Urban Forms in the Age of Tourism*, London and New York: Routledge.

Anderson, B. (1983) *Imagined Communities: Reflections on the Origins and Spread of Nationalism*, London: Verso.

Anon. (1935) *Lusaka: The New Capital of Northern Rhodesia*, London: Jonathan Cape.

Appadurai, A. (1990) 'Disjuncture and Difference in the Global Cultural Economy' in Featherstone, M. (ed.) *Global Culture: Nationalism, Globalization and Modernity*, London, Newbury Park, New Delhi: Sage: 295–310.

—— (1996) *Modernity at Large: Cultural Dimensions of Globalization*, Minneapolis: University of Minnesota Press.

—— (2000) 'Grassroots Globalization and the Research Imagination', *Public Culture* 12, 1: 1–19.

Appiah, A. and Gates, H. L., Jr. (eds) (1996) *The Dictionary of Global Culture*, Harmondsworth: Penguin.

Archer, J. (1997) 'Colonial Suburbs in South Asia 1750–1850 and the Spaces of Modernity' in Silverstone, R. *Visions of Suburbia*, London and New York: Routledge: 26–54.

—— (2000) '*Paras*, Palaces, Pathogens: Frameworks for the Growth of Calcutta 1800–50', *City and Society* 12, 1: 19–54.

Arnold, D. (2000) '"Illusory Riches": Representations of the Tropical World, 1840–1950', *Singapore Journal of Tropical Geography* 21, 1: 6–18.

Ashcroft, B. (2001) *Post-Colonial Transformation*, London: Routledge.

Ashcroft, B., Griffiths, G. and Tiffin, H. (1989) *The Empire Writes Back: Theory and Practice in Post-Colonial Literatures*, London and New York: Routledge.

—— (1995) *The Post-Colonial Studies Reader*, London and New York: Routledge.

—— (1998) *Key Concepts in Postcolonial Studies*, London and New York: Routledge.

Ashley, J. (2002) 'Global Culture has Squeezed Royalty out of Our Hearts', *The Guardian* April 3: 6.

Atal, Y. (1981) 'The Call for Indigenization', *International Social Science Journal* 33, 1: 189–97.

Attoe, W. (1981) *Understanding and Moulding Urban Silhouettes*, Chichester: Wiley.

Augé, M. (1995) *Non-Places: An Introduction to the Anthropology of Supermodernity*, London: Verso.

August, O. (2002) 'Freewheeling China Shanghai's London Eye', *The Times* July 5: 1.

Axford, B. (2000) 'The Idea of Global Culture' in Beynon, J. and Dunkerly, D. (eds) *Globalization: The Reader*, London: Athlone Press: 105–7.

Bacon, M. (1985) *Ernest Flagg: Beaux-Arts Architect and Urban Reformer*, Cambridge, MA: MIT Press.

Balandier, G. (1966) 'The Colonial Situation: A Theoretical Approach' in Wallerstein I. (ed.) *Social Change: The Colonial Situation*, New York: Wiley (originally 1951).

Ballantyne, T. (2002) 'Empire, Knowledge and Culture: From Proto-Globalization to Modern Globalization' in Hopkins, A. G. (ed.) *Globalization in World History*, London: Pimlico: 115–140.

Bamyeh, M. (2001) *The Ends of Globalization*, Minneapolis: University of Minnesota Press.

Bannerjee, S. B. and Linstead. S. (2001) 'Globalization, Multiculturalism and Other Fictions: Colonialism for the New Millennium', *Organization* 8, 4: 683–722.

Barker, F., Bernstein, J., Coombes, J., Hulme, P., Stone, J. and Stratton, J. (eds) (1981) *1641: Literature and Power in the Seventeenth Century* (Proceedings of the Essex Conference on the Sociology of Literature, July 1980), Colchester.

Barnett, R. and Cavanagh, J. (1996) 'Homogenization of Global Culture' in Mander, J. and Goldsmith, E. (eds) *The Case Against the Global Economy*, San Francisco: Sierra Club: 71–8.

Barthes, R. (1973) *Mythologies*, trans. A. Lavers, London: Paladin.

Basu, K. (2000) 'Immigration Check', *India Today (International)* May 29: 38.

Bater, J. H. (1976) *St Petersburg*, Montreal: McGill/Queen's University Press.

Baudrillard, J. (1988) 'For a Critique of the Political Economy of the Sign' in Poster, M. (ed.) *Jean Baudrillard: Selected Writings*, Stanford, CA: Stanford University Press.

Beaverstock, J. V., Smith, R. V. and Taylor, P. J. (1999) 'A Roster of World Cities', *Cities* 16, 6: 445–58.

Beidecke, K. (1896) *London and Its Environs*, London: Dulau.

Benjamin, W. (1978) 'Paris, Capital of the Nineteenth Century', in Benjamin, W. *Reflections, Essays, Aphorisms. Autobiographical Writings*, New York: Harcourt Brace Jovanovich.

Bennison, A. K. (2002) 'Muslim Universalism and Western Globalization', in Hopkins, A. G. *Globalisation in World History*, London: Pimlico: 74–97.

Bentmann, R. and Muller, M. (1992) *The Villa as Hegemonic Architecture*, trans. by T. Spence and D. Craven, New Jersey and London: Humanities Press. Originally published as *Der Villa als Herrschaftsarchitektur*, Surkamp Verlag: Frankfurt am Main, 1970.

Berger, J. (1972) *Ways of Seeing*, Harmondsworth: Penguin.

Berman, M. (1988) *All That is Solid Melts into Air: The Experience of Modernity*, Harmondsworth: Penguin.

Bhabha, H. (1983) 'The Other Question: The Stereotype and Colonial Discourse', *Screen* 24: 18–36.

—— (1994) '"Race", Time and the Revision of Modernity', in Bhabha, H. *The Location of Culture*, London and New York: Routledge: 236–56.

Bharat Savak Samaj Delhi Pradash (1958), *Report of the Socio-Economic Survey of the Slum Dwellers of Old Delhi City*, Delhi: Atma Ram.

Bhatia, G. (1994) *Punjabi Baroque. And Other Memories of Architecture*, New Delhi: Penguin.

Bigott, J. C. (2002) *From Cottage to Bungalow: Houses and the Working Class in Metropolitan Chicago, 1869–1929*, Chicago: University of Chicago Press.

Bingaman, A., Sanders, L. and Zorach, R. (eds) (2002) *Embodied Utopias*, London and New York: Routledge.

Bishop, R., Phillips, J. and Yeo, W. W. (eds) (2004) *Beyond Description: Singapore Space Historicity,* London and New York: Routledge.

Black, C. E. (1966) *The Dynamics of Modernization. A Study in Comparative History*, New York: Harper and Row.

Black, I. (1999) 'Imperial Visions: Rebuilding the Bank of England, 1919–39' in Driver, F. and Gilbert, D. (eds) *Imperial Cities: Landscape, Display and Identity*, Manchester: Manchester University Press: 96–116.

Blakely, E. and Snyder, M. (1997) *Fortress America: Gated Communities in the United States*, Washington DC: Brookings Institute Press.

Blaut, J. M. (1993) *The Colonizer's View of the World. Geographical Diffusionism and Eurocentric History*, New York: Guilford Press.

Blunt, A. (1994) *Travel, Gender and Imperialism: Mary Kingsley and West Africa*, London and New York: Guilford.

Blunt, A. and Rose, G. (eds) (1994) *Writing Women and Space: Colonial and Postcolonial Geographies*, London and New York: Guilford.

Bose, S. and Jalal. A. (1998) *Modern South Asia: History, Culture, Political Economy*, London and New York: Routledge.

Boulding, E. (1989) *Building a Global Civic Culture: Education for an Interdependent World*, New York: Teachers' College Press, Columbia University.

Bourdieu, P. (1977) *Outline of a Theory of Practice*, London: Cambridge University Press.

—— (1984) *Distinction*, London and Boston: Routledge and Kegan Paul.

Boyce Davis, C. (1994) *Black Women, Writing and Identity: Migrations of the Subject*, London and New York: Routledge.

Bozdoğan, S. (2001) *Modernism and Nation Building: Turkish Architectural Culture in the Early Republic*, Seattle: University of Washington Press.

Bradbury, M. and McFarlane, J. (1976) *Modernism, 1890–1930*, Harmondsworth: Penguin.

Brand, S. (1994) *How Buildings Learn: What Happens After They're Built*, London and New York: Penguin.

Breckenridge, C. (1995) *Consuming Modernity: Public Culture in a South Asian World*, Minneapolis: University of Minnesota Press.

Bremner, A. (2003) '"Some Imperial Institute": Architecture, Symbolism and the Ideal of Empire in Late Victorian Britain, 1887–93', *Journal of the Society of Architectural Historians* 62, 1: 50–73.

Briggs, R. A. (1891) *Bungalows and Country Residences*, London: Batsford (later editions 1894, 1895, 1897, 1901).

—— (1894) 'Bungalows', *The Studio* April 1894: 20–7.

Broudehoux, A-M. (2001) 'Learning from Chinatown: The Search for a Modern Chinese Identity' in AlSayyad, N. *Consuming Tradition, Manufacturing Heritage: Global Norms and Urban Forms in the Age of Tourism*, London and New York: Routledge: 156–80.

Brunner, O., Conze, W. and Koselleck, R. (1978) *Geschichtliche Grundbegriffe*, Stuttgart: Klett-Cotta.

Buchanan, K. (1972) *The Geography of Empire*, Nottingham: Russell Press.

Bunnell, T. (1999) 'Views from Above and Below: The Petronas Twin Towers and the Contesting Visions of Development in Contemporary Malaysia', *Singapore Journal of Tropical Geography* 20, 1: 1–23.

Cain, P. J. and Hopkins, A. G. (2001) *British Imperialism 1688–2000* New York: Longman.

Cairns, S (1998) 'Postcolonial Architectonics', *Postcolonial Studies* 1, 2: 211–35.

—— (2003) 'Introduction' to Cairns, S. *Drift: Architecture and Migrancy*, London and New York: Routledge.

Campbell, C. (1999) 'The Easternization of the West' in Wilson, B. and Cresswell, J. (eds) *New Religious Movements*, New York and London: Routledge.

Castells, M. (1996) *The Rise of Network Society*, Vol.1. Cambridge, MA: Blackwell.

Castillo, G. (2001) 'Building Culture in a Divided Berlin: Globalization and the Cold War' in AlSayyad, N. *Consuming Tradition, Manufacturing Heritage: Global Norms and Urban Forms in the Age of Tourism*, London and New York: Routledge: 181–205.

Çelik, Z. (1997) *Urban Forms and Colonial Confrontations: Algiers under French Rule*, Berkeley: University of California Press.

Chakrabarty, D. (1992a) 'Postcoloniality and the Artifice of History: Who Speaks for "Indian" Pasts?', *Representations* 32 (Winter): 1–32.

—— (1992b) 'Provincializing Europe: Postcoloniality and the Critique of History', *Cultural Studies* 16, 1: 337–57.

Chakravarty, S. (1998) 'Time to Get the Boot. Urban Affairs Minister Jethmalani Serves Final Notice on VIPs Refusal to Vacate Official Bungalows', *India Today (International)* June 9: 18.

Chakravorty, S. (2000) 'From Colonial City to Globalizing City: The Far from Complete Transformation of Calcutta' in Marcuse, P. and van Kempen, R. (eds) *Globalizing Cities: A New Spatial Order?*, Oxford, and Malden, MA: Blackwell: 56–77.

Chatterjee, P. (1994) 'Whose Imagined Community?' in Balakrishnan, G. (ed.) *Mapping the Nation*, London: Verso: 214–25.

—— (2003) 'Is the Indian Population Becoming Bourgeois?', Paper given at *City One: South Asian Conference on the Urban Experience*, Sarai, Delhi, January 9–11.

Chatterjee, S. and Kenny, J. (1999) 'Creating a New Capital: Colonial Discourse and the Decolonization of Delhi', *Historical Geography* 27: 73–98.

Chattopadhyay, S. (2000) 'Blurring Boundaries: The Limits of "White Town" in Colonial Calcutta', *Journal of the Society of Architectural Historians* 59, 2: 154–79.

—— (2004) *Representing Calcutta: Modernity, Nationalism and the Colonial Uncanny*, London and New York: Routledge.

China Daily 1994–2000.

Clark, T. J. (1984) *The Painting of Modern Life: Paris in the Art of Manet and His Followers*, Princeton, NJ: Princeton University Press.

Clifford, J. (1988) *The Predicament of Culture*, Cambridge, MA: Harvard University Press.

—— (1998) *Routes: Travel and Translation in the Late Twentieth Century*, Cambridge, MA: Harvard University Press.

Cohn, B. S. (1987) *An Anthropologist Among the Historians and Other Essays*, Delhi: Oxford University Press.

Collins, J. (1980) 'Lusaka: Urban Planning in a British Colony, 1931–64' in Cherry, G. C. (ed.) *Shaping an Urban World*, London: Mansell: 227–42.

Coquery-Vidrovitch, C. and Goerg, O. (eds) (1996) *La Ville Europeène Outre Mers: Un Modèle Conquerant?*, Paris and Montreal: Harmattan.

Crane, D., Kawashima, N. and Kawasaki, K. (eds) (2002), *Global Culture: Media, Arts, Policy, and Globalization*, London and New York: Routledge.

Crawford, A. (1985) *C. R. Ashbee: Architect, Designer and Romantic Socialist*, London: Yale University Press.

Crinson, M. (1996) *Empire Building, Orientalism and Victorian Architecture*, London and New York: Routledge.

—— (2003) *Modern Architecture and the End of Empire*, Aldershot, Hampshire and Burlington, VT: Ashgate Press.

Cromley, E. (1990) *Alone Together: A History of New York's Apartments*, Ithaca, NY: Cornell University Press.

Crouch, D. P. and Johnson, J. G. (2001) *Traditions in Architecture: Africa, America, Asia, Oceana*, New York and Oxford: Oxford University Press.

Crush, J. (1994) 'Post-colonialism, Decolonization and Geography' in Godlewska, A. and Smith, N. (eds) (1994) *Geography and Empire*, Oxford: Blackwell: 330–50.

Crysler, C. G. (2003) *Writing Spaces. Discourses of Architecture, Urbanism and the Built Environment 1960–2000*, London and New York: Routledge.

Crystal, D. (1997) *English as a Global Language*, Cambridge: Cambridge University Press.

Cumming, E. and Kaplan, W. (1991) *The Arts and Crafts Movement*, London: Thames and Hudson.

Cvetkovich, A. and Kellner, D. (eds) (1997) *Articulating the Global and the Local: Globalization and Cultural Studies*, Boulder, CO: Westview Press.

Davey, P. (1995) *Arts and Crafts Architecture*, London: Phaidon.

Davies, P. (1985) *Splendors of the Raj: British Architecture in India 1680–1940*, Harmondsworth: Penguin.

de Vries, J. (1983) *European Urbanization 1500–1800*, London: Methuen.

Dick, H. W. and Rimmer, P. J. (1998) 'Beyond the Third World City: The New Geography of Southeast Asia', *Urban Studies* 35, 12: 2303–21.

Dirks, N. (1992) 'Introduction' in Dirks, N. (ed.) *Colonialism and Culture*, Ann Arbor: University of Michigan.

—— (1996) 'Foreword' in Cohn, B. S. *Colonialism and Its Forms of Knowledge*, Princeton, NJ: Princeton University Press.

Dirlik, A. (1994) 'The Postcolonial Aura: Third World Criticism in the Age of Global Capitalism', *Critical Inquiry* 20: 328–56.

Dirlik, A. and Zhang, X. (eds) (2000) 'Introduction: Postmodernism and China' in Dirlik, A. and Zhang, X. (eds) *Postmodernism and China*, Durham, NC, and London: Duke University Press: 1–20.

DLF News (2001–2). See also www.DLF.com.

Dobson, J. (1990) The Role of Ethics in Global Corporate Culture', *Journal of Business Ethics* 9: 481–88.

Domosh, M. (1988) 'The Symbolism of the Skyscraper: Case Studies of New York's First Tall Buildings', *Journal of Urban History* 14, 3: 321–45.

Dovey, K. (1996) 'Tall Towers and Short-Sighted Cities', *Tirra Lirra* Winter: 2–3.

—— (1999) *Framing Places: Mediating Power in Built Form*, London and New York: Routledge.

Downing, A. J. (1969) *The Architecture of Country Houses*, New York: Dover (original publication, 1850).

Driver, F. (1992) 'Geography's Empire: Histories of Geographical Knowledge', *Environment and Planning D: Society and Space* 10: 23–40.

Driver, F. and Gilbert, D. (eds) (1999) *Imperial Cities: Landscape, Display and Identity*, Manchester: Manchester University Press.

Driver, F. and Yeoh, B. (2000) 'Constructing the Tropics: An Introduction', *Singapore Journal of Tropical Geography* 21, 1: 1–5.

Duncan, J. S. and Gregory, D. (eds) (1999) *Writes of Passage: Reading Travel Writing*, London and New York: Routledge.

Dupont, V. (2003) 'The New 'Chic' Residential Areas of Outer Delhi: Publicity Hype and Suburban Reality'. Paper presented at *City One: First South Asian Conference on the Urban Experience*, Sarai, Delhi, January 9–11.

Dupont, V., Tarlo, E. and Vidal, D. (eds) (2000), *Delhi: Urban Space and Human Dimensions*, Delhi: Manohar, Centre de Science Humaines and Institut de Reserche pour le Development.

Dupré, J. (1996) *Skyscrapers. A History of the World's Most Famous and Important Skyscrapers*, New York: Black Dog and Leventhal.

du Prey, P. R. (1982) *John Soane: The Making of an Architect*, Chicago, IL: University of Chicago Press.

Durant, A. S. (1992) *C. F. A. Voysey*, London: Academy Editions and New York: St Martin's Press.

Durham, J. (1992) 'Cowboys and . . . Notes on Art, Literature and American Indians in the Modern American Mind' in Jaimes, M. Annette (ed.) *The State of Native America. Genocide, Colonialism and Resistance*, Boston: South End Press: 423–38.

Easwaran, E. (1973) *Gandhi the Man*, San Francisco: Glide Publications.

Elvin, M. (1986) 'A Working Definition of "Modernity" ?', *Past and Present* 113, November: 209–213.

Environment and Planning D (2003) 'Introduction: Tracking the Power Geometries of International Critical Geography', *Environment and Planning D: Society and Space* 21, 2: 131-68.

Evenson, N. (1989) *The Indian Metropolis: A View Towards the West*, New Haven, CT: Yale University Press.

Fainstein, S. (1994) *The City Builders*, Oxford: Blackwell.

Faison, S. (1995) 'China Stands Tall in the World and Here's Proof', *New York Times* (International section), July 26.

Fanon, F. (1967) *Black Skin, White Masks*, New York: Grove.

—— (1968) *The Wretched of the Earth*, New York: Grove

Featherstone, M. (1990) 'Global Culture: An Introduction' in Featherstone, M. (ed.) *Global Culture: Nationalism, Globalization and Modernity*, London, Newbury Park, New Delhi: Sage: 1–14.

—— (1995) *Undoing Culture: Globalization, Postmodernism and Identity*, London and Thousand Oaks, CA: Sage.

—— (1996) 'Localism, Globalism, and Cultural Identity' in Wilson, R. and Dissanayake, W. (eds) *Global/Local. Cultural Production and the Transnational Imaginary*, Durham, NC, and London: Duke University Press: 46–77.

Featherstone, M. and Lash, S. (1995) 'Globalisation, Modernity and the Spatialization of Social Theory: An Introduction' in Featherstone, M., Lash, S. and Robertson R. (1995) *Global Modernities*, London, Thousand Oaks, CA, and New Delhi: Sage: 1–24.

Featherstone, M., Lash, S. and Robertson, R. (eds) (1995) *Global Modernities*, London, Thousand Oaks, CA, and New Delhi: Sage.

Fenske, G. and Holdsworth, D. (1992) 'Corporate Identity and the New York Office Building: 1895–1915', in Ward, D. and Zunz, O. *The Landscape of Modernity. Essays on New York City 1900–1940*, New York: Russell Sage: 129–59.

Finkelstein, M. J., Seal, R. and Schuster, J. H. (1998) *The New Academic Generation*, Baltimore: The Johns Hopkins University Press.

Fisher, J. (ed.) (1995) *Global Visions: Towards a New Internationalism in the Visual Arts*, London: Kala Press.

Fishman, J., Conrad, J. and Rubal-Lopez, J. (eds) (1996) *Postimperial English: Status Change in British and American Colonies 1940–1990*, The Hague: Mouton.

Fishman, R. A. (1987) *Bourgeois Utopias: The Rise and Fall of Suburbia*, New York: Basic Books.

Fleming, J., Honour, J. and Pevsner, N. (eds) (1991) *Penguin Dictionary of Architecture*, 4th edition, London: Penguin.

Foucault, M. (1980) *Power/Knowledge. Selected Interviews and Other Writings 1972–7*, Gordon, C. (ed.) New York: Pantheon.

Frampton, K. (1985) *Modern Architecture: A Critical History*, London: Thames and Hudson.

Franck, K. and Schneekloth, L. (eds) (1994) *Ordering Space: Types in Architecture and Design*, New York: Van Nostrand Reinhold.

Franklin, S., Lury, C. and Stacey, J. (eds) (2000) *Global Nature/Global Culture*, Cambridge: Polity.

Freeman, D. B. (1999) 'Hill Stations or Horticulture? Conflicting Imperial Visions of Cameron Highlands', *Journal of Historical Geography* 25, 1: 17–35.

Frenkel, S. and Western, J. (1988) 'British Tropical Colony: Sierra Leone', *Annals of the Association of American Geographers* 78, 2: 211–28.

Friedmann, J. (1986) 'The World City Hypothesis', *Development and Change*, 17, 1: 69–84.

—— (2002) *The Prospect of Cities*, Minneapolis: University of Minnesota Press.

Friedmann, J. and Wolff, G. (1982) 'World City Formation: An Agenda for Research and Action', *International Journal of Urban and Regional Research* 6, 3: 309–44.

Frisby, S. (2001) *Cityscapes of Modernity: Critical Explorations*, Cambridge: Polity.

Fuchs, R. and Herbert, G. (2001) 'A Colonial Portrait of Jerusalem: The British in Mandate-Era Palestine' in AlSayyad, N. *Consuming Tradition, Manufacturing Heritage: Global Norms and Urban Forms in the Age of Tourism*, London and New York: Routledge: 83–110.

Fukuyama, F. (1996) 'Review of Appiah, A. and Gates, H. L., Jr. (eds) (1996) *The Dictionary of Global Culture*. Harmondsworth: Penguin' in *Foreign Affairs* 76, 3: 122.

Furnivall, J. S. (1948) *Colonial Policy and Practice*, London: Cambridge University Press.

Futagawa, Y. (1997) *Global Architecture. An Encyclopaedia of Modern Architecture*, Tokyo: ADA Edition.

Gad, G. and Holdsworth, D. (1987) 'Corporate Capitalism and the Emergence of the High Rise Office Building', *Urban Geography* 8, 3: 212–31.

Galtung, J. (1999) 'A Multicultural Global Culture: Not a Question of When but How. Some Roads to Cultural Integration for Peace', *Biography* 22, 1: 104–12.

Gaonkar, D. P. (1999) 'On Alternative Modernities', *Public Culture* 11, 1: 1–18.

Garnham, N. (1989) *Capitalism and Communication. Global Culture and the Economics of Information*, London, Newbury Park, New Delhi: Sage.

Garreau, J. (1991) *Edge City: Life on the New Frontier*, New York: Doubleday.

Geyer, M. (1993) 'Multiculturalism and the Politics of General Education', *Critical Inquiry* 19, 3: 499–533.

Giddens, A. (1990) *The Consequences of Modernity*, Cambridge: Polity.

—— (2002) *Runaway World: How Globalization is Reshaping Our Lives*, London: Profile Books.

Gill, G. (c.1901) *The British Colonies, Dependencies and Protectorates*, London: George Gill and Sons.

Gilroy, P. (1987) *There Ain't No Black in the Union Jack*, London: Hutchinson.

—— (1993) *The Black Atlantic: Modernity and Double Consciousness*, Cambridge, MA: Harvard University Press.

Girouard, M. (1985) *Cities and People*, New Haven: Yale University Press.

—— (1990) *The English Town*, London: Yale University Press.

Glancy, J. (1998) 'Urban Bullies', *The Guardian* December 14.

—— (2000) 'Tower and the Glory', *The Guardian* May 15.

—— (2002) 'Reach for the Sky', *The Guardian* September 15.

Glick Schiller, N., Basch, L. and Blanc, C. S. (1995) 'From Migrant to Transmigrant: Theorizing Transnational Migration', *Anthropological Quarterly* 68, 1: 48–63.

Godlewska, A. and Smith, N. (eds) (1994) *Geography and Empire*, Oxford: Blackwell.

Goh, Beng-Lan (2002) *Modern Dreams: An Inquiry into Power, Cultural Production and the Cityscape in Contemporary Urban Penang*, Ithaca, NY: Cornell University Southeast Asia Program Publications.

Graburn, N. (1997) 'IASTE 1996: Retrospect and Prospect', *Traditional Dwellings and Settlements Review* 9, 1, Fall: 60–4.

Gradidge, R. (2002) 'Baker and Lutyens in South Africa, or the Road to Bakerloo' in Hopkins, A. and Stamp, G. (eds) (2002) *Lutyens Abroad: The Work of Sir Edwin Lutyens Outside the British Isles*, London: The British School at Rome: 147–58.

Graham, S. and Marvin, S. (2001) *Splintering Urbanism: Networks, Infrastructures, Technological Mobilities and the Urban Condition*, London and New York: Routledge.

Grant, R. and Short, J. R. (eds) (2002) *Globalization and the Margins*, New York and Basingstoke: Palgrave Macmillan.

Grant, R. and Yankson, P. (2003) 'Accra', *Cities* 20, 1: 65–74.

Gregory, D. (2000) 'Postcolonialism', in Johnson, R., Gregory, D. and Smith, D. M. (eds) *The Dictionary of Human Geography*, Oxford: Blackwell.

Gregotti, V. (1996) 'In our Skies Devoid of Ideas', *Casabella* LX, 630–631: 3–11.

Griswold, C. L. (1986) 'The Vietnam Veterans' Memorial and the Washington Mall: Philosophical Thoughts on Political Iconography', *Critical Inquiry* 12 (Summer): 688–719.

Groll, C. L. T. and Alphen, W. V. (2002) *The Dutch Overseas: Architectural Survey*, Zwolle: Waanders Publishers: Netherlands Department for Conservation.

Gubler, J. (1996): 'The Grand Manoeuvres of the International Avant-garde', *Casabella* LX, 630–631: 13–19.

Gu, F. R. and Tang, Z. (2002) 'Shanghai: Reconnecting to the Global Economy' in Sassen, S. (ed.) (2002) *Global Networks/Linked Cities*, New York and London: Routledge.

Guan, M. and Zhu, P. (2002) *Neighborhood Villas. I Guang Dong and II Shanghai*, Nanchang: Jianxi Kexue Jishu Chubanshe.

Guha, R. (1987) 'Introduction', to Cohn, B. S. (1987) *An Anthropologist Among the Historians and Other Essays*, Delhi: Oxford University Press: i–xxiv.

Guinness Book of Records 1492, New York: Facts on File.

Guinness Book of Records (1996) New York: Sterling Publishers.

Gupta, A. and Ferguson, J. (1997) *Culture, Power, Place: Explorations in Critical Anthropology*, Chapel Hill, NC: Duke University Press.

Gupta, N. (1994) 'Kingsway to Rajpath: The Democratization of Lutyens' Central Vista' in Asher, C. and Metcalf, T. (eds) *Perceptions of South Asia's Visual Past*, Delhi: Oxford and IBH: 257–69.

—— (2000) 'Concern, Indifference, Controversy: Reflections on Fifty Years of Conservation' in Dupont, V., Tarlo, E. and Vidal, D. (eds) *Delhi: Urban Space and Human Dimensions*, Delhi: Manohar, Centre de Science Humaines and Institut de Reserche pour le Development: 157–72

Gutierrez, J. and Lopez-Nieva, P. (2001) 'Are International Journals of Geography Really International?', *Progress in Human Geogaphy* 25, 1: 53–70.

Hagerstrand, T. (1983) 'In Search for the Sources Concepts' in Buttimer, A. (ed.) *The Practice of Geography*, London: Longman: 238–356.

Haggett, P. (1990) *The Geographer's Art*, Oxford: Blackwell.

Halbwachs, M. (1992) *On Collective Memory*, Chicago: University of Chicago Press (Originally published as *La Memoire Collective*, Paris: PUF 1968).

Hall, P. G. (1998) *Cities in Civilization*, New York: Pantheon Books.

Hall, S. (1991a): 'The Local and the Global: Globalization and Ethnicity' in King, A. D. (ed.) *Culture, Globalization and the World-System*, London: Macmillan and Binghamton: State University of New York at Binghamton: 19–40.

—— (1991b) 'Old and New Identities, Old and New Ethnicities' in King, A. D. (ed.) *Culture, Globalization and the World-System*, London: Macmillan; and Binghamton: State University of New York at Binghamton: 41–68.

Hamadeh, S. (1992) 'Creating the Traditional City: A French Project' in AlSayyad, N. (ed.) *Forms of Dominance: On the Architecture and Urbanism of the Colonial Enterprise*, Aldershot: Avebury: 241–60.

Hancock, J. (1980) 'The Apartment House in Urban America' in King, A. D. (ed.) *Buildings and Society: Essays on the Social Development of the Built Environment*, London and Boston: Routledge and Kegan Paul: 151–92.

Hannerz, U. (1989) 'Notes on the Global Ecumene', *Public Culture* 1, 2: 66–75.

—— (1993): 'The Cultural Role of World Cities' in Cohen, A. and Fukui, K. (eds) *Humanizing the City: Social Contexts of Urban Life at the Turn of the Millennium*, Edinburgh: Edinburgh University Press.

—— (1996) *Transnational Connections: Culture, Peoples, Places*, London and New York Routledge.

Harley, J. B. (1988) 'Maps, Knowledge and Power', in Cosgrove, D. and Daniels, S. (eds) *The Iconography of Landscape*, Cambridge: Cambridge University Press.

Harvey, D. (1973) *Social Justice and the City*, London: Arnold.

—— (1985) *The Urbanization of Capital*, Oxford: Blackwell.

—— (1989) *The Condition of Postmodernity. An Enquiry into the Origin of Cultural Change*, Oxford, and Cambridge, MA: Blackwell.

Held, D., McGrew, A., Goldblatt, D. and Perraton, J. (1999) *Global Transformations: Politics, Economics and Culture*, Cambridge: Polity.

Hexham, I. and Poewe, K. (1997) *New Religions as Global Cultures*, Boulder, CO: Westview Press.

Hitchcock, H. R. and Johnson, J. (1966) *The International Style*, New York: W. W. Norton.

Hitchmough, W. (1995) *C. F. A. Voysey*, London: Phaidon

Hobsbawm, E. J. and Ranger, T. (eds) (1983) *The Invention of Tradition*, Harmondsworth: Penguin.

Hobson, J. A. (1938, first published 1902) *Imperialism: A Study*, (1988 edition with new introduction by P. Siegelman), Ann Arbor: University of Michigan Press.

Hogan, T. and Houston C. (2002) 'Corporate Cities – Urban Gateways or Gated Communities Against the City? The Case of Lippo, Jakarta' in Bunnel, T., Drummond, L. B. W. and Ho, K. C. (eds) (2002) *Critical Reflections on Cities in Southeast Asia*, Singapore: Times Academic Press: 243–64.

Holston, J. (1989) *The Modernist City. An Anthropological Critique of Brazilia*, Chicago, IL: University of Chicago Press.

Home, R. (1997) *Of Planting and Planning: The Making of British Colonial Cities*, London: Spon.

'Home Counties' (1905) *Country Cottages. How to Build, Buy and Fit Them Up*, London: Heinemann.

Hopkins, A. G. (ed.) (2002) *Globalization in World History*, London: Pimlico.

Hopkins, A. and Stamp, G. (eds) (2002) *Lutyens Abroad: The Work of Sir Edwin Lutyens Outside the British Isles*, London: The British School at Rome.

Hooper, C. (2000) 'Masculinities in Transition: the Case of Globalization' in Marchand, M. and Sisson Runyan, A. (eds) (2000) *Global Restructuring. Sightings, Sites, and Resistances*, London and New York: Routledge: 59–73.

Hosagrahar, J. (2000) 'Mansions to Margins: Modernity and the Domestic Landscapes of Historic Delhi, 1847–1910', *Journal of the Society of Architectural Historians* 60, 1: 24–45.

—— (2004) *Indigenous Modernities*, London and New York: Routledge (forthcoming).

Howe, S. (1998) 'Review of Appiah, A. and Gates, H. L., Jr. (eds) (1996) *The Dictionary of Global Culture*, Harmondsworth: Penguin' in *New Statesman* 127, 4385: 48.

Howes, D. (1996) *Cross-Cultural Consumption*, London and New York: Routledge.

Hudson, B. (1977) 'The New Geography and the New Imperialism', *Antipode* 9, 1: 12–19.

Hulme P. (1981) 'Hurricanes in the Caribee: The Constitution of the Discourse of English Colonialism' in Barker, F., Bernstein, J., Coombes, J., Hulme, P., Stone, J. and Stratton, J. (eds) (1981) *1641: Literature and Power in the Seventeenth Century* (Proceedings of the Essex Conference on the Sociology of Literature, July 1980), Colchester.

Hung, W. (1991) 'Tiananmen Square: A Political History of Monuments', *Representations* 35: 84–117.

Hunt, J. D. (1978) *Gandhi in London*, New Delhi: Promilla.

Ibelings, H. (1998) *Supermodernism: Architecture in the Age of Globalization*, Amsterdam: NAI Publishers.

India Today (International), 1992–.

International Publications (2001) *Delhi and its Surroundings*, New Delhi: International Publications.

Irving, R. G. (1981) *Indian Summer: Lutyens, Baker and Imperial Delhi*, New Haven: Yale University Press.

Jackson, P. and Jacobs, J. M. (1996) 'Postcolonialism and the Politics of Race', *Environment and Planning D: Society and Space* 14: 1–3.

Jacobs, J. M. (1993) '"Shake 'em this Country": The Mapping of the Aboriginal Sacred in Australia: The Case of Coronation Hill' in Jackson, P. and Penrose, J. (eds) *Constructions of Race, Place and Nation*, Minneapolis: University of Minnesota Press: 100–20.

—— (1996) *Edge of Empire: Postcolonialism and the City*, London and New York: Routledge.

Jacobs, J., Dovey, K. and Lochert, M. (2002) 'Authorizing Aboriginality in Australia' in Lokko, L. N. N. (ed.) *White Papers, Black Marks: Architecture, Race, Culture*, London: Athlone Press: 218–35.

Jagmohan (1975) *Rebuilding Shahjahanabad: The Walled City of Delhi*, Delhi: Vikas.

Jameson, F. and Miyoshi, M. (eds) (1998) *The Cultures of Globalization*, Durham, NC, and London: Duke University Press.

Jencks, C. (1986) *What is Post-Modernism?*, New York: St Martin's Press.

Jiang, H. and Cheek, T. (2002) 'Introduction' to Li Longyun (2002) *Small Well Lane: A Contemporary Chinese Play and Oral History*, trans. and edited by H. Jiang and T. Cheek, Ann Arbor, MI: University of Michigan: 1–12.

Joffe, M. (1951) *Britain Builds Abroad: Constructional Engineering in the Service of World Civilization 1850–1950*, London: Constructional Steelwork Export Group.

Judd, D. and Fainstein, S. (eds) (1999) *The Tourist City*, New Haven: Yale University Press.

Kennedy, D. (1998) *The Magic Mountain: Hill Stations and the British Raj*, Berkeley: University of California Press.

Kenny, J. (1995) 'Climate, Race, and Imperial Authority: The Symbolic Landscape of the British Hill Station in India', *Annals of the Association of American Geographers* 85, 4: 794–815.

King, A. D. (1976) *Colonial Urban Development. Culture, Social Power and Environment*, London and New York: Routledge and Kegan Paul.

—— (ed.) (1980, 1984) *Buildings and Society: Essays on the Social Development of the Built Environment*, London and Boston: Routledge and Kegan Paul.

—— (1984) *The Bungalow. The Production of a Global Culture*, London and New York: Routledge and Kegan Paul. (2nd edition, Oxford University Press, 1995)

—— (1990a) *Urbanism, Colonialism and the World-Economy: Cultural and Spatial Foundations of the World Urban System*, London and New York: Routledge.

—— (1990b) *Global Cities. Post-Imperialism and the Internationalization of London*, London and New York: Routledge.

—— (1990c) 'Architecture, Capital and the Globalization of Culture' in Featherstone, M. (ed.) *Global Culture. Nation, State, Modernity*, London, Newbury Park and Delhi: Sage.

—— (ed.) (1991a) *Culture, Globalization and the World-System*, London: Macmillan and Binghamton: State University of New York at Binghamton (second North American edition, with new preface. Minneapolis: University of Minnesota Press, 1997).

—— (1991b) 'Spaces of Culture, Spaces of Knowledge' in King, A. D. (ed.) *Culture, Globalization and the World-System*, London: Macmillan and Binghamton: State University of New York at Binghamton (second North American edition, with new preface. Minneapolis: University of Minnesota Press, 1997): 1–18.

—— (1994) 'India's Past in India's Present: Cultural Policy and Cultural Practice in Architecture and Urban Design' in Asher, C. and Metcalf, T. (eds) *Perceptions of South Asia's Visual Past*, Delhi: Oxford and IBH: 271–86.

—— (1995a) 'Writing Colonial Space: A Review Essay', *Comparative Studies in Society and History* 37: 541–54.

—— (1995b) 'The Times and Spaces of Modernity (or Who Needs Postmodernism)' in Lash, S., Featherstone, M. and Robertson, R. (eds) *Global Modernities*, London, Newbury Park, and New Delhi: Sage: 108–23.

—— (1995c) 'Re-Presenting World Cities: Cultural Theory/Social Practice' in: Knox, P. and Taylor, P. (eds) *World Cities in a World-System*, Cambridge: Cambridge University Press: 215–31.

—— (1996a) 'Introduction: Cities, Texts and Paradigms' in King, A. D. (ed.) *Re-Presenting the City: Ethnicity, Capital and Culture in the Twenty-First Century Metropolis*, London: Macmillan: 1–22.

—— (1996b) 'Worlds in the City: Manhattan Transfer and the Ascendance of Spectacular Space', *Planning Perspectives* 11: 97–114.

—— (1997) 'Excavating the Multicultural Suburb: Hidden Histories of the Bungalow' in Silverstone, R. (ed.) *Visions of Suburbia*. London and New York: Routledge: 55–85.

—— (1999) 'Commentary: (Post)Colonial Geographies: Material and Symbolic', *Historical Geography* 27: 99-118.

—— (2000a) 'Postcolonialism, Representation and the City', in Watson S. and Bridge, G. (eds) *Blackwell Companion to the City*, Oxford: Blackwell: 261–9.

—— (2000b) 'Cities: Contradictory Utopias', in Pieterse, J. N. (ed.) *Global Futures: Shaping Globalization*, London: Zed Books: 224–41.

—— (2003) 'Actually Existing Postcolonialism: Colonial Architecture and Urbanism after the Postcolonial Turn' in Bishop, R., Phillips, J. and Yeo, W. W. (eds) *Postcolonial Urbanism: Southeast Asian Cities and Global Processes*, London and New York: Routledge: 167–86.

King, A. D. and Kusno, A. (2000) 'On Bei (ji) ng in the World: Globalization, Postmodernism and the Making of Transnational Space in China' in Dirlik, A. and Zhang, X. (eds) *Postmodernism and China*, Durham, NC: Duke University Press: 41–67.

Knauft, B. (2002) 'Introduction' to Knauft, B. (ed.) *Critically Modern: Alternatives, Alternates, Anthropologies*, Bloomington and Indianapolis: Indiana University Press: 1–42.

Knox, P. L. and Taylor, P. J. (eds) (1995) *World Cities in a World-System*. Cambridge: Cambridge University Press.

Kornwolf, J. D (1972) *M. H. Baillie Scott and the Arts and Crafts Movement*, Baltimore and London: The Johns Hopkins University Press.

Kosambi, M. (1990) 'The Colonial City in its Global Niche', *Economic and Political Weekly* December 22: 2275–81.

Kostof, S. (1995) *A History of Architecture. Settings and Rituals* (second edition), New York: Oxford University Press.

Kuper, H. (1972) 'The Language of Sites in the Politics of Space', *American Anthropologist* 74, 3: 411–25.

Kusno, A. (2000) *Behind the Postcolonial: Architecture, Urban Space and Political Cultures in Indonesia*. London and New York: Routledge.

Lamprakos, M. (1992) 'Le Corbusier and Algiers: The Plan Obus as Colonial Urbanism', in AlSayyad, N. (ed.) (1992) *Forms of Dominance: On the Architecture and Urbanism of the Colonial Enterprise*, Aldershot: Avebury: 183–210.

Lancaster, C. (1985) *The American Bungalow*, New York: Abbeville Press.

Lang, J., Desai, M. and Desai, M. (1998) *Architecture and Independence: The Search for Identity: India 1880–1980*, Delhi: Oxford University Press.

Langlands, B. W. (1969) 'Perspectives on Urban Planning for Uganda' in Safier, M. and. Langlands, B. W. (eds) *Perspectives on Urban Planning for Uganda*, Department of Geography, Makerere University College, Uganda.

Lash, S. (1990) *Sociology of Postmodernism*, London and New York: Routledge.

Lash, S. and Urry, J. (1994) *Economies of Signs and Spaces*, London, Thousand Oaks, CA, and New Delhi: Sage.

Leaf, M. (1994) 'The Suburbanization of Jakarta: A Concurrence of Economics and Ideology', *Third World Planning Review* 16, 4: 341–56.

Lee, L. O. (1999) *Shanghai Modern. The Flowering of a New Urban Culture in China 1930–45*, Cambridge, MA: Harvard University Press.

Lefebvre, H. (1991) *The Production of Space*, Oxford: Blackwell.

Leisch, H. (2002) 'Gated Communities in Jakarta', *Cities* 19: 341–50.

Levy, M. J. (1966) *Modernization and the Structure of Societies. A Setting for International Affairs*, Princeton, NJ: Princeton University Press.

Lewis, M. (1994) *Melbourne. The City's History and Development*, Melbourne: City of Melbourne.

Li Longyun (2002) *Small Well Lane: A Contemporary Chinese Play and Oral History*, trans. and edited by H. Jiang and T. Cheek, Ann Arbor: University of Michigan.

Li Rongxia (2000) 'Beijing Becoming an International Metropolis', *Beijing Review* 43, 5, January: 12–15.

Li, Wei (1998) 'Anatomy of a New Ethnic Settlement: The Chinese *Ethnoburb* in Los Angeles', *Urban Studies* 35, 3: 479–501.

Liu Kang (1995) 'Is There an Alternative to (Capitalist) Globalization? The Debate about Modernity in China', *boundary 2* 23, 3: 193–218.

Liu, L. G. (1989) *Chinese Architecture*, New York: Rizzoli.

Livingstone, D. (1991) 'The Moral Discourse of Climate: Historical Considerations on Race, Place and Virtue', *Journal of Historical Geography* 17, 4: 413–34.

—— (1999) 'The Spaces of Knowledge: Contributions Towards an Historical Geography of Science', *Environment and Planning D: Society and Space* 13: 5–34.

—— (2000) 'Tropical Hermeneutics: Fragments for a Historical Narrative. An Afterword', *Singapore Journal of Tropical Geography* 21, 1: 92–98.

Logan, J., Bian, Y. and Bian, F. (1999) 'Housing Inequality in Urban China in the 1990s', *International Journal of Urban and Regional Research* 23, 1: 7–24.

Logan, W. S. (2002) 'Introduction: Globalization, Cultural Identity and Heritage' and 'Introduction', Part II in Logan, W. S. *The Disappearing 'Asian' City: Protecting Asia's Urban Heritage in a Globalizing World*, New York: Oxford University Press: xii–xxi, 71–3.

Loomba, A. (1998) *Colonialism/Postcolonialism*, London and New York: Routledge.

Lyotard, J.-F. (1984) *The Postmodern Condition. A Report on Knowledge*, trans. G. Bennington and B. Massumi, Manchester: Manchester University Press.

Ma, M. C. K. (1998) 'Chinese Canadian Cultural Identity and Cultural Practice: Explorations in Ethnic Identity and Theories of Transmigration', MA thesis, State University of New York at Binghamton.

McClintock, A. (1992) 'The Angel of Progress: Pitfalls of the Term "Post-Colonialism"', *Social Text* 31/32: 84–98.

McGee, T. G. (1967) *The Southeast Asian City*, London: Bell.

Malik, B. (1995) 'Downside of the Mantra of Liberalisation', *Indian Express* July 4.

Mannoni, O. (1956) *Prospero and Caliban: The Psychology of Colonialism*, London: Methuen.

Markus, T. A. (1993) *Buildings and Power: Freedom and Control in the Origin of Modern Building Types*, New York and London: Routledge.

Markus, T. A. and Cameron, D. (2002) *The Words Between the Spaces: Buildings and Language*, London and New York: Routledge.

Marshall, R. (2002) *Emerging Urbanity: Global Urban Projects in the Pacific Rim*, London: Spon Press.

Massey, D. (1988) *Spatial Divisions of Labor*, Cambridge: Polity.

—— (1994) *Space, Place and Gender*, Cambridge: Polity.

Mathews, G. (2000) *Global Culture/Individual Identities. Searching for Home in the Global Supermarket*, New York and London: Routledge.

Memmi, A. (1965) *The Colonizer and the Colonized*, New York: Orion Press.

Menon, A. G. K. (2000) 'The Contemporary Architecture of Delhi' in Dupont, V., Tarlo, E. and Vidal, D. (eds) *Delhi: Urban Space and Human Dimensions*, Delhi: Manohar, Centre de Science Humaines and Institut de Reserche pour le Development: 143–56.

Merriman, N. (1993) *The Peopling of London*, London: The Museum of London.

Metcalf, T. R. (1989) *An Imperial Vision. Indian Architecture and Britain's Raj*, Berkeley: University of California Press.

Mills, S. (1991) *Discourses of Difference: An Analysis of Women's Travel Writing and Colonialism*, London and New York: Routledge.

—— (1994a) 'Gender, Knowledge and Empire' in Blunt and Rose 1994, op. cit.: 29–50.

—— (1994b) 'Gender and Colonial Space', *Gender, Place, Culture*, 3: 125–47.

Mirzoeff, N. (2000) *An Introduction to Visual Culture*, London and New York: Routledge.

Mitchell, K. (2000) 'Global Diasporas and Traditional Towns: Chinese Transnational Migration and the Redevelopment of Vancouver's Chinatown', *Traditional Dwellings and Settlements Review* 11: 7–18.

Mitchell, K. and Olds, K. (2000) 'Chinese Business Networks and the Globalization of Property Markets in the Pacific Rim' in Yeung, H. W. and Olds, K. (eds) (2000) *Globalization of Chinese Business Firms*, London: Macmillan: 195–217.

Mitchell, T. (1988) *Colonizing Egypt*, Cambridge: Cambridge University Press.

Mongia, P. (1995) *Contemporary Postcolonial Theory: A Reader*, London: Arnold.

Moore-Gilbert, B. (1997) *Postcolonial Theory: Contexts, Practices, Politics*, London: Verso.

Morris, J. (1995) 'The Islanders: Manhattan 1979', in Morris, J. *From the Far Corners*, Harmondsworth: Penguin Books.

Moses, M. V. (1995) *The Novel and the Globalization of Culture*, Oxford: Oxford University Press.

Myers, G. A. (1995) 'A Stupendous Hammer: Colonial and Post-Colonial Reconstructions of Zanzibar's Other Side', *Urban Studies* 32, 8: 1345–59.

—— (1999) 'Colonial Discourse and Africa's Colonized Middle: Ajit Singh's Architecture, *Historical Geography* 27: 27–55.

—— (2003) *Verandahs of Power. Colonialism and Space in Urban Africa*, Syracuse, NY: Syracuse University Press.

Nabar, V. (1990) 'The Raj Nexus. The Influence of British Culture on the English-educated in India in Terms of the Global Culture', *Indian Horizons* 41, 1–2: 22–27.

Nalbantoğlu, G. B. and Wong C. T. (eds) (1997) *Postcolonial Space(s)*, Princeton, NJ: Princeton University Press.

Nasr, J. and Volait, M. (2003) *Urbanism: Imported or Exported? Native Aspirations and Foreign Plans*, Chichester: Wiley-Academic.

Masser, N. (2003) 'The Space of Displacement: Making Muslim South Asian Place in British Neighborhoods', *Traditional Dwellings and Settlements Review*, 15, 1: 7–21.

Nilsson, S. (1968) *European Architecture in India 1750–1850*, London: Faber.

Norindr, P. (1996) *Phantasmic Indochina: French Colonial Ideology in Architecture, Film and Literature*, Durham, NC and London: Duke University Press.

Nurse, B. (1994) 'Planning a London Suburban Estate: Dulwich 1882–1920', *London Journal*, 19, 1: 54–70.

Nurse, K. (1999) 'Globalization and Trinidad Carnival: Diaspora, Hybridity and Identity in Global Culture', *Cultural Studies* 13, 4: 661–90.

Oakey, A. F. (1883) *Building a Home*, New York: D. Appleton and Co.

Ogata, A. F. (2001) *Art Nouveau and the Social Vision of Modern Living*, Cambridge and New York: Cambridge University Press.

Olds, K. (2001) *Globalization and Urban Change*, New York and Oxford: Oxford University Press.

Oliver, P. (1969) *Shelter and Society*, London: Barrie and Rockcliffe.

Olwig, K. F. (1993) *Global Culture, Island Identity. Continuity and Change in the Afro-Caribbean Community in Nevis*, Philadelphia: Harwood Academic Press.

Öncü, A. (1997) 'The Myth of the "Ideal Home" Travels Across Cultural Borders to Istanbul' in Öncü, A. and Weyland, P. (eds) *Space, Culture and Power: New Identities in Globalizing Cities*, London: Zed Books: 56–72.

Oxford English Dictionary (1989) Oxford: Oxford University Press.

Patterson, O. (1994) 'Ecumenical America: Global Culture and the American Cosmos', *World Policy Journal* 11 (Summer): 103–17.

Pellow, D. (2003) 'New Spaces in Accra: Transnational Houses', *Cities and Society*, 15, 1: 59–86.

Pennycook, N. (1998) *English and the Discourses of Colonialism*, London and New York: Routledge.

(The) People's Illustrative and Descriptive Family Atlas of the World (1889) Rochester, NY: W. H. Stewart and Co.

Perera, N. (1998) *Society and Space: Colonialism, Nationalism and Postcolonial Identity in Sri Lanka*, Boulder, CO: Westview Press.

—— (2002) 'Indigenizing the Colonial City: Late Nineteenth Century Colombo and its Landscape' *Urban Studies* 39, 9: 1703–21.

Perry, N. (1998) *Hyperreality and Global Culture*, London and New York: Routledge.

Philo, C. and Kearns, G. (1993) 'Culture, History, Capital: A Critical Introduction to the Selling of Places' in Philo, C. and Kearns, G. (eds) *Selling Places: The City as Cultural Capital, Past and Present*. Oxford: Pergamon: 1–32.

Pieterse, J. N. (1992) *Empire and Emancipation*, London: Verso.

—— (1995) 'Globalization as Hybridization?' in Featherstone, M., Lash, S. and Robertson, R. (eds) (1995): *Global Modernities*, London, Thousand Oaks, CA, and New Delhi: Sage: 45–68.

—— (2002) 'Global Inequality: Bringing Politics Back In', *Third World Quarterly* 23, 6: 1–24.

—— (2004) *Globalization and Culture*, Lanham, MD: Rowman and Littlefield.

Poovendran, P. (1994) *A Road Guide to Delhi*, Madras: TTK Pharma.

Poewe, K. (1994) *Charismatic Christianity as a Global Culture*, Charleston: University of South Carolina Press.

Population Crisis Committee (1991) *Cities. Life in the World's Largest Metropolitan Areas*, Washington, DC: Population Crisis Committee.

Port, M. H. (1995) *Imperial London: Civil Government Buildings in London 1850–1915*, London: Yale University Press.

Porter, B. (1977) *The Lion's Share. A Short History of British Imperialism 1850–1970*, London: Longmans.

Prakash, V. (2002) *Chandigarh's Le Corbusier: The Struggle for Modernity in Postcolonial India*, Seattle and London: University of Washington Press.

Pratt, M. L. (1992) *Imperial Eyes: Travel Writing and Transculturation*, London and New York: Routledge.

Progressive Architecture (1995) 'Asia Bound', March: 40–88.

Rabinow, P. (1989) *French Modern. Norms and Forms of the Social Environment*, Boston: MIT Press.

Ramesh, J. (2000) 'Ubiquitous Indians', *India Today (International)* May 1: 25.

Raychaudhuri, S. (2001) 'Colonialism, Indigenous Elites and the Transformation of Cities in the Non-Western World: Ahmedabad (Western India), 1890–1947', *Modern Asian Studies* 35, 3: 677–726.

Redfield, R. S. and Singer, M. (1954) 'The Cultural Role of Cities', *Economic Development and Cultural Change* 3: 53–73.

Renbourne, E. T. (1961) *Life and Death of the Sola Topee: Protection of the Head from the Sun*, London: War Office: Directorate of Physiological and Biological Research, Report 117.

Reynolds, D. (2002) 'American Globalism: Mass, Motion and the Multiplier Effect' in Hopkins, A. G. (ed.) (2002) *Globalization in World History*, London: Pimlico: 243–60.

Richardson, M. (1983) *Architects of the Arts and Crafts Movement*, London: Trefoil Books.

Ridley, J. (1998) 'Edwin Lutyens, New Delhi and the Architecture of Imperialism', *Journal of Imperial and Commonwealth History* 26: 67–83.

—— (2002) 'Lutyens, New Delhi and Indian Architecture' in Hopkins, A. and Stamp, G. (eds) (2002) *Lutyens Abroad: The Work of Sir Edwin Lutyens Outside the British Isles*, London: The British School at Rome: 181–90.

Rieff, D. (1993) 'A Global Culture?' *World Policy Journal* 10, 4, Winter: 73–81.

Robertson, R. (1990) 'Mapping the Global Condition: Globalization as the Central Concept' in Featherstone, M. (ed.) *Global Culture: Nationalism, Globalization and Modernity*, London, Newbury Park, New Delhi: Sage: 15–30.

—— (1991) Social Theory, Cultural Relativity and the Problem of Globality' in King, A. D. (ed.) *Culture, Globalization and the World-System*, London: Macmillan and Binghamton: State University of New York at Binghamton: 69–90.

—— (1992) *Globalization. Social Theory and Global Culture*. London, Newbury Park, New Delhi: Sage.

—— (1994) 'Globalisation or Glocalisation?' *Journal of International Communication*, 1, 1: 33–52

—— (2002) 'Opposition and Resistance to Globalization,' in Grant, R. and Short, J. R. (eds) (2002) *Globalization and the Margins*, New York and Basingstoke: Palgrave Macmillan: 25–38.

Robinson, J. (1999) 'Postcolonialism' in McDowall, L. and Sharp, J. P. (eds) *Feminist Glossary of Human Geography*, London: Arnold: 208–10.

—— (2002) 'Global and World Cities: A View from off the Map', *International Journal of Urban and Regional Research* 26, 3: 531–54.

Roche, M. (2000) *Mega-Events and Modernity: Olympics and Expos in the Growth of a Global Culture*, London and New York: Routledge.

Roy, A. (2001) 'Traditions of the Modern: A Corrupt View', *Traditional Dwellings and Settlements Review* 12, 2: 7–20.

Rufford, N. (1995) 'Towering Hong Kong Reaches for the Sky', *Sunday Times*, May 14.

Sabine, N. (1943) *The British Colonial Empire*, London: Collins.

Saha, S. K. (1995) *Conservation Based Development of Shahjahanabad: The Historic Capital City of India*, UNCRD Research Report No. 9. Nagoya: UN Center for Regional Development.

Said, E. (1978) *Orientalism*, London: Penguin.

—— (1993) *Culture and Imperialism*, London: Vintage.

Sardar, Z. (1992) 'Terminator 2. Modernity, Postmodernity and the "Other"', *Futures* 24, 5: 493-506.

Sassen, S. (2001) *The Global City: New York, London, Tokyo*, 2nd edition, Princeton, NJ: Princeton University Press.

—— (ed.) (2002) *Global Networks, Linked Cities*, London and New York: Routledge.

Scriver, P. (1994) *Rationalisation, Standardisation and Control in Design*, Delft: Technische Universiteit.

Service, A. (1977) *Edwardian Architecture*, London: Thames and Hudson.

Shermer-Smith, P. (2000) 'Helene Cixous', in Crang, M. and Thrift, N. (eds) *Thinking Space*, London and New York: Routledge.

Short, J. R. (2001) *Global Dimensions: Space, Place and the Contemporary World*, London: Reaktion Books.

Short, J. R. and Kim, Y.-H. (1999) *Globalization and the City*, New York: Addison Wesley Longmans.

Sidaway, J. (2000) 'Postcolonial Geographies: An Exploratory Essay', *Progress in Human Geography* 24, 4: 591–612.

Siegelman, P. (1998) 'Introduction' to Hobson, J. A. (1938, first published 1902) *Imperialism: A Study*, (new introduction by Siegelman, P.), Ann Arbor, MI: University of Michigan Press.

Signler, J. (ed.) (1995) *Small, Medium, Large, Extra-Large. Office for Metropolitan Architecture*, Koolhaus, R. and Mau, B., Rotterdam: The Monacelli Press: 363–9.

Silverstone, R. (1997a) 'Introduction' in Silverstone, R. *Visions of Suburbia*, London and New York: Routledge: 1–25.

—— (ed.) (1997b) *Visions of Suburbia*, London and New York: Routledge.

Simon, D. (1998) 'Rethinking (Post) modernism, Postcolonialism, Postcolonialism and Posttraditionalism', *Environment and Planning D: Society and Space* 16: 219–45.

Simpson, D. (1979) *C F A Voysey: An Architect of Individuality*, London: Lund Humphries.

Singh, P. (2002) 'Sir Edwin Lutyens and the Building of Delhi', *Icon*, Winter 2002/2003: 38–43.

Sklair, L. (2001): *The Transnational Capitalist Class*, Oxford: Blackwell.

Slater, D. (1998) 'Post-colonial Questions for Global Times', *Review of International Political Economy* 5, 4: 647–78.

Smith. A. D. (1990): 'Towards a Global Culture?' in Featherstone, M. (ed.) *Global Culture: Nationalism, Globalization and Modernity*, London, Newbury Park, New Delhi: Sage: 171–92.

Smith, G. R. (1988) *The Valley of Opportunity: A Pictorial History of the Greater Binghamton Area*, Virginia Beach, VA: Donning Co.

Smith M. G. (1965) *The Plural Society in the British West Indies*, Oxford: Oxford University Press.

Smith, M. P. (2001) *Transnational Urbanism: Locating Globalization*, Malden, MA: Blackwell.

Smith, N. (1984) *Uneven Development: Nature, Capitalism and the Production of Space*, Oxford: Blackwell.

Soni, A. (2000) 'Urban Conquest of Delhi: Beneficiaries, Intermediaries and Victims' in Dupont, V., Tarlo, E. and Vidal, D. (eds) (2000), *Delhi: Urban Space and Human Dimensions*, Delhi: Manohar, Centre de Science Humaines and Institut de Reserche pour le Development: 75–96.

Spencer, J. E. and Thomas, W. I. (1948) 'The Hill Stations and Summer Resorts of the Orient', *Geographical Review*, 39, 4: 637-51.

Spivak, G. C. (1985) 'Three Women's Texts and a Critique of Imperialism', *Critical Inquiry* 18, 4: 756–69..

—— (1988) *In Other Worlds. Essays in Cultural Politics*, London and New York: Routledge.

—— (1990) *The Post-Colonial Critic. Interviews, Strategies, Dialogues*, Harasym, S. (ed.), London and New York: Routledge.

Spybey, T. (1996) *Globalization and World Society*, Cambridge: Polity.

Stamp, G. (2002) 'Introduction' to Hopkins, A. and Stamp, G. (eds) (2002) *Lutyens Abroad: The Work of Sir Edwin Lutyens Outside the British Isles*, London: The British School at Rome: 1–6.

Steedman, C. (1992) *Past Tenses. Essays on Writing, Autobiography and History*, London: Rivers Oram Press.

Stieber, N. (1998) *Housing Design and Society in Amsterdam: Reconfiguring Urban Order and Identity 1900–1920*, Chicago: University of Chicago Press.

Storkey, M. (1994) *London's Ethnic Minorities: One City, Many Communities. An Analysis of the 1991 Census Results*, London: London Research Center.

Street, J. (2000) 'The Myth of Globalization' in Beynon, J. and Dunkerly, D. (eds) *Globalization: The Reader*, London: Athlone Press: 103–4.

Sudjic, D. (1992) *The Hundred Mile City*, New York: Harcourt Brace.

—— (1996) 'The Height of Madness', *The Guardian*, March 1: 6.

Sundaram, R. (2001) 'Recycling Modernity: Pirate Electronic Cultures in India' in Sarai Media Lab (ed.) *Sarai Reader 01*, Delhi: Sarai: 93–99.

Surin, K. (1995) 'On Producing the Concept of a Global Culture' in Mudimbe, Y. (ed.) 'Nations, Identities, Cultures', Special Issue of *South Atlantic Quarterly* 94, 4: 1179–1200.

Tarlo, E. (2000) 'Welcome to History: A Resettlement Colony in the Making' in Dupont, V., Tarlo, E. and Vidal, D. (eds) (2000), *Delhi: Urban Space and Human Dimensions*, Delhi: Manohar, Centre de Science Humaines and Institut de Reserche pour le Development: 51–74.

Taylor, P. J. (1996) 'Embedded Statism and the Social Sciences', *Environment and Planning A* 28, 11: 1917–28

—— (1999) *Modernities: A Geopolitical Interpretation*, Cambridge: Polity.

Taylor, P. J., Walker, D. R. F. and Beaverstock, J. V. (2002) 'Firms and Their Global Service Networks' in Sassen, S. (ed.) (2002) *Global Networks, Linked Cities*, London, and New York: Routledge: 93–115.

Teather, D. (2003) 'High Drama: Warring Architects Invent Compromise Tower', *The Guardian*, December 20, 2003.

Therborn, G. (2000) '"Modernization" Discourses, Their Limitations and Their Alternatives' in Schelke, W., Krauth, W-H., Kohli, M. and Elwert, G. (eds) (2000), *Paradigms of Social Change: Modernization, Development, Transformation, Evolution*, Frankfurt/New York: Campus Verlag and St Martin's Press: 49–72.

Thompson, F. M. L. (ed.) (1982) *The Rise of Suburbia*, Leicester: Leicester University Press.

Thrift, N. J. (1986) 'The Internationalization of Producer Services and the Integration of the Pacific Basin Property Market' in Taylor, M. J. and Thrift, N. J. (eds) *Multinationals and the Restructuring of the World Economy*, London: Croom Helm.

Thurner, M. and Guerrero, A. (2003) *After Spanish Rule: Postcolonial Predicaments of the Americas*, Durham and London: Duke University Press.

Timms, E. and Kelley, D. (eds) (1985) *Unreal City: Urban Experience and Modern European Literature and Art*, Manchester: Manchester University Press.

Tomlinson, J. (1991) *Cultural Imperialism*, London: Pinter.

—— (1999) *Globalization and Culture*, Cambridge: Polity.

Trouillot, M-R. (2002) 'The Otherwise Modern: Caribbean Lessons from the Savage Slot' in Knauft, B. (ed.) *Critically Modern: Alternatives, Alternates, Anthropologies*, Bloomington and Indianapolis: Indiana University Press: 220–40.

Turner, V. (ed.) (1971) *Colonialism in Africa*, London: Cambridge University Press.

Tyack, G. (1996) 'Villa' in Turner, J. (ed.) *The Dictionary of Art*, New York: Grove, 34 vols. Vol 32: 239–40.

Tyrwhitt, J. (1947) *Patrick Geddes in India*, London: Lund Humphries.

Tzonis, A., Lefaivre, L. and Stagno, B. (2001) *Tropical Architecture: Critical Regionalism in the Age of Globalization*, London: Wiley.

UNDP (1999) *Human Development Report*, New York: Oxford University Press.

Urry, J. (2000) 'The City and the Senses' in Bridge, G. and Watson, S. (eds) *Companion to the City*, Oxford: Blackwell: 388–97.

—— (2002) 'The Global Complexities of September 11th,' *Theory, Culture and Society* 19, 4, 57–69.

Vacher, H. (1997) *Projection Coloniale et Ville Rationalisée. Le Role de l'Espace Colonial dans la Constitution de l'Urbanisme en France 1900–1931*, Aalborg: Aalborg University Press.

Vale, L. J. (1992) *Architecture, Power and National Identity*, New Haven: Yale University Press.

van Leeuwen, T. A. P. (1988) *The Skyward Trend of Thought*, Cambridge, MA: MIT Press.

Walker, R. A. (1981) 'A Theory of Suburbanization: Capitalism and the Construction of Urban Space in the United States', in Dear, M. and Scott, A. J. (eds) (1981) *Urbanization and Urban Planning in Capitalist Society*, London: Methuen: 383–430

Wallerstein, I. (1980) *The Modern World System II. Mercantilism and the Consolidation of the European World-Economy 1600–1750*, New York, San Francisco, London: Academic Press.

Wallock, L. (1988) 'New York City: Capital of the Twentieth Century' in Wallock, L. (ed.) *New York: Culture Capital of the World, 1940–1965*, New York: Rizzoli.

Ward, S. V. (2003) 'Learning from the US: The Americanization of Western Urban Planning' in Volait, M. and Nasr, J. (eds) (2003) *Urbanism: Imported or Exported? Native Aspirations and Foreign Plans*, London: Wiley: 83–106.

Waters, M. (1999) *Modernity: Critical Concepts*, London and New York: Routledge.

—— (1995) *Globalization*, New York, and London: Routledge.

Watkin, D. (1980) *The Rise of Architectural History*, London: Architectural Press.

Webster, C., Glasze, G. and Frantz, K. (2002), 'The Global Spread of Gated Communities', *Environment and Planning D: Society and Space* 29, 3: 315–20.

Websters New Universal Unabridged Dictionary, (1984) New York: Simon and Schuster.

Wee, C. J. W-L (2003) *Culture, Empire and the Question of Being Modern*, New York and Oxford: Lexington Books.

Weiner, M. (1966) *Modernization: The Dynamics of Growth*, Voice of America Forum Lectures.

Weisman, W. (1970) 'A New View of Skyscraper History' in Kauffman, E. (ed.) *The Rise of American Architecture*, New York: Praegar: 115–62.

Weldes, J. (2001) 'Globalization as Science Fiction', *Millennium. Journal of International Studies* 30, 6: 647–56.

Wertheim, W. F. (1964) *Indonesian Society in Transition*, The Hague: W. van Hoeve.

Western, J (1985) 'Undoing the Colonial City?' *Geographical Review* 73, 3: 335–57.

—— (1997) *Outcast Cape Town*, 2nd edition, Berkeley: University of California Press.

Williams, P. and Chrisman, L. (1994) *Colonial Discourse and Postcolonial Theory*, New York: Columbia University Press.

Williams, R. (1985) 'The Metropolis and the Emergence of Modernism' in Timms, E. and Kelley, D. (eds) *Unreal City: Urban Experience and Modern European Literature and Art*, Manchester: Manchester University Press.

—— (1974) *Television, Technology and Cultural Form*, London: Fontana.

—— (1984) *Keywords. A Vocabulary of Culture and Society*, London: Fontana.

Winter, R. (1980) *The Californian Bungalow*, Los Angeles: Hennessey and Ingalls.

Wolfe, P. (1997) 'History and Imperialism: A Century of Theory from Marx to Postcolonialism', *American Historical Review* 102: 388–420.

Wolff, J. (1995) 'Eddie Cochran, Donna Anna and the Dark Sister: Personal Experience and Cultural History' in Wolff, J. *Resident Alien: Feminist Cultural Criticism*, Cambridge: Polity: 23–40.

Wolff-Phillips, L. (1987) 'Why "Third World"? Origin, Definition and Usage', *Third World Quarterly* 9, 4: 1311–27.

Wood, J. S. (1997) 'Vietnamese American Place-Making in Northern Virginia', *Geographical Review* 87, 1: 58–72.

Woodruff, W. (1993) *Beyond Nab End. An Extraordinary Northern Childhood*, London: Abacus.

Works, M. (1993) 'Trade and the Emergence of Global Culture in Spanish Colonial New Mexico' in Mathewson, K. (ed.) *Culture, Form, Place*, Baton Rouge: Louisiana State University.

Wright, G. (1991) *The Politics of Design in French Colonial Urbanism*, Chicago: University of Chicago Press.

www.SkyscraperPage.com.

Yardley, J. (2001) 'Symbol of Greed and Sky-High Vanity', Review of *M. Pacelle, Empire: A Tale of Obsession, Betrayal and the Battle for an American Icon*, New York: Wiley, 2001), *Guardian Weekly*, November 29–December 5: 34.

Yeang, K. (1987) 'Regionalist Design Intentions' in Yeang, K. *Tropical Urban Regionalism. Building in a Southeast Asian City*, Singapore: Mimar: 12–33.

—— (1991) 'The Malaysian Skyscraper Reconsidered', *Solidarity* 131, 2: 16–31.

Yeoh, B. (1996) *Contesting Space: Power Relations and the Urban Built Environment in Colonial Singapore*, Oxford: Oxford University Press.

—— (2001) 'Postcolonial Cities', *Progress in Human Geography* 24, 3: 456–468.

Young, L. (1998) 'The Color of Ivory Towers', *The Times Higher* June 5: 17.

Young, R. J. C. (1990) *White Mythologies. Writing History and the West*, London: Routledge.

—— (2001) *Postcolonialism: An Introduction*, London: Blackwell.

Yule, H. and Burnell, A. C. (1968) *Hobson-Jobson: A Glossary of Colloquial Anglo-Indian Words and Phrases*, London: John Murray (first edition, 1903).

Zandi-Sayek, S. (2000) 'Struggles over the Shore: Building the Quay of Izmir 1867–75', *City and Society* 12, 1: 55–78.

Zha, J. (1995) 'A City without Walls,' in Zha, J. *China Pop: How Soap Operas, Tabloids, and Best Sellers are Transforming a Culture*, New York: The New Press.

Zhang, X. (2000) 'Epilogue: Postmodernism and Postsocialist Society: Historicizing the Present' in Dirlik, A. and Zhang, X. (eds) *Postmodernism and China*, Durham, NC: Duke University Press: 399–442.

Zukin, S. (1991) *Landscapes of Power*, Berkeley, CA: University of California Press.

Zwingle, E. (1999) 'Goods Move, Ideas Move, and Cultures Change' in 'Global Culture', special issue of *National Geographic* 196, 2: 12–37.

Name Index

Abaza, M. 34
Abel, C. 130
Abercrombie, N. 185
Abeyasekare, S. 100
Abu-Lughod, J. 20, 79, 83, 100, 201, 202
Ackerman, J. 111–12, 123
Aden 162
Adshead, S. D. 167
Afghan(istan) 101, 147
Africa 7, 28, 33, 50, 53, 61, 67, 76, 82, 86, 88, 97, 162, 168, 198, 203, 208
Agra 142
Ahmedabad 87
Albany 198
Algiers 47
All Saints' Cathedral, Khartoum 168
Alphen, W. V. 69, 85
AlSayyad, N. 92
Alto, A. 34
Alwares, C. 154
America/s 28, 139, 162, 183; see also United States
America On Line (AOL) 104
Amin, I. 203
Amsterdam 69, 70, 82
Anandale 104
Anderson, B. 5, 31
Andrews, C. F. 215
Angkor Wat 33
Ankara 13
Anon 167
Appadurai, A. 23, 26, 28, 29, 32, 36, 38, 85, 92, 127, 128, 132, 171, 208
Appiah, A. 33–4, 38
Archer, J. 84, 100, 101, 123
Argentina 169
Arlington Boulevard 105
Armstrong, L. 33

Arnold, D. 50, 51
Arts and Crafts Exhibition Society 163
Arts and Crafts Movement xiii, 163–86
Ashbee, C. R. 168
Ashcroft, B. 46, 48, 49, 63, 91
Ashley, J. 27, 37
Asia/southeast Asia 13, 17, 33, 50, 56, 67, 82, 86, 88, 114, 141, 142, 162, 164, 198, 203, 208
Aswan Dam 168
Atal, Y. 86, 89
Ataturk 113, 123
Atlanta 35
Attoe, W. 6
Augé, M. 41
August, O. 17
Australia/Australasia 15, 52, 56, 59, 76, 86, 98, 101, 103, 106, 119, 131, 137, 138, 142, 146, 157, 162, 164, 170, 192, 196
Australia Building 13
Axford, B. 26
Ayodhya 5

Babylon 33
Bacon, M. 10
Baghdad 15, 90, 224
Bahrain 138
Baker, H. 148, 164, 166, 167
Balandier, G. 49
Ballantyne, T. 84
Baltic Exchange 5
Bamyeh, M. 117
Bangalore 127, 130, 132, 134, 135, 137, 138, 152
Bangkok 15
Bangladesh 53, 137
Bannerjee, S. B. 35, 36
Barclays 159
Barnett, R. 31

Subject Index